she first smiled & laughed – her
first taste of soup – carrot – &
as she loved her spinach – & how
(?)ly she looks in white, & how she
hates having her hair rubbed dry.
She won't remember – will I?

Monday Jan 25th

Up at 8.20 played, will & dressed baby
fed her – raining – put her to bed. Made
(?) etc had dinner – fed baby –
her to bed – did some knitting
(?)ched Sara & put her to bed. All
went out to pics – I did knitting –
finished right side – & listened to
wireless – lots of songs – thought
of Alex – very good programme
– at 10.30 or 45. Discussion
about Love & married life – with
illustrations in the form of plays
taken from Juliet – Cleopatra.
(?) & the Dolls house – Candida
– & others. Went to bed 12.

Tuesday Jan 26th

Usual day, did a little knitting
in evening but not much.

ginal 1943 Diary

Best Wishes

Cynthia Kahn

WILD WATER LILIES

WILD WATER LILIES

A Young Girl's War-time Diary
1940–1945

Cynthia Kahn

BEACK PUBLICATIONS

Published by Beack Publications
114 Roebuck Road
Chessington
Surrey KT9 1EU
Tel: 020 8397 8397

British Library Cataloguing in Publication Data

A C.I.P. for this book is available from the British Library

ISBN 0–9550293–0–9

Front cover illustration:
Designed by Cynthia B. Kahn, executed by Tamara T. Kahn

Designed, typeset and produced by The Studio Publishing Services Ltd, Exeter EX4 8JN

Printed in Great Britain by Cromwell Press Trowbridge Wiltshire

With gratitude to my husband Bernard, whose presence in South Wales during the war influenced so many lives

ACKNOWLEDGEMENTS

In 1995, during a creative writing class at the Institute, Hampstead Garden Suburb, our tutor, Sonia Ribeiro, asked those students who could remember the war to write a short article about their memories of VE Day, 8 May 1945. On hearing that I had kept a diary throughout the war years, Sonia encouraged me to copy out the contents of my six small notebooks, which had lain untouched for more than five decades. After hearing me read parts of the manuscript in class, she and the other members of the group agreed that it would be worth publishing. My thanks to her for this and also for her unstinting help with the final editing of the *Diary*. I also wish to thank members of the writing class for their encouragement and constructive comments, especially Mary Huttrer, Patrick Gibson and Gwen Leigh.

Thanks are due to Sarah Ansbacher for editing my transcript in its early stages.

I am indebted to several members of my family for checking the manuscript for accuracy and making many sound suggestions, particularly my son Yaacov, my daughter Miriam and my daughter-in-law Mirjam. My granddaughter Tamara gave invaluable help in executing my design for the cover.

This book could not have been printed without the help of my eldest son, David; from the first typed copy to this final edition, he carried out the major task of correcting and editing the diary, and arranging the layout of the illustrations.

Dr Gerry Black, who appears in my diary as a young boy, gave me sound advice and help in bringing it to final publication.

Finally, I would like to give thanks to the men and women who fought and worked to overcome the forces of evil in the Second World War.

INTRODUCTION

I began writing my *Diary* in January 1940, four months after the beginning of the Second World War. I wrote down the events of the war as experienced in South Wales and various parts of England, right up to the final victory over Japan, making the last entry in my diary on Victory Sunday, 19 August 1945. I was a Welsh–Jewish girl who survived the war years, and was able to experience the "ordinary" life of a young girl growing up in extraordinary times.

When the war began, I was living with my grandmother, Ida Britz, together with my older sister Joyce, in a small mining village called Penrhiwceiber. My mother Ruth, who had been born in Penrhiwceiber, was living, with her second husband Harry, above her dress shop in Aberdare, about five miles further up the valley. Joyce and I arrived in Penrhiwceiber from Llanelli, the town where we were born, when I was seven years old; I soon became known to everyone in this warm and friendly village.

The early months of the war found seven of us crammed into the small living quarters above my grandmother's shop. Apart from Gran and her unmarried son Ben, my sister Joyce, and myself, there were also Gran's brother Solly and his wife Alma, who were recent refugees from Nazi Germany. In addition, Gran had taken in a twelve-year-old refugee girl named Berta Oppenheim.

Three of Gran's sisters are mentioned in the diary: Mary, who lived on her farm above Swansea; Fanny, who lived in Cardiff, and Ray, living in London. Gran's married son, Charlie, had a grocery shop in Aberaman, a short distance from Aberdare.

We lived on the main road with a few other streets above and below us on the steep hillside. Our Hardware Store, the only one for miles around, was built into the hillside and had a steep flight of steps next to it leading from Penrhiwceiber Road to the street above. These steps were often referred to as the "Britz Steps". Like most of the families in the village, we had one unlit, outside toilet, though we did have a bathroom upstairs, provided with lukewarm water by a small coal fire down below.

We would never have believed that this relatively unknown and secluded corner of Wales would soon be experiencing the all-too-frequent sight of German bombers flying overhead, bringing the war right to our front door.

During those years, most of us went to the cinema frequently to enjoy a few hours of warmth and respite from the deprivations of the war. Newsreels shown with the films were of great importance in keeping us up to date with the latest news from the front.

While the dates and places mentioned in the *Diary* are correct, some of the names of people have been changed. I have followed the text and style of the original as closely as possible, adding illustrations and including extracts from letters and poems referred to in my *Diary*. For clarity, I have used italics and inserted explanatory notes in parentheses.

Cynthia Kahn
8th May, 2005

Explain none can
Life's pending plan:
Thou wilt thy ignorant entry make
Though skies spout fire and blood and nations quake.

Thomas Hardy (1840–1928)

1940

Sunday 7th January
Packed my case ready to go to the farm tomorrow. Taking a few books – *Dumb Witness* by Agatha Christie, *Old St. Paul's* by Harrison Ainsworth and *Silas Marner* by George Eliot – and my gas mask. Leaving early.

Monday 8th January
Caught the first train to Swansea, then bus to Fforestfach. Arrived at Caerithin Farm at 2 p.m. Glad it wasn't yet dark, as the long lane leading to the farm is very lonely; it must be even darker now in the blackout, the only sound being the eerie hum of the telephone wires above. Had lunch with Aunty Mary [Gran's sister] and Ivor and Owen, two of the farm workers; Uncle Harris was in Swansea for the day.

Walked down to the stream – drew a quick pencil sketch; a few brilliant sunny moments, racing clouds; too cold to stay out long. After 8 p.m., Rifka – Aunty Mary's daughter – and quite a few of her friends and cousins, gathered in the piano room. Rifka played all the latest tunes. She's a brilliant pianist. We all sang together; no one wanted to stop – for when shall we all be together again? Two of the cousins are leaving for the Army. Rifka's fiancé Jeff may be called up. Expected to sleep in the room with the hissing gaslights, but Uncle had changed them to electric. Stubbed my toe on the stone hot-water bottle at the bottom of the bed.

Tuesday 9th January
This morning I visited my friend the bull for the *last* time. He looked at me with his big liquid eyes, rattled his chain, and ignored me. When he was let out into the yard to service the cow, he took one look at Aunty Mary coming out of the cowshed, broke the gate, jumped the steel bars, and charged. Aunty ran for her life, screaming, straight through the kitchen door with the bull roaring after her. He was so big he got completely wedged in the doorframe. Trembling with anger, he snorted and bellowed; Aunty collapsed in hysterics. The wood began to creak and some of the stones on the sides of the doorposts began to crumble. I ran to get Uncle Harris. We heard a shot. Ivor had climbed in through the kitchen window with his gun and shot my old friend. We heard Owen running from the cooling parlour shouting " 'Ave you shot a German (pilot, parachutist) then?" and,

"Duw! Oh! Duw!" when he saw the large brown backside of the slumped bull filling the doorway. (Ivor and Owen are in the Civil Defence and Ivor is the sole owner of a gun.) Uncle threw off Aunty's milking cap and apron, exclaiming: "No wonder the bull chased you!" Then he put her to bed with a mug of hot tea.

Wednesday 10th January
Aunty stayed in bed today. Uncle took Yetta [his youngest daughter] and me to the pics. in Swansea. We saw *Stowaway* with Shirley Temple and Alice Faye. Yetta enjoyed it and I did too. Uncle Harris had built the first cinema in Llanelly – the Regal. Mum, Joyce and I had attended the opening night [*The Jazz Singer* with Al Jolson – the first talking picture]; afterwards there had been a reception and speeches. Tonight, during supper, Aunty talked about buying a new bull. "No need," said Uncle, "the vet can do it." Aunty's eyebrows rose! Then Uncle read out an article from the *Farmer's Weekly* about a more modern method of breeding calves without keeping a bull. Aunty shook her head in amazement – and disbelief.

Thursday 11th – Friday 12th January
Went to Llanelly [Welsh spelling and modern usage: Llanelli]. Everyone there pleased to see me – insisted I stay the night. Went to see Monty Landy and then met Wilfred Myron. We talked about the Russian war against Finland. Wilfred thought he might volunteer again to defend Finland. (He fought in the Spanish Civil War and came back weighing only seven stone! He said he'd lived on oranges for months!) Saw all Llanelly Uncles and Aunts and little cousin Pam. Sorry to leave.

Monday 15th January
Returned to Aberdare by bus and train. It was 9 p.m. and quite dark when I got to Penrhiwceiber. Had hoped to see Alex while I was in Swansea, but he never came. School tomorrow. Must remember to take my gas mask. [We had to be prepared for the Germans using poison gas against us as they had done in the trenches in the First World War.]

Tuesday 16th January
Back to school again. Decided to make use of my Pocket Diary. It's quite small. Only four lines for each day. I shall have to précis everything.

Sunday 21st January
Spent the morning practising script writing with calligraphy nibs. Wrote a poem on cardboard and stuck a small calendar onto it. Might give it to Joyce for her birthday. Finished knitting gloves. Went with Gran to see her friend Mrs. Davies. Bitterly cold on the way home; snowing again. Coldest winter for 50 years!

Poem and calendar given to Joyce on her 17th birthday

Monday 29th January
Got to school late, everything snow and ice, fields look like frozen ponds: no bus – so had to walk two miles to school. A lot absent. I almost slipped on the railway lines at the crossing.

Thursday 1st February
Had gym instead of games. Grandma Cohen died [my father's mother]. Fell down after school; limped home soaking wet. No buses, as the roads are like ice tracks.

Friday 2nd February
Stayed home, read *Tess of the D'Urbevilles* by Thomas Hardy.

Saturday 3rd February
Ed Morgan came to see Uncle Ben to have him take the last of his teeth out. Ed sat in the kitchen, I held the bowl of mouthwash. Uncle Ben said that I could help him choose the colour and shape of the teeth to go into the new set. The false teeth Uncle Ben makes look so natural – he boils them up on Gran's kitchen stove.

Tuesday 6th February
Managed to skip gym, leg still stiff. Went to Aberdare shop to see Mum, then to pics. to see Deanna Durbin in *Three Smart Girls Grow Up*.

Thursday 8th February
First day of spring. Went for a walk after school as far as Cwmpennar, then went to Betty's [my school friend] to catch up on homework. Mrs. Gladys Thomas, her aunt, was there. Amazed at her size, I said to Betty, "She was always so thin." "She's not fat now," Betty replied, "just having a baby – looks like any day now." Surprised at my ignorance, Betty filled in the gaps in my knowledge of life. – Well! … I shall have to read *Tess of the D'Urbervilles* again!

Friday 16th February
Snowing heavily. Hockey cancelled; did gym. My gym clothes were awfully small; almost couldn't get them off.

Tuesday 27th February
Had awful toothache today – nearly went crackers.

Wednesday 28th February
Had to see the dentist. He didn't do much except prod and "tut-tut". Peggy came up after school. Did a lot of homework together, then went to pics. Saw *Tarzan Finds a Son* with Johnny Weissmuller. It was lovely.

Friday 1st March
Took Berta for a walk after school. Her English is getting better. She's been with us six months! No news of her family.

Tuesday 5th March
Stayed home – my neck is stuck somehow. Read *Man in the Iron Mask* by Alexandre Dumas.

Thursday 28th March
Prize day today. I was given a book of *English* poetry for getting top marks in *Maths*! Mum didn't come. Went home early, then walked five miles to Aberdare to see her. Caught bus back to Penrhiwceiber. Took Berta to pics. Saw Shirley Temple in *Suzanna of the Mounties*.

Wednesday 10th April
Heard on the wireless that the Germans have invaded Denmark and Norway.

Friday 12th April
Went to pics. with Mum, saw Carole Lombard in *Only in Name*. Uncle Harry [my stepfather] went to London. Mum would like him to sell his upholstery factory and find work here. Megan's brother has been sent to France (Territorial Army).

Sunday 14th April
Got an awful cold. Joyce says it's from living in "Pneumonia Corner": our living room has three doors to the outside – one to the shop, one to the back kitchen and one to the back lane, where eighty steps go up to Tanycoed Street. Mum's father died here of pneumonia when he was thirty-four. Mum was three-and-a-half years old. Our small fire is surrounded by three cats, two dogs, and Mrs. Prosser, who comes to write up Gran's books. She smokes non-stop, so I have to do my homework in a smoky haze. Went to bed and read.

Monday 22nd April
Took the Pesach [Passover] can up the mountain to get fresh milk from Dylan's Farm. Picked a bunch of wild violets. I had to watch that no breadcrumbs got into the milk (because of Pesach). Dai said, "There's twp [stupid], how can I milk with two 'ands and eat bread at the same time?" Ran down the mountain like a goat without spilling a drop. Went to Aberdare and then to pics. with Mum. Saw *Lady of the Tropics* with Bob Taylor and Hedy Lamarr. She has the most perfect face.

Monday 29th April
Didn't feel at all well. Went to bed at 6. Wonder if it's from eating Matzos [unleavened bread] for a week and Gran's kneidlech [dumplings].

Wednesday 1st May
Felt ill. Went to doctor's – gave me awful medicine and pills.

Thursday 2nd May
Half-day closing, so Mum came from Aberdare. I told her about feeling "ill". She told me what to do and said she was glad to know that I was normal. Well! I don't feel a bit "normal". I'm thoroughly annoyed and upset – and it seems I don't even have a choice. Wish I'd been born a boy! Mum wrote a note so that I can miss games tomorrow – so my cloud has a small silver lining.

Tuesday 7th May
Mum has decided to open a new shop in the centre of Aberdare. It is to be called Barbara Gold. Barbara after me [my middle name] and Gold after Uncle Harry (Golding). I read a play by J. M. Barrie, *What Every Woman Knows*. Well, I also know now! Also read *The Admirable Crichton* by the same author. I liked this play very much.

Thursday 9th May
Rifka's wedding. Had a lovely time as a bridesmaid. Our frocks looked beautiful – white organza trimmed with blue velvet ribbon, embroidered with coloured flowers. Came home very late. Tomorrow, in school, we start rehearsals for *A Midsummer-Night's Dream*.

Saturday 11th May
The Germans have attacked Holland and Belgium. There have been air-raids on some French towns. Mr. Churchill has taken over as Prime Minister.

Uncle Solly and Aunty Alma look very worried. Uncle Solly and his wife have come from Stavenhagen, Germany; he is to be the Minister and teacher for the Aberdare Jewish Community. I am the only one who can speak German to Aunty, who knows only two words of English, "Kettle Boiling", which she calls out loudly whenever she wants Gran to make her a cup of tea.

Tuesday 14th May
Supposed to have a holiday today, but because of the war had to go to school. Only half the school turned up. More practice. I'm a fairy!

Saturday 1st June
Holland and France have been occupied. Our forces are being evacuated from Dunkirk (France).

Sunday 2nd June
Evacuees came to Penrhiwceiber today from London. Given out to families. Some of them were as young as five. None was given to us as we already have

Yetta Wyman and I as bridesmaids

Berta, Uncle Solly and Aunty Alma, and of course, Joyce and me – plus Uncle Ben.

Wednesday 12th June

Midsummer-Night's Dream went off well. Weather stayed dry. Acted on the lawn between two large oak trees. Puck "flew" down from one of them; Bronwen played Titania and Emrys was Bottom – he made a great ass! I danced barefoot on the grass with the other fairies to the sound of our orchestra playing Mendelssohn's *Midsummer Night's Dream*. Many of the older boys from the orchestra were absent – they're already in the Air Force.

Oberon and Puck in A Midsummer-Night's Dream

Thursday 13th June

Repeat performance of *A Midsummer-Night's Dream.* Mum came to see it and enjoyed it very much. It was 10.30 p.m. by the time I had changed and taken off my make-up – Mum had left straight after the performance so I had to walk the two miles home alone in the dark. Felt tired and awfully stiff.

Sunday 16th June

Aunty Ray's daughter Sal came from London for a break. She works for an electricity company and after work has been helping with the wounded that escaped from France. She's Mum's double cousin, as two sisters had married two brothers. She's good fun and has a wonderful singing voice like Gracie Fields. ('Sing As You Go'; 'Sally, Sally, Pride of Our Alley' etc.) We sing together all the time and even Uncle Ben jokes with her. Usually he ignores women – except for his Scotch Terrier bitches, Lady and Pam, now both dead. Only two dogs left – Pat and Mac. Sal has got red hair and uses bright red nail varnish.

Tuesday 18th June

Met Dai "the Farm" on the way home. He wants to join up. Said he has been told to take a pitchfork and pike with him when he's working on the farm – in case German parachutists appear floating down on the mountains. "Twp!" he said. (He speaks almost no English – only Welsh.) "At least in the army I'll be given a gun." Took Berta to pics.; saw *Daughters Courageous*, with the Lane sisters in it. Listened to Winston Churchill on the wireless. Very stern and powerful.

> [...The Battle for France is over. I expect the Battle of Britain is about to begin. Upon this battle depends our own British life and the long continuity of our institutions and our Empire. The whole fury and might of the enemy must very soon be turned on us. Hitler knows that he will have to break us in this island or lose the war. If we can stand up to him, all Europe may be free, and the life of the world may move forward into broad, sunlit upland; but if we fail, then the whole world, including the United States, and all that we have known and cared for, will sink into the abyss of a new dark age made more sinister, and perhaps more protracted by the lights of a perverted science. Let us therefore brace ourselves that if the British Empire and Commonwealth last for a thousand years men will still say, "This was their finest hour".]

Italy has declared war on us; the Germans have taken over Paris. Megan's brother, who was wounded at Dunkirk, has been sent home. Berta and I hope to visit him in Abercwmboi on Sunday.

Saturday 22nd June
Went with Sal to see *The Wizard of Oz* with Judy Garland. Wonderful film, fantastic colour. We came home singing 'Follow the Yellow Brick Road' and 'Somewhere over the Rainbow'. Our good mood vanished when we listened to the news. France has given in – signed an armistice with Germany. Sal is going back to London tomorrow.

Sunday 23rd June
War services in chapels, churches and synagogues; I went to shul [synagogue] in Aberdare.

Thursday 27th June
Mum came from Aberdare very worried – said she'd heard that a bomb had been dropped on Wales but she doesn't know where. It could be a rumour.

Saturday 29th June
Cable from America [Mum's cousins – the Resniks]. They want Joyce and me to go there. We both refuse!

Aberdare Synagogue 1899–1957

Sunday 30th June
Did fourteen pages of History summary, ditto Geography, and some French and German vocabulary. Felt very happy after I'd finished. Exams start this week.

Monday 1st July
Had two long air-raids during the night. Stayed downstairs. Went to school late. Took Berta to pics. Saw the Dead End Kids in *Angels Wash Their Faces* and *Proud Valley* with Paul Robson and Rachel Thomas – a film about a Welsh mining valley like ours.

Tuesday 2nd July
Another air-raid last night. The all-clear went after about an hour. Today our German teacher called me out in class. She asked: "What has happened to your German accent?" I told her that I was getting a lot of practice talking to my great-uncle and aunt who had come from Germany. "I don't know where they come from," she said with disgust, "I only allow *Hoch-Deutsch* to be spoken in my class, not some southern dialect!" And I thought I was improving! Anyway Uncle Solly has found a house in Clifton Street, Aberdare. They'll be moving in next week. Went to pics. to cheer myself up – saw *The Stars Look Down*, with Michael Redgrave and Margaret Lockwood. Wonderful film.

Thursday 4th July
Went to school. Found we had no terminals [exams] because of the war. Air-raid practice instead. One of our ships, the *Arandorra Star*, was sunk on its way to Canada. It was taking prisoners of war and German internees to camps there. Many of them were Jewish refugees from Germany. Most were drowned. Since France signed the Armistice with Germany, German troops have reached as far as the Channel Islands and occupied them.

Wednesday 10th July
Had air-raid but NO WARNING! Bombs dropped in Cwmbach. Our shop shook a lot.

Thursday 11th July
Walked to Aberdare after school. The shop girls were all upset. Customer from Cwmbach brought back daughter's wedding dress. Daughter killed by a bomb. She was in bed with her sister. Sister quite unhurt. All the family changed their new clothes for black. Mum very shocked.

Friday 12th July
Had air-raid about 4.30 a.m. again. No warning. Didn't bother to go back to bed. Read *The Vicar of Wakefield* by Oliver Goldsmith.

Sunday 14th July
Uncle Solly and Aunty Alma left for their new home. We all went to see Gran's sister, Aunty Fanny, and her family, in Cardiff. I wore my new yellow tweed coat. Glad I finished making my pleated skirt yesterday, as nothing else fits me. We came back at 6. Listened to Churchill on the wireless. There were more subs. in the Channel trying to sink our convoys. Some German planes were brought down.

Friday 19th July
Another air-raid in the afternoon. Mum came home from London. She's bought three dozen siren-suits [all-in-one garments for wearing in air-raids or on war work] as well as the usual stock.

Saturday 20th July
Didn't get up until late as air-raid in the night. We all slept on the floor under the metal table. Bombs were dropped on *our school*! Four big craters in the playing field. No damage to the building, except all the windows were broken from the blast. No one was hurt.

Sunday 21st July
My BIRTHDAY. 14 today. Got up late because of air-raid last night. Went to Aberdare Park. Had some cards and presents. Mum has already sold *all* the siren-suits.

Tuesday 23rd July
Air-raid for over an hour in the night. Went to school. Teachers checking our school books. I was sent home for one of mine. Had to wait ages for a bus. Very annoyed!

Wednesday 24th July
Broke up for Summer Holidays. Went to Mountain Ash Palace – saw *The Terror of Toytown*. All midgets in it!

Thursday 25th July
Went to Cardiff this afternoon with Mum to buy shoes. Bought two pairs instead of one. Assistant said to me, "You've got a hammer toe." She's right – it comes from wearing shoes that are too small. We went to pics. to see *The Untamed* with Ray Milland, Patricia Morison and Akim Tamiroff. Called in to see Aunty Fanny & Co.

Wednesday 14th August
Went to Aberdare, to the dentist. Had six teeth out. Feeling awful. I was very frightened. Went alone. Had gas and had a terrible dream while having it. Vowed never to have gas again.

Thursday 15th August
Almost fainted in the bathroom. Mouth still very sore. Ben says he will take an impression tomorrow for my new front teeth.

Wednesday 21st August
New teeth look great. Looking forward to smiling again. Went to pics. to celebrate. Saw *The Real Glory* with Gary Cooper and David Niven and *I Stole A Million* with George Raft and Claire Trevor. (Quote from my Pocket Diary: Keep smiling; a smile is like a ray of sunshine.)

Monday 26th August
Heard on the news – heavy raids on London. Uncle Harry is there this week to be with his sisters. Mum is extremely worried. Our airmen and ack-ack guns have destroyed more than seven hundred German planes. We have lost about two hundred.

Saturday 31st August
One year since Berta came to us from Germany. This week we had new visitors. Mrs. Davis and her daughter Sheila have come to escape the London bombing. Sheila is my age – Mrs. Davis is the same age as Uncle Ben – born in 1900. Both her parents died young of typhoid fever in Palestine. They emigrated there, from the same village that Gran lived in, at the same time that Gran went to New York. This week there have been raids on all the large cities in Britain. Eighty-six German bombers have been shot down.

Tuesday 3rd September
Anniversary of the start of the war. Listened to special services on the wireless.

Monday 9th September
German invasion expected this week. Govt. leaflet given out says: Do not give a German anything. Do not tell him anything. Hide your food and bicycles. Hide your maps!!

Tuesday 10th September
Raids have continued on London – a very big one yesterday. Uncle Harry still there. School started again. In assembly the Headmaster read out a list of former M.A.C.S. [Mountain Ash County School] boys killed in the war. Mainly Air Force. Sang hymns: 'Abide With Me', 'A'r hyd y nos' … ['All Through the Night']. We filed out in silence. Using cloakroom for air-raid shelter. Have to lie under the benches.

Ruth Golding circa 1935

Wednesday 11th September

Nasty experience today! Air-raid. Heard bomber circling the school – only big building for miles. Lay on the floor of the cloakroom thinking how upset Mum will be when she hears I've been killed. John Morgan, one of the watchers on duty, ran in to tell us "It's one of ours!" The plane had been doing a victory roll over our school after shooting down a German plane. We all laughed with relief, but we were also a bit cross – still, who knows, it might have been a Mountain Ash County School boy greeting us from the sky. We'll never know.

Thursday 12th September

Went to Aberdare after school. Uncle was back. We all went to pics. to see *The Women* with Joan Crawford, Norma Shearer – Mum's double [See photo] and Rosalind Russell. I enjoyed it – but, as expected, as soon as there was the first hint of unfaithful behaviour, Uncle was out of his seat like a shot, trailing Mum behind him; he's such a puritan – he was fifty when he married Mum. Later I told Mum about the film and how it ended.

Saturday 14th September

Yesterday a German bomber was shot down over Newport. It crashed into a house, killing a woman and her two children. What awfully bad luck! This week part of Buckingham Palace was destroyed by a bomb, but not badly, and no one was injured.

Sunday 22nd September

Joyce and I discussed, until late at night, what we should do when (if?) the Germans come. To my surprise she has been making plans for weeks, as I have. We decided not to tell each other what our plans are, in the event of one of us being captured.

Monday 23rd September

School as usual. Much talk of invasion. Headmaster gave us an encouraging talk in assembly. Told us to listen to the King's Speech tonight. Mum said she's sorry she didn't insist on us going to Canada or America.

Tuesday 24th September

Mum has changed her mind after hearing the awful news about the evacuee ship *City Of Benares*. The Germans torpedoed it, causing the death of over eighty children and crew. Except for a few, they all drowned … Joyce and I could have been on that ship!

Wednesday 25th September

REALLY BAD NEWS!

Aunty Ray's daughter Sal was killed in the London raid! She was living with the Robins family in Dalston. When the raid started they were supposed to go to the Anderson shelter in their garden but Sal went to the large communal shelter to sing and cheer everyone up. Mrs. Robins went with her. The shelter had a direct hit and there were no survivors. In the morning the milk bottles were still standing unbroken outside their house – they could have all stayed in their own beds! (All I can think of is the memory of Sal singing her favourite song – 'Sing as You Go and Let the World Go By'.) Her brother and sister, Max and Phoebe, went to look for her but there was absolutely nothing left – the whole warehouse where the shelter was sited had been completely destroyed! All the family is upset and shocked. Very sombre Diary Quote: "Life is a one-way street – you're not coming back."

Saturday 28th September
A few children, survivors from the evacuee ship, have been rescued – Uncle said: "If your name is on it," etc. He's a Fatalist as well as an Atheist.

Tuesday 15th October
Uncle Harry came back from London last night. I walked to Abercynon on the old road on the other side of the river. Went to see Gran's friend "one-eyed" Joe [an elderly Jewish miner]. No one knows much about him except that he lost his eye at Mafeking in the Boer War. I find him very interesting. Took him some Cornish pasties that Grandma had made. He was delighted to see me and accompanied me part of the way back. Later I went with Berta to pics. Saw *They Flew Alone* with Anna Neagle as Amy Johnson. Very good film.

Wednesday 16th October
Full moon tonight. Hope it'll be cloudy, so the German bombers can't see down. Heavy raids have continued, mostly in London. At least four hundred German planes have been destroyed this month. Joyce and I don't bother to undress at night in case the sirens go. Mrs. Davis went back to London, but Sheila is still here. She says she's so bored. I can't understand her, I'm *never* bored.

Saturday 19th October
Went to pics. in Mountain Ash with Peggy. Saw *Ebb Tide* with Ray Milland and Frances Farmer and *First Love* with Deanna Durbin and Robert Stack. Both very well acted. Saw newsreels of London burning; so many buildings destroyed. This week part of St. Paul's Cathedral was hit. Came home to find Sheila packing. She's homesick for London! She wants to travel back with Uncle Harry tomorrow.

Monday 11th November
ARMISTICE DAY FOR THE FIRST WORLD WAR!
Peggy forgot her gas mask and was sent home from school to get it. I re-read the poem I had written last year to commemorate those who died:

The Unknown

We will remember
When brown leaves fall,
Those who went
At the first bugle's call.

We will remember
Those who went down,
With only a thought for
Their country and crown.

With grey skies above them
That day in November,
When the last shot was fired
We will remember.

Voices are lifted,
Praising things said
Of the brave men immortal
Who lay cold and dead.

In a lone field in Flanders,
Covered with red
Of the poppies which were coloured
By the blood that was shed.

When they've all turned to dust
'Neath the flowers on the hill,
Though names are forgotten,
We'll remember them still.

That was mainly a military battle. I could never have imagined a war like this in which civilians are killed – women and children who have nothing to do with the fighting – and their homes destroyed.

Sunday 24th November

Mum and Uncle came down to see us for a few hours – Mum still red-eyed and blowing her nose – still grieving over Sal. Gran sighing and Uncle Ben stamping in and out with his dogs, swearing. After Mum and Uncle had left, alone in my bedroom I burst into tears – me – who never cries. Suddenly I so missed my father (!), which is quite silly, as I can't really remember him – I was only two. I hardly know what he looked like, Uncle Harry having torn up all his photos in a jealous rage; he wants to think he's the only man in Mum's life – which is why he doesn't allow Joyce and me to see our Llanelly Aunts and Uncles. I feel sad too, about Sal – and about this awful month – the destruction of Coventry by the

Germans – the massive raids on Birmingham, Manchester and other towns and cities. Glad no one heard me, particularly Berta, who really has much more than I to cry about.

Monday 25th November
Went to pics. with Berta. Saw *In Old Chicago* with Alice Faye, Tyrone Power and Don Ameche. The film was great, especially the fire scenes – the Great Fire of Chicago. (Really cheered us up!!!) The last scene was so moving and powerful.

Sunday 1st December
Normal day. Grandma ill. Fed the chickens and collected the eggs. Joyce asked for my pocket money to buy sweets – she's worried they are going to be rationed. Everything's on ration now. Have to carry an identity card and gas mask everywhere. Anyone owning a gun (ancient or otherwise) asked to hand it in to the police station for our defence!

Saturday 14th December
Birthday of George VI. Grandma finds old gun that belonged to her son Sam who died in 1927 [from T.B.]. Took it to the police station. VERY WRONG MOVE!! Police charged her for having *no licence* and for being an *Alien* without registering! Grandma protested that she had lived in Penrhiwceiber since 1897 – before most of them were BORN! Never been naturalised. "What for?" Gran said, "I never travel anywhere!" "You won't now!" they told her. Now she has to get a special permit whenever she wants to go to Cardiff. Gran livid. (Diary Quotation: "Everything worthwhile has its risks"!!)

Monday 16th December
New German teacher (two years' study in Germany) called me COHEN every time it was my turn to read. She calls the others by their first names. My friends were furious! She has started to teach us the 'Horst Wessel Song' and 'Deutschland Über Alles' [Germany over everyone]!!! Howell Davies said we should complain to the Headmaster. We did. Hope she gets the sack.

Saturday 21st December
Spent most of the day serving customers in Jane Cooper's. Finished reading *The Man in the Iron Mask*. Very good. Everybody told; "Careless words cost lives!" All road directions have been taken down or changed. Diary Quote: "A lie is too big a price to pay for anything!" Ha! Now we have to confuse the Germans at whatever cost. It is thought that if the Germans descend on us they won't know where they are!??!

Monday 23rd December
Very cold. Went to pics. with Berta. Saw *Honeymoon Merry-go-round.* Laughed myself sick. Used a covered torch to find our way home – no moon or stars.

Tuesday 24th December
Worked all day in Jane Cooper's; didn't sit down once. Stayed open late. Put on my mac to catch the last bus to 'Ceiber. Mum remarked, "Must you always wear that old mac?" Told her that nothing else fits me. (I am already four inches taller than her – but I don't think she's noticed.) "Try this one," she said, handing me a beautiful grey winter coat. It looked great; very smart, with buttons crossing over the front and a flared skirt. I'm thrilled. Hope I don't grow any more.

Wednesday 25th December – **Xmas Day**
Spent the day knitting – balaclavas for the troops and finishing Joyce's cardigan. Street very quiet. No lights anywhere. Blackout! Uncle Charlie and Aunty Gwen came in the evening to bring us presents. It seems that Charlie (Grandma's eldest) is exempt from war duty because he was born in America. He was two when he came to Wales. Gwen, his wife, is also exempt although she's never been out of Wales in her life! She's an American citizen by marriage. It's a strange war!

Thursday 26th December
Mum and Uncle Harry came down from Aberdare. Read *The Four Feathers* by A. E. Mason most of the day. Gran of course, seeing me reading, made her usual comment: "Might as well talk to the wall as talk to her!" Gran has never been to school and she can't read or write (although she's taught herself to sign her signature). She thinks reading books and doing one's homework are a complete waste of time. Made some models in Plasticine this evening [dolls dressed in foreign costumes]. Very last Diary Quote: "Think before you ink." It's started to snow, hope it'll be all white when I get up tomorrow.

Tuesday 31st December
Stayed awake until New Year.

1941

Wednesday 1st January

Bought a notebook to use as a diary so that I can write as much or as little as I need. Uncle Harry went to London today to see his five sisters. They live at 100 Cazenove Road, N.16 and go to the Underground every night to sleep (to be safe from the bombing raids). He also has a brother and brother-in-law who have an upholstery factory in the East End. Joyce and I went to pics. Saw Errol Flynn and David Niven in *Dawn Patrol*. The newsreel showed the incendiary bomb attack on London. The city was engulfed in flames; the oldest buildings made of wood – some of them six to eight hundred years old – could not be saved. We have to learn fire drill and look in the loft every night after a raid in case an incendiary bomb has dropped through the roof.

Thursday 2nd January

Very cold today. Started reading *Jane Eyre* by Charlotte Brontë. Cardiff had a BIG raid – terrible damage! The flames and explosions could be seen from Ponty, twelve miles away. Tydvil said the whole sky was red. A few bombs dropped near us (German bombers trying to get away from our fighter planes ditch their cargo of bombs to lighten their load, to be able to get away over the mountains). One bomb hit our local Infants' School half a mile away. Lucky it was early, so only a few children had turned up! Don't know about casualties – there were a lot in Cardiff.

Friday 3rd January

Uncle Harry came back from London. Went to Aberdare to see him and Mum. We all went to the Regal. Saw *The Man in the Iron Mask* with Louis Hayward and Joan Bennett. Not a bit like the book! Saw newsreel about the ships that have been sunk by submarines and mines. Uncle told us about his time in the Merchant Navy during the First World War. Says he walks with a roll from balancing in heavy seas. (He does!) He worked as a stoker.

Saturday 4th January

Went to Aberdare and helped serve some customers in the shop (Jane Cooper). Decided to go to the farm tomorrow before school starts again. Met Ted [my Maths teacher] on the bus back to Penrhiwceiber. He's a good friend of Uncle

Ben and has a marvellous sense of humour. He's the only teacher in M.A.C.S. who doesn't have a degree; he's also the best!

Sunday 5th January
Took the first bus to Swansea, then on to Fforestfach. Got to Caerithin Farm about 1 p.m. Heard that both Myer and Benny Wyman [Uncle Harris's nephews] are in the forces. Eva Winter came up, but Alex didn't, as he's too busy with exam work. Eva, Alex's sister, has become so pretty! Went for a walk down to the brook. Very muddy – the pasture fields have all been ploughed up! Made myself drink Aunty Mary's borscht [beetroot soup]. It wasn't as bad as I remembered. (Must be growing up!) Can't be so fussy in war-time.

Monday 6th January
Caught the bus from Sketty to Llanelly. Aunty Sarah [my father's sister] and Uncle Myer were thrilled to see me! At first they thought I was Joyce, I've grown so much. After lunch I went for a long walk along the seashore. Cold wind, but wonderful to be there. Tide far out; no one except me. Saw, on the sand dunes, new bunkers built against the invasion. Went back to 3 Mina Street and then to Uncle Harry [my father's brother] and Aunty Beaty. Aunty was in bed as usual, looking very beautiful and sad. (She has a bad heart.) Then my feet took me to 10 Cowell Street – the place where I was *born*. It is now a wool shop! I went in

Aunty Mary and Uncle Harris Wyman at Caerithin Farm

and bought a cardigan pattern. Very strange to be inside after all these years. Vivid memories of my last day there, HALF my life ago!! (The day we left, Joyce had scarlet fever and the cat had 5 kittens that the milkman drowned in a bucket – he kept one, a ginger tom, for himself.) Went across the road to visit the Days – Mrs. Day is the exact opposite of Mum – she's so motherly, Joyce and I had always wished that she really *was* our Mum. Mr. Day was out. Big hug from Mrs. Day. Vera and I compared Matric subjects. Mrs. Day made me welsh-cakes on a griddle. She remembered how much I liked them! Telephoned Mum to say I would be back tomorrow. Wish I could stay forever – I LOVE Llanelly!!!

Tuesday 7th January
Took ten o'clock train back to Aberdare. Got out at the Upper Level station, so had to walk down. Didn't tell Mum I'd been to Llanelly, but I'm sure she guessed. Wore the new jumper Aunty Sarah had given me – Uncle Harry would have a fit if he knew! Went on to Penrhiwceiber. Heard Pat, Ben's dog, got badly scalded yesterday. Think she'll have to be put down. Ben in a filthy mood! Mac, Pat's twin, looks so sad and just lies there in front of the fire.

Wednesday 8th January
Pat was taken to the vet. Uncle Ben came back alone and stayed all day in the Billiard Hall next door. Mac very subdued, had to be coaxed to eat.

Thursday 9th January
Went to pics., saw *The Hardys Ride High* with Mickey Rooney. Jolly good!

Saturday 11th January
Went collecting for Grandma. [Weekly payments for goods bought in her hardware shop.] Taught Berta some English spelling. She is finding it very difficult. It's not logical like German.

Sunday 12th January
Drew for a while and then started my first OIL PAINTING – view of a thatched cottage and 'Ye Olde Country Garden' ON CANVAS! Went over my French vocabulary. Expect a test this week.

Tuesday 14th January
Started reading this term's Shakespeare play in English Literature. Of all things it has to be *The Merchant of Venice*! Miss Edwards is very fair to Shylock, but the cruelty and anti-Semitism of the Nazis has made me think of what would happen to us if, like the Channel Islands (occupied last June), the Germans would set foot here! I've been given the part of Portia, which I like very much. I would like to do law or perhaps medicine IF I go on to Higher (or even Art). I wish we

were doing *Macbeth* – tomorrow, and tomorrow … and tomorrow … I'd love to be a witch!

Friday 17th January
School as usual. Had a bad cold. Sniffed a lot. Missed the first bus on the way home as I had to wait for a long goods train to go by at the level crossing. Met David Powell on the next bus (the bus owner's son). He sat next to me and we talked all the way down. He stopped the bus for me, right outside Grandma's shop.

Saturday 18th January
Read *Little Dorrit* by Charles Dickens. Lots of rain – Station Road was flooded. Ben and Mrs. Prosser had a row over cigarettes – nothing new! Mrs. Prosser said Ben had taken her last two Woodbines – they both smoke like chimneys. Have decided I shall *never* smoke.

Sunday 19th January
Aunty Fanny and Uncle Harris came up from Cardiff. Grandma still tells her sister to "Sit up straight – you'll get a hump!" Aunty Fanny is very quiet and sweet. She must be at least 60! Her daughter is getting married at Easter and she asked Mum to find her a dress – "Something for the wedding that I can use afterwards to clean the house in," she said. Mum replied indignantly: "I don't sell clothes for scrubbing floors!"

Monday 20th January
Rhys Thomas, from opposite, died last night (T.B.). He's had it for three years. He was just 17. I always waved to him every day. Teresa Alberti, from the Italian ice-cream shop three doors up, also has T.B. now. I hope she gets better. Mrs. Thomas had to be brought from the chapel when it happened. Gran often gives Dai, her 8-year-old son, egg and chips when Mrs. Thomas comes home late from choir practice.

Tuesday 21st January
Nearly cracked my shoulder walking home – no buses because of the snow – satchel full of books. History test tomorrow.

Wednesday 22nd January
Joyce's birthday. She's 18, and is doing an art course in Cardiff School of Art. I baked her a sponge cake with a new recipe. Dried eggs, liquid paraffin (instead of fat), saccharine and brown flour. It came out so-so. We ate it with custard.

Saturday 25th January
Finished *Jane Eyre*. Watched Uncle Ben making teeth in the kitchen. He does a perfect job! Colour, shape and fit are like a work of art. Gran complained about

the mess – bits of wax everywhere. Ben never takes any notice. Saw film *Dark Victory*, with Bette Davis and George Brent. Very moving!

Tuesday 28th January
The TRIO came to school today. Everyone groaned when they heard about it. I thought they played wonderfully. I really LIKE classical music – but would never dare tell anyone!

Saturday 2nd February
Saw *Alexander's Ragtime Band* with Alice Faye and Tyrone Power – songs by Irving Berlin were great – still in my head: ('C'mon a hear – c'mon a hear …') Collected rent for Gran as she has a cold. I'm glad all the miners have work now (because of the war), and there's no unemployment for a change. Miners are a reserved occupation. At least they are appreciated!

Sunday 3rd February
Gran, Berta and I visited Gran's only brother. He lives in Aberdare with his wife Aunty Alma; they have no children. I spoke German to them and they seemed to understand me! Very pleased with myself! They came here from Germany just before the war. At the time Gran hadn't seen her brother for 50 years or more, since he left Lithuania at the age of 6 to escape being sent to the Russian Army. (They took boys as young as 10!) Now he had had to leave his home again.

Wednesday 5th February
On the way to the library I saw a young man riding a tall Shire-horse, crossing the bridge surrounded by a flock of sheep. He looked very foreign. I think he's the refugee who lives in Llwydcoed. He was wearing a small brimmed hat and a thick tweed jacket. I had on my gymslip and blazer and must have looked about twelve! He looked very serious – about 18, and made me think of Heathcliff from Brontë's *Wuthering Heights*.

Sunday 9th February
Mrs. Winter came from Swansea with Aunty Mary. BROUGHT Alex with her!!! We (Alex and I) talked in the shop (closed) – only quiet place. We are both doing the same subjects for Matric. He wants to do Higher and then go on to university, if he's not called up before. I wore the brown dress that I hate – Mum's taste!

Saturday 15th February
Took Berta to pics. Saw Greer Garson in *Remember*. We both enjoyed it. Did quite a lot of homework and started reading *The Tower of London* by W. Harrison Ainsworth. All about the Black Plague and The Great Fire of London. Wonderful book!

Monday 17th February

Heard *Curiouser and Curiouser* on the wireless and also *Monday Night at 8*. On the news – more heavy bombing raids last night This time Portsmouth and Plymouth were the main targets. [My father was brought up in Plymouth. My grandfather had sewn handmade officers' uniforms for the Navy there, before he moved to Llanelli.]

Tuesday 18th February

Managed to skip gym. Gym teacher, Miss Gordon, writes in a book whenever girls say they are "not well". She looked at me and said: "AGAIN? It's not four weeks!" I said "I'm irregular," and she let me off. Got a lot of work done instead.

Thursday 20th February

Swansea was heavily attacked last night!!! We telephoned the farm and they are all O.K. Many deaths and casualties. A lot of people fled to the mountains around the town. Worried sick about Alex and Co. Couldn't ask the Wymans because the telephone went dead in the middle of the call.

Friday 21 February

School as usual. Couldn't concentrate. Mum phoned the farm again. They said the WHOLE centre of Swansea is in ruins! Alex's street has been completely destroyed except for two houses – his and the one next door. The Winters are staying at the farm. Mr. Winter, Alex and Eva are all O.K., but Mrs. Winter is very upset. For many people it will be the third night sleeping in the open on the mountains. The Germans did not destroy the port however, which was really their target (like Plymouth and Portsmouth last week).

Saturday 22 February

Our bombers have dropped bombs on German cities this week – Cologne etc. (Australian and New Zealand troops are fighting with our troops in Africa.) Wrote to Alex c/o the Farm – I doubt he can get post at his home address, as the street isn't there!

Sunday 23 February

Alex PHONED ME – he's been helping his parents clear the dust from their house. The bombing caused many fires from broken gas mains and flooding from water pipes; electricity and telephone lines were made useless. Men from the whole area were helping to get people out from under the rubble, and to stop the fires etc. A group of men, including Bernard Cann [*sic*: Kahn] of Llwydcoed (the horseman I had seen), went down with picks and shovels, to help.

Monday 24th February
Long assembly this morning. Saw Spencer Tracy in *Fury*.

Tuesday 25th February
Had two hours of hockey this afternoon!!! All aches and pains after it. Got knocked to pieces! Read *Story of an African Farm* by Olive Schreiner. It was really marvellous – quite different to what I'd expected – full of great ideas, far too many to copy down – but gave me a lot to think about. I'm always interested in any book that has "Africa" in its title. [At the age of thirteen my father was taken by his uncle to South Africa to be a tutor to his children.]

Friday 28th February
John Johns has broken a bone again – for the sixteenth time! This time it is his right arm. He has had brittle bones since birth and always has to be careful. David Roberts, who sits behind me and has a wooden leg, is going to take work home to him every day and coach him for the exams. David wants to be a Methodist minister. They are both brilliant! David learns a page of the dictionary every day. (Saint David Roberts!)

Saturday 1st March – St David's Day
All the Junior School children dressed up in their red and black [Welsh] costumes. Went to pics. with Berta. Saw *Oh, Mr. Porter!* with Will Hay. Nearly

fell off the seat laughing when "One-Eyed Joe" appeared as an Irish ghost/gun runner complete with black eye-patch. *Our* One-Eyed Joe, who has never been to a cinema, looks exactly like the wizened Moore Marriott who played the Assistant Stationmaster.

Sunday 2nd March
Had a bust-up with Uncle Harry over Women's Careers. He says the ONLY THING for a girl to learn is shorthand and typing! Violent argument! Mum says: "Agree with him – don't make a row." She hates rows – me too!

Monday 3rd March
Lots of incendiary bombs were dropped on Cardiff. None here! Many of them started fires in the roofs of the houses they dropped on. Heard on the wireless how to deal with an incendiary bomb and what to look for. Not every bomb or incendiary device goes off. A special unit has been trained to de-fuse unexploded bombs [UXBs] – very dangerous and tense job.

Tuesday 4th March – Mum's Birthday
Came up to Aberdare after school. Raid last night … Mum went into the loft to look for incendiaries. She LOVES lofts! Came down beaming! She found two cooking pots; a pile of old dishes; two feather beds; a roll of thick material (good for blackout) and a bag of odd stockings! Says there's lots more up there. Uncle Harry said it'll all have to be cleared out because of fire hazard.

Wednesday 5th March
Mum very happy with the two old pots. We gave all our saucepans etc. to be melted down for armaments. All the railings went too. Pots and pans covered the Aberdare Clock Tower (about the size of a house). It was an amazing sight!

Thursday 6th March
Finished my German homework in the Maths lesson. This term we have a new German teacher. She's a well built spinster with grey hair tied back severely into a bun – not openly German influenced – so no problem for me – only she is iron-strict. She gives us hours of homework; I have nightmares about not finishing it for her next lesson.

Saturday 8th March
Went to pics. with Peggy. Saw *Mutiny on the Bounty* with Charles Laughton and went back to her home afterwards. (She has been my BEST friend for seven years!) Mr. Evans is a pithead winder. He asked me if I'd like to go down the pit in "his" lift. I said: "No thanks, Mr. Evans, that's one thing I definitely DON'T want to do!"

Photograph courtesy of the Imperial War Museum, London

Sunday 9th March

We all went to the farm today in a hired car. Pleased to see everyone O.K. Didn't meet Alex but saw the ruins of Swansea as we passed on the way to Fforestfach. Looks much worse than I imagined. You can see right across the city; it's almost flattened!

Monday 10th March

At lunch-time, six boys from the top form skipped school and went to a café in Mountain Ash. When they came back Mr. Carter-Smith, our headmaster, met them. They all had to queue up outside his study to get "six of the best!" "Whish, Swish!" went the cane. They are all TALL and going to be called up in a few months. Mr. C. is VERY short and ENGLISH! "Bad example," he muttered – he's usually very nice.

View of Swansea after the Blitz on the night of 20th February 1941

Wednesday 12th March

Tonight Mrs. Hoskins came in to do the ironing. Seeing her unhappy face, Gran put her arms around her and Mrs. Hoskins burst into tears. Gran and Mrs. Hoskins are best friends, they have so much in common. Listening to them talk to each other is like hearing Italian opera on the wireless – Gran speaks in Welsh/English/Lithuanian/Yiddish style and Mrs. Hoskins in Welsh/English with a Maltese accent. She comes from a very high-born family in Malta – fell in love with a sailor, married him and came back to his home – a terraced house in Penrhiwceiber where the sun never has a chance to shine through the almost constant grimy rain. In Malta Mrs. Hoskins rode her own horse. Gran too was made to leave the bright lights of New York to come to this small mining village where Grandfather soon died from the damp weather. Now Malta is being besieged by the Germans – bombed – starved – our convoys of food and ammunition blown up by submarines and bombers. So far they are holding out, but life there must be very grim. Mrs. Hoskins worries about her family; odd to think she's safer here in 'Ceiber!

Thursday 13th March

We all went to Cardiff to see Uncle Harris, Aunty Fanny & Co. Everyone was very shaken by the huge fire raids. Shocked to see all the damage – even the Cardiff Hospital has been struck. Got home in time to hear the 9 o'clock news.

Started reading *Mr. Deeds goes to Town* by Clarence Budington Kelland. It's the best book I've read this year – and the last for the moment as I'll have to swot for Matric, which is in four months' time.

Saturday 15th March
Saw *The Adventures of Robin Hood* with Errol Flynn. Errol Flynn is so handsome! Served in Jane Cooper's and was NOT A SUCCESS! Woman, la-di-da type, came in, very short and fat – at least a size 16. I showed her some smart slimming dresses, but SHE chose a bright green dress with stripes across, which was exactly wrong for her. "I like this," she said twirling round in it, "don't you think it's out of the common?" "Yes," I replied, "like GRASS!" Mum told me NEVER to tell a customer what I think, and always try to flatter them.

Saturday 29th March
Ben missed the football results on the wireless so he gave me money to get an *Echo* [*South Wales Echo*]. I waited outside for the *Echo* boy to pass. He is a half-caste boy, the only one in the valleys, with lightly tanned skin and tightly curled ginger hair. Every evening, as he runs along the valley as fast as a greyhound shouting "*Echo*, *Echo*!", everyone has their money ready for him. I have no idea where he lives (his father might have docked in Tiger Bay in Cardiff). He passes like the wind up Penrhiwceiber Road. I've never seen anyone run so fast.

Tuesday 1st April – April Fool's Day!
Mr. C. said in assembly: "No jokes please, unless they're harmless." He doesn't want false alarms etc. After the raid on Cologne in Germany we are expecting more trouble here.

Saturday 5th April
Finished making my white chiffon blouse. It's copied from a Hedy Lamarr film (*The Ziegfeld Follies*: 'You Stepped out of a Dream') – long wide sleeves caught at the wrist. It came out very well: I shall wear it with my red and white tartan skirt.

Monday 7th April
Greece and Yugoslavia have been invaded by the Germans. So many countries are now in the war. Ushy, our Geography master, is in his element! He has put up a map showing us how many countries the Germans have over-run! He and Churchill are quite sure we'll win! Well, we have *no choice*! Ushy (Llewellyn Lewis) is very tall, very bald, and has absolutely ruined my handwriting! His idea of a lesson is to read out long passages from a textbook while we write them down in our rough books like mad! At least I love drawing the maps. Quite a lot of bombing again last night – but not near here.

Tuesday 8th April
Got a surprise visit today! I shall ALWAYS remember this day – the 8th APRIL! Alex came in the late morning. The rain had stopped and I took him for a walk up the Cwm. It was so peaceful there. We walked over the green hills as far as the clear rushing brook and stood on the old bridge watching the water hitting the stones beneath. We talked for ages, about everything, and then, suddenly, we both knew how we felt for each other. The sun came out, the wet leaves sparkled; we walked to the old abandoned village (four houses and a chapel). We read the names on the overgrown tombstones, some from the 1700s. The world seemed to stop there, and time had no meaning. We promised to write to each other. A few wild violets stared at us, and we returned to the valley. I wore my grey Cossack coat with grey and red socks. Of course my new blouse. (I felt very glam!)

Wednesday 9th April
Poured today, but who cares. I AM IN LOVE! Every sentimental song I know is in my head. Thought of one person all day. Went over every second – couldn't concentrate on schoolwork – or anything. Wrote Alex a long letter.

Friday 11th April
Birmingham and Coventry were bombed again last night. Helped Gran to clean the kitchen and wash the dishes [to use on Pesach]. All the rooms have new wallpaper on them – rolls from the shop. Mrs. Rees did the wallpapering. I walked three miles up the mountain to a farm to get a bucketful of milk; carried it back without spilling a drop. Enjoyed the walk remembering Tuesday …

Saturday 12th April
A letter from Alex, written at 8.40 p.m. Tuesday evening. He wrote: "This morning I shall remember as long as I live as one of the happiest. Do you think that if I wrote *3* times a day it would be enough? (No?) Please answer quickly for I shall be waiting." – The sun came out – to suit my mood, so I walked to the shop in Aberdare, my head in the clouds. Bought two writing pads and diary paper next door. Served in Jane Cooper's, then went to pics. with Gwyneth. Saw Judy Garland in *Strike Up The Band*. It was STUPENDOUS! We came out dancing 'La Congo'.

Sunday 13th April
Helped Gran with the cooking. She is a wonderful cook! She made kneidlech, and showed me how to make them, rolling the dough into balls and dropping them into the soup. Read *Anna Karenina* and did some swotting.

Monday 14th April
Back to school. Assembly very solemn – long list of names read out [of former pupils killed, injured or missing] – prayers etc. Have to work hard, as it's so near to exams. Last term. Nose to the grindstone.

Tuesday 15th April
Awful day today. Weather suddenly turned very hot. Tried on last year's cotton school dress. I must have grown at least three inches (in all directions!) Wore my gymslip with white SOCKS. Bopa John [our headmistress] called me out and told me off, of course! "You will wear your black woollen stockings with your gymslip until you have a dress made!" she said. Went to Mrs. Thomas "Tanycoed" and begged her to make a dress quickly. Found an old one of Joyce's; spent some time shortening it; washed and ironed it, but it's still the wrong shape for me. Mum says it's not worth having a new one made for just one term!

Saturday 19th April
Went to Mrs. Thomas for my dress and collected rent for Grandma on the way there. Bought two more Collins Classics (from my saved bus money) to add to my collection – *Vicomte de Bragelonne* by Alexandre Dumas and *De Profundis* with *Salomé* by Oscar Wilde.

Monday 21st April
Peggy and I walked in the woods behind school. They are covered with daffodils – late this year. (A host of golden daffodils, dancing and fluttering in the breeze.)

Tuesday 22nd April
Replied to Alex's three letters. In one he'd written: "I found out that about 25 years ago your mother took my father over the same walk! She had an unfortunate "accident" – her heel broke and Dad had to carry her home! There's fun, eh? About your concern re: your possible visit next Sunday, I don't think you need worry. Mum knows that I would get to you within 1½ mins if I heard that you were within a five miles radius of me. About breaking engagements – I'd break prison bars if I had to. I'm so excited and impatient thinking you may come."

Sunday 27th April
Stayed home. Did a lot of revision for the Mock. Listened to wireless. Reports from Greece confirm that the Germans have occupied Athens. Read *Bubble Reputation* by P. C. Wren.

Thursday 1st May
Portsmouth had very heavy raids this week – terrible damage by night bombers. Plymouth was also attacked again.

Saturday 3rd May
Just now, two months before my exams, Mum has decided that Joyce and I should move to Aberdare – after seven years living with Gran. (Joyce says we've served "seven years penal servitude" since leaving Llanelly, moving to Gran's place at

160 Penrhiwceiber Road after Mum's shop closed and she vanished to work in London.) Mum wants to put two beds in the stockroom above the shop. There's a dressing table that I can use as a desk. Wondering how it'll work out with Uncle Harry. (He and Mum have been on their own for three years.)

Saturday 10th May
Listened to Alvar Liddell reading the news. There has been a big raid on London. Bombs have hit Westminster Abbey, the Houses of Parliament and the British Museum. Winston Churchill spoke – very stirring as usual.

Sunday 11th May
Sal's sister Gerty and husband Archie are coming to Penrhiwceiber from London; they are going to open a small grocery shop opposite. Wrote to Alex and then got down to some work.

Monday 12th May
Went from school to 'Ceiber, then packed and took the 6 o'clock bus to Aberdare. Very strange feeling. Bedroom opposite the cinema. Heard the sounds of the film *Beau Geste,* with Gary Cooper's deep voice, all evening.

Tuesday 13th May
Travelled DOWN to school instead of up. Mr. Powys (the Latin teacher) was on the bus – I asked him if I could "drop" Latin. He said no, he's sure I can pass it. I told him that I'm doing too many subjects and have to drop something. He said: "Well not mine!"

Wednesday 14th May
Did Physics and Chemistry homework in the Maths lesson. Ted (the Maths teacher) lets me do whatever I like. (I got very high marks for Maths in the Mock.) He knows I have almost no free periods. I do appreciate his attitude!

Friday 16th May
Joyce had a big row with Uncle Harry. Uncle had the sulks and said he's going to London. I told Mum: "I hope he doesn't come back!" Mum was cross with me but didn't say much. Asked me to do some alterations after school – hems and waistbands. Rush job for a customer.

Saturday 17th May
Went down to Gran's for a bath. She promised to heat the water for me. There is no bathroom in Aberdare and only one cold tap in the cellar for the whole building. The lavatory is on the other side of the yard – only one for 18 staff (and us). Our living room is in the back cellar – very good for safety. The radio is

blaring all day. The dance hall next door is very noisy, although only at night, cinema ditto. Still, who's complaining? There's a war on! Went to the Regal and saw Veronica Lake in *The Glass Key*. All the girls are copying her hairstyle – long, peroxide blonde, hanging down over one eye – not my type.

Sunday 18th May

Mum asked me to dress the window of Jane Cooper. She was amazed at how well I did it. So was I! I also did the other shop, Barbara Gold's, on the corner of Trecynon Street, for separates (blouses, skirts etc.).

Tuesday 20th May

Washed and styled my hair. Tried a new style – pageboy. It looks a bit severe, but makes me look older. Veronica Lake style has been officially banned after two women got their long hair caught in machinery in a munitions factory. Both were badly injured! Now factory girls have to wear cotton turbans or cut their hair very short.

Wednesday 21st May

Report from Alex on the evacuation of the children of Swansea to a safer area:

Ruth Golding's first shop at No. 11 Cardiff Street, Aberdare, in 1936

"On Thursday the children went away quite happily and left extremely mournful mothers. It was very moving – this parting. I've been trying out a song on the piano – the words are:

Here we are, two very bewildered people,
Here we are, two Babes that are lost in the Wood,
Something has happened to us,
A thing that's too marvellous,
And from now on the future looks wonderfully good.

"To which I say (??) … I'm afraid that now I have to report some bad news. A bitter controversy has been raging in our family over the question of us two. My mother says that I should not write to you till after C.W.B. [Central Welsh Board] I say that this is not only impossible, but that I wouldn't be able to take the exams because of my health. If possible could you try to answer so that I get the letter by first post on Monday, June 2nd? I'll be waiting for it. Oh dear … isn't life hard??? Cheer up, old man! You're not dead yet!

All the luck possible for your Exams.

DON'T FAIL!"

Saturday 24th May
Gwyneth called, with her boyfriend Frank and his brother John, to take me to a dance. Enjoyed it very much – danced every dance, either with John or other girls – especially liked the tango. John brought me home. Very quiet boy – not much to say – why does Alex have to live so far away?

Tuesday 27th May
Heard on the news about the sinking of the *Bismarck*, one of Germany's most advanced battleships. Everyone was in a good mood for the rest of the day; even Bopa John only gave me a "ticking off" about my brown shoes ("BROWN shoes in SCHOOL!!!") and didn't send me home.

Monday 2nd June
Clothes rationing has been announced. Mum is very worried, as she has just bought a lot of new stock. She soon cheered up when my friend Moira Vincenti from the fish and chip shop called and bought some expensive clothes. She is very well paid in the munitions factory in Hirwaun. She complains that ALL her clothes smell of fried fish oil! Mrs. Powell came in and offered Mum 2 lbs of butter instead of coupons. We all had a good laugh; Mum couldn't agree, but Mrs. Powell ordered a good Sunday best outfit for when she does receive her coupons.

Wednesday 4th June
Letter from Alex. He wrote:

"I found a most beautiful song the other day, this is my favourite now because the tune is lovely too. Tell me what you think of it.

Do I love you, do I?
Doesn't one and one make two?
Do I need you, do I?
Does July need a sky of blue?
Would I miss you, would I?
If you should go away
If the sun should desert the day
What would Life be?
Will I leave you? Never!
Could the ocean leave the shore?
Will I worship you forever?
Isn't Heaven for evermore?
Don't I want you, don't I?
Oh my darling it's plain to see
Don't you know I do
Don't I show you I do,
Just as you do me."

I wrote a few words in answer, in an old exercise book, as I do not intend sending any replies until the exams are over.

Friday 6th June

Uncle Harry came back from London. He told us about a spring manufacturer that his brother buys from. He was ordered by the government to make thousands of rolls of barbed wire instead of springs – then they realised that he was a refugee from Germany, so they interned him on the Isle of Man behind his OWN barbed wire! The fact that he was Jewish and an enemy of Germany didn't count.

Saturday 7th June

We all went to the cinema opposite and saw *The Adventures of Sherlock Holmes* with Basil Rathbone. There was a newsreel before the second feature about the big raid on London. It showed the night sky full of searchlights; bombers; fighter planes; barrage balloons; anti-aircraft fire; buildings in ruins and on fire, and fire fighters with their long jets of water. It looked horrific!! When we came out, Uncle, who never says much, exclaimed: "They don't tell you the half of it! … You hear the narrator, but when you're in it you hear the crash of falling masonry; the crackling of flames; the shouts and the explosions – and if you're hit by blast you don't hear anything for days. In the Underground it's all orderly and cheerful, but you know that everyone is wondering if the exits will be free and whether they can find their way home after the raid."

What remains in my mind was the sight of baths and beds tottering on the edge of floors that had no walls left, and the sad knowledge that as many as 1,500 people had died, including our Sal. I shall stop complaining about 11 Cardiff Street.

Tuesday 10th June

Our troops have evacuated Crete – the Germans have occupied it using parachute regiments. Bardia [in Libya] has also been taken, but Tobruk is holding out. Received a short note (not a letter!) from Alex, written on the 3rd, saying: "Despite our sad decision, I find that I absolutely must write. I've been asked to do farm work in the summer hols. My pay will be 5d [five old pence] an hour! Visited the farm today to see the new tractor. (Another first for Uncle Harris.) It's exactly like an ordinary Ford with no springs and a top speed of 8 mph. It's so simple that a baby could drive it (and Uncle Harris does – !!-?). Owen won't go near it. I offered to drive it, but my idea was repulsed (I wonder why?) … Yes, I *did* smash my specs coming off my bike at 50 mph! Still, I shall have new ones in a week. I do believe that this is the first tractor in Wales – so it has to be treated with respect!"

Friday 13th June

Really Friday the 13th as Mum fell down a manhole this morning! The workmen had left the cover off! She's quite bruised and scraped, and aching all over. Uncle put a long couch in the shop so that she can tell the shop girls what to do. She should have gone to bed. The doctor called at six.

Saturday 14th June

Mum, still in a lot of pain, stayed on the couch; I made lunch and supper. Made my first flan.

Thursday 19th June

Joyce boiled a chicken that Aunty Gwen had bought. When it was soft she sent me upstairs to ask Mum how to make the soup. Mum said the water we had boiled the chicken in WAS the soup. I ran down to the cellar just in time to stop Joyce throwing the "water" out!

Friday 20th June

A man came from the council to see about the "manhole accident". He said that as Mum's been in work every day he doesn't think she's entitled to any compensation. Poor Mum! She's been lying in pain for a week and has to be helped upstairs every night.

Saturday 21st June

Uncle Harry has been very good to Mum. He has taken over all the clothes alterations (by trade he's an upholsterer). He is a perfectionist, and when he measures a hem he throws 40 or so pins into his mouth and takes them out one at a time to pin up the hem. He uses a measuring stick, and everyone is delighted when they come back for a garment.

Sunday 22nd June

Grandma came up [with Berta] to see Mum. She brought her own homemade bread, cinnamon cake, chopped fried fish and homemade vermicelli. I miss Gran's cooking since coming to Aberdare. We mostly live on baked beans and chips! Berta and I walked as far as the Cynon and I showed her the bungalow with the beautiful garden. We never had a garden.

News: This month at least forty German bombers have been shot down – Merseyside was badly hit. We've been warned to be vigilant, as we can still expect an invasion from the Germans. These months of June to September are the best months for them to cross over by sea. I wouldn't wonder if they're massing again on the other side of the Channel. (It's only *22 miles* across!) Is this news a hint of something big being planned?

Photo taken by Berta of me by the Cynan

Monday 23rd June

Heard that the Germans have attacked RUSSIA!!! Another front (not us!). Hope it draws their bombers away from us. Winston Churchill said we would fight together with anyone to defeat Hitler – even the Russians. Almost caught the Penrhiwceiber bus after school out of habit, instead of the Aberdare bus! In four weeks today I will have finished school! One week to Matric.

Tuesday 24th June

Alex wrote describing his amazing experience last Sunday:

> "The aerodrome bus took us [the Air Cadets] as far as the apron outside the Control Tower. Outside, two Hurricanes were lined up, two new special Spits, one Anson and two Airspeed Oxfords.
>
> "After some standing about, at 4.33 on Sunday the 22nd of June I entered the cabin of an Airspeed Oxford:
>
> At 4.34 we moved down the approach road.
> At 4.35 we moved up the runway.
> At 4.36 we were off!!!!!
>
> "It was really wonderful. There was I, standing beside the pilot, while the altimeter rapidly changed from 0 to 1200ft. Below me I could see the beautifully green vale of Gower and, in the distance, the sea. Soon we were over the sea, and looking down I could see the deep brownish yellow sands, the deep blue sea and the green fields. I just can't tell you how wonderful it was. We travelled east, having made a complete circle. Then below me appeared a crescent of red roofed houses – our street! At 4.46 we landed and were whisked home by bus. Never in all my life have I had such a thrill (except perhaps once – you know when). That 10 minute flight standing under the Perspex roof of the Oxford will ever be in my mind."

The Airspeed "Oxford" Advanced Training Monoplane

Can I dare to hope that the war will be over before Alex gets his call-up papers and that he will fulfil his wish to become a pilot in peaceful skies?

Saturday 28th June
Took my books to Aberdare Park to study, as it's impossible to learn anything in the shop, especially on Saturday when everyone's rushing around.

Sunday 29th June
Stayed upstairs all day swotting.

Monday 30th June
Matric started today. English Grammar, French Oral. Three weeks of exams ahead.

Monday 7th July
Went over French paper with Bryan Griffiths. Since he went on the Student Exchange programme to France he has been top of the class. I'm still sorry I didn't go as arranged, but as Bryan came back only three days before the start of the war I can understand Mum not wanting me to go. Twenty other students all cancelled, so Bryan went by himself.

Saturday 12th July
Really fed up with the cinema opposite. Have heard the same sound track three times over. Have a lot of swotting to do. Helped a bit in the shop to get away from the noise.

Boating Lake, The Park, Aberdare

Sunday 13th July
Lovely sunny day. Stayed in all day revising. Mum and Uncle Harry went to see Gran, so I had the whole place to myself.

Monday 14th July
Exams all day.

Tuesday 15th July
Ditto.

Wednesday 16th July
Latin exam tomorrow. Fed up. Decided to do no work tonight; went to pics. instead! Saw *Scarlet Pimpernel* with Leslie Howard. Have not even opened my Latin book!

Thursday 17th July
Surprise! Easiest Latin paper they have ever given. If I had revised a bit I'm sure I would have passed – as it is, I doubt I've done well.

Sunday 20th July
Swotted like mad all day. Last exam tomorrow!

Monday 21st July
Heat-wave! It's *my 15th birthday*, and wouldn't you know, I had German exams all day – written and oral – *and* it's the last day of school for me! THE last day I shall wear this uniform and turn up at Mountain Ash County School. Cleared my desk and got to Aberdare absolutely finished.

Tuesday 22nd July
Today I have forgotten everything I have ever learned!

Monday 28th July
Helped in the shop all day. Big row with Uncle Harry over my future plans. They want me to enrol in Clarke's College, Cardiff, to take a secretarial course!!!

Tuesday 29th July
Walked down to Aberaman to see Uncle Charlie and talk to him about Uncle Harry. He said one can't always do what one wants. He had wanted to be a lawyer and now he runs a village grocery shop. Maurice (his little boy), said: "*I'm* going to be a *doctor*!" Uncle Charlie promised: "I'll make sure you do!" [And he did!] I ate half a tin of custard creams and went for a long walk to cool off.

Thursday 31st July

Uncle Harry and Mum went to London to buy stock. Gwyneth came with her bike and taught me to ride – a bit wobbly.

At last – a letter from Alex. He wrote:

> "Thanks a million for your 'book'. 'Poor thing!' You must think an awful lot of me to write that diary, but really I'm ever so pleased because now I KNOW. I read it all night and once again our thoughts make a parallelogram … Well, how do you like being 15? Somehow I wish this letter was 10 years hence and that you were 25 and me 25½ – don't you? I've been trying to get a bike ever since May, and I've failed. When I do get one I've promised myself that I'm going to see the Cwm again – meanwhile I've been doing some song writing,
>
> Oh, I've been struck by Cupid's dart,
> 'Cos I love a little girl with all my heart,
> I hope that we two never part,
> It's Foolish but it's Fun.
> I know she loves me too
> Because she said the other day,
> I only hope that this is true
> And it always stays that way.
> And so I go around I find,
> You'd think that I was out-of-my-mind,
> And p'raps I am, 'cos love's not kind.
> It's Foolish but it's Fun."

Saturday 2nd August

Wandered about in the back streets of Aberdare. Found a partly opened large wooden door at the end of a leafy lane. Went inside. Looked like an old foundry with lots of rusty iron around and a very large open tank more than 20 feet long, filled with water and crammed full of water-lilies! Large, round, shiny, green leaves, with both yellow and white lilies floating on top. Sat there in the sun. Going to be my secret place. Hummed 'Wanting You' from *New Moon* and thought of Alex.

Monday 4th August

Stayed up late until Mum came back from London. She brought 2lbs [pounds weight] of Viennas [cocktail sausages] which, of course, I immediately boiled. I must have eaten at least a lb (It's 11.30 p.m.!) She also brought HALVA!

Tuesday 5th August

Asked Mum if I could buy a bike. She said: "No, I've had enough trouble with Joyce always having accidents." But Joyce is clumsy and I'm not – but *no* bike.

Wednesday 6th August
It has been arranged for me to start in Clarke's College in September. Typing, Shorthand and Bookkeeping. I have NO say in the matter!!!

Friday 8th August
Worked in the shop. Getting better at not saying what I think!

Saturday 9th August
Mrs. Brodie and her daughter Stella have come to Grandma's from London for a few weeks' break. They let Gran wait on them hand and foot! Stella (one year older than me) complained that she has nothing to do, so I took her up the Cwm. She actually wore high heels to go on a mountain walk! One heel broke off on the way down, so she had to take both shoes off and walk barefoot.

Sunday 10th August
Went to Aberdare Park. Read *The Citadel* by A. J. Cronin. Beautiful day. Replied to Alex's three letters which arrived this week from Harvest Camp. Last week he was promoted (in the A.T.C.) to Acting Sergeant Instructor – Instructor of Aircraft Recognition, and gave a lecture to his Squadron – he also sent a short note from:

> "Harvest Camp. Abergavenny.
> CURSE CAMP COMPANY!
>
> "Once again I've had to sneak out on my bike to write to you because I can't in camp. But – why didn't I see you this weekend? I rode to Pontypool twice and waited two hours each day, but no Cynthia – I know I'm asking rather a lot, but it's too much to ride 34 miles, and be back in camp late, and not even having had a glimpse of you! …"

I explained to Alex that "our" Ponty is Pontypridd in the Taff Valley [30 to 40 mins away] while Ponty*pool* is almost as far away as England!

Friday 15th August
Worked in Barbara Gold's; came home about six and walked into a seething volcano. Joyce and Uncle Harry were having a violent row. Joyce ran up the stairs as Uncle Harry took off his belt. "I'll thrash that girl," he shouted, shaking it about. Mum came in from the back kitchen, as if nothing was happening, with a cup of tea! "Here's a cup of tea, Harry," she said, putting it down in front of him. I stared at the large oval grease-spot on the wall behind his chair made by his Brylcreemed hair, and tried to make myself invisible. I have no idea what the row was about!

Monday 25th August
Exam results!!! Passed in all 12 subjects that I'd hoped for. (Failed in Latin as expected!) All Credits in: Arithmetic, Geometry, Algebra, Physics, Biology,

Chemistry, History, Geography, English Grammar and English Literature, German and French. I don't intend to collect my certificate from M.A. County as the Headmaster will want to know what I'm going to do – and I can't say "Secretarial College". He'd be shocked! Told Mum about my results. She said rather offhandedly: "Well, I expected you to pass."

Thursday 28th August

Mum decided to go to London for the day, as it's half-day closing here. She was late for the train, so she sent me to tell Morgan the Station to hold the train for her. We chatted until she came running, dressed up to the nines. I waited until the train had disappeared. I love the smell of stations and trains. On the way home I met Mr. Davies. I feel sorry for him, as his son is a conscientious objector. I discussed this with Frank when he called round to collect Gwyneth. Frank said that *we* are fighting so that people like Mr. Davies' son can be free to have their OWN opinion. Gwyneth said that if everyone was a conscientious objector Hitler would be here in less than a week and then no one would be free to do anything! My trouble is, I think they are both right!

Saturday 30th August

Great letter from Alex this morning:

> "Your letter of the 26th fixed things for me nicely, made me happy all day. – Incidentally …
>
> **CONGRATULATIONS!**
>
> I'm so glad to hear of your success, I was thrilled. *Thank Goodness* you passed! But I hope you continue to succeed in Cardiff, and go to both America and Paris. I'm just listening to Carmen Miranda, and appropriately she's singing 'I-I-I-I-I-I-I- like you *very* much!' Still 1951 (or '48) draws on apace – something to look forward to P.G. [Please G-d]. But, I'm afraid that I'm at a disadvantage here, because 22 is a very marriageable age for a girl but not for a boy. How horrible if you were Mrs. Somebody [else]. Anyway there are still 7 years to go …
>
> Stop Press. *May* have uniform this afternoon – because big Parade to meet tanks tomorrow.
>
> P.S. Saw *I Wanted Wings* (at last). Thoroughly enjoyed it. Jolly fine film.
> P.P.S. Guess what? I have made plans for Sunday so please wait in for me – in case – etc, etc, etc."

Very excited thinking about tomorrow.

Sunday 31st August

Alex kept his word and CAME TODAY! He cycled all 26 miles from Swansea and was pretty tired when he arrived. We went to the lily-pond, which looked even lovelier as the white lilies were quite open and their tips had turned pink. Alex was surprised that I had found such a quiet, secluded spot in Aberdare, but a sudden thunderstorm put an end to our walk and we ran back to the shop. It was a good ending as I enjoy thunder and lightning. On the way to the station he showed me a poetry book he was reading by Dylan Thomas, who was a former student at Alex's grammar school in Swansea. I shall try and get it from the Library tomorrow. The train left at six – who says "Parting is such sweet sorrow"?!

Sunday 7th September
One year since the first big air attack on London. The Blitz really seems to be over. Uncle Harry went to London and brought back a large biscuit tin full of saccharines. He also brought thousands of tiny envelopes; we are supposed to put 100 saccs. into each one and sell them in the shop, to be used instead of sugar.

Monday 8th September
Counted saccs. all day today. Had the radio on, so didn't go quite mad! They sold very well – people are coming back for more and, better still, some are tempted to buy a dress or coat.

Tuesday 9th September
Got up at seven (!) and caught the 8.25 train to Cardiff. Got to Clarke's College. I felt very new. Didn't like the Typing lesson – very boring! Shorthand quite interesting. Don't know anyone!

Wednesday 10th September
Today at college they were teaching us how to SPELL!!!! E.g. Address, 2 Ds 2 Ss, and Sincerely, 1 S, 1 C, 2 Es. Feel I'm back in Penrhiwceiber Infants'. Quite disgusted! Managed to read on the train home, as it's still quite light: *Sons and Lovers* by D. H. Lawrence.

Sunday 14th September
Discovered that I have NOTHING decent to wear for college. Having lived in school uniform for four years and grown (5ft 5½), I'm really short of ordinary clothes! I refuse to wear any more of Joyce's old things.

Monday 15th September
Finished seventeen Shorthand exercises at the weekend. Very pleased with myself. The teacher was very cross. Says she hasn't time to mark so much work! Told to do less and more thoroughly. She doesn't believe I find it so easy.

Tuesday 16th September
Have made a few friends, both in college and on the train. Had baked beans on toast with a fried egg at the Kardomah Café at lunch-time. Enjoyed looking at

the shops – got new ideas for dressing the windows of Jane Cooper. Read *Sons and Lovers* until Ponty. Saw *Goodbye Mr. Chips* with Robert Donat and Greer Garson in the cinema opposite. Reminded me of wonderful Miss Evans, who had taught me to love books, and opened up a whole world of new ideas to the dreamy ignoramus aged seven, who had arrived in her class from Llanelly – I owe her so much. Wrote to Alex.

Wednesday 17th September
Saw super dress today in Howells' window. Too late to go in, so shall try tomorrow. Listened to news tonight. The Germans are approaching Odessa where Uncle Harry's parents came from. His father had spent some time in Turkey making all the upholstery furnishings for the Sultan's Palace. His parents both died in London the year he was 18, leaving him, the eldest, to look after his eight younger brothers and sisters! Uncle Harry says that since then he became an atheist.

Friday 19th September
Bought THE Dress! It's yellow, with red, green and black paisley stripes going across it. Shirt-waister – looks wonderful! Very happy on the way home. Mum was furious! "With *two thousand* dresses in our shop, you have to waste money buying one somewhere else …! And RETAIL TOO!" (Oh, dear, oh, dear!!!)

Saturday 20th September
Tried to slow down Shorthand exercises. Finished fourteen. Shall only hand in seven or there'll be complaints! Went to Aberaman to see Uncle Charlie. Aunty Gwen has gone to Aldershot to work in an Amusement Arcade. Loads of soldiers there with time and money to spend. Went on to Gran's for a bath. Water not very hot. (Gran says cold water is healthier!) Helped Berta with her homework. Gran thinks Gwen should stay home and look after her family. I told Mum about Aunty Gwen … she said: "Good for her!"

Monday 22nd September – Jewish New Year
Went to shul . Didn't understand much, so I got very bored. Mum and Gran can't understand Hebrew either. Joyce and I went for a walk and came back to hear the shofar [blowing of the ram's horn]. Uncle Solly conducted the service. Quite a few new faces.

Tuesday 23rd September – second day of Jewish New Year
Today I read some of the English in the Prayer Book. Arranged with Dita Ilsberg to go for a walk in the afternoon. Dita is one year older than me; we took Berta with us and saw Bernard Kahn, but didn't speak to him.

Saturday 27th September
Helped in the shop. Wrote to Alex. (He's doing Higher School Certificate.) Went to pics. with Meg Beynon. She's getting married in a few weeks' time. Mum has given her the wedding dress from the Cwmbach girl – no one wanted to buy it. Meg was very pleased, she saves all her money for her bottom drawer – £2 a week.

Monday 29th September
Learning Bookkeeping and Accounting in College. Started typing Jane Cooper's letters and entered the day's takings into the Accounts Book.

Tuesday 30th September
Got up in good time to catch the train – for once! All the gang were there, Connie, Pat, Dylis, Idris, Bill and John. We always try to get a compartment to ourselves. (Pat and Bill join the train at Ponty.) Letter from Alex – with a poem from Goethe's 'Maileid':

Oh Mädchen, Mädchen,
Wie lieb' ich dich!
Wie blickst dein Augen,
Wie liebst du mich!

Oh Maiden, Maiden
How I love thee!
How your eyes sparkle
How much you love me!

Happy all evening – even nice to Uncle Harry!

Wednesday 1st October – Day of Atonement (Yom Kippur)
We all fasted – even Uncle Harry, who doesn't believe in anything! Glad we didn't have to walk the five miles from Penrhiwceiber. Grandma and Berta came and stayed the night with Uncle Solly. The Brodies are going back to London tomorrow!!!

Friday 3rd October
My friends asked me if I'd enjoyed my day off! Didn't explain we had fasted and prayed all day etc.

Saturday 4th October
Modelled a dress for a customer (she didn't buy it). Looked so good on me, Mum said I could KEEP it. It's soft blue wool with printed coloured squares. Mum took one for herself – in red, one size smaller. Went to pics. and saw *Thief of Baghdad* with Sabu and Conrad Veidt in glorious Technicolor. Marvellous spectacle! Amazing newsreel! Saw MYER WYMAN in officer's clothes disembarking from

a ship somewhere in Egypt. He smiled and looked so handsome. I never expected to see one of the family on the newsreel! Phoned the farm to tell them – they're going to try to see it too!

Monday 6th October
Very bad report from the Russian Front – the Germans are outside Moscow! Listened to the 9 o'clock news: counted saccharines afterwards. Reading one of Leslie Charteris's "Saint" books.

Tuesday 7th October
Letter from Alex. His parents have found a new house (their house is too unsafe to sleep in after the bombing). Eva is still in Tredegar: Alex, on the farm. Alex wrote partly in French: "I was à la ferme hier parce que vôtre cousine Yetta est très malade. She has been bleeding for two weeks since she had a tooth out. Poor kid, she looks awful."

Yetta has long blonde curls, blue eyes and is very pretty.

Saturday 11th October
Mac got run over today!!! [Ben's black Scotch Terrier.] Went to 'Ceiber for a bath and heard the news. I liked Mac best of all the three dogs. Mac was never really himself after Pat, his twin died – he's from the last litter that Ben bred. Everyone is upset for Ben. He was out when I arrived and I didn't meet him.

Monday 13th October
Guess what?!! The whole of Penrhiwceiber is talking about Uncle Ben. He's joined up for the Army! Ben??!!

> Run, 'Itler, run 'Itler, Run, Run, Run,
> Here comes our Ben with his Gun, Gun, Gun!

We're bound to win the war now.

Tuesday 14th October
Quite sunny today. Took the tram to Roath Park in my lunch-time. Saw Joyce there boating on the lake with a boyfriend. I pretended not to see her. Usual gang on the way home in the train. Sang all the way to Ponty, as it's getting too dark now to read on the journey home.

Friday 17th October
Letter from Alex. He wrote:

> "I'm going to send you pieces in both French and German to keep you up to scratch, for you can't afford to lose what knowledge you have."

Also a long typed poem called 'Nähe Des Geliebten' written when Goethe was away from his wife for a short while around 1828:

> Ich denke dein, wenn mir die Sterne Schimmer (gleam)
> Vom Meere strahlt; (shines)
> Ich denke dein, wenn sich des Mondes Flimmer (glitter)
> Im Quellen malt.
> Ich bin bei dir, du seist auch noch so ferne,
> Du bist mir nah!
> Die Sonne sinkt, bald leuchen mir die Sterne,
> O wärst du da!
>
> I think of you, when the stars shine on me
> Beamed from the sea;
> I think of you, when the moon glitters
> Reflected in the spring water.
> I am with you, however far you are,
> You are near to me!
> The sun is setting, soon the stars will light up,
> If only you were here!

This comes as a cry from the depth of my heart ever so often – "O wärst du da! If only – !"

According to Alex, Goethe fell in love at 15 and almost married …! Also Lamartine. Alex's parents have at last been able to buy poles for the blackout curtains, so they are moving this week.

Sunday 19th October

<u>JOYCE'S STORY!</u>

Very odd occurrence today: The Tale of the *Evil Spirit.*

Joyce, Mr. Kahn and his son Bernard, Mr. Bowden who lives with them, Uncle Solly, Mr. Schwartz, Mr. Freed, etc. all went down to Mountain Ash to EXORCIZE A GHOST!! Mr. Jacobs, a widower who lives alone, says his dead wife comes back every night and beats him when he's asleep. He didn't treat her well when she was alive and now she's taking revenge on him. He's so scared he hasn't slept for a month and goes to bed wearing long fishing boots to stop her scratching his legs! So ten men and Joyce went down to say some prayers in the house – and Mr. Jacobs asked his wife for forgiveness in front of them. They all came back on the bus laughing and singing: "She'll be coming round the mountain when she comes, YIPEE-AY, she'll be wearing pink pyjamas when she comes …" etc., etc.

(Strange how seriously we take ghost stories in fiction, like the ghost of Hamlet's father, but in real life we think it's a big joke.) Anyway, I hope it's done the trick, otherwise he's for Bridgend! [Mental Institution.]

Joyce said Bernard Kahn's first words to her were: "WHAT are you?" To which she replied: "I'm a Neo-Lamarckian!" Of course HE meant what kind of Jew was she? Religious, liberal etc. Lamarck – Jean Baptiste Pierre Antoine de Monet, Chevalier de Lamarck (!) produced his book on the theory of evolution which preceded Darwin's Theory of Evolution and became known as Lamarckism. Trust Joyce to be way-out (or way back!) She's also an agnostic. I can't imagine what Bernard Kahn, who comes from a VERY religious family, thought of her answer. As far as Judaism is concerned, we are both only Jewish by birth; and irreligious "by ignorance". Our knowledge can be summed up in three words – Passover, New Year and The Fast – and eating Kosher food (almost) – except for Uncle Harry, who doesn't on purpose. Couldn't get to sleep thinking about the above. Concluded that, unlike Joyce, I know exactly what I believe – that G-d exists, but my ideas on religion are very personal and NOT to be written about.

Monday 20th October

Almost missed the train this morning – Mr. Morgan kept it waiting for me! Visited Aunty Millie [my father's sister] at lunch-time. She has started a small restaurant to support her family. My Uncle and cousin Zena were both killed in a car crash a few weeks before his eldest daughter's wedding! Aunty Millie was pleased to see me, but was too busy serving to spend much time with me. Went home and saw *Bringing Up Baby* in cinema opposite. Cary Grant and Katharine Hepburn – very good comedy. Shall hear it in my bedroom for the rest of the week!

Tuesday 21st October

Letter from Alex. He wrote:

> "On Thursday they blew up an unexploded bomb behind our house – we had to evacuate. It blew all our replaced windows out and covered everything with three inches of dust. Mum can't sleep because 300 yards behind our house they have set up a gun park. Whenever Liverpool has it, the planes always pass over Swansea both ways. The last three nights have been one long bang. The guns are 3.7s and 4.5s and make an awful din, and with all the other gun parks at work, you can't imagine the row. Last night I had the satisfaction of hearing one plane brought down – my fifth since January. It crashed not far away but no bombs dropped here; anyway there is nothing much left to bomb in this shell of a town. The roads have all been cleared of rubble; gas pipes and water mains have been repaired, so it's comparatively easy to cycle from home to school, but impossible to ignore the bleakness that surrounds me – I can see the whites of my knuckles on the handlebars and feel the anger blazing from my eyes – how I wish I already had my pilot's wings. Passing the bombed out devastation of my hometown I am not my usual complacent self – but in a fiendishly vengeful mood. I mourn for the familiar shops – no more W. H. Smith's to wander round looking for something to read; no Boot's the Chemist or Dr. Scholl's. Not one shoeshop left, for Upsons' Shoes, Lennards' Boots, Trueform, R. E. Jones, all gone – along with Stead & Simpsons, Potter Gilmore Gowns, Dean's Tailor and Burton's

(where my new jacket was waiting for an alteration). College Street has vanished with its row of shops, Welsley Chapel and our dear old Kardomah Café. In Castle Street, Lloyds Bank has gone – the list is endless – suffice it to say I feel a stranger in the town of my birth. How does this mindless destruction rank as a war victory for Germany, the mighty conqueror? ... If you have time, read Drayton's 'Agincourt', you'll find it in your book of Longer Poems (p. 72) – extract –

And turning to his men
Quoth our brave Henry then:
Though they to one be ten,
Be not amazed:
Yet have we well begun,
Battles so bravely won
Have ever to the sun
By fame been raised.

The siren has just gone so 'I must away and to my post'. Do come in the holidays, the farm is relatively quiet and with a bit of luck it might even snow."

Thursday 23rd October

A lovely long letter from Myer today. Poor Wy! He's had Malaria from Aug. 20th to Sept. 10th. He's now in a convalescent home in Palestine after being in hospital. It made me think, though, of those *wonderful* "peace" days up on the farm. When will those days return? I wait and wish.

Saturday 1st November

Ben came home today wearing his khaki uniform. He's much thinner! He was to be sent to Egypt, but ended up in Nottingham where he's been put into the Dental Corps, which makes sense. Told Grandma that he had met Hilda (Gran's former help) working in a grocery store. She wants to introduce him to a nice girl (!) she knows – (about 40, I expect!).

Wednesday 5th November

Definitely NO FIREWORKS tonight!

Wednesday 12th November

Have started reading *None But the Lonely Heart* by Richard Llewellyn. Quite a few of our ships have been sunk this week, including the aircraft carrier *Ark Royal*. Alex had a surprise last Sunday – he was in the middle of his homework when a large red piece of bomb shrapnel dropped onto the table in front of him, missing him by inches. Now the Winters need another new window and a new tabletop.

Friday 14th November

ABSOLUTELY GREAT NEWS! A registered letter came from America! *Two* of Berta's brothers are alive! They traced her address through Bloomsbury House.

They sent photos of themselves (one is VERY handsome). Made a special cake for her, to celebrate. Took it to 'Ceiber and helped her to write a reply. Got back to Aberdare late, but extremely happy.

Saturday 15th November

Went to see Berta, talked a lot and showed her how to crochet. We unpicked an old jumper for the wool, as there's almost none to be bought in the shops. Met Miss Evans [my former teacher]; she *hugged* me. She thinks I'm still at M.A.C.S. doing Higher. Luckily the bus came, so I didn't have time to disappoint her.

Thursday 20th November

Bad news for my *teeth*! *Milk* is to be rationed. From now on only 2 pints a week allowed for each adult – that means ⅓ pint a day. No cream can be sold by the farmers as it must be used to make butter and cheese (also rationed), as obviously none can be brought in from abroad.

Friday 21st November

Started knitting a new jumper – green and cream – lovely pattern. Heard that Ben is getting quite serious about Rae (Hilda's bright idea). It seems there are two sisters, one pretty and 38 years old and one not (40 or so). When Ben went to visit them, Rae, the older one, sent her sister out so that *she* could meet the possible suitor – OUR BEN (!) – she must be desperate!

Thursday 27th November

Went with Margaret and Idris (two of the "train gang") to see the Carl Rosa Opera. It was *La Bohème* and was so good I came out walking on air! Most wonderful theatre I've ever seen. The Philharmonic Orchestra will be playing here next week. We've planned to get tickets. Shall write to Alex to see if he can join us.

Saturday 29th November

Served in Barbara Gold's. Came home lunch-time as I started sneezing and coughing. Went to bed. Read *None But the Lonely Heart* (that's me all right).

Monday 1st December

All tinned foods are to be sold on a points system now. Food situation getting quite bad. Dream of white bread and MELONS! (Even one slice!) Almost no fruit to buy. Mum and Uncle have started an allotment and work there every Sunday. (Uncle does the digging and Mum, in thick gloves to protect her nails, gives orders.) They are growing potatoes, carrots and onions – the cabbages were full of slugs. Gran brings us eggs from her chickens, but mostly we have to use dried egg, which tastes awful. Not bad in cakes. Fish is also scarce because the German submarines and mines make fishing dangerous. Uncle Solly has an allotment – he's really expert at it. No letter from Alex today.

Tuesday 2nd December
Started reading *Gone with the Wind*, by Margaret Mitchell, in the train. It is over 1,000 pages. Knitted on the way home as it's too dark to read and I have taught myself to knit by feel! (Eat carrots and you can see in the dark!)

Wednesday 3rd December
Letter waiting for me from Alex, written on the farm last Sunday. He wrote:

> "I love going to the farm because of the 'associations' –as in 'Tintern Abbey' by W. Wordsworth:
>
> Once again I see
> These little hedgerows, hardly hedgerows, little lines
> Of sportive wood run wild: these pastoral farms,
> Green to the very door; and wreaths of smoke
> Sent up in silence, from among the trees!
>
> "After some time I went to the piano and played the tunes the 'gang' used to play – you know them. An especial favourite of mine is 'I have Lost my Heart in Budapest' – but I substitute 'Aberdare'. (I only wish I could come and find it.) Not only do I like the tune, but also the fact that I can really play it helps to make it a favourite. However since I played to you in Pen'ceiber I've progressed a lot. Other favourites are 'Bei mir bist du schön' (apt wording – especially the introduction) and 'When that man is dead and gone' (You can guess why.) By the way, I shall make every effort to meet you in Cardiff on Thursday."

That's tomorrow! I'm trying *not* to get too excited – so many things may go wrong.

Thursday 4th December
Alex managed to get a direct train from Swansea to Cardiff. We went with Marge and Idris to hear the Philharmonic Orchestra. They played *Scheherazade* by Rimsky-Korsakov. No words to describe it. Ran to Cardiff station to catch our respective trains. Still in a dream when I arrived in Aberdare.

Friday 5th December
LETTER for Berta from her brothers. They are so happy she's found a good, loving family. Well, she's almost like a sister to me, and Gran really loves her. (Now that Ben, Mum, Joyce and I have left, Berta is a great companion for her.)

Saturday 6th December
Helped in Barbara Gold's. Two women came in today, arm in arm, one with long curly hair and the other in trousers, shirt, tie and her hair cut like a man. The curly-haired one bought a very fussy frilled blouse; Glenda finished serving them then nudged me, and when they had gone she told me about them. Very surprised! Had never heard that name used before! It seems everyone in Aberdare knows about

them. (Dictionary definition: pertaining to the Island of Lesbos in the Aegean Sea, the home of a famous school of lyric poets including Sappho; amatory, erotic.)!?

Sunday 7th December
Visited Gran. We heard on the radio that Japan has declared war on us!!! They have bombed an American port called Pearl Harbour. America is now IN the war with us – I think I'm pleased, as we do need America to be fully behind us. (I can imagine Ushy getting out his maps in M.A.C.S. Pacific, etc. etc. Malaya, Philippines etc.)

Thursday 11th December
Gloomy news. Japs are VERY dangerous enemies. Advancing rapidly. It really is a WORLD WAR now. Spent the evening drawing – and filling saccharine packets. Listened to wireless – the Germans have declared war on America! Went to bed before 10 p.m.

Friday 12th December
Spent the whole evening drawing (mainly fashion designs). I hope to try for a place in the London School of Fashion next year. I have written to them for an Application Form. Mum absolutely against me going to London.

Thursday 18th December
Finished in Clarke's today until January. Learned quite a lot, can type at a good speed; and shorthand is simple. The train was very dark on the way home. [No lights were allowed because of the blackout.] Full compartment emptied out at Ponty – except for one man. No corridors on these valley trains so I felt a bit worried – but had my knitting needle ready in case he would try anything. Glad to arrive in Aberdare.

Saturday 20th December
Had a reply from the London School of Fashion. They have accepted me for September, BUT they are only accepting payment for one month at a time in case they get bombed out. Very negative reaction from Mum to this news.

Sunday 21st December
Freezing weather. Can't write much tonight – my writing is so bad as my hands are so cold.

Monday 22nd December
Served in the shop until 9 p.m. – worked late because of Xmas – people came to buy from all over the valley. Our shop 'Jane Cooper' has become very well known. We always get the newest, smartest stock from London. (I am now "Jane Cooper's daughter"!)

Thursday 25th December
Joyce went for a walk today with Bernard Kahn. She told me that "*today*" is his BIRTHDAY! On *Xmas Day*! What a laugh! He's 18. He came back with her for a few minutes – down to our cellar – our cat took one look at him and dived under the easy chair with fright! The Kahns are moving from Llwydcoed to a house in Clifton Street exactly opposite Uncle Solly and Aunty Alma. Bernard has a job on a farm above Abernant. Had a long letter from Alex yesterday, but was too exhausted to answer it last night.

Friday 26th December
Shop closed. Sorted out my books – threw away school exercise books – found a small book of poems written when I was 12. One was called 'Stanzas Written While Wandering', another was called 'Why?' … I have a lot more questions to ask now. Five more days until I'll be in Swansea.

Saturday 27th December
Yesterday we listened to the King's Speech at 3 p.m. Tonight the news was not "of good cheer" as the Japanese captured Hong Kong on Xmas Day – they have also invaded Borneo, Sarawak and Kuching. On the Russian front, the bitter winter snows have halted the German advance, but the fighting around Leningrad continues. This is our third Xmas of the war – miss the sound of bells, and, suddenly, also the wonderful smell of tangerines – they were always imported at this time of year individually wrapped in blue, red and silver paper – Mum always bought a box. The memory was so powerful – it almost seemed real.

Sunday 28th December
Berta has had another letter. Her two brothers want to join up, but I think only the older one has been accepted. Imagine if he would be sent here! I hope NOT to the Pacific.

Tuesday 30th December
Can hardly believe I am going to Swansea tomorrow. Staying with Rochale [Aunty Mary's daughter] and Hymie. They have a grocery shop near the farm. Phoned Alex to tell him what time I shall arrive.

Wednesday 31st December
What a year – my school days are over – and what a way to end it! Alex met the bus and took me to Fforestfach. There was a clear moon; the trees and ground were covered with hoarfrost. Complete silence, except for the sound of our footsteps and conversation. I am so glad to be away from Aberdare, and too happy to write much. New Year's Resolution: – to leave home when I'm 16!!!

1942

Thursday 1st January
Phoned Alex this morning and arranged for him to come for lunch. We took the bus to Swansea and went to the Maxime to see *Cheers for Miss Bishop* and *In the Navy*. Got back at about 8 p.m. Jenny Seal was there, and when she asked Alex if he liked *Cheers for Miss Bishop* he said "You'd better ask her (me), *I* didn't see it," meaning that he hadn't taken much notice of it. Jenny coughed – as it did seem rather suggestive!

Friday 2nd January
Norma [Rochale's little daughter] woke me up at 6.30 this morning. Went to catch the bus for Llanelly at 11 but it didn't come until 12. Ever so windy, and raining slightly. Found Aunty Sarah in bed, but she got up to see me. Aunty Beaty is ill again. Played with Pam. Left at 7 p.m. On the way to the bus I saw Mr. Jones and he told me my doll's house was ready – he's been making it in his spare time for years – since I was six! I told him to keep it for my grandchildren (?) (!)

Saturday 3rd January
Norma woke me up at *five a.m.* this morning! Went over to Rifka's at 3 p.m. Absolutely pouring. Alex came, wearing his A.T.C. [Air Training Corps] uniform. The rain was now coming down in buckets, and Jeff told him it would shrink in the rain. Standing under the porch of the Rialto waiting for the bus, Alex started whistling and then sang: "You're in my arms and I thrill to your touch while we're dancing." It was so dark I couldn't see his face. Got back to Rochale's soaked but happy. Alex is coming over tomorrow to take me out for our traditional walk down by the stream, so I do hope it keeps fine.

Sunday 4th January
Alex came at 3 p.m, rushing up the stairs a few at a time. We went over to the farm and I dragged him off towards the stream. The ground was terribly mucky. We got down as far as the last field but found the mud formed a practically impassable barrier. We walked over to the heather ditch in the old quarry and tried to get down onto the road. It was a fairly good jump, so Alex went first and then caught me – right into his arms. Took the 8.05 p.m. bus back to Aberdare. The moon was out, and it was a full one – I've never seen it so low before and it was very bright. In spite of the blackout I could see the whole countryside bathed in light. When I got

home I found no one in. A few minutes later Joyce arrived. She'd been out for a walk with Bernard Kahn. Strangely, Uncle and Mums said nothing about my overstay, although Mum gave me a lecture about not writing – but no wisecracks were made at all. Fancy getting up at 7 a.m. for college tomorrow!

Monday 5th January
Got up at the unearthly hour of 7 a.m. Only Handel and John were on the train, so it was very quiet. Read *Flotsam* by Erich Maria Remarque. Listened to the wireless. The Japanese are now in New Guinea.

Tuesday 6th January
Went to Church Club Dance at 8 and had quite a nice time. Danced the fox-trot with Miss Thomas and one with Denis, the only boy there until Freddy came in with a pal. They talked together for most of the evening – so Gwyn was rather nasty to him. Thought of Alex … he's delightful … delicious … de-lovely. Had a terrible row when I got home for being out so late. I DO think I deserved it. Made a late New Year's resolution – to be more considerate to others, and to have a little more sense.

Thursday 8th January
When I came home from college at five I found a letter from Alex waiting for me. It was the nicest letter I have yet received from him – and that's saying something! Afterwards I got ready for the Hospital Ball. The taxi came at 7.30 p.m. and we all went. I definitely did *not* enjoy myself one bit, as I couldn't help wishing all the time that Alex was there. It was 1.30 a.m. when we came home and I wasn't in bed before 2. The nicest thing I enjoyed today was Alex's letter.

Saturday 10th January
Worked in Barbara Gold's this morning, then went to Penrhiwceiber for a bath. Buses were all full on the way back, so I had to take a train. Went to the Club dance and had a lovely time. Danced nearly all the time with the Vining family, mostly John. Left early. Mum was still up. She told me the Japs have taken Manila in the Philippine Islands and captured parts of Borneo. Mum and Uncle are going to London tomorrow. There have been fewer raids there in the last few months. Got to bed at 11.30. Alex – I can't get you out of my mind – and I don't want to.

Friday 16th January
School – snowed and rained. Bought gloves for Joyce (her birthday is next week). Finished knitting the jumper; then listened to the wireless. Russians fighting hard in the Crimea, taking many prisoners. Went to bed; my cold seems to have suddenly disappeared.

Sunday 18th January

Did a lot of Shorthand today. Went to Judy Schwartz's first birthday tea party at about 4. Mrs. Schwartz is a lovely person. She's American. They live in a large house called Ty-Clyd. It has both a front and back garden. There is a stream in the back that has a Japanese style bridge crossing it. At the end of the apple orchard one can see the fields of Aberdare Hospital with a few cows grazing on them. Of course they have a modern bathroom etc. and I suddenly realised that I have *never* lived in a house. Born in Llanelly above the gown shop – then seven years with Gran behind the hardware store – and now, above and below Jane Cooper's. Our living room is a converted cellar; the "kitchen" – one gas cooker and a dresser – has an open grating to the outside pavement above so that the coal can be poured down; when there's a delivery the dust gets everywhere. Our one tap (cold) is in a corner cupboard; the shop is kept warm with paraffin stoves. Upstairs Joyce and I sleep in the stock room. At the other side of the back yard is our one lavatory, complete with regulation cobwebs and spiders, and of course no electric light. On icy nights the tank freezes and has to be blow-torched back to life. The Kahns were also at Ty-Clyd. Mrs. Kahn is a beauty and very elegant. Mr. Kahn looks like a professor.

Mr and Mrs Sam Kahn

Bernard, Joyce and I went up to Abernant to see a young Jewish boy who has been evacuated there. By the time we arrived the snow had made our feet very cold. Bernard was trying to persuade the boy to come down to his house on Thursday so that he could talk to him about the Jewish religion. On the way back Bernard talked to us and explained a lot of things about Judaism. He is absolutely dynamic where that is concerned! Joyce and I are going to his house on Saturday to talk things over.

Wednesday 21st January
Slept terribly last night. At 2 a.m. our cat came upstairs crying the house down. Mum got up – and all the cat wanted was to be let out! Mum didn't go to London after not sleeping! Post came very early and with it a letter from Alex. Of course, nothing more interesting than that happened today! Went to the dance but didn't enjoy myself. Every time I even SPEAK to another boy I'm thinking to myself – now why couldn't it be you, Alex? If only you were here we'd have such a nice time. Wrote a reply and got to bed very late.

Thursday 22nd January
Snowing heavily. Bought a pair of warm gloves in Cardiff. Idris went into another compartment on the way home to swot for exams (with a torch). News of Myer (Wyman): he and two other officers left Derna (North Africa) on 9th January to return to base (Derna had been captured from Rommel's forces on January 2nd after heavy fighting – more than 7,000 prisoners were taken). They picked up a lorry in the desert and drove 800 miles in three days. On the third day they drove into Bardia, quite unaware that it had only surrendered (to our troops) less than *half an hour* before! What an escape!

Friday 23rd January
Joyce's birthday today. She went to the Fire Station on fire duty. Later we both met Bernard and went for a long walk in the rain as far as Hirwaun. Talked continuously about religion. Came back late – usual row! I'm deeply impressed by what he said, but somehow don't want to be.

Saturday 24th January
Went to dance. John brought me home; he's no conversationalist. Joyce came in – she had been to Bernard Kahn's for tea. Had an argument with Uncle about intermarriage. I say – you're more drawn to someone the same as yourself, but Uncle says that, when that "certain time" comes, you don't care what the man's background is – anyway, I suppose he's right! Re-read Alex's letter, hummed song he sent – it's been in my head all day.

Why do robins sing in December,
Long before the springtime is due?
And even though it's snowing,
Violets are showing,
I know why and so do you.

Oh! I DO, DO, DO wish you were here. Alex – why do you have to live in one place and I in another? It's so maddening!

Monday 26th January
Passed exam in college. Went to pics. – saw *Hold Back the Dawn* with Charles Boyer, Olivia de Havilland and Paulette Goddard. I liked it very much. Moon shining brightly tonight. Read till late.

Wednesday 28th January
Went to Bernard's at 8. Gerry Black, the evacuee, was there. We had quite an interesting conversation. Bernard was surprised that Gerry had not had a Bar Mitzvah – he's almost 14. Bernard's going to teach him, and we shall all make him a party. I've never been to a Bar Mitzvah so it'll be a "first" for me too.

Friday 30th January
Listened to a play on the radio while counting saccs. It was called *Inspector Silence Takes the Air*. It was one of the best radio plays I've ever heard. Joyce is *still* interested in Bernard Kahn. Advised her that he is definitely NOT her type – he's much too serious!

Saturday 31st January
Went to Penrhiwceiber to help Gran. Mrs. Prosser was there doing the books. She's very worried, as she hasn't heard from her son Alan for some weeks. His ship has been sent to the Pacific to bring home women and children from XXXX (censored) before the Japs get there. Later went with Bernard Kahn, his sister Ellen (very pretty), her boyfriend Adolf (WHAT a name!!! AND he's over THIRTY!) and Joyce to see *Lady Hamilton* with Vivien Leigh. I was the only one who had seen it before and I wasn't struck by it the first time. At home Joyce told me that Bernard had been looking at me the whole time – I just didn't believe her.

Sunday 1st February
Mum not too well today. She stayed in bed – IN BED! It's the first time I've ever known her take a day off however sick she feels! Took her meals upstairs and gave Uncle his. Went to the Kahns' at 8 p.m. and started learning Hebrew (it's much more difficult than Shorthand) – also some Jewish History. Went for a

walk up the Craig with Bernard and had quite a nice chat. Landed home at about 10.30 p.m. – Mum was a bit better. Talked with Joyce in bed about Bernard and his views till 1.30!

Thursday 5th February

Met Joyce after college. Went to see *Kiss the Boys Goodbye* with Don Ameche and Mary Martin and was rather disappointed. Bernard had called and left a book for us – *A History of the Jewish People*. Uncle said Joyce is seeing too much of Bernard. Joyce replied: "It's only platonic!" "There's no such thing between a boy and a girl!" snapped Uncle. He doesn't approve of Bernard. "Stuffing your heads with religious nonsense!" he said, thumping the table. Of course Joyce then persuaded me to do some Hebrew – it was very late when I finally went to sleep.

Saturday 7th February

Was in Barbara Gold's today when Gwyn came to say there was a very large letter from Alex. I couldn't think what it was. At last I realised it must be his photo. Ran all the way to Jane Cooper's. It was – and the rest of the Air Cadets with him. Went to Kahns' as usual at 8 p.m. and did some Hebrew. Quite fascinating, the alphabet also stands for numbers, e.g. aleph (A) = 1, bet (B) = 2, etc.

Sunday 8th February

The Japanese have taken Singapore! It doesn't seem possible! I hope Mrs. Prosser has had some news of Alan. Went for a walk with Joyce, Dita and Bernard at 3 p.m. up the mountain towards Merthyr. Suddenly Bernard told us to go on, so we did. After about 15 minutes he caught up with us and was in a bad mood. I suppose he expected us to "run after" him! I think his self-esteem was hurt that we didn't wait for him. He thinks too much of himself.

Monday 9th February

Forgot my season ticket was up, came home on a half-single – me! Mary sacked for thieving. My heart-shaped locket and green Victorian watch (my only two pieces of jewellery) are gone!

Wednesday 11th February

Bought wool for my jumper. Gerry was at the Kahns'. On the way home Bernard told me the reason for his rudeness on Sunday. I shall never forget it – I was utterly amazed – I never dreamed of anything of the sort. He said he was cross because he HAD FALLEN IN LOVE with me – that he knew it was an unsuitable match (you bet!) and he didn't know how I'd feel about it. I told him my affections were completely elsewhere (in Swansea) as he well knew. "Yes," he said, "That's another reason I'm so annoyed!" Then he leaned towards me in the shop doorway – I was just getting a slap ready – real Bette Davis me – when he suddenly rushed off – for the second time this week. What a relief!

Thursday 12th February

Went to see Disney's *The Reluctant Dragon* and liked it ever so much. Passed by the Liberal Club where the Zionists were having a whist drive. Only stayed a few minutes.

Saturday 14th February

Went to Kahns' and argued the whole evening. I found something to say against everything that Bernard said (it was quite a sword fight). Joyce was quiet – later she said she was quite impressed – with Bernard's point of view – (naturally!) Example: Reading the first chapter of Genesis …

Me: "Why were Adam and Eve put into the Garden of Eden together with the Tree of Knowledge and told not to eat from it? Surely an all-knowing G-d would know that they *would*!"

Bernard's answer: "Because unlike animals, who were created with only instincts, Man was given freedom of choice, so that they could have *chosen* not to eat the fruit."

Me: "I don't believe we have *much* freedom of choice. For instance, I didn't choose to be born; or to be female; or to be short or tall!"

Bernard: "Freedom of choice is of the mind and the spirit. That is, both a tall or short person can *choose* to do good or evil."

Me: "We are in the middle of a world war; there's great Evil not of our choosing, and how do you account for Fate, Accidents (like me) and Destiny?" and so on …

Sunday 15th February

The weather was awful so I stayed in and did a lot of knitting. Painted a Pinocchio and a few other Disney characters. Wrote a long letter to Alex in answer to his six-page letter. I agreed with him about Bacon's essay 'On Love' – Bacon despised love (poor man! Evidently he'd never walked up the Cwm in April). Started reading *Rebecca* by Daphne du Maurier. Was quite engrossed in it when, at 9.25 p.m., Bernard called to ask me out for a walk. Talked in general for quite a while and then continued the conversation of Wednesday night. He practically proposed marriage, at least so I gathered. Wants an answer tomorrow when I go to the Club. Haven't got an earthly idea what to do!

Monday 16th February

Didn't go to the Club, to avoid answering Bernard. Joyce said the evacuees had a great evening. I was glad, as some of them live in very difficult circumstances in their foster homes and nearly all of them are homesick. Bernard asked why I wasn't there!

Wednesday 18th February
Uncle went to London today. I stayed home with a cold. Stayed in bed until 6 p.m. so I didn't go to the Kahns'. Read more of *Rebecca*.

Thursday 19th February
Got up at midday. Bernard called in the afternoon to see how I was. We talked about usual subject (our marriage) … he said he knows I'm avoiding him. When I told him that I was only fifteen-and-a-half his big doe eyes nearly dropped out of his head! He'd assumed that, as Joyce was nineteen, I might be about his age – eighteen, or at least seventeen! I said that it's probably because I'd looked after myself since I was seven, was used to thinking for myself, and that growing up in war-time makes everyone grow up so fast (also a year of Liebe und Sehnsucht – love and longing). He nodded. "I also grew up too fast in the war." He promised not to speak of it again for three months – his idea – I hope he keeps to it – for good!

Monday 23rd February
Took Mary's place today and helped in the house. Gran closed the shop and came up to tell us that Mrs. Prosser had received a telegram about Alan – he's missing! Joyce, Alan and I were together at least once or twice a week, whenever his mother came to Gran's. He was (*is*?!) an only child and rather spoilt. Joyce and I used to tease him, and now I can't think what may have happened to him. Even if he's alive and a prisoner of the Japs – that's an awful thought. I hope he copes well, whatever happened. Said a deep-felt prayer for his safety. Couldn't sleep for hours.

Thursday 26th February
Last night at the Kahns' we read from The Book of Esther in preparation for Purim [Festival of Joy]. Bernard explained what it was all about – also the similarity between Haman and Hitler. He showed us a parchment Megilla [scroll] that was written in the 15th century. It was very well kept. They use it every year. Each page is surrounded by beautiful decorations – flowers, leaves, and scroll patterns in black ink. It had been given to Bernard for his Bar Mitzvah. Thursday was half day closing so we all went to 'Ceiber to visit the Prossers – a very harrowing visit.

Sunday 1st March
Cleaned the house and made lunch. Mum wants me to stay home and not go to college anymore. Suddenly I DO want to go to Cardiff – I shall miss it! Dita came in the evening and promised to call tomorrow night to take us to shul.

Monday 2nd March
Did housework all day. Dita called at 6.30 p.m. and we went to shul for the Purim service. She had been fasting today. I followed the Scroll [of Esther] in German and understood it quite well, especially having read it once before in English.

Tuesday 3rd March
Phoebe and Eva came today. Eva [Alex's sister] said Alex is now 5ft 11ins. I surmise that he's grown ½ inch since Xmas, or he must be holding himself straighter. Measured myself today – I'm 5ft 5 ins tall, but I don't think it's very accurate. Mum's birthday tomorrow – she'll be 44, but would *never* admit it. The Kahns had made a Purim party and many of them were in fancy dress. Left at 10.40 and went home to "Out Late Again!" – Mum in her dressing gown waiting up for us! It was such a contrast in atmosphere that Joyce blew up: "But you knew where we were!" she said, stomping up to bed.

Wednesday 4th March
Mum and Uncle went to London to buy stock. Joyce and I went to the Kahns' to discuss the Purim Play. Reggie Freed and Dita were there. Later started reading *Within Four Walls* by Major M. Harrison DSO and Capt. H. A. Cartwright MC.

Friday 6th March
Mum went up to the doctor's today. He said she must go straight to bed for a fortnight, so I am now hired as the private housemaid. Made dinner. Took some up to Mum (up two flights) who said it was very good. Put Uncle's in front of him. He looked at it for about ten minutes as if I was trying to poison him, then got up without saying a word and went out.

Saturday 7th March
Tidied rooms and made the meals today – also helped in the shop. Reggie, Mr. Bodenheimer, Ellen, Bernard, Joyce and myself were in Kahns' at 9.30 p.m. *starting* to rehearse the play for *tomorrow*. Went home at 11.15 – made crowns and costumes for tomorrow. Went to bed extremely late.

Sunday 8th March
Cooked dinner and started to serve it – then came X. (Black Maria Day!) Dreadful quarrel with Uncle about religion – not me, but Joyce – then I joined in – crumbs, what a commotion! Uncle can always be relied upon to spoil any day of celebration! Went to Aberaman to fetch the [evacuee] children, but Berta had already taken them. Then went to the Club. Party went off very well, and so did the play and the film. Went to bed VERY tired.

Monday 9th March
Made meals today and tidied around. Sat down for the first time (excepting meals) at 9 p.m. Read a little of *Within Four Walls*. Washed my hair. Atmosphere very strained between Uncle and everyone else. Doctor came today and told Mum she must stay in bed for another fortnight. Grandma came up to see her. Arranged to go to 'Ceiber for a bath on Sunday. Gran said: "Don't forget to bring your own soap!" *Soap* is now rationed!!! What next?

Wednesday 11th March
Uncle a lot better tempered today. Too tired to go to the Kahns', so stayed in and read. Went to the library for Mum; she usually likes 'Improve Yourself' books (Improve your Memory; Charm; Brain Power etc.) so she has decided that, now she has the time, she wants to learn psychology. I got her the most difficult book I could find. Her bookmark has stuck on page two, but she's very happy with it, for it looks very impressive lying on her bed when she has visitors.

Thursday 12th March
Joyce went to Cardiff to buy meat. In the butcher's she met Estelle (our cousin) who talked to Joyce about Uncle Abe. He and Aunty Rosie [my father's sister] lived opposite the beautiful old shul in Merthyr and had seven children. Some years ago he was watching his daughters, Leah and Sadie (twelve-and-a-half and eleven years old at the time) acting in a pantomime in a hall. They were so good, he was filled with joy – suddenly he coughed badly, collapsed and died. I didn't think one could really die from happiness. He was only 52 – Aunty was 42. She had to bring up all our cousins alone, as does Aunty Millie [Estelle's mother]. We decided not to tell Mum about Joyce meeting Estelle, as we can never mention my father's family in front of Uncle – he's so jealous.

Friday 13th March
Friday the 13th! Joyce told me what was wrong with Mum. I am in a state of shock, disgust, and anger! I've never so much as seen Uncle give Mum a kiss – and now *this* news – and he's nearly 55!! Slammed out of the shop and walked the hills all day. I've decided if the baby is a boy (like him) then I shall have nothing to do with it – but if it's a girl I shall help Mum if she needs me to. Anyway, it seems that Mum is just as upset about it as I am. Can't get over how naive I've been. Uncle comes from a family of nine and NONE of them had had any children. (Six never married!) No wonder he's been more disagreeable than usual.

Saturday 14th March
Got over last night's lapse and don't really mind now. At least Mum's illness is not serious! Went with Joyce to Kahns'. We have started reading Genesis. Came home at 11 p.m. and went to bed late.

Monday 16th March
Did housework again and went to pics. this evening to see *Fantasia*. Was I thrilled with it! Occasionally I forgot to breathe and came back up just in time to remind myself to. It was really wonderful.

Tuesday 17th March
Letter from Alex. He is upset that I am likely to become a nursemaid as well as household amanuensis. He heard rumours from the farm and, putting two and two together, realised that now would not be a good time to cycle over. Joyce came in from Cardiff very excited. She had been to an Art Show with John Roberts and seen a painting she liked very much by a French painter called Cézanne. She asked Mum if she could borrow £25 to buy it as it was for sale. "£25 for a PAINTING!" said Mum, amazed. I was sorry for Joyce as she has a very good eye for art and if she thought it was worth it, then I'm sure it was.

Thursday 19th March
New girl came today to work in the house. She seemed rather awkward, but of course it was her first day. Finished making supper. Went with Bernard to see a new room for the Youth Club. It was in a terrible state. Bernard was nearly caught by the police on the way home, but he dodged into a doorway and the policeman followed a man who had been walking in front of him. What an escape, eh? It was long after Bernard's curfew. [Aliens were not allowed on the street after 8 p.m.]

Friday 20th March
Dressed the windows with Phyllis. The new spring clothes look lovely and I copied the way I had seen the smart shops in Cardiff arranged. Mum came down in the afternoon ever so grumpy and nagged all day. She went back to bed before supper. Later when I took her a cup of tea she said she MUST have some peaches and cream! Well!! It's March, and there's a WAR on! Went back down and opened a tin of fruit salad that I had been keeping for Sunday, found a small tin of condensed milk (both now on points) and took some upstairs. Mum picked out the peaches and only ate those. "Go and see if there's some more," she demanded. I stood in the back cellar taking out small pieces of peach from the rest of the tin, wondering if I was quite mad! Mum devoured the lot as if she was starving. Aunty Gwen popped in for a few minutes – she had come from Aldershot for the day to see her family in Aberaman. I told her about Mum's peculiar behaviour. She laughed. "It's quite normal to get strange food cravings when you're having a baby," she said. "Come on, let's eat the rest." So we did. Aunty Gwen always puts me in a good mood.

Saturday 21st March
It was very busy in the shop all day with people buying clothes for Easter. Because of the rationing customers are buying more expensive clothes with their few

coupons so, unexpectedly, the rationing has been good for us. Went to Kahns' at 8 p.m. and carried on learning Exodus ready for Pesach. Bernard said that all the great empires that have persecuted the Jews have disintegrated – the Byzantine Empire; the great Land of the Pharaohs; the vast Roman Empire; the Spanish Empire and Tsarist Russia. While *our* small nation, which doesn't even have a land to call its own, keeps together, surviving through all the generations. It follows, says Bernard, that the great German Reich will also fall, without a doubt. He also said Joyce and I have no Weltanschauung – "What?" whispered Joyce, who has never learned German. "World-outlook," I explained. Bernard's right – we don't! Read a few more chapters of *My Antonia* before I went to bed.

Sunday 22nd March
Mum had a lot of visitors this afternoon. Uncle Solly didn't stay long, as Uncle can't stand him – "He shakes hands like a flabby, dead, wet fish," is Uncle's complaint. I offered to accompany him part of the way home. We started talking about Bernard, as Uncle Solly lives opposite the Kahns'. He told me Bernard had had a very hard time. First, at the age of fourteen, he was sent to Dachau [concentration camp]. Then, on his release, he escaped via Holland to England as a stowaway on a ship, as he had no passport or entry papers. A few days after the war started he was put in prison in case he was a Very Dangerous Spy – 15½ years old at the time! Then to Prisoner of War camp and, after that, to an Aliens' Detention Camp on the Isle of Man. No wonder he's so serious! Cleared up after the visitors. Wanted to write to Alex but was too tired to do anything – except make designs of his name.

Monday 23rd March
Went to see *Manhunt* with Walter Pigeon in the Palladium. Super film! Uncle went to London. I lost my fountain pen on the way to the post – rather upset over it too. Have to continue this in pencil. Joyce came back from Cardiff and SHE had LEFT the Pesach butter and tea on the train! However she still had Gottlieb's black bread with her, which we all love. Tried creaming my face before I went to bed (at Mum's suggestion – to improve my sallow skin).

Tuesday 24th March
Cleaned cupboards and washed all the Pesach dishes. Our REFRIGERATOR came today! Went to pics. tonight and saw *Hatter's Castle* – marvellous film, but could be described as "horribly fascinating" – very well acted. Uncle came home from London – brought big box of lipsticks [to sell in the shop], so we put them in cases till 12.20 a.m. when we all went to bed.

Saturday 28th March
I was very busy in the shop all day. Went with Joyce to the Kahns'. Continued with Exodus. Didn't understand why "G-d hardened Pharaoh's heart" so that he

wouldn't let the Israelites go. Bernard explained that Pharaoh had no intention of really letting his slaves go, as even after the plagues he sent his soldiers to get them back – his army drowned in the Red Sea. Came home and went to bed really late – 12.35! Next time I see Bernard I shall ask him why G-d didn't harden *Adam's* heart so he would have refused Eve's fruit – and saved us all a lot of trouble! (Bernard takes my teasing so seriously!)

Sunday 29th March

Made dinner early and went for a walk to Abernant. Then Grandma, Gerty, and Uncle and Aunty Schlachter came to see Mum. What a noise – tried to listen to *Big Times* on the radio, but it was impossible. Read a little, then, after supper, Mum came down for a drink – she missed the top step of the kitchen stairs and *fell* eighteen steps right to the bottom! Uncle lifted her up and put her in his chair. She kept saying: "I'm all right, I'm ALL RIGHT!" I ran to fetch the doctor, just in case. He examined her and said she was *very*, *very* lucky. Couldn't sleep for hours. Really pleased that she didn't lose the baby.

Uncle Solly and Aunty Alma Schlachter

Wednesday 1st April – April Fool's Day
Busy all day. Lovely letter from Alex:

> "So you learn Hebrew!!! Cynthia sweet, you surprise me more every day. How I would like to HUG YOU!!!" And continued: "Cara Mia – about 'Popping the Question' – never you fear – for if necessary I shall (don't laugh) drop on my knees before you – well!!??"

Stayed up until 1 a.m. writing a reply.

Thursday 2nd April
Uncle Solly came in to ask Joyce and me to go to his house for the Seder [Passover night service] tonight. Went for a long walk up the Craig – very sunny – enjoyed myself; followed the "yellow brick road" all the way down. Went to Uncle Solly at 8 p.m. Was rather bored, I must admit, although I was glad I went.

Friday 3rd April
This morning Joyce tipped a pan of boiling oil over her right arm when she was making latkes. It was very bad, but Uncle plastered it up all right. When she did it, all she said was: "I'm sorry." I bet she was too! Went down to Pen in the afternoon. Pouring raining. Did a few errands for Gran and got soaking wet. Grandma gave me two flour sacks, that she had cut open and washed, for Mum to embroider and make into tablecloths. Mum's embroidery is absolutely beautiful – it'll keep her happy while she's resting. Ben was home on a few days' leave. He's lost more weight and looks very nice in his uniform.

Saturday 4th April
Still raining. Did saccs. until lunch-time, then helped in the shop as it was rather busy. Went to Kahns' at 8.15 p.m. Shabbos [the Sabbath] WAS STILL IN! They were all sitting in the dark, as they don't switch on lights on a Saturday. Couldn't do any learning – just talked. Went to bed after 12.

P.S. Have come to a final conclusion, that I, personally, do *not* like Bernard Kahn!

Sunday 5th April
Got up late. I forgot the clocks were put forward last night, and getting up at 10 a.m. I discovered, to my great surprise, that it was 11! What a sell! Was just getting ready to go out when Becky walked in and said, "Come on, you're coming to Swansea with me for company – quick the bus is waiting, grab a coat quick!" I didn't know what to do, but Joyce was all for it, so I went. Arrived at the farm at 7 p.m. and found everyone there, except of course the one I wanted. Went to bed at 1 a.m. and to sleep at 2.30.

Monday 6th April
Fay, Becky's friend, phoned up Winters' but, she said, Alex had gone out on a picnic and wouldn't be in till very late. Extremely downcast but hate the "poor Cynthia" conversations of everyone there. Left at 6 p.m. and had to stand all the way home. More "poor Cynthia" stuff again. Went to bed feeling mad and VERY annoyed and sorry for myself.

Tuesday 7th April
Saw *Appointment for Love* with Margaret Sullivan and Charles Boyer; quite enjoyable, but still upset about yesterday.

Wednesday 8th April
"Anniversary Day INSIDE me." (A year ago today, Alex and I walked up to the Cwm together – unforgettable!) Had a letter from Alex. He also remembered our walk up the Cwm last year. Very happy! I wish I could have answered it, but it was Yom Tov [Jewish Festival]. Started reading *How Green Was My Valley* by Richard Llewellyn.

Friday 10th April
Letter from Alex – in a *murderous* mood. He'd visited the farm and heard I was there on Monday. Fay had spoken to HIM on the phone, and told him I was NOT there, only the cows were! She thought it would be a joke! Alex has vowed not to visit the farm until he's calmed down – otherwise …

Sunday 12th April
Had many visitors today: Grandma, Berta, Uncle Solly and Aunty Alma; Uncle Harris and Aunty Fanny; Mr. and Mrs. Marcus from Pontypool; Mr. and Mrs. Winter – but alas – no Alex! Made supper for ALL. Mrs. Winter said Alex was in Llandudno so I can't write now. She also invited me over to Swansea for Whitsun, and am I looking forward to it.

Monday 13th April
Saw *Hi Gang* with Bebe Daniels, Ben Lyon and Vic Oliver – very funny. Beautiful weather. Uncle left for London.

Tuesday 14th April
Went out on a bike ride with Gwyn and rode pretty well, except for one fall that nearly knocked off my posterior! Whew!! Am I aching!

Wednesday 15th April
Had a stiff neck today, as well as a stiff underneath! Can't sit down at all comfortably. Walked to Clifton Street to tell Bernard that I would not be there

this evening. He hadn't come home from work (on the farm). Only his grandparents were in. Mr. Ginsberger opened the door and – at last, my four-year slog learning German in school paid off. Mrs. Ginsberger was sitting as usual in the kitchen. I took courage and spoke to her in German. She was so amazed she started to *speak* to me! I told her I was Uncle Solly's great-niece and she told me about her father, who had been a miller and owned the mill-house built into the main bridge crossing the River Main in Frankfurt. Her family had lived there for hundreds of years. Mrs. Ginsberger knows no English and rarely speaks to anyone except her immediate family. Her husband had been the principal Shamas [Beadle] in the main shul. (Seating for 4,000 orthodox members!) They had lived in rooms above the synagogue. When the Nazis burned down the building in 1938 they had tied Mrs. Ginsberger to her bed. Bernard, who had told me about this, had gone with his father into the burning building to save her – she was in her nightdress; they lost everything in the fire. The shock of this and moving to Wales was too much for Mrs. G., who mostly sits all day peeling vegetables or darning a huge pile of socks (like poor Dr. Manette from *A Tale of Two Cities*). When Mr. Ginsberger came in – he is the most NOBLE person I have ever met – he lit up with pleasure to hear his wife talking to me – a stranger! Went to bed early as I was aching too much to knit.

Photo of the Brückenmühle on the River Main taken in 1914

Synagogue burning after Kristallnacht 9th November 1938

The Ginsbergers' flat

Adass Jeshurun Synagogue before the war

Thursday 16th April
Went to pics. with Mum and saw a very good show: *Tall, Dark and Handsome* with Cesar Romero and *Hello Sucker* with Hugh Herbert. It was very amusing. Held Mum's arm tightly to make sure she didn't fall in the dark – she's still very unsteady.

Saturday 18th April
Very happy all day today. Reason? Alex of course! Lovely letter and snap. Gwyneth was the only one who noticed it. Went to Kahns'. They had Yahrzeit [Anniversary of death of a close relative]. There was a candle burning in memory of one of their parents. Went home very late. Bernard took me right to our door.

Monday 20th April
Did a mountain of housework all morning. After lunch counted saccs. and for once I appreciated sitting down. Went with Mum to see *Blossoms in the Dust* with Greer Garson and Walter Pigeon. It was really marvellous. I cried once, and almost a second time. The newsreel showed the Island of Malta, which has had heavy German bombing. It has been awarded the George Cross. The Germans are also advancing into Russia and North Africa. Read more of *How Green Was My Valley* and wrote to Alex.

Tuesday 21st April
Started doing Jane Cooper's business papers and entering up the books. Wrote to some of the firms, ordering new Spring clothes, as Mum can't travel to London to visit them. She is now wearing flowing dresses, but is beginning to look like a round ostrich with very fine dainty legs. Electrician came this afternoon to connect the fridge. I always get engrossed watching all the wires being joined up and ask loads of questions. When the fridge started to hum all the shop-girls ran down to see, shouting, "It's working!" Gran came up in the evening to see Mum but was more impressed with the fridge. It stands in the back cellar near the cooker.

Wednesday 22nd April
Went to the Kahns' as usual – carried on reading from Exodus. Bernard translates every word from Hebrew to English as he says that the English text is unreliable and sometimes distorts the real meaning. I'm surprised at his command of both languages.

Thursday 23rd April
Went to Cardiff with Joyce. Saw *Chu Chin Chow* at the Prince of Wales Theatre. Very enjoyable; I went into raptures over one of the girls in it, she was so sweet. Met Thelma and Gwyneth on the train home; sang most of the way.

Saturday 25th April
Very busy day in the shop. Swansea cousins came to see Mum. Went to Kahns' at 8 p.m. We have started on the Ten Commandments and AM I having a hard time with them! Lots of questions on "Keep the Sabbath day holy" and "Do no manner of work on it." Questions about what is considered "work" and what makes a day "holy"? After a hectic day in the shop, the Kahns' house seems like a quiet haven after a storm. When we got to the 5th Commandment – "Honour your father and mother" – I interrupted: "How can I possibly …?" Getting a kick from Joyce under the table I stopped, for we don't talk about this subject – except with each other. Bernard explained that "Honour" does not mean "Love" – honour is harder and is a two-way contract. The parent has to be worthy of the honour by teaching the children the right way to behave *by example*. For once I was satisfied with his explanation.

Tuesday 28th April
Sorted out all Mum's papers and filed everything properly; had a good clean-out – tons of salvage paper. The books really look in order for once. Went to pics. Saw *Great Man's Lady* with Barbara Stanwyck. It was very good. Did some knitting afterwards. Nearly finished jumper – now I'm not sure I like it.

Wednesday 29th April
Went to Kahns' at 8 p.m. Listened to Gerry practising his Parsha [chapter of the Bible]. Bernard was in a very good mood. He's started work at Evan's Farm, Llwydcoed, and even though he's an enemy alien the police have given him a permit to "ride a pedal cycle" to and from work and also to be out later than curfew time (8 p.m.) in the summer months. Went home at 9.30 p.m. As light as day out tonight, lovely moon.

Thursday 30th April
Letter from Alex this morning. He's been reading M.M.'s [Michel de Montaigne 1533–92] Essays and quoted long passages from them in French. I shall try to get an English translation from the library. In the afternoon I went out on a bike ride with Thelma [Jane Cooper shop assistant] as far as Mountain Ash along the Cwmbach Road. Passed my old school and saw my former teachers Ted and Beaky going home. I waved to them. We were followed by a very good-looking boy who stopped every time we did. I think he wanted to talk to Thelma. Met Cliff Pritchard near Mountain Ash Bridge. He and I used to play for hours every evening with "the gang" up and down the dark streets of 'Ceiber. He's been working down the pits for two years and looks a real *man*, strong and muscular. I felt very strange talking to him and hardly knew what to say. He told me he wants to join up and hopefully drive a tank. He laughed when I said: "Not much different to the pits!"

He said, "We must have been twp [daft] when we crossed the river (Cynon) balancing on top of the pipeline, we could both have drowned – I still can't swim." We did some crazy dares when we were together!

Went to pics. and saw *A Yank in the R.A.F.* with Betty Grable and Tyrone Power. It was quite good, especially the last part – about the evacuation of Dunkirk.

Friday 1st May

Did Mum's hair this morning. Listened to Tommy Handley, in *Handleydrome,* on the wireless. It was very good. Four months today since I last saw Alex. Wrote a long letter.

Saturday 2nd May

Went to shul this morning for Gerry Black's Bar Mitzvah. He read very well considering that he hardly knew a word of Hebrew until Bernard taught him. His uncle had come from the Isle of Man, but his mother couldn't manage to come. We are making him a party tomorrow.

Sunday 3rd May

Made a cake for Gerry and took it to the hall. To my amazement Ellen said they couldn't use it. "You don't use Kosher margarine," she explained. "*Of course* we buy Kosher food," I told her, but actually I didn't know margarine had to BE Kosher. This evening I went for a long walk with Bernard to tell him how annoyed I was with his sister's behaviour. He said that she was right and told me the following facts. Margarine is mostly made from whale oil: the cheese *we* use contains rennet which is made from animal intestines. Jelly contains gelatine made from animal bones! Cakes and biscuits have fat, usually lard, chips – ditto. Dishes have to be washed in different bowls when used for milk or meat, etc. etc. Therefore, even though Mum goes specially to Cardiff to buy Kosher meat, our home is definitely *not* Kosher. Ah me! Shall I ever enjoy a Kunzle cake again?!!! There is no way that Joyce and I can keep the dietary laws at home – Uncle would have a fit! Anyway, I'm not sure I'm convinced of how important these things are.

Monday 4th May

The mason knocked a large doorway through to the next door rooms today. The enlarged shop does look grand! I'm getting quite good at judging a customer's size and know all the stock. Mum asks me to model the dresses (as she can't), which is quite fun. Saw *All That Money Can Buy* with Edward Arnold. Not bad. Mum didn't like it. It was strange coming back in through the "new" shop, there's dust everywhere and all the rails are covered up.

Wednesday 6th May

Paper woman came today and started papering the downstairs room. Ever such a mess everywhere. I cut the edges of the rolls and did some pasting. Went to the

Kahns' at 8 p.m. Too tired to be argumentative. Came home at 11 with Bernard. Room not quite finished. Bernard said he didn't like the wallpaper, but *we* all like it.

Thursday 7th May
Made lunch, went out on my bike with Thelma as far as Penrhiwceiber on the New Road. Lovely going down, sunny and cool. We took some snaps there and then turned around. The wind was against us and we had a very hard job getting up the steep hills. Dreadfully tired and hot. Wrote to Alex in the evening.

Saturday 9th May
Went to the Kahns' early as Mrs. Kahn had asked me to come to tea. Murderous looks from Mum and Uncle as I walked through the shop filled with customers. Mrs. Kahn sliced the cake into very fine pieces and offered it with a serviette and *cake knives* and *forks*! She poured tea out of a silver pot. Dita was also invited. After tea we sat in the garden, as it was quite warm. Bernard does all the gardening. We talked about the 'Giving of the Torah (Law)' on Mt. Sinai. I asked how laws given 3,000 years ago could be relevant in the 20th century? Bernard agreed that man-made laws *would* be out of date and old-fashioned, but laws made by G-d would last for all time and would not date. He gave a few examples. Next to Dita I felt very ignorant and decided I must learn as much as possible about my own religion. All my friends (chapelgoers) know everything about theirs from attending Sunday school.

Sunday 10th May
Saw a show in the Palladium. L.O.U.S.Y. Supposed to be a Variety – of what I wouldn't say – or rather could, but won't!

Monday 11th May
Went to the library to get M.M.'s Essays. They didn't allow the book to be taken out, so I read it there. It was so interesting I stayed for over two hours taking notes …

On marriage:

> I see no marriages that sooner are troubled and fail than those that progress by means of beauty and amorous desires. It needs more solid and stable foundations, and we need to go at it circumspectly; this ebullient ardour is no good for it.
>
> The foundation of a good marriage, and its real proof, is how long the association lasts and whether it has been constantly pleasant, loyal and agreeable.

Other quotes:

> I hate a gloomy spirit that slides over the pleasures of life and seizes and feeds on its misfortunes like flies, which cannot cling to a smooth body but attach themselves to the rough uneven places.

A note to his wife:

Michel de Montaigne, Sept. 10 1570.

To Madame de M., my wife …

Regarding my writings – I do not want stingily to enjoy them all alone, nor do I deserve that they be useful only to me. For that reason I have wished to communicate them to my friends.

Very pleased that Alex introduced them to *me.*

Tuesday 12th May

Ellen Kahn and Mr. Bodenheimer got engaged today. Very long letter from Alex. He is training by cycling 10–20 miles a day so that he can cycle to Aberdare and back – 27 miles each way. On Sunday he went to hear the famous pianist, Moiseiwitsch, and the Welsh Philharmonic Orchestra, at the Maxime. The audience of 2,000 clapped for almost half an hour and Moiseiwitsch had to take three encores. Re. films, he thought *A Yank in the R.A.F.* was the worst film he has ever seen! He took his A.T.C. exam on Saturday – said the Maths paper was a real stinker! Thelma was sacked today for leaving the shop (Barbara Gold's) to have a perm. She cried, but Mum wouldn't give in. Thelma thought no one would have found out as she went while she was over at Barbara Gold's – that's why she got the sack!

Wednesday 13th May

Raining heavily. Took engagement present to Kahns' – a biscuit barrel. Bernard offered to take me home but took me as far as the small park. We sat and talked. He had the funny idea I was ashamed to be seen with him in his working clothes! Came home at 9.30 p.m. and helped clear up some of the mess. Joyce came home from London when everything was finished! She promised to help me paint our living room.

Thursday 14th May

Went to Penrhiwceiber to get paint from Gran's. I took a snap of Berta and Grandma. If it comes out Berta can send it to her brothers in America. Zena was there from Cardiff – lipstick and high-heels! Joyce and I painted the room, first cream and then green. Then we dragged a comb over the nearly dried paint in a wavy motion so that the cream showed through the green; it looks terrific! Went to pics. in the evening, saw Bette Davis in *The Great Lie* – very good! Lovely ending. My *bed* came today. What a pleasure sleeping in it! Like lying on a cloud after a stone floor! Going to call her MAY – blossom time – blue skies – bright stars – green leaves – spring-time – Alex!

Friday 15th May

Mrs. Prosser started working in Barbara Gold's today instead of Thelma. It helps to take her mind off Alan who's still missing (in the Pacific). Uncle finished making our curtains. They look marvellous. His handiwork is always so perfect. Both bed-heads were polished and sent over – first bed of my own!! The wood is light walnut and the style is Queen Anne.

Saturday 16th May
Went collecting rent in the morning and worked in Barbara Gold's in the afternoon. Didn't sit down once till closing time. Made supper, then went to the Kahns' at 8.30. We are learning about Shavuoth [Pentecost – the giving of the law on Mount Sinai]. Came home at 11.30. Electrician had fitted a light in the stock room so that we don't have to "feel in the dark" to get to our bedroom.

Friday 22nd May
Trying to persuade Joyce to come with me to Swansea on Sunday. I just can't believe it – Saturday and then – it doesn't seem true! Finished sewing my jumper, lengthened the sleeves of my coat and had a Blue Mask – a mud pack!

Saturday 23rd May
Rained all day. I got soaked twice! Bernard took me home and kept asking if Alex was coming for Whitsun; he refused to go away until I'd promised to bring Alex up if he *did* come – I knew he wouldn't. I wish Bernard would mind his own business more! Didn't say that I was going to Swansea.

Sunday 24th May
Got up early today. Gave everyone tea and got my case and myself ready by 11 a.m. Made a rhubarb flan. Day started fine but it rained by lunch-time. After Joyce had eaten my flan she decided to come (they *do* say "Feed the Brute"). Waited half an hour for the bus and got to Swansea at 4 p.m. Couldn't see Alex at the depot – we had given up hope, but at ten past he turned up. I was very stuck for words, don't suppose I shall warm up until tomorrow. Went to Winters' for tea, and then Alex came with us to the farm. He left at about 9.30. Lots of teasing from Rifka afterwards. Wind howling terrifically – hard to get to sleep.

Monday 25th May
Absolutely pouring! Very dirty weather. 2.30 p.m. and still no Alex – *very* down-hearted. Came from the farm to Rochale's to find – impossible of impossible – Alex there. We took Joyce to the bus at 5 then talked in the lounge until 9 when the weather cleared up. Clear skies – so we *had* to go out for a walk. Wind blew all my shyness away (Huh, Huh!) and Alex caught the 10.25 bus to Swansea. We decided to go for a picnic tomorrow, weather permitting. Wind howling, but I do hope it'll be nice tomorrow.

Tuesday 26th May
Went to the farm to get lettuce to make sandwiches. Started to pour, so alas – we couldn't go! Very annoyed with the weather. At 4 p.m. the sun started to shine!!! We *were* mad. Went for a short walk, then stayed in – and talked and talked! He can't see me tomorrow so I shall go to Llanelly.

Wednesday 27th May
Woke up late – at 9.30, and got dressed. Rochale came in and started talking to me about Alex's mother. What she told me upset me a great deal – I didn't know if I was standing on my head or my toes. It quite unbalanced me. She did quite right to tell me what she did, but still I can't say I liked hearing it. It does make me feel mad! I don't know how I can tell Alex – I'll have to manage it somehow. Walked to the Cross to get the Llanelly bus. Waited twenty minutes before it came. Wind blew some of my disturbing thoughts away and I decided on a course of action which, although it doesn't seem a *bit* satisfactory to me, will have to do. The journey to Llanelly was completely spoilt by the words scorching through my head. Mrs. Winter had told Rochale that it's obvious that I'm a flirt, and no good for her son – the sort of girl who will make a man head over heels in love and then leave them flat for someone else. She said much more which was so bad I couldn't ever write it down and will *never* be able to forget. I've known her since I was three and thought she *liked* me. Anyway, there's to be no more romantic goings-on with her son – and if I write to him, she'll make sure she reads my letters! (MRS. WINTER guarding her delicate plant from a frosty fate!) If Alex knew, I know he'd leave home straight away and join the Air Force, then she'd definitely lose him. She told Rochale to tell me that she would never allow him to marry me. It's true I've never seen a proper home life, but I'm sure I could make a reasonable job of it. Her home is always perfect, but you don't have to be a genius to do that! Mum and Gran are both too busy making a living to be concerned about house-keeping. They are generous, warm, and hospitable, have a great sense of humour and lots of spunk, and *that's* what I admire. Still inside me I am *very*, *very* cut up. Got to good 'ole Llanelly at 11.50. Still the same as ever. I do love it and everyone here. I wish I could live here. The sea air made me feel light and lifted my spirits. Had dinner in Aunty Sarah's and went over to Aunty Beaty where I was to stay. Saw Monish Landy on the way. He is now a Major! Also met [cousin] Renée and her husband (R.A.F.). Wrote a letter home and rang up Alex. He was alone in the house. Spoke for at least ten minutes. He said he missed me today and cannot wait until I get to Swansea tomorrow.

Thursday 28th May
Had breakfast with Pamela and Estelle [cousins]. Went to Aunty Sarah's and had a singsong till lunch. Uncle Myer's a dear. Ran to Aunty Beaty's to get my things and rushed to catch the bus for Fforestfach. Met Mr. Day on the bus. He told me

Vera was studying for Higher, Gwen was a nurse in Manchester, and Michael was in the forces as a Catholic minister. After he got off, the journey seemed very long. Alex and I met at 6 and went to the pics. Saw *Penn of Pennsylvania* with Clifford Evans and Deborah Kerr and then *Sullivan's Travels* with Veronica Lake and Joel McCrea. They were both very good, and I must say I enjoyed the show very much. We came out at 10 p.m. – it had lasted 3½ hours! We walked back to Sketty the long way. I came to the point straight away and told Alex that letters from then onwards would be – well – just letters. He was rather upset, especially when I said I couldn't tell him the reason why, and that he himself wouldn't want me to tell him (he would hate his mother if I did). He was very good about it and never once asked what had happened, although he said it would be very difficult. I told him that it had nothing to do with him or myself. He said it would be awful getting letters that wouldn't really be mine. I told him: "You said yourself that I was a lot different to my letters." "Yes," he said, "but I like the two 'yous' equally as much." We talked for a few minutes until the bus came. Alex said he'd try to meet me at the depot tomorrow. We said "Good bye" and I left, feeling very strange. The walk up to Caerithin seemed endless. It started to rain. I was glad. The rain was nice and cool, but did not entirely settle my slightly muddled mind. I didn't want to think of anything, – but couldn't help thinking of one thing! I realised how I'd been duped by Mrs. Winter into going to Swansea so that Rochale could speak the unspeakable to me! I can never tell Alex what his mother had said about my family and me. I feel judged and sentenced without the possibility of saying one word in my defence. My self-esteem is at a very low point!

Friday 29th May

Alex wasn't at the depot. Waited until the 12 o'clock bus, then I saw a tall, curly-haired figure rushing into the depot. The bus started up and I jumped on. The flying figure in a light grey suit continued running, but, seeing the bus go, finally stopped. I didn't feel too well, occasionally tried to read *Lilliput,* but couldn't seem to take in what I was reading. Raining – got home to find only Joyce and Mum there. Uncle had gone to London. Must say I was somewhat relieved. Did some cooking with Joyce for Sunday and counted how many people have been invited (Ben and Rae's engagement party). Altogether we'll be 20!! The music from the dance hall is maddening, and I do feel so lonely. I want to write a letter but I am not sure how. I can't believe that I was in Swansea this morning and saw Alex and most probably won't see him for at least four months or more! I don't want to think about it either. Joyce said Bernard had called in on Monday to see if Alex was here. She said: "I think Bernard has a soft spot for you." Thought how *real* was Shakespeare's plot when he wrote about the Montagues and the Capulets in *Romeo and Juliet.* Pinned Alex's mascot to my coat and went to bed. My new bed is so inviting – is it only two weeks since it came? Felt so full of joy then, and now I feel so empty and can't get to sleep.

Saturday 30th May
Got the upstairs room ready for tomorrow. Made lunch, but couldn't eat anything. Went to the Kahns' at 8 p.m. Bernard told me it was very unmannerly of me not to let him know that I wouldn't be coming on Wednesday. He was quite right, but the way he said it made me boiling mad – I seem to be in everyone's bad books! Went to bed at 11.45 – didn't sleep for a long time. Realised that, looking after myself since I was seven, I have come to regard myself as a person quite apart from family influences – but Mrs. Winter only sees me as a product of every family problem that's come our way. She doesn't know the *real* me (as Alex does). To me *she* has been "Alex's mother", but now I see her in a different light. I wonder if *she's* ever been in love?

Sunday 31st May
Worked hard all morning. Gwyn and Berta came to help. We did have quite a do! Altogether we had, Uncle, Mum, Joyce, Grandma, Aunty Ray and Becky from Swansea, Uncle Charlie, Uncle Solly and Aunty Alma, Martin and Gerty, Gwyn and myself. Rae seems quite nice and Ben and Rae seem *very* fond of each other. It's very strange to see Ben catch her hand and start playing with her fingers. Tea was at 5.30 p.m. and supper at 7.30. Everything went very successfully except for one incident – Joyce fell *up* the stairs carrying Mum's silver tea service (that she'd spent months saving up for) – not much damage except a dent in the hot water jug! Amazing what a difference the Army has made to our fat, uncouth Uncle Ben, who is now thin and almost good-looking! In contrast, Rae looks older than her age (42) and has dark rings around her eyes. Becky, who's staying the night, said Rae's "Lucky" and "Plucky"! Somehow Becky got onto the subject of Mrs. Winter. She upset me rather by saying *exactly* what Rochale had told me. When I said, "Well, she needn't live with her son when he's married!" she said, "*That* kind of mother *would* – but then he'll have to marry someone!"

In bed I told Joyce what Rochale had said and how similar it was to Becky's. But Joyce said not to take any notice of anyone – if Alex was any sort of a man he would never let his mother interfere, however much he liked her – but I wish I knew. I *do* feel like ringing him up – I so wish I could!

Monday 1st June
Whew! JUNE already! Got up late (9). Uncle Ben's friend, Mostyn, called to see if Ben was here. When he found that Ben had left he asked me if I'd like to go fishing with him. I quickly made some sandwiches and hopped into his beautiful car. The seats are wine leather and the hood was down. We drove for about ¾ hour and stopped at a quiet trout stream. Mostyn took off his officer's uniform, rolled up his sleeves and trouser legs and cast his rod. Ben and Mostyn had often taken me on their fishing trips before the war. Ben never used a rod, preferring to catch the fish with his hands by "tickling their bellies". Mostyn let me try with the rod

and I managed to catch three trout. The quiet and the calm were just what we both needed! When he dropped me off I saw Gwyn's boyfriend Frank coming to fetch her. He was away yesterday and she missed him – Hmm – only *one* day! Alex, if I could see you one twentieth the amount they see each other *I'd* be satisfied. Went to pics. at 6.45. Didn't feel like going but didn't want to miss *Suspicion* with Joan Fontaine and Cary Grant. Didn't enjoy it one bit. The news consisted of the same shot I saw with Alex – a newsreel about the fighting in Burma – I didn't enjoy that either. Came out before the end and didn't want to go home. No one in. Must admit I cried – not much – but still – I feel torn up inside. Hope I get a letter tomorrow.

Tuesday 2nd June
Helped Mum with papers nearly all day. No letter, but you never know what tomorrow will bring. Started reading *Mortal Storm* by Phyllis Bottome. I seem to have got a queer saddish feeling inside me and I *do* feel tired. Quote from *Mortal Storm*: "It is a good thing to learn early that other people's opinions do not matter unless they happen to be true."

Wednesday 3rd June
No letter again today! Heat wave! Now why couldn't we have had this weather a week ago! Three Board of Trade men came to see Mum about our saccs. and cosmetics. Joyce is going to London tomorrow to tell Uncle about them.

Great event!! Cut my hair about 2½ inches – felt awful doing it. My hair combed doesn't look much different though. Uncle Charlie came up to advise Mum about the saccs. etc. Joyce and I went to the Kahns' and had a lesson in the garden. I liked it very much. Another *Mortal Storm* quote: "All persecution is a sign of fear, for if we did not fear the power of an opinion different from our own, we should not mind others holding it." No one noticed that I'd cut my hair!!

Thursday 4th June
Dreamt nasty dream last night. Alex deserted me – but came back in the end. *No* letter again this morning. Oh Alex, I wish you would write! Glorious day today – summer has really arrived. Went as far as Aberdare Park but came home without going in. Frank came to fetch Gwyn. She looked marvellous in a pale blue frock – I've never seen her look so radiant before! Uncle and Joyce came back from London with summer stock.

Friday 5th June
Waited for post, but still no letter! Alex, I do miss you now that summer has come – I don't feel like going out for walks with anyone else – and I just hate staying in. Dance hall next door has been playing 'I Don't Want To Walk Without You' – and

it's true. They're playing 'Yours' now – that's true too! Stayed in and did nothing in particular.

Saturday 6th June
Worked in Barbara Gold's. Went with Joyce to the Kahns' at 8 p.m. Had lesson – Bernard accompanied us home and talked to Joyce about her wish to join a Hachsharah [agricultural training centre for Jewish youth who intend to go to Palestine]. I was very surprised! I can't imagine Joyce doing farm work, or fitting in with a communal settlement. It would be a shame if she didn't complete her Art Teacher's Course.

Tuesday 9th June
Did papers this morning, then *had a letter from Alex!* Wrote three quarters of a letter back to him. Don't know how to continue ... Alex wrote:

> "A week and two days have passed since your departure from Swansea and however sentimental it sounds 'The light has gone out of my life.' I have read no books, seen no films, can't study, and am feeling particularly low. With your leaving my good luck went. I heard that I have failed the exam for Leading Cadet. I am leaving the next page blank as I shall make a complete fool of myself if I say what I would like to put in it... But – are you *not* writing of your own free will? Is the embargo you have brought about self-imposed, or is it due to extraneous circumstances? Please give me *some* hint however small – I really need it. I *must* know how things stand between us. Sorry this letter is so disjointed but I don't know how to write you an 'ordinary' letter."

After a few tries I finished my letter. Wrote: "In answer to your questions … 1) The embargo is definitely *not* self-imposed; 2) Not *my* wish and 3) Impossible to write about. To conclude: think of certain poems by Goethe and every song we've sent to each other – as always, Cynthia."

Wednesday 10th June
Posted letter. Ordered patterns for my summer whites. Went to Kahns' at 8 p.m. Bernard was very persuasive about Joyce and I starting to keep Shabbos etc. Read some more of *Mortal Storm*. Quote: "It is very dangerous to have an idea that you will not practise. It may well make you angry with those from whom the idea came." – How true!

Thursday 11th June
Went to Cardiff at 2 p.m. Met Harold Shipman (my cousin). His likeness to me is quite remarkable – it's very queer talking to someone who looks *very* much the same as oneself. Bought material for frocks and a yard of fawn leather. Thought I saw Harold again, only he seemed to have grown by inches – it was Bernard Schwartz, another cousin. I look more like them than I look like Joyce (all three

of us have lost our fathers). Met Mum, who had been to see her doctor. Did some knitting on the train.

Saturday 13th June
Served in the shop. Did some alterations (waistbands mostly), which gave me too much time to think. Very strange how sometimes I feel quite queer – a funny pain above my waist and a sort of longing to see Alex. Went to the Kahns' as usual. Had a fit of the giggles! Bernard said he's *very* anxious to see Alex. He wants me to ask him to come to Aberdare to see him. (See if he's good enough for me?? Look over the opposition??) Thanks to Mrs. Winter, Aberdare is strictly "verboten"!!!

Sunday 14th June
Quite a few visitors for Mum. The noise was terrific. Retired to my bedroom which, although it is only the next room, is really in a different house, and it's absolutely perfectly quiet here (on Sunday). Heard a new singer on the wireless, Jean Williams, who is only 14½ years old – I think she's going to be very popular. Bernard called at 9 p.m. and Joyce and I went for a walk with him. We tried to make him understand how difficult our home circumstances are, making it almost impossible for any great changes to it.

Monday 15th June
Rifka came from Swansea to buy some dresses. She has a marvellous sense of humour and Mum had to beg her not to make her laugh too much. I gave her a note to give to Alex. I know she'll be careful that no one else sees it. Everyone went to see *Sullivan's Travels* after Rifka left. I stayed home, feeling a little lonely – remembering seeing the film in Swansea – then I phoned Alex!! Not really of course. I amused myself for a quarter-of-an-hour making up a telephone conversation with him to last for 3 minutes [maximum allowed duration of war-time phone calls]. I put down the things I knew he would say – and they seemed so much like him that after I'd repeated it out loud, trying to imitate his voice, it really seemed as if I *had* been talking to him. Gave me a good feeling – went downstairs quickly not to spoil the mood with hearing the film's soundtrack. Am going to play tennis with Cissie tomorrow. She's going to lend me her racket and teach me.

Wednesday 17th June
Finished sewing my handbag. It looks quite nice – a little big I think, but no one else does. [Handbags, tablecloths and other household and personal goods were not available – manufacturers were required to make war supplies.] Started on my white shorts. Bernard was working late on the farm, so no lesson tonight. Heard *Sullivan's Travels three* times!! After the third time I went into Mum's room. There the band music from the dance hall filled the air. We *do* live in an awkward

place. Hope I get a letter tomorrow. Wonder what Alex will reply to my note. Hope he sends me [his friend] Steven's address so that I can send at least one letter a month there. Listened to the news. A few weeks ago more than 1,000 bombers destroyed Cologne and dropped bombs on the Ruhr where a lot of German munition and steel works etc. are sited. Our bombers are beginning to retaliate for Coventry, London, Swansea, Portsmouth … I suddenly thought of Mostyn, picturing him high in the night sky, leading his squadron through the searchlights, flak and enemy fighter planes, finding his target, then flying back home. My own problems seem small by comparison! I must try and keep a better sense of proportion.

Friday 19th June

Books in the morning, rent collection in the afternoon. Had a letter today – I *knew* I would! Went to the Coliseum to hear the BBC Orchestra conducted by Sir Adrian Boult, Leader, Paul Beard. It was really wonderful! Met Cissie and discussed arrangements with her about what to do with the evacuees on Sunday 28th. We shall take the 11.20 a.m. train to Cardiff, taking lunch with us; back on the 9.30 p.m. train.

Saturday 20th June

Very busy in the shop. Went to Bernard's at 8.30 p.m. We talked about each individual's purpose in life. I replied: "As I'm only an accident I'm not expected to have a *purpose*." To be truthful, I've never given it much thought until now. Bernard said I was definitely "meant" to be. My purpose is to be an example to others of how to live a decent life. (Of course he means that I should keep all the Jewish laws and customs.) The idea of *me* being "a good example" is just what I needed to hear … I came home feeling much better. (11.30!) Lovely moon out tonight.

Sunday 21st June

Went out with Joyce on the bike as far as Abercynon – about 13 miles. Feel quite at home on the bike now, but still wouldn't like to ride through town on a busy day. Cissie called at 8 p.m. and then Bernard came in!!! Joyce, Cissie and Bernard argued until 11 p.m! Joyce took Bernard home. Went to sleep by 1 a.m.

Monday 22nd June

Tonight I nearly got crippled for life!!! Mum went to bed at 6 p.m. I took her supper upstairs; gave Uncle chicken soup etc. Went upstairs again to fetch the dishes … downstairs Joyce and Uncle were arguing. Joyce had refused to give Uncle his usual tea with milk but made him a lemon tea (without lemon) instead. Joyce is trying to keep the dietary laws of not eating meat and milk together. "If you want milk, then make it yourself!" she flared at him. Uncle got so mad he picked up the heavy oak table – with all the dishes on it, and threw it at her. Joyce escaped up the stairs, I was caught in the middle and luckily jumped back in surprise – to see the edge of the table crash down less than half an inch from my feet; plates and glasses broke all around me!! Fortunately Mum, two floors up, heard nothing. I left Uncle, white with anger, to find Joyce red-faced and furious! "I'm definitely leaving college and going away," she cried. I wish I could leave too – we've been living here almost a year and it's *not* been a great success!

Tuesday 23rd June
Came downstairs to find the table upright, all the mess cleared up – and Uncle gone to London on the early train! A lovely morning, so I walked to the Lily Pond and sat there trying to enjoy the sunshine; did some knitting and wished Alex was there with me. Listened to the 9 o'clock news – it seems that the Germans are advancing towards Tobruk (North Africa). Hope Myer's nowhere near.

Wednesday 24th June
This morning Mum gave me her wedding photos and a few pictures of my father to keep in my room. It seems that Uncle found some and tore them up! He's so jealous! I asked Mum why she lets Uncle get away with it when he gets into a rage. She said: "You wait until you're married and we'll talk again!" I said: "I would *tell* my husband if I thought he was in the wrong …" (Anyway, Alex has a gentle temperament.) Mum just said, "We'll see!" I know Uncle adores her; I expect it's quite difficult for him having Joyce and me around... (He can't tear us up too!)

News: Germany has captured Tobruk, which is an important position.

I smashed a light bulb and shade; I hardly ever drop things, however, I'm still jumpy from Uncle's violent outburst of Monday night – a few more bits of glass for the bin! Went to the Kahns', came home and went to bed very tired.

Thursday 25th June
Letter from Alex. He has been flying a plane! Only at ground level! Hopes to get into the air next week. Other news from Alex:

> "The last couple of weeks American soldiers have arrived in Swansea – and are they smart! The ordinary English private looks, and is amazed – they really shine from cap rim to toe cap, and they're so handsome! Last night, while I was digging in our garden, there was a terrific BANG and, looking up, I saw a plume of smoke rising from a nearby hill and a 'stone' came flying past me through the air to smash into our neighbours' door. A few of us went to inspect it and found three B.D.S. (Bomb Disposal Service) men just leaving. They had set off a mine, and the 'stone' which I had seen was actually a piece of *hot* metal from the casing of the thing. For the next two hours people kept arriving to have a look and the army lieutenant who had done it was delighted that the explosion had set a record by blowing a

splinter over *500* yards! One more thing: Steven is going to live in Cardiff at the end of July …"

So my plans to write to Alex c/o Steven can only work for one month! Walked to the Lily Pond, then met Meg and went to pics. to see *Dumbo*. Went for a stroll by myself afterwards and was amazed to find that I was rather frightened to go anywhere quiet away from all the people, in case – well – in case anything happened. So although I longed for quiet fields or woods, I just walked along Cwmbach Road and back. Felt very lonely seeing lots of couples pass by.

Saturday 27th June

Worked in Barbara Gold's all day. Tomorrow's Sunday!! I *am* excited, but have a nasty feeling that nothing will happen, or rather something *will* happen, to spoil my hopes of seeing Alex in Cardiff. Went to the Kahns' – stayed until 10 p.m.

Sunday 28th June

One month ago today (since Swansea)!! It seems more than four weeks – ages more! Wore my new costume – it fits perfectly. Went to the station with about 14 [evacuee] children. Joyce, Cissie and Bernard were there. Had a job keeping the children together when we changed trains at Ponty. The trains were very crowded. Went to Trinity Hall and had lunch. The children from a hostel in Merthyr were also there. They seem ever so healthy. I'm sure they love being there. Their Rev. seems a lovely chap and fond of the kids. The show started at 2 p.m. An *excellent* play and the acting was extremely good. The hostel children then put on their show and they were also very good. Alex didn't come – I suppose transport was too difficult. After the show we all went to Windsor Place and played games, danced etc., then walked back to the station. My feet ached as if I was treading on pins and needles. Had to stand all the way to Abercynon. Nearly dropping when I got home. Most marvellous moon out tonight – an orange globe. Looked ever so low and only about 300 yards away.

Monday 29th June

Continued with the books most of the day. I *do* like doing them once I get started. Mum has given me some money for bringing the books up to date!! I went straight out and bought a new fountain pen! These last two months I've had to write with a pencil and have not enjoyed it – two very apt lines from my book of Elizabethan Verse:

> And where the pen fails, pencils cannot show it,
> Only the soul may be supposed to know it.

Wednesday 1st July

July!! Already!!! Exactly a year ago today I started exams for C.W.B. Am I glad I'm not doing them this year. It does seem longer than a year ago. Bernard was working late on the farm, so I stayed in tonight and cut out shorts; finished tacking them. I think I'll be extremely pleased with them.

Thursday 2nd July
Went down to Penrhiwceiber early because Gran has got phlebitis. Normally she stands in the shop for at least 10 hours a day and has the largest varicose veins I've ever seen – like the roots of an old oak tree; the rest of her is straight and solid, topped by a glorious head of greying hair in small regular waves. Unlike Mum, she took her "day in bed" with a laugh and asked me if there'll be time to teach her to read. (I always promised I would!) Served in the shop – mainly selling wallpaper – I *do* like the dry, pasty smell of new rolls. Everyone in 'Ceiber knows me as "Ruth's girl" and I know everyone by name, unlike Aberdare where I'm known as "Jane Cooper's daughter" and where I know less than half of them. Sold a set of plain, ugly, cream dishes – war-time variety i.e. no variety, and no pattern at all on them! As it was half-day closing, I popped down to see Rhiannon (one of my closest school friends). Her father, Evans "The Pit-Head", was in his Evans "The Poet" role – composing a poem for the Eisteddfod. We persuaded him to read it out to us – it was like music. He read it full of hwyl (passion), and I couldn't understand a word!

Friday 3rd July
'Ceiber all day. Stayed until Berta came home from school. I got a shock when I saw how she's suddenly grown – from a spindly underdeveloped twelve-year-old looking like ten, to a healthy normal fourteen-year-old. I wondered if she knew what to expect, as Gran would never talk about "female matters". After tea I explained things to her as well as I could. Berta took it all calmly, looking at me through her thick 'specs, with not much curiosity. "Well," I said, "you can always come and ask me if you've any questions." Got home by 7.30 to find that Mum had come downstairs and cooked supper. No saccs. tonight because of the Board of Trade fuss, so I managed to finish sewing my waistcoat.

Sunday 5th July
It's raining – just lightly. I love summer rain! Had a bath, made lunch, then at about 2.30 Joyce says, "Oh, Cynthia, there's something that came yesterday – I forgot to give it to you." It was a letter from Alex to say he would try and cycle over *today* and be here at 2!! I was really excited, but as time wore on, my excitement wore off. Something must have happened to stop him coming. Maybe the weather – or his mother. Did I say I liked summer rain? Bernard called at 7.30 p.m. We went out for a walk and got soaked. Came home looking like a drowned rat! Joyce had fire duty at the fire station. I don't expect anything to catch fire in this downpour! [Young women between the ages of eighteen and twenty acted as firefighters to put out fires caused by bombs or incendiaries. They carried out duties on roofs to

watch for falling incendiaries and deal with them. Women from the age of twenty onwards were called up to the forces and munitions factories.]

Thursday 9th July

More fuss about the Board of Trade this morning. I'm up to date with the Account Books at last!! Joyce went to Cardiff this afternoon to see the Anglo-Polish ballet. I wish I could have gone but she didn't get a ticket for me, so I stayed in reading a book that Bernard had lent us on *The Social Order in the Torah* [Bible]. Very interesting – e.g. everyone should give 10% of their earnings to charity – even if one only earns 10d! [Ten old pence.] Mum in P'ceiber, Uncle in London. Shop closed for half-day – so it was *very* peaceful.

Sunday 12th July

Made tarts etc. this morning with *brown* flour. It was awful – the dough kept crumbling all the time, but it turned out O.K. in the end. After 5 p.m. Bernard came to talk to Uncle and Mum. He told them (at last) what Joyce is going to do, i.e. go to a Hachsharah to be trained ready for emigrating to Palestine. Uncle and he argued and quarrelled till 9 p.m. After he had left, Uncle began to call Bernard everything he could think of; but as Uncle Solly and Aunty Alma came in he had to restrain himself a little, though not much!!! Uncle and the rest of us talked (argued) till late. Both Mum and Uncle are very shocked and surprised. Firstly, because Joyce hates any kind of exercise and the life in a kibbutz in Palestine is very hard. Secondly, we have *no* family there and, from Aberdare, Palestine seems further away than the moon (some of my friends have never even been to England!) so we would probably never see her again. We all calmed down by 12, for in any case she couldn't go until after the war! Wrote to Alex to find out what he thinks on the subject. Hate the uncertainty of never knowing when we shall see each other again. Oh well! It's very late now and my feet are getting cold, so lights out. (Cynthia – I hope your thoughts will have straightened themselves out by the morning.)

Tuesday 14th July

Went to see Gary Cooper in *Sergeant York* tonight. I enjoyed it very much. Saw Gwyneth and Frank there – in the back row! The newsreel was rather depressing: Germans advancing in North Africa; they have also taken Sebastopol (Black Sea, Russia); large number of our ships were sunk on their way to Russia. The other film was a comedy with George Formby. Alex does a marvellous impersonation of George Formby singing 'When I'm Cleaning Windows'.

Saturday 18th July

Rained all day, as it has all week. Zena Shane from Aberaman came with us to the Kahns'. We read some chapters of Isaiah. It fitted in very well at this moment in time. Very powerful and prophetic. "… Your cities are burned with fire, your land – strangers devour it: it is desolate – except the L--d had left unto us a very small remnant, we should have been as Sodom and Gomorrah … And they shall go into holes of the rocks and into caves of the earth – when He arises to shake the earth terribly." (Quite a few families are using *caves* every night as air-raid shelters!)

And a few words of hope!

"And it shall come to pass; because of the abundance of milk he shall eat butter: for butter and honey shall everyone eat that is left in the land.

"… And it shall come to pass; they shall beat their swords into ploughshares … nation shall not lift up sword against nation, neither shall they learn war anymore."

Zena, who had not been to Bernard's lessons before, was surprised when he said that Judaism is not a religion, but a "way of life". One doesn't necessarily have to have a strong faith as long as one keeps the Mitzvot [Commandments]. Through this action one can attain a "nearness to G-d". I'm not sure that I agree with this idea. We walked home with Zena, had a chat with her father and walked back from Aberaman, arriving home after 12. Luckily Mum was already asleep.

Sunday 19th July

Got up very late today, 10.30! After lunch I started making a skirt from a piece of silk I had found in the remnants box. Grandma and Berta came up. Gran is much better. Later, Uncle Solly and Aunty Alma came to bring vegetables from the allotment. Uncle Solly is now looking after our plot, as Mum can't. Uncle Solly and Uncle started talking about Jewish matters, and Uncle (as usual when talking on that subject) got into a temper and started shouting. Joyce and I went out for some quiet. We went up the Craig – it was lovely there – *but* I had my wedge-heeled shoes on and, walking down, I fell and twisted my ankle and bruised my knee. Ankle hurt terribly on the way home.

As we came in, Mum instantly asked us if we had been to the Kahns' – we said, "No," and she replied, "Well, you're *never* going up there again, and you're not to speak to Bernard or dare bring him in the house!" The reason: Uncle Solly had told them that Bernard had gone to him and said that Joyce wanted to go to the Hachsharah because she could not keep the Torah in our house; she had to go away because Mum was not "frum" [religious] enough for her. While Mum was speaking Uncle kept quiet, then just shouted in jerks. He said that if Bernard came into the house again he'd throw him out. Mum said we were as frum as anybody else in Aberdare except for the Kahns; that we didn't eat pig – so what more do they want! Joyce and I didn't say very much. I bathed my ankle, washed my knee and went to bed.

Monday 20th July

Got up at 8.30, foot still hurting. Mum came into the bedroom to tell us that Uncle and she hadn't slept a wink all night, they were so upset over the insulting remarks Bernard had made. Uncle believes we told Bernard that as long as we were in this house we could never be orthodox. (It was more or less true, though why on earth Bernard said it to Uncle Solly or what result he expected to come of it, I can't understand.) Mum said we'd better write Bernard a note telling him not to come here, as Uncle really *will* throw him out, and she said, "He'd be quite right to do it too!"

At lunch-time the shop girls were eating their sandwiches downstairs (bought from the shop over the road) when we heard a loud scream. Meg, who always lifts off the top slice of bread to see how much Spam she's got, saw the Spam was crawling with wriggling white maggots!! The other girls were all sick, or tried to be. Meg took her sandwich back to the shop to be told, "Sorry! But it's the heat." Later Joyce and I went for a walk up the Craig (me hobbling) and met Bernard on his "farm". He was sowing mushroom spawn. He told us that Uncle Solly was wrong to tell Mum and Uncle what he had said and he would ask Uncle Solly to try to put it right. Went home at 11.15 p.m. and to bed soon after. Who said nothing ever happens in Aberdare?!!!

Tuesday 21st July

Joyce woke me up this morning asking if I wanted Tea or Lettuce first? Wondering, I really woke and found she meant letters or birthday cards. It's strange, but I can't really feel that today's my birthday. I've been *waiting* to be 16, but can't feel any birthday spirit today. Joyce and Mum gave me two cards that I had previously bought because I thought they were nice and that we might not be able to get any any more. Had a *very* nice one from Alex. Rather enjoyed the idea of him going out looking for one *for me*, and therefore only thinking of me right then. Otherwise today is the same as any other day – unless of course events prove it to be different – and they certainly did!

This morning Uncle Solly came in to try to make matters better, saying that Bernard never really said that our house wasn't Kosher – however he managed to make matters worse by saying that Joyce and I both wanted to keep the Sabbath but couldn't tell Mum and Uncle – but could tell a friend (Bernard) – at that Uncle flared up!! In the afternoon Aunty Gwen [Mum's sister-in-law] called to see if Mum wanted to go with her to see Howard [Aunty Gwen's son] in hospital. He has just had his tonsils out. Mum told Gwen she'd not slept well, so I went with her instead. I told Aunty Gwen a little of what was happening.

"Oh! You must do as your conscience tells you – like me!" Aunty Gwen loves all the Jewish customs and lights candles every Friday night (we don't!), buys Kosher meat, fasts on Yom Kippur etc. and has read books on Judaism. "Only now's not a good time to make a stand," she added, referring to Mum's condition.

Walked back with her to Aberaman. Came home about 6 p.m. to find Mum upstairs in tears with her eyes all puffed up. I said, "You'll make yourself ill," to which she replied between sobs: "I'll never get better while this sort of thing is going on here." Went to bed at 11. Well! What a birthday! I am exactly three months younger than Princess Elizabeth who has already registered for war service. Of course Bernard says I should celebrate my birthday on the Jewish day, which he has worked out is on the 10th Av – this Friday, in the year 5702!!

Wednesday 22nd July

Uncle and Mum were silent most of the day. Aunty Ray came from Swansea for a few hours, so Mum brightened up. In the evening Joyce went to the pics. I stayed home and went to bed at 9.30! Read a little about Tisha B'Av [the destruction of the Temple in Jerusalem]. Suited my gloomy mood – fell asleep very dissatisfied.

Thursday 23rd July

Wanted to fast today [Fast of 9th Av – Tisha B'Av]. Uncle went to London as usual after a row! When I asked Joyce if she wanted to eat lunch, Mum started shouting, so we had to eat in order not to upset her. Supposed to see Bernard this afternoon, but couldn't leave Mum. Gran came up and, of course, Mum told her the whole story. Slept in Mum's bed tonight and talked long into the night. She said that Gran was disgusted with Joyce thinking this place wasn't good enough for her, as she earned good wages, had *everything*; nearly £100 in the bank, and 2 houses in Tanycoed (2 terraced pit-houses that Gran had saved up for). What more could she want?!!

I said: "Thank goodness Joyce *hasn't* got a materialistic mind." Mum said: "I know neither of you have ever valued money." "No," I replied, "we're not materialistic like Mr. Corb, Mr. Jacobson or Mr. Landau." I asked her if she thought that, after they'd been to shul on Shabbos, they'd starve to death if they kept their shops closed for the rest of the day? She said, "No, they wouldn't; but they only go to shul to make up the Minyan [quorum of 10 needed for prayers], and in any case they'd make themselves more conspicuous if they kept shut." "Jews!" I told her. "People admire the Jewish religion, and they would admire a few *keeping* it – but they only despise them when they don't – and keep open on Shabbos." "I'm sure," I said, "our Temple only fell thousands of years ago because the Jews of that time became irreligious. If they had kept the Torah there would have been no exile, no persecution of Jews, no Hitlerites – if we had kept our faith – and our Temple."

I was then told to go to sleep – so I did – at about 1 a.m!

Friday 24th July

Nothing particular. My Jewish birthday according to Bernard.

Saturday 25th July

Usual busy day. Uncle came back. Joyce and I went to the Kahns'; helped a bit, laying tables etc. for tomorrow. Uncle didn't know we'd been.

Sunday 26th July
Ellen's wedding day. Rained in the morning, but very luckily it cleared up and stayed fine all day after that. The wedding was lovely – in the garden. Bernard had worked for weeks planting Virginia Stock and other flowers. Rev. Gray (Mum's old flame) was there, and we spoke to him a lot. Helped with the reception. Ellen looked beautiful. She wore a silver belt on her wedding dress – said to be a family heirloom – it looked quite uncomfortable. Bernard was too excited to speak to anyone most of the time!!! A girlfriend of his came from London, Miriam Weiss – very nice; rather plumpish, but quite pretty. Family Hechsher also came from London with their two children, about 4 and 6 years old. Heard them bensch [say Grace after Meals] by heart, *and* in Hebrew, after their supper and was absolutely amazed! Came home, had supper, went upstairs and started writing to Alex.

Tuesday 28th July
Went to pics. Saw *Sundown* with George Sanders and Gene Tierney. It was very good – but the film with it was so old you could smell the mothballs it had been kept in! We were all bored stiff, and it spoiled the whole evening. Uncle was in London so I sat in Mum's bedroom. Told her that I really think the families we know are kind, generous people, and if they don't keep much, it's really not their fault as there's no one here in the valleys to teach them anything. Bernard calls us "diluted Jews", i.e. our grandparents were religious and they passed down the good principles of Torah to their children and grandchildren, but what will future generations have to guide them? Shall we lose still more Jews to assimilation? Bernard says that the only solution is a return to the keeping of the Torah [religious law].

Wednesday 29th July
Very hot today! Aunty Annie and Shirley came in the afternoon. Shirley looks very like me, and everyone said we could be taken for sisters. She used to live in Swansea. During our conversation we started talking about Swansea people. She asked "Do you know Alex Winter – and do you like him?" I said: "Why?" "Oh! I *hate* him," she said. Well! I was flabbergasted! We dropped the subject – then I realised she must have been about eight years old when she left Swansea. I promised to call on her next time I go to Cardiff. Joyce and I went to the pics. to see *Hoppity goes to Town*. It was quite enjoyable. Joyce, however, is full of gloom, as we now have sweet rationing! However will she manage!? She can eat ½lb of chocolate at one go! Listened to the wireless. Our bombers made a big raid on Hamburg yesterday – we lost over 30 of them.

Thursday 30th July
Uncle still in London. Kept Mum company – talked about the sweet rationing. She told me how Gran had kept large sacks of flour and sugar during the First

World War. I suddenly realised that Mum was exactly 16 when it started. I asked her: "What did you do in the war – roll bandages – knit for the troops?" Her blue-grey eyes opened wide. "Oh no, – nothing like that," she said disparagingly. "Much more important work! I put my hair up; dropped the shoulders of my dress – just a little – held a rose at my bosom and had my photo taken. Then I sent it together with a cheerful, boosting letter to every man I knew in the trenches." (She showed me the photo: she must have been about 17 or 18.) "And *all* my boys came back alive! Of course some of them expected to marry me …"

I thought of poor Rev. Gray who had thrown himself under a train when she turned him down – he now walks with a limp. "One of them," she added, "was Alex's father." I sat there in shock! Was that why Mrs. Winter (who's very plain compared to Mum) has reacted so violently to my writing to Alex? Started on a letter, got stuck – feel rather guilty for not replying to his letter of last week yet. What can I write when I know Mrs. Winter will be reading it? Went to bed at about 11 p.m. – I wish Alex would come over.

Saturday 1st August
Very busy in the shop today. Ankle hurting a lot and very swollen by the evening. Went to the Kahns' and told Bernard that I shall be away next week. Feel sorry Mum will miss her brother's wedding. Started reading *Jew Süss* by Lion Feuchtwanger. Quite good so far.

Sunday 2nd August
Got up, had a bath – started collecting my clothes together etc. for tomorrow. Got Berta's birthday present ready. Gran and Berta came to stay the night as we're leaving early tomorrow.

Monday 3rd August
Got up at 6.30 this morning and started getting ready to go to Nottingham. Gave Berta her presents – she's very pleased with them. Fussed around, wore a costume. Caught train to Cardiff – we were surprised at getting seats – not many people for a Bank Holiday! Uncle Charlie joined us at Aberaman. We changed at Ponty and then at Cardiff Station to the General and caught the Gloucester train. For the first quarter of an hour only Grandma had a seat, so we sat in the corridor on our trunks. Uncle Charlie kept us in fits of laughter all the way. After Gloucester we were extremely lucky, having seats and direct connections at every change. Met Aunty Mary and Yetta at Gloucester. Four American servicemen also got on – my first sight of these well-dressed smiling soldiers – and three of them were BLACK! They had wonderful teeth (I was quite jealous!) and an easy-going manner. Got to Nottingham at 3.15 and were met by Aunty Alma and Uncle Solly. We all went straight to Rae's house, which was not far from the station, and were greeted by Ben (looking very clean and smart in a new suit etc.) and Rae and her sister, who seemed very nice. Also a sister-in-law of Rae's, who is an extremely charming woman. Had tea, and then visited some relatives of Aunty Alma. Stayed there until 8 p.m. and then walked back. The buses here run on electricity – very smooth running, and almost silent. The shopping centre of Nottingham is really wonderful – about four times the size of Cardiff's and much smarter. Went to our hotel (!?) at 11. Joyce, Yetta and I slept in *one* double bed and Grandma and Aunty Mary in another – both in separate rooms of course. The hotel smelt *very* boarding house-ish, and it was quite late by the time I went to sleep.

Tuesday 4th August
Got up at 8.30 – washed and went downstairs. We were all extremely surprised when we were told that Rae had arranged for us to have breakfast in the hotel. Aunty Mary and Grandma, especially the former, looked very disgusted. We sat down to the table and at intervals people walked in, said "G'morning" and then – silence, in typically English fashion. Aunty Mary said: "This milk is mixed with water!" We had bread and butter (!), a tomato and watery tea – and then we walked

out of the place – very glad to get out of that electric atmosphere into the fresh air. Called at Rae's to be told that the car would call for us at the hotel about 1.15 p.m., meaning we'd have to find our lunch as best we could. Well – Joyce, Yetta and I walked around town – Joyce bought a nightie and then we tried to find a Jewish club where we could have lunch. We looked for a telephone box and looked up the address in a directory. After 15 minutes we found one, at Carrington Street, 2 City Buildings. We soon found Carrington Street, but no one knew where City Buildings were. In the end we had to ask a policeman before we finally found the place. It was very dark inside; we walked up some stairs and into a room where a man was cleaning. He informed us that the club was only open Tuesday and Thursday evenings and only tea was served. Well!! It was by now 12.15 p.m. We tried to get into a café – but they were all full. In the end we had to walk right back to where our hotel was, running the last fifteen minutes, as we had to change; we arrived at 1.05 to find Grandma very annoyed as *she* couldn't change because Joyce had locked the room and taken the key. The landlady told Joyce off, as she should have handed the key in at the desk! We changed in about 10 minutes.

Arrived at shul at 2 to find all the Leeds family there – Max, Becky, Sarah, Doreen, Miriam, Alan – and Hilda who had made the "match". We were thrilled to see her again. Rae, the bride, looked really lovely, and Ben – very shy and schoolboyish. He didn't know what to do – as he explained: "I've never been married before." Rae looked rather unconcerned, and of course Aunty Mary and Aunty Ray had a good cry and Grandma a watery eye – while I looked on, disbelieving my own eyes. I wonder why women cry at weddings? After the ceremony we all went to a restaurant for a meal. The speeches were very good and *short*. Max spoke very well as usual, and when Ben answered the toast he was red in the face and could hardly get a word out. He began by saying: "Well, I'm stuck before I begin – er – I thank all our relations and friends for toasting us – and I hope that I'll be all those things the chairman said." Went back to Rae's where we played Truth or Dare. Estelle asked Becky (who's in her thirties) how many boys she'd had before she married her husband? When Becky said she wasn't married Estelle said, "Well, you're pretty enough to be married!" Went to the "Hotel" at 10.30 and after a short walk with Max, went to bed at 11.

Wednesday 5th August

Got up at 7.30 – took Grandma to the station, then Joyce and I had an early breakfast with Max. Went to pack – the digs cost us 9 bob [45p] a night – shocking! They even charged Yetta the same, and she'd slept with Joyce and me in one small double bed! Caught the 2.30 p.m. train for Leeds. The journey took us 4 hours! It went very quickly for me, as I wrote to Alex on the way and posted it. Got to Chapeltown and was really amazed to see so many Jewish people compared to Aberdare. Miriam was very glad to see us. She gave me a postcard from Alex saying he was not at home and that I should write! In the evening we went to pics.

to see *Santa Fé Trail* – Errol Flynn and Olivia de Havilland – quite good. Went to Sarah's to sleep.

Thursday 6th August
Slept marvellously well till 11 in the morning! We went to the Jewish bookshop – Levi's – and bought a couple of books, then to Robinson's where we saw a lovely blouse in the window and Joyce bought it for me for my birthday (my 16th one). Like Leeds *very* much. Went to pics. again and saw Deanna Durbin, Charles Laughton in *It Started with Eve*. It was very nice – Deanna sang beautifully. Afterwards we went to the Jewish Chip Shop where Sarah works in the evening. Really lovely chips there, and nearly full inside – seems a very popular place.

Friday 7th August
Went to Miriam's. Helped in the grocery shop – Alan's a little tyke! Went to town and bought presents for the shop-girls – all eighteen of them … bought a lovely basket of artificial flowers for Mum. Later Mum rang to say she's going into the Nursing Home on Monday evening. Arranged to leave Monday morning.

Saturday 8th August
In the morning we went to two of Leed's shuls – marvellous places, really beautiful buildings inside – not like ours! In the second, a Reverend was talking. He was an officer in the Army, and he *did* speak well. We stayed until he'd finished. In the evening we saw *To Be or Not to Be* – not thrilled with it. Miriam's brother-in-law Izzy and his wife called and started to argue about communism. He is a strong believer in it, but he didn't make much headway with Joyce or me. He used to be an Agudist [member of strictly Orthodox movement] but is now an atheist! Day's comment: I had thought that in Leeds the shuls would be filled on Shabbos, being a big Jewish centre, but they were empty and many of the women carried handbags into shul [against Sabbath laws]!!! I *was* surprised! Raid in the night. Went to bed after 1 a.m.

Sunday 9th August
Got up late today. Although the clocks were put back this morning I didn't benefit from the extra hour. After lunch we went to Temple-Newsam to see a mansion there. There was an exhibition of Jacob Epstein's sculptures, and the heads and busts were really wonderful. The house was full of antique furniture etc. and we saw a carved horse in perfect condition from 618 C.E.! The paintings were wonderful too, especially one by Romney of a lady in a satin gown. Alan, of course, was thrilled with the gunroom. Went back to Chapeltown to visit Louis's brother (Miriam's brother-in-law). He has a lovely little daughter, also called Cynthia, and a son, Bernard, who wants to be a film producer. Had dinner there and Bernard put on a Mickey Mouse film. Had an argument with Louis's brother

about "women, home and children". He thinks that women hate working in the house and think that it's drudgery, and that even children are tiresome and a bother to their parents – although he seems to like his own! We, of course, strongly contradicted all that – and then we asked him why he had become an atheist after going to a Yeshivah [Talmudical College]. He told us that, at first, he too had been very fanatical, but began to question things and found no answers until he met some communist friends who converted him to their ideas of Communism and Atheism. Much to my dismay we had to stop and leave, as it was gone 11 p.m. I then had a lovely hot bath – it was really delightful (not lukewarm like Gran's!) – except that the sirens went off while I was in the middle of it – so I had to hurry, dress, and get down to the shelter! The raid continued until 12.45 a.m. with heavy gunfire and bombs, but none anywhere near us. Flares were dropped not too far away – we could see a fire they had started. Alan had long trousers on over his pyjamas, and he looked lovely. Helped him to do a jigsaw puzzle until the all-clear came.

Monday 10th August

Got up at 8.15 this morning; said "G'bye" to Sarah and went to Miriam's for breakfast. Louis took me by car to the station. Had to make a few detours around bombed buildings etc.; some streets were closed off. Raining heavily – Ah, me – August! Station undamaged – looked normal and organised – left on time and had a through train all the way from Leeds to Gloucester. Becky, Aunty Ray, Joyce and myself talked and laughed all the way – the other passengers hid behind their newspapers or sat stony-faced. Had slow train from Gloucester to Cardiff. At Newport, a cheerful crowd came on and asked us where we'd been? One of them came from Aberaman and knew Uncle Charlie. Joyce and I parked our parcels in the station and went on to the Nursing Home to see Mums – Uncle was there. Mums looked marvellous. She's to have the operation tomorrow: a Caesarean *and* a hysterectomy! Came home on the 8 p.m. train – very slow – very tired. Waited half an hour at Ponty and got home at 10. Unpacked and went to bed. Gee – my bed's nice!

Tuesday 11th August

Got up at 8.30 a.m. Did some books. Went to Aberaman for rations and came back at about 11.30. I was just peeling apples for lunch when Miss Beynon came rushing downstairs, her eyes all shining. Wesley [her boy friend] has come, I thought, but then she said: "It's a girl – and everything's all right!" I was too stunned to think – I didn't think it would happen *this morning*! I was *so* relieved – all the months of waiting over – and a *girl*! Just what I'd wanted – I'm so happy – and Mum is O.K. too. Uncle went down to Cardiff at 2 p.m. and I caught the bus to 'Ceiber to tell Gran, as she has no phone – I feel like telling the world. She's going to be called Rebecca after Uncle's mother – I think it's a lovely name

– couldn't be nicer. Gran relieved and thrilled – went on to Aberaman to tell Uncle Charlie – got home by 5. Uncle was back. He said he'd seen the baby and it yelled at him. First thing Mum said: "Is it ginger?" Uncle said: "No, it's black, like you and me." (His brother is ginger.) He was disappointed it wasn't a boy – but I'm ever so glad it wasn't. Stayed in and did embroidery in the evening and went to bed at 12.30.

Wednesday 12th August
Up early. Joyce was not feeling well this morning. Started on the papers and got a lot done. Uncle went to see Mum at 11 and came back at 4. He seems very thrilled over baby Rebecca and T.G. [Thank G-d] Mum is not too bad either – although she is not allowed to lie flat in bed and had to sit up all night. Went to see *Bahrain Passage* in the evening. Quite nice. I'm going to see Mum and baby tomorrow.

Thursday 13th August
Grandma went to the Nursing Home with Uncle, so I stayed home with Joyce and continued knitting a matinée coat for baby. Also made a toy bear. Grandma said Mum looks "not too bad" and "the baby's the nicest she's ever seen". Went to pics. with Joyce and Uncle. Saw Greta Garbo and Melvyn Douglas in *Two-faced Woman* and – well, *was* I glad I was only with Joyce and Uncle because – well, it was so *bluntly* suggestive – and yet, it was *very* amusing and well acted. Still

Harry with baby daughter

… (I was surprised Uncle didn't walk out. Maybe he's still in a daze from being a Dad!)

Friday 14th August
Did papers in the morning and went to Cardiff in the afternoon. Mum doesn't look too bad; the baby is so sweet. I nursed her for a little while. She's ever so much like Uncle – the shape of her head and the way her hair grows back at the sides. She has Mum's fingernails though – and they're tiny – about this size: ⊂ Came home at 6 p.m. Uncle asked me to phone the farm (in Swansea) as he hates speaking on the phone. I told Aunty Mary, but she already knew, as Aunty Fanny had rung her on Wednesday with the news. Aunty Mary had also had a baby – Yetta, when she was in her early forties. Rebecca is to have a second name – Sara, after Sal who was killed in the Blitz last year.

Saturday 15th August
Went to Cardiff with Uncle and Joyce. Mum looks better than ever now. Baby Rebecca sleeps most of the time. Went alone to the Kahns' to tell Bernard that we wouldn't be coming. Made me stay until Shabbos was out and then came with me as far as our door. He left at 10 p.m., Uncle and Joyce came in at 10.25!

Wednesday 19th August
Heard Polly [Mum's cousin] has had a baby boy. Ever so pleased – Max must be dancing for joy – I'm so happy for them. (Polly's lost three, either in the 8th month or stillborn.) Went to pics. and saw *Banana Ridge* – it was awful! Read more of *Jew Süss* – quite interesting. Uncle went away today.

Thursday 20th August
Went with Joyce to Cardiff. Everyone in our compartment was talking about the big attack by our troops on the French coast. There have been many casualties, over 100 aircraft missing! One man noticed Joyce reading a book on Zionism. He said he knew a bit about it and admired the Jews' history very much. He said that Britain could never lose this war, as, so far, who ever had fought against the Jews had been defeated by those that had defended them! Both Mum and Rebecca looked lovely. Went to pics. to see *Joan of Paris,* which was really good – excellent cast, Michel Morgan, Paul Henreid, May Robson and Alan Ladd. We missed the 8.55 p.m. train as we only came out at 9.15. Joyce knew there was a bus going at 9.15, so we ran from Capitol to the bus stop so quickly that I'm sure we got there at 9.10! Anyway, the bus was still there – but full up, and crowds were waiting for the next bus. Ran to the station and caught the train – got home at 11.20.

Saturday 22nd August
Usual day today – except that we heard that Polly's baby had died after 5 hours. Feel awful about it. Went down to Pen. to tell Grandma. She said, "Poor Ray!"

[Aunty Ray is Gran's sister, Max's and Sal's mother. She was left a widow, with six children when her husband died of pneumonia when he was 34!] Helped Berta with some homework and finished a jigsaw puzzle with her. Went to Peggy's and talked with her non-stop for about an hour. (Had the wantums badly this week!)

Monday 24th August
Went to pics. with Gwyneth. Saw *Tarzan's Secret Treasure*. Not bad. Came home and started a letter to Alex.

Tuesday 25th August
The Duke of Kent, the King's brother, was killed yesterday in a plane crash. He has three small children, the youngest just two months old! Uncle went to London this morning. Bernard Schwartz [my cousin] came with Mr. Lush to bring some dresses. I *was* surprised. He's got a moustache and looked so handsome. Miss Beynon asked me if we could marry cousins. He's going into the army and hopes to be an officer. Went up to Bernard Kahn's and did some learning. His parents are very annoyed with him – a few weeks ago he secretly turned his bed into an incubator and put two dozen eggs under it. Today, while he was at work, they all hatched!! His bedroom was full of broken eggshells and cheeping chicks. Bernard is quite thrilled and took me upstairs to see them. Went to bed at 12 and to sleep at 1.30.

Wednesday 26th August
Saw Mum in the afternoon, then went to see *The Lady Has Plans – very* good show. Uncle came home tonight. I continued reading *Grand Hotel* by Vicki Baum. Joyce came up and took it from me – "That's not a suitable book for someone your age!" she said. I finished it when she was asleep!

Thursday 27th August
Caught the train to Cardiff with Miss Beynon. Helped her pick a hat, gloves, and shoes for her wedding. Went to see Mum and Rebecca. Want her to be called Rebecca Ann. Mum said *definitely* Sara. Went with Uncle, Joyce and Gwen to see a Dorothy Lamour film in colour! Very good film with it: *St. Martin's Lane* with Charles Laughton and Vivien Leigh. Had to stand all the way home – terribly tired – terrifically hot day at last!

Saturday 29th August
Hot today. Usual busy Saturday. Made a carrot flan – my own recipe: flour mixed with dried egg, 1oz cooking fat, 2 crushed saccs. (for the base). Grated carrots mixed with 2 real eggs (from Gran's chickens), 1 spoon liquid paraffin, 1oz sugar, 2 crushed saccs., almond essence and a little water. Baked for 35 minutes. Shall

serve with hot cherries from a jar that we bottled last year. Mum and baby may be coming home tomorrow – terribly excited. Oh, Alex dear, I wish you'd write.

Sunday 30th August

Up at 9 this morning. Tidied everywhere. Waiting for 4 p.m. to come in order to go to Cardiff to fetch Mum and baby. Car came at 4.15. Pouring. At Abercymboi the roads were flooded – never seen anything like it. People staring out of upstairs windows, their downstairs rooms under water. All of Treforest Estate was one big lake with trees poking out – even a few *boats* on it moving old people from their homes. Had to drive along a cycle track to get to higher ground. Just as we got to a top path, the engine conked out! Uncle said he hasn't seen such heavy rain since he was in Africa. After forty minutes the engine dried out and we continued for another five minutes on the *pavement!* Then O.K. for ten minutes until we came to a place over 2 foot deep in water! Rain stopped after a while and the water subsided a little. The driver wanted to turn back, but was persuaded to drive higher up the mountain. In the end we got through and arrived at the Nursing Home at 7! Mum was so worried – the forty minutes drive had taken us three hours! I held Rebecca all the way home. Mum had to be helped upstairs. Went to bed at 11 very tired – forgot to serve the flan. Wish Alex would write – can't understand it – shall have to write tomorrow.

Monday 31st August

Didn't sleep well last night. Got up at 9 and took Mum breakfast. Rebecca sleeps, cries, eats (repeats), but she's lovely. This evening I bathed her with Mum's supervision and put her to bed. We had all our meals upstairs today. Flan was a great success. Went to bed at 10.30 p.m. but feel as tired as if it was 3.30 a.m.!

Tuesday 1st September

Busy with Rebecca all day. Mrs. Schwartz came in today with Judy and brought a lot of her first size clothes for Rebecca – tiny vests and terry and muslin nappies. She had a chat with Mum and then watched me bath the baby. Showed me exactly where to put my hand under the baby's neck to support her in the water; also how to test the warmth of the water with my elbow. Read in the evening.

Thursday 3rd September

Three years since the war started!! Very quiet; almost no cars on the road. [On July 31st all driving for pleasure was banned – only doctors, firemen and emergency services were given petrol coupons.] National Day of Prayer. Uncle Solly came in after a special service in the synagogue. He brought us some vegetables from their allotment. Gran came up too. Both brother and sister delighted with baby Rebecca.

Friday 4th September
Letter from Alex and a photo too! Feel *much* better! In fact I feel marvellous! Didn't do much except think about him *all* day. Took Rebecca out for the first time today. Pram quite heavy to push. Uncle said it's really *solid* and won't tip over. Went to get baby's gas mask! It's horrible! Much worse than ours. It covers the whole baby – there's a pump outside to pump air into the contraption. Quite sure a baby would suffocate inside it before being gassed. What if the person pumping was knocked out by a bomb? A lot of people think Hitler won't use gas – he knows he'll get it straight back on Germany.

Sunday 6th September
Lovely weather – took baby to Aberaman, then helped in the house. Mr., Mrs. and Miss Cohen came up in the evening and talked to Uncle about Joyce going to a Hachsharah. Everyone against it. I went to bed and read *The Apple Cart* by G. B. Shaw. Re-read Alex's letter written from the A.T.C. camp. He wants to meet me in Cardiff, but, as he wrote:

> "There are a few
>
> **SNAGS**
>
> 1) I've no idea what time I'll have off, if any.
> 2) I don't know how far the camp is from Cardiff, I don't know Cardiff, and even if it was possible to get there, where could I meet you? If you have time, write to me AT ONCE. OH DAMN ALL THESE ——— SNAGS!!!!!! Why in Heaven's name can't I see you as easily as any other boy or girl???? And I *do* want to see you. Do you realise that I haven't seen you since May 28th, exactly 14 weeks 3½ MONTHS. Nearly one-third of this year of 1942?
>
> "Do you remember a wonderful evening which began half an hour ago 14 weeks back? I do. Do you remember how I rushed down that precipitous path? I do. I see the end of my hols in sight and I won't have another opportunity of seeing you until Xmas. Even that thought is torture.
>
> "OH. DAMN SUCH TALK! Now to something more cheerful. First, congratulations on the safe arrival of your new sister. I have no doubt that she will grow up as pretty, as successful, and as good as her sisters – but why another Becky?"

I have only *one* major SNAG! I definitely can't go to Cardiff until Mum has recovered.

Monday, Tuesday, Wednesday, Thursday, Friday – 7th to 11th September
Took baby out most of the week. Impossible to leave her outside the shop as all the customers stop and peer into the pram to see "Mrs. Cooper's" baby. Had letter from Alex on Tuesday. Went to pics. once and saw Clark Gable and Rosalind Russell in *They Met in Bombay* – quite good. Thursday night I saw a shooting star and wished.

Saturday 12th September – Jewish New Year
Went to shul at 10 a.m. with Berta, Joyce, Grandma and Becky. New Year service finished at 1.15 p.m. Seemed like Sunday in the house, or should I say like a *real* Shabbos. All the Jewish shops were closed for the day. This week our bombers carried out a very heavy raid on Dusseldorf. Over 30 did not return. The mood in shul was quite sombre, everyone wishing – "a *really* good New Year".

Sunday 13th September – second day of Jewish New Year
Went to shul at 11 a.m., ditto yesterday. Went up the Craig with Joyce, Berta and Bernard to feed his chicks. Mum not feeling too well. Mr. and Mrs. Marcus, Gerty, Uncle and Aunty Schlachter came to visit her.

Monday 14th September
Mum very ill – sent for doctor – baby stayed at Mrs. Schwartz's in the night. Doctor came again and said that Mum has diphtheria. Grandma and Uncle stayed up with her all night.

Tuesday 15th September
Went for baby. Mrs. Schwartz offered to keep baby for a while – ever so good of her. Took baby out. Mum was taken to Merthyr Isolation Hospital this afternoon. Uncle looks awful! Doctor stayed to show me how to make up baby's feeds. Meg went out to buy six feeding bottles and the Doctor showed me how to make a hole in the teats with a red-hot needle. Boiled up milk, water, meal and sugar, poured it into bottles and put them in the fridge. I wrote down the recipe. Have to warm the bottles in a pan of hot water as I need them. Doctor also showed me how to hold the bottles when baby is feeding so that she doesn't gulp air. Took baby back to Mrs. Schwartz, came home at 11 p.m. Uncle Charlie "Aberaman" had been and brightened Uncle up a little. Uncle doesn't want Mrs. Schwartz to keep the baby.

Wednesday 16th September
Uncle went to Merthyr at 12. I went to Mrs. Schwartz for the baby. Took her to the clinic – she weighs 9lb 9½ oz. Uncle came home very pleased – Mum getting a lot better – ever so relieved! Went to pics. to see *Reap the Wild Wind* with Paulette Goddard and Ray Milland. Very good. *Ever* so glad Mum is a little better.

Thursday 17th September
Had toothache all night. Decided to have tooth out this morning. Dreadfully scared. Gwyn came with me. Sat waiting, not really believing one bit that I *would* have a tooth out. Had *gas*! Afterwards I still didn't believe it. Stayed in the rest of the day. Uncle and Joyce cross because I had it out and therefore couldn't take baby for a walk. So Joyce took her out – with a long face! Did some of the books in the afternoon.

Friday 18th September
Took Rebecca out for most of the day. Drizzly day today. Took her to The Rembrandt Studio to have her photo taken – also started a letter to Alex. Mrs. Schwartz told me that I have to feed baby every four hours "on the dot", and not to take any notice if she cries for her feed before it's due – to get her used to a routine. At the moment baby has no idea of routine! Took some books on baby-care out of the library.

Saturday 19th September
Took Rebecca out for most of the day again. She seems to like the movement of the pram and settles down better between feeds. Didn't finish supper until 9 p.m. Feel very tired … 10 p.m. Last feed!

Photo taken in The Rembrandt Studio

Sunday 20th September
Made lunch, then took baby to Mrs. Schwartz. Told her that the baby seems to cry a lot at night. She advised me to give her boiled water. Definitely *no* dummy! Raining. Grandma and Berta came up. Uncle Solly had slaughtered a chicken for Gran that had stopped laying. (A rare treat!) Had a good supper!

Monday 21st September
Yom Kippur [Day of Atonement]. Drizzly day. Felt hungry from 12 to 1 p.m. but after that I felt O.K. Went to shul in the afternoon. Bernard had given me a prayer book with English translation. He says I should read the English while my Hebrew is still so poor; enjoyed the "old English" style of the prayers. Saw to Rebecca. Broke my fast at 9 p.m. instead of at 8, as I didn't get back from Mrs. Schwartz's till then. Had another good supper – *more* chicken. Re-read Alex's letter which had come this morning. He had heard how ill Mum is and that I am looking after baby Rebecca. Said he will pray for Mum's recovery and for all of us to be "freed" by "Victory".

Wednesday 23rd September
Finished a reply to Alex's letter this morning. Took baby to the clinic. When I put her on the scales one of the mothers said: "What a lovely baby you have Mrs. … er … er …" and stopped in confusion when she noticed that I had no wedding ring! Told Gwyneth that I had met Maire "the Farm" in the clinic. She held her baby Welsh fashion in a shawl, which, to me, looked very practical and comfortable. The baby's father is a prisoner-of-war and he's never seen the baby. Went to Merthyr in the afternoon to see Mum. Had to stand outside a window to see her. She looks much better for her rest. Sent the photo of Rebecca in to her – she was delighted! Saw Aunty Rosie and Sadie. Got to Aberdare, bathed baby, etc. Got home at 9.45 p.m. Uncle is going to London tomorrow. Missed the 9 o'clock news. Joyce said it was mainly about the heavy fighting in Stalingrad and the large number of casualties, dead and missing, in the Dieppe raid. Most of these were Canadian soldiers. Aunty Gwen knows two brothers fighting with the Canadian forces. She's very worried about them.

Friday 25th September
Looked after baby. Life one big hurry – hurry to Schwartz's at 8.30 in the morning – hurry to feed baby – hurry back – and hurry back to Schwartz's again at 12.30 p.m. [1½ miles uphill and back.] Feed baby, back to Cardiff Street at 2, home for lunch, which is either not made, or cold. Hurry back to baby at 4 p.m. for her feed. Hurry home for nappies – hurry back at 7 for baby's bath – hurry home at 9 for supper – Oh, dear! But I do love Rebecca – she's worth it all. I'm sleeping in Schwartz's tonight. Hope baby sleeps. Fed her at 11.30 p.m. Went to bed at 12.10.

Saturday 26th September
Baby wasn't good last night. Woke up at 2.40 a.m. and cried till 4! Gave her water. She woke again at 5 and cried until 5.30 when I gave her her feed – woke me up at 8.30! Amazed I don't feel very tired. I am *sure* that when the baby cries for over half an hour she is too tired to drink all her feed and therefore wakes up too early for the next one. Told Mrs. Schwartz that the Penrhiwceiber mothers feed their babies whenever the baby *stirs* and the babies are very contented. Mrs. Schwartz said that it's very "primitive" to feed like that, feeding in the bus or shops or wherever they happen to be. I don't agree, but didn't say so. Mrs. Schwartz told me I must *never* put the baby down until I've winded her by patting her back to bring up any wind, as she could choke on milk coming back up. Also, baby has to be laid on her side so that any milk would dribble out (and not back down) – a different side after each feed. When I stroked baby's back for a few minutes to bring up her wind Mrs. Schwartz laughed. "Not like that," she said. She gave Rebecca a quick firm tap on her back – and "Burp", up it came!

Sunday 27th September
Rebecca was a little better last night – woke up at same times as Friday night but went straight back to sleep each time. This afternoon I changed into a pale blue frock. Feel glorious after my dowdy brown one that baby quite often uses as a nappy etc. Uncle, Joyce and I went up to the Schwartz's and took snaps of Judy and Rebecca. Hurried home at 6.30 to make supper and be back at the Schwartz's by 7.30. Just made it. Bathed and fed baby. Had just put her to bed when I heard the telephone ringing and Mr. Schwartz answering said, "Miss Cohen? Which one?" I could hardly wait till he called me before I rushed down. It was Alex of course, and I just loved to hear his voice again. I also spoke to Mrs. Winter who asked about Mum and the baby. Alex said he'd try to ring tomorrow and that in any case I'd be getting a letter tomorrow – something to look forward to. Rebecca is sleeping in a different room tonight. Couldn't sleep for quite a while thinking of Alex.

Monday 28th September
Rebecca slept well – only waking up at 5. Decided to feed her – so all feeds will be one hour early today. I find that when I sleep my ears seem to keep awake listening for the slightest sound. Even the absence of sound gets me bounding out of bed to see if baby is still breathing. By the night light I see the slight rise and fall of the cream blanket and fall back into bed relieved – I wonder if "real mothers" act the same – or is it because I feel the responsibility of looking after someone else's baby?

Had a *lovely* letter from Alex. He wrote:

> "When I heard that you were looking after the baby – to say that you could have knocked me down with a feather would have been a gross understatement. You

> surprise me every day; there seems to be no end to the things you can do – and do well … I agree that 'Becky' is – er – well – 'not done' and that the name *is* Rebecca but surely one could call her Rifka? Because I absolutely FORBID Rebecca! Anyway, she has a second name hasn't she? Tell me next time you write."

Tuesday 29th September

Baby can really *see* today! I'm so excited. She's too busy looking around to drink her milk. Took her for a walk along the Cwmbach Road. I've found a wonderful garden there, belonging to a bungalow – a splash of colour among the grey, soot-covered hedges. The vegetable garden is hidden behind a trellis of climbing roses. As I stood there the owner came out, said "Ow be," then picked me a bunch of autumn flowers. Returning, we passed Aberdare Grammar [School]. A crowd of girls in their navy uniforms swirled around us, laughing and giggling, passing around the pram as if we were invisible objects. Strange to think that just over a year ago I was still in M.A.C.S.! Went to see *Night in New Orleans* – it wasn't bad – didn't stay for the second star – a cowboy film.

Wednesday 30th September

Joyce and Uncle went to see Mum – I sent her the flowers. Went with Uncle to see *Corsican Brothers*. *Very good*! Enjoyed every minute of it. In fact, the picture held your attention every second – didn't even think of Alex once till we went out – so it *must* have been good. Douglas Fairbanks played in it.

Thursday 1st October

Baby's first smile today!!! Looked so sweet. Alex rang up – I didn't know what to say I was so excited – only for three minutes, and didn't that go quickly! Started a letter this evening. Lovely day today!

Friday 2nd, Saturday 3rd, Sunday 4th October

Usual routine. Must walk miles every day from the shop to Abernant Road and back. Saw Mum on Saturday – looking better. Simchat Torah [Festival of Rejoicing of the Law] Party on Sunday. Didn't go, as Aberdare parties are always overcrowded and very boring, with people continually chipping at one another. Baby getting prettier every day – she only woke up twice last night.

Thursday 8th October

Joyce and Uncle went to Cardiff. I stayed in Schwartz's with baby as it's raining. Felt cross with Uncle for waking baby up just to hold her – although I couldn't really blame him as he sees so little of her. Saw Charles Boyer and Loretta Young in *Caravan* – it was awful – about 5 years old or more!

Friday 9th October

Grandma came up and saw baby. She had the cheek to say she looked pale and small, and that I don't give her enough food! Baby started crying at lunch-time – Uncle wanted to fetch her downstairs. I said: "NO, I'm taking her her feed in a second." Uncle said to baby: "Never mind, you'll only have to suffer another fortnight till T.G. your mother comes home!" Felt very hurt, especially as I don't feel exceptionally A1 after getting up at nights with baby. Felt really sick and dizzy last night when getting water for her at 4 a.m. – I had to stop and sit down in the dining room before I felt I could go upstairs. Feel a bit better today, but think it unfair of Gran and Uncle to say what they did. Told Mrs. Schwartz what Grandma had said. She said we'd take baby to the Doctor's tomorrow just to satisfy them. When I got home for supper Uncle said that we'd better have baby home, as Joyce could look after baby in the night to give me a rest. He said I looked ill and Joyce said I was getting very snappy, which I know is true – but I can't help it. I suppose it's because of broken sleep – but I still think baby's worth it. Joyce said Uncle was going to London on Monday so she'd need my help in the shop. She's managing both Jane Cooper's and Barbara Gold's. Told Joyce I didn't like to tell Mrs. Schwartz because she might think it's because of what Grandma said. Had a good cry tonight – and feel 100% better for it.

Saturday 10th October

Took baby to the Doctor's – he says she's lovely – as good as any baby could possibly be! Uncle told Mrs. Schwartz about wanting me home to help Joyce and that Joyce could help see to baby at night. Mrs. Schwartz said I'd have to look after baby in any case, as Joyce wouldn't know what to do – and the baby wasn't used to her handling and would feel strange. Gwyneth will keep Joyce company at night, as Joyce is frightened to be alone.

Sunday 11th October

We all went to see Mum today and were surprised how well she looked. She said she's only a 35″ hip and she was always 38″! She'll only be there another fortnight T.G.

Tuesday 13th October

Helped in the shop. Mrs. Schwartz fed baby at 2 p.m. Went to see *Dive Bomber* with Errol Flynn and Fred McMurray in the evening. Quite good, but a little too much "plane" in it. We heard this week that 100 American planes bombed Lille (Northern France) *in daylight*; 500 Allied fighters escorted them. Feel good that the Americans are now helping us. Berta's brother is still trying to get over here, but is having problems because he's German born.

Wednesday 14th October

They told me today that Alex rang up last night – feel very disappointed – but he must have been too. Mrs. Schwartz went to Cardiff with Aunty Gwen who went to see her friend in a Military Hospital: he was wounded in both legs in the Dieppe raid. Stayed at Ty-Clyd to look after Judy and baby Rebecca. Lovely to be in one place all day. Made zoo animals for Judy out of plasticine, potatoes and matches. Mr. Schwartz helped me with supper, then left to meet the train. Bernard called in with a book at about 9 p.m., but didn't have much to say – and neither did I.

Monday 19th October

Saw Mum yesterday; she's put on weight and is now her usual size. Coming home in about 10 days. Cheers!! Out with baby most of the day – she's beginning to imitate sounds now, and smiles often. Stayed in Schwartz's in the evening. Wish Alex would ring or write. Bernard came in and asked me to go for a walk. He looked very serious – I hoped he wasn't going to start proposing again! (He didn't!) Told me he was having difficulties with his job at the Farm. I said: "I thought you liked it."

"I do," he replied, "but because of the dark mornings I leave home early and say my morning prayers in the barn before I start work. Mr. Evans saw me standing there in my Tallis and Tefillin [prayer shawl and phylacteries]. He waited until I had finished, and then said: "Blessed be the seed of Abraham!" He called me into the farmhouse and told me that a few months ago he had had a vision on the mountain. Je. Ch. had appeared to him, and he was SAVED and REBORN! Now he's convinced that he has to convert me to Christianity."

"He'll have his work cut out," I said, laughing.

"Don't laugh," said Bernard. "What does 'cut out' mean? – I may lose my job!!"

Today Mr. Evans has been following Bernard around while he was ploughing, quoting from the Old and New Testament. Well! Mr. Evans doesn't know Bernard's skill with religious arguments!

Tuesday 20th October

Uncle was very ill this morning – grey faced and *shaking like a leaf*. Joyce called the Doctor. The doctor says he has *malaria* – of all things. First case he's seen in Aberdare. (Uncle originally caught it in Alexandria, Egypt, during the First World War.) Told us to keep him warm, give him plenty of hot drinks and prescribed some medicine for him.

Wednesday 21st, Thursday 22nd, Friday 23rd October

Running between Ty-Clyd (baby) and Jane Cooper's (Uncle). Uncle is ever so ill – he's got bronchitis as well as malaria. He looks so bad. Mum might be home on Sunday – but I can't believe it. Took baby to the clinic – she weighs 11lb 6oz now. Court Case (Board of Trade) was postponed as neither Mum nor Uncle could attend.

Saturday 24th October
Helped Joyce tidy up – Mum is *really* coming home tomorrow. Got back to Schwartz's at 9.45 in time to give 10 p.m. feed.

Sunday 25th October
Went on my own to Merthyr to collect Mum – it was pouring. Mum looks well but can't walk much. It's hard to believe she's really home. Uncle got up for the first time today. I brought baby's things back from Schwartz's. Grandma came up – she was awful – nagging about everything anyone does. Put up a camp bed in the front room so that I can sleep there with baby. Went to sleep at about 11.30 p.m. Baby woke at 3 a.m. and again at 6.30. I didn't go back to sleep afterwards. The camp bed folds like a concertina and leaves ridge marks across my back.

Monday 26th October
Lovely having Mum home – but baby doesn't quite fit in with the shop-cum-home yet. Joyce's and my bedroom is too small for a cot – and being in the next house one couldn't hear her. There's no place for the pram to go except *in* the shop – and the kitchen in the cellar is quite far to go to get her her 6 a.m. feed. She is also quite strange with Mum. Uncle is not much better. 8.30 p.m. on my own downstairs I started crying uncontrollably – felt I had to relieve myself – ever so tired; felt better afterwards.

28th October – 1st November – Wednesday, Thursday, Friday, Saturday, Sunday
Much too busy for anything. Mum getting about a bit; doesn't seem to bother much with baby – but *has* decided to call her SARA! Alex will be pleased. Uncle is much better. He has to go to court tomorrow. Morgan "The Sweet Shop" came in and suggested that *he* would sell the saccharines if Uncle would buy them for him. Uncle said he dare not as he's in enough trouble. Morgan said Uncle had done the whole town a service – selling them the saccharines and "no harm to anyone". Baby has gained 9oz this week.

Tuesday 3rd November
Noticed baby had a septic thumb – took her to the Doctor's – he said just to bathe it. Baby cried nearly all day. Put a mitten on her hand so that she can't suck it – baby got very cross and cried *all* night!

4th–23rd November
EVENTS
Baby's thumb better. Saw *Gun for Hire* with Veronica Lake – very good. Took whole day off to see *Gone with the Wind* in Cardiff. Four hour show – didn't notice

it – terrific cast. Alex didn't write, so I wrote. Mum said I could go to Rifka's baby's Brit [circumcision] in Swansea. Rang Alex to tell him. He said he was very busy, so I didn't go. Rommel's army has been defeated and most of North Africa has surrendered to our troops. U.S. forces have landed on the Pacific Island of Guadalcanal. Japs are very deadly fighters; they don't believe in showing "a white flag", even if they're losing.

Wednesday 25th November
Joyce and I went to the Kahns' for the first time since Sara arrived! We had just started the lesson when the sirens went. Mr. and Mrs. Kahn crept under the Morrison steel table [specially designed as a shelter]; Bernard put his Grandparents safely under the stairs. Joyce and I said we'd take a chance and run for it. The streets were empty and we raced down the hill. Joyce went straight to the fire station. I got home to find Mum downstairs (in the cellar) with the baby. Sara was screaming and red in the face – she hates being woken up so I decided to give her her 10 o'clock feed even though it was only 9 o'clock. Mum put on the wireless to hear the 9 o'clock news. The all-clear went at 10.30. Joyce told me that now Mum is home she is leaving to go to a Hachsharah.

Thursday 26th November
Uncle Solly called in at lunch-time, white in the face, to tell us that a land mine had dropped onto the allotments! His shed was shattered and the whole ground churned up, with a big hole in the middle. He was surprised we hadn't heard the thud! The Bomb Disposal Service (B.D.S.) are coming to defuse it, or blow it up.

Sunday 29th November
Went to help Uncle Solly clear his plot and was amazed to find all the allotment keepers helping him. Uncle's plot was always the neatest, his shed upright, as if guarding the vegetables. Now, all was a shambles, glass from the glass-houses strewn everywhere. When it got dark Uncle Solly (who rarely talked to anyone because of his German accent) shook hands with each one, saying, "Sank you, sank you very much." I have *never* seen him look so happy! Joyce left for Hachsharah – with *very* little opposition! Now that Mum is back in the shop Joyce would have to do war work somewhere, as she left Teacher's Training College in July.

Monday 30th November
Bought a book (World Classic Series), *The Mutiny and Piratical Seizure of H.M.S. Bounty* by Sir John Barrow, written in 1830. It's small enough to hold in my hand while I'm giving Sara her feed. I usually sit with "baby, bottle and book", as otherwise I find feeding Sara very boring.

Thursday 10th December
Went to the Palladium. Saw *All Through the Night* with Humphrey Bogart, Peter Lorre and Conrad Veidt. Very well acted. Saw part of the news – the rout of

Rommel's forces in North Africa. Came out before the end to be home for Sara's 10 o'clock feed.

Thursday 24th December
Letter from Alex at last. Feel glorious! Alex apologised for not writing, but, he wrote: "The sight of a very large and bright moon rising majestically, silhouetting the chimneys of a large house and the bare branches of the trees, has put me into the mood necessary for writing a letter such as this – please I *must* see you, or fail my exams entirely. You have got to have a rest, so try and come down soon."

Rang him to say I can go to Swansea next week. Went up to Bernard's last Wednesday night. He has had to leave Evan's Farm (or convert) and has found a job at Cross-Bychan. Tomorrow is his 19th birthday.

Friday 25th December
Xmas Day – and a surprise visit from Uncle Harry's only brother Morrie. He came from London to see baby Sara. Morrie is the exact opposite of Uncle Harry in every respect. He is gentle, with a quiet voice and, while Uncle has black hair and very hairy arms, Morrie wears a bright ginger *wig* and has no eyebrows! When he was eleven the house he was living in caught fire – Morrie jumped from a window and was quite unhurt except that the next day all his hair fell out and never grew again. Morrie spent hours holding Sara on his lap, a big, happy smile on his face; Sara reached up and stroked his cheek and altogether behaved beautifully. Baby Sara smiles, laughs, and practically sits up now.

Tuesday 29th December
Caught 12.25 bus for Swansea – arrived at 2 p.m. Waited for Alex to arrive. Had tea at his house with Mr. and Mrs. Winter. We went to catch the bus for the farm. Bitterly cold. Had to wait a whole hour. Arrived there at 7 p.m. Alex stayed until 9. I walked with him as far as Ravenhill. Didn't notice the cold – walked back on air!

Wednesday 30th December
Went for a walk on the farm with Norma. Yetta liked the book I had bought her. Alex came at 3 p.m. Went for a walk in the top farm. From there one can almost see the Mumbles and the sea. It was very windy, but we didn't mind. Seven *months* since we last saw each other. So much to catch up on. Had supper in Rochale's. Alex left at 9.

Thursday 31st December
Had tea at Alex's, then to pics. to see *This Above All* with Tyrone Power and Joan Fontaine. Not very good – however, we were together, so nothing else mattered. Alex stayed late and had to run to catch the last bus. New Year's Eve – tomorrow will be the 1st January 1943!

1943

Friday 1st January

Went over to the farm this morning. Had lunch there. Feasted my eyes on bowls of fresh eggs, muslin bags full of cream cheese and a larder stocked with butter, bottled fruit and vegetables – pickled beef!!! Aunty Mary told me she "gave Yetta two pints of milk a day, straight from the cow, when she was a baby." She's sure I don't give Sara enough – however, I didn't argue … (New Year's Resolution – quote from *Mortal Storm*: "Think a great deal – but do not think it is necessary to always say what you think!")

Went back to Rochale's. Alex came at 2.15 p.m. and stayed until 5. Talked about Higher (Alex's difficulties in concentrating on his work) … our future plans … Palestine … War … the rumours of terrible atrocities meted out to Jews in German occupied Europe.

Statement in Parliament, December 17th, 1942

> There have been numerous reports from Europe that the German authorities are now carrying into effect Hitler's oft repeated intention to exterminate the Jewish people in Europe. From all the occupied countries Jews are being transported in conditions of appalling horror and brutality. None of those taken away are ever heard of again. The number of victims is reckoned in many hundreds of thousands of entirely innocent men, women and children.
>
> ANTHONY EDEN in the House of Commons.

Could have stayed there talking for hours. Had tea and then caught the bus for Sketty. Had a very nice supper at Winters'. Went about 9.15 p.m. to catch a bus – Mrs. Winter said if I couldn't get one I'd have to sleep there – very surprised! I suppose, seeing me looking so tired after looking after Mum, Uncle, and a new-born baby, she decided to show a little warmth towards me. Extremely windy out – but didn't mind. Rather cold too. We waited almost an hour. Started raining. As we stood close together in the gusty rain Alex's black umbrella turned inside out – it looked like a demented palm-tree blowing about in a hurricane on a desert island. The dark streets were deserted, and for us time stood still and the whole world receded. After so many months of separation, we were both surprised at the strength of our feelings. In the grip of such new and powerful emotions, I willed the bus not to come – but when at last it did, I couldn't make myself get on it! Went back and phoned the farm. Hymie rang at 11. Felt bad about worrying Hymie. Slept very well considering – no stone hot water bottle either!

Saturday 2nd January

Got up at 9 a.m., had breakfast and then went to town with Alex. Walked through streets of cleared rubble to the Winters' shop – their former home. Alex, now used to the sight of it stuck together with its neighbour like Siamese twins overlooking the destroyed town where he had spent a sleepless week helping to get out the injured and dead from the blitzed and burning buildings – me – shocked anew, with a deep pain inside me – for after Llanelly this had been my favourite place: the large stores, busy town centre – now, acres of NOTHING, only wet mounds of cleared space.

I pressed Alex's hand. "I can see why you find it hard to study," I said, "especially the Romantic 16th century poets."

"Well, at least they remind me of you," he answered, "but yes, everything I do seems so futile – unless of course you are here." He quoted a poem from Drayton and then wrote it down for me:

Mortimer and Queen Isabella at Nottingham Castle

She laid her fingers on his manly cheek,
The Gods' pure sceptres, and the darts of Love,
That with their touch might make a tiger meek,
Or might great Atlas from his seat remove;
So white, so soft, so delicate, so sleek,
As she had worn a lily for a glove,
As might beget life, where was never none
And put a spirit into the hardest stone.

Michael Drayton (1563–1631)

Went to see Rifka and her new baby, Malcolm. Baby was very sweet, with delicate fingers and serious eyes. Went with Yetta and Norma to the Empire to see *Mother Goose* – bored stiff. Alex left Rochale's at 9 p.m. I went to bed about 10.

Sunday 3rd January

Walked over to the farm. Didn't do much. Alex came at 3 p.m. – helped me wash up after tea. Rochale and Hymie went over to the farm. We baby-sat. Talked about lots of things, mainly Higher and us. Went as far as Ravenhill bus stop at 8, but Alex took me back as it was very dark and there were few people about. Rochale and Hymie teased me when I got back. Hymie said that Mrs. Winter had expected me to go there for tea. I hope not, or Alex *will* be in hot water! Went to bed at 10 p.m., but didn't sleep well.

Monday 4th January

Packed, had breakfast, said "Good bye" to everyone. Alex came at 11. Called in at Alex's home. Mrs. Winter not too agreeable after yesterday. It seems she really had expected Alex to take me there for tea. Went to depot and waited half an hour before bus went out – didn't have much to say ('Thanks For The Memory'; 'I Double Dare You') … Got home at 2 p.m. Queried about letters home (which, of course, I hadn't written – or even thought to write) – only lasted quarter of an hour. Baby had grown immensely. Took her out in the afternoon. Very grumpy as she's evidently teething. Had the weepums about 6.30, but on the whole very glad to be out of the awkward atmosphere I had felt in Swansea – can't say I feel less tired than if I'd never been away. Mum and Uncle went to see *Holiday Inn*. I stayed home with Sara – and my thoughts. Can't bear to think I won't see Alex for at least another seven months – horrid thought – but I suppose it'll pass – even if very slowly. This morning, in the bus depot, I told Alex, "It'll rain this afternoon." He said, "I don't think so – I think it'll snow." And, for the first time this year, it did! It's about three inches thick now and I'm as pleased as punch. I don't feel half as far away from him now – as if he had something to do with it – the snow came to keep me company … Fed baby at 10.30 – went to bed about 12.

Tuesday 5th January

Uncle went to London this morning. Snow very thick everywhere. Mum went to Cardiff. Sara very restless – awake from 12 to 6.30 p.m. Naturally thought about Alex a lot – strange, but, except for many memories, it now seems as if I've never been away. Songs: 'I Have Nothing New To Tell You'; 'And So Do I'. Wish I could think of some way of helping both Alex and myself out of our very complex worries. Namely:

1) How to help Alex to work and get his Higher – and also to get his outlook for the future straightened out a bit.

2) Whether I should write or not before Higher? His parents don't really want me to – Alex will be hurt if I don't. The danger is that if I write and he fails, his parents will blame me for taking his mind off his work.

3) Our own future outlook is none too grand. If I see him in the summer it may only be for a day – after that he will be in University or the Forces – and after the war, University again. Therefore the chances of seeing him are very poor for the next three years at least – so – what can we do?

4) His parents: If I did marry Alex, would I really be happy – or would they come between us and spoil it? I'm sure they would be the only subject we may ever quarrel over. Of course they've not said anything nasty *to* me – but, what I think is worse – to other people. If only I could let Alex know what they really think about us two – but it would disillusion him about them so much – I should hate to. I can imagine what it must feel like to despise one's parents – even one of them – and you would wish you'd never been told anything about them, but would have preferred to have been left in a fool's paradise. Of course, I'm not referring to my mother, but I must say, since Uncle has been here – he has made the longing for one's real father much more acute and makes one naturally have a grudge against Fate for being fatherless – and therefore, mostly, motherless!

5) The emotional problem. I really adore Alex's affections, but can't define my emotions – they're so different and more demanding than I expected.

Went to bed at 12. (Sara just woke up – she's teething.)

Thursday 7th January

Letter from Alex this morning. Very disturbing one too. Tried to answer it four times. In the end I got so mad, I just sat down and wrote. Evidently that was the mood needed – his letter was so reasonable it was maddening! He wrote:

> "Since you left I am in a bad state of Cynthyitis. Have started my 1943 diary (an exercise book) with a question … Why should this have happened to us *now*? Couldn't the Fates have postponed it for just a few years? Why couldn't I have walked thro' the Cwm in April 1945 instead of 1941? P'raps it's because we two are unsuited to eternal friendship. THEY think that such a step as marriage must be avoided. Anyway, it's fairly obvious that this is just what *will* not take place. Were we 21 and 22 instead of 16 and 17 I'm sure we'd have been well on the way to that step, but as it is, we've got to wait. Just think that, feeling the way we do now, then at a very early age, say 18, we'd either *have* to marry, or decide to marry … The facts must be faced, and the undeniable truth is that for our age we are far ahead of schedule … Despite all I've said, you are still to me, my 'Belle Idée', my goal, my Everest, my aim, ambition – my life … I've been listening to the wireless today, so I wrote out the words of a couple of songs:
>
> At 17, he falls in love quite madly
> With eyes of brightest blue,
> At 21, it is quite another
> With eyes of a different hue.
> At 35, you find him flirting sadly
> With two or three more,
> And then when he's passed love,
> Well – it's then he finds his last love,
> And he loves her like he's never loved before.
>
> (Not a very bright thought for us!) Here's a happier one by Noël Coward:
>
> I'll see you again,
> Whenever spring
> Breaks through again,
> Time may lay heavy between,
> But what has been is past forgetting.
> Each sweet Memory,
> Across the years will come to me,
> Though my world may go awry,
> In my heart will ever lie,
> Just the echo of a sigh –
> Good-bye."

Monday 11th January
Baby had her first taste of soup today and drank orange juice from a cup. Had to have a quiet laugh when Uncle was shaving – remembering Alex shaving Thursday and having to answer the phone in the middle – and leaving out his chin – at least the groove in the middle of it. Happy memories! Only a week ago – it seems like a year. Read *The Greatest People in the World* this evening. Very good reading.

News from North Africa by Flying Officer "X": "our forces are advancing across the desert." I wonder where Myer is now? His letters (so I'm told) have become very formal, not the old jolly Myer, but he's been away so long fighting, it's hardly surprising.

Friday 15th January
Cleaned out shelves in the scullery today. Came into contact with *two spiders* (ugh!) – but didn't lose courage (not much!). Drew quite a few dress designs, practised some Hebrew and started reading *Children of the Ghetto* by Zangwill.

Saturday 16th January
Worked really hard in the scullery, and by 6.30 p.m. everything was perfect. Can hardly recognise the place. Very pleased with myself. Explained to Mum that flour is now kept in the tin marked FLOUR, salt in the one marked SALT, and so on. Mum nodded and dashed upstairs to serve a customer – I expect everything will be mixed up again by next week. Sara had carrot today – can't say she was very thrilled; she can almost sit up now and laughs and smiles. Went up to Kahns' and did some learning. Bernard was of course *very* sarky because I wasn't there for the last two weeks. Had very funny thought in bed about thinking – *where* do we think? It feels as if it's inside our forehead, but does not take up any space – nothing is noticed working in our heads manufacturing our thoughts – our thoughts can't be known for they are nothing solid. Yet I feel my mind working somewhere behind my eyes. Confusing? … But it makes yer think!

Sunday 17th January
Listened to Tolstoy's *War and Peace* on the wireless – did a lot of dress designs – seem to be improving. Changed hair parting to middle – look more serious! Mum and Uncle went to 'Ceiber to see Gran. I suddenly heard the shop door open and close just as I finished Sara's feed. There, looking like a pale bedraggled ghost, was Joyce – back from Hachsharah. "I couldn't stand it another day," she said. As she ate, she told me how miserable she had been. "They were all refugees, mostly from Germany; talked German or Hebrew amongst themselves and pretty well ignored me. I was an outcast because I knew so little of Jewish observance, couldn't even 'daven' [pray] properly; the food was awful; the place primitive and cold, and the work unorganised and dull. I'm going to sleep for a

Some of the dress designs I did in January 1943

week." Mum and Uncle delighted that Joyce has come home. Went to bed at 11.30. Wonder if Alex is keeping his diary every night.

Monday 18th January

Joyce slept until 4 p.m. Mum and Uncle had smug "I told you so!" faces on all day – however Joyce told me that the only thing that really impressed her was the dedicated and beautiful way the members of the Hachsharah kept Shabbos and other religious requirements. She is more determined than ever to do likewise! I feel quite cross I haven't done any of the things I wanted to do. We never finish till 8 p.m. i.e. Sara's bath 5.30, feed 6, bed 6.45, then supper 7.30, washing up till 8, then before I can turn around to do anything it's 9.30 and the milk's to be put on the fire and baby seen to at 10! (Mum has made no attempt to help with any "motherly duties"!) Tonight I was actually in bed by 10.40 – but I had hoped to finish knitting Gran's cardigan; practise Hebrew; read about four books; write to Alex; practise typing; revise my shorthand and German; make a few blouses out of Uncle's old shirts, and finish a dress I'm making for Sara – well, I *think* that's *all*. Can't help thinking of 14 days back from today. 347 hours since I last saw Alex – of which at least 347 minutes have been spent thinking of him. I wonder what I'll be doing in 300 months! Will I be settled in life and happy? Or will I still be in a fog where my future is concerned? Still, how can I tell when I don't know what will happen in 300 days? Last year so many things happened that altered the whole course of my life – so how *can* anyone plan ahead? I really would like to go to London to study dress designing, but I don't see much chance while the war is on.

Wednesday 20th January

Heard that Grandma has broken her arm. Later was told she's only dislocated her shoulder. She had it re-set this afternoon; Joyce went down to Penrhiwceiber to sleep with her. Took baby to clinic. She now weighs 16lb. Berta came with me to Bernard's. He was quite cheeky as usual. When talking about Rosh Hashanah [New Year] he said everyone passes before G-d for judgement like sheep – ("As the shepherd mustereth his flock, and passeth them under his crook, so dost thou cause to pass, number, appoint, and visit every living soul, limiting the period of life of all creatures, and prescribing their destiny.") – Berta, as if waking up, interrupted: "Do the sheep get killed?" Well, we roared! Read some of *Children of the Ghetto* (Zangwill) till 12. Went to sleep around 1 a.m.

Thursday 21st January

Very bad news today. German bombers have dropped their bombs on a school (like they did on Miskin Junior, and M.A.C.S.). More than 30 children were killed; some are still missing – also some teachers. Do the German pilots think they've achieved a great victory? Everyone is more determined than ever not to give in!

Saturday 23rd January
Joyce's birthday. Gave her a gold propelling pencil. XX-day Uncle! (If there's something to celebrate Uncle can be trusted to flare up into a temper over very little.) Grandma came up with her arm in a sling. Went to Kahns' at 8.30 p.m. with Joyce and Berta. Talked about the Resurrection. I had always thought this was a Christian belief, but Bernard said "the revival of the dead" was an important part of Jewish doctrine. He showed us the prayer (from the daily prayer book): "Thou art mighty for ever, thou revivest the dead, thou art mighty to save – and keepest thy faith to them that sleep in the dust." Also from Isaiah, who likens the dew that revives the parched earth of summer to the dew that restores the dead to life. Bernard also said that Adam was formed from the dust of the earth, so it's possible that one could be made anew from "our" dust at the time of the Resurrection. I can believe that my spirit/soul could be eternal and return to its immortal sourcc, but MY BODY? … Once I'm dead – that's it! Once round is quite enough for me! Looked up Resurrection in the dictionary: Rising of Ch. from the grave; rising again of men at the last day. Resurrection-pie, made from remains of previous meals. (!!!)

Sunday 24th January
Helped in the house in the morning. (Made some Resurrection-pie!) Uncle Charlie, Uncle Solly and Aunty Alma came and stayed until 7 p.m. I finished

Reproduced courtesy of the Imperial War Museum

War-time Government poster

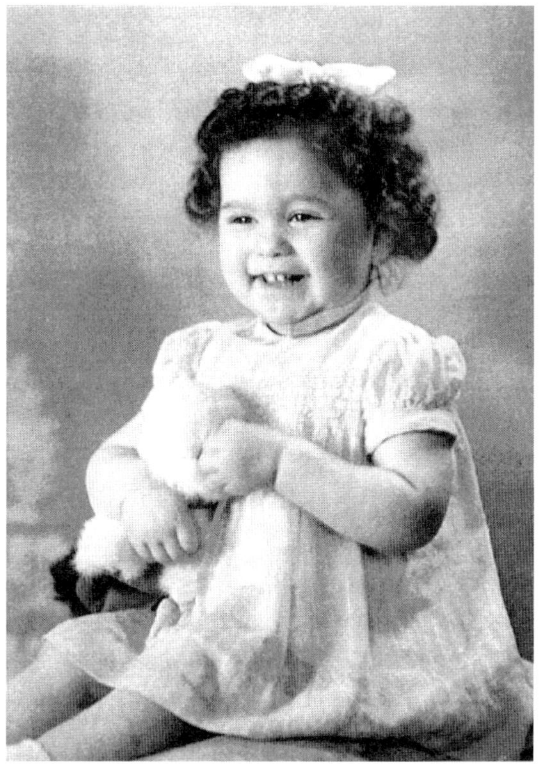

Baby Sara

knitting the back of a cardigan and started on the front. Went to bed at 11. When feeding baby Sara tonight I began to think about her – what will she be like when she's my age – what will she think about – will she be as close to me then as I am to her now? I'll be 32 then – what will I be like? Will I remember the way she is now – the way she smiles when "Boo" is said to her – the way she cries when put down in her pram – how happy she is after her feeds – and how most of her orange juice goes down her neck – the face she makes when she has her cod liver oil – and the way she touches my face when I put her to bed – and, most especially, the way her thumb finds its way to her mouth the moment the blankets are tucked in – will I remember? Will I forget the day she first saw – the day she first smiled and laughed – her first taste of soup – carrot – and how she loved her spinach – and how lovely she looks in white; how she hates having her hair rubbed dry. *She* won't remember – will I?

Monday 25th January

Very good programme on the wireless; discussion about love and married life – with illustrations in the form of plays taken from *Romeo and Juliet*, *Cleopatra*,

Norah and *The Doll's House*, *Candida* and others. Read from *The Book of Joad* by Professor Joad. Went to bed at 12.

Thursday 28th January
Uncle went to London, Joyce to Cardiff. I started getting the books (Jane Cooper's) up to date. Listened to radio – Judy Garland sang 'Zing! Went the Strings of My Heart'. Rather a good line in *Children of the Ghetto*: "… and the years pass by – the children grow up – and here and there, an adult." Also – "A man whose wife continually threw up her better parentage to him told her 'When our marriage was made in Heaven one of your three uncles complained that you were too good for me – so to make us equal he took away one of your eyes. The second one complained, and you were made deaf in one ear – the third objected, so you were made lame in one leg – Oh! If only you had had a fourth Uncle!' " – As he explained, she only has one mouth. This reminded me of an incident in a play – a woman was trying to marry a girl to one of six men she had on her list. "Oh! There's Finkelstein – a lovely fellow – marvellous!! Good looking – plenty of money – but he stutters – oh, but *only* when he speaks – oh, and of course he has a wooden leg." "Not for me, then," said the girl. "What! Look at the expense he'll save you – what if you married a man with two legs and on your honeymoon a car knocks him down, he's taken to hospital – they carve him up – look at the expense – and you have to buy a wooden leg – and here's Finkelstein, already made for you!" Joyce said: "You may as well marry a corpse to save the expense of a funeral!"

Friday 29th January
In the evening I listened to *ITMA* [comedy programme, *It's That Man Again,* with Tommy Handley]. They're hot stuff! Went to bed about 10 p.m., but must have heard 12 striking. Alex – 'You Are Always In My Thoughts.'

Saturday 30th January
Went to Kahns' at 8 p.m. Talked about Mohammedanism and why the Arabs are still our foes. Dates back to Isaac and Ishmael – the latter sent by Abraham into the desert with Hagar, his mother. Also Isaac's twin sons, Jacob and Esau – when Jacob was blessed as the first-born, Esau was told that he would live in the open and be a hunter; for many centuries this prophecy held true. The Arabs (or Moslems) also believe in a Unity – one G-d, and they accept the Old Testament and are in many ways like us – Kosher meat – no pork – but *they* believe in Mohammed as their Prophet. Bernard has been given a small plot of land up the Craig, where he has built a hencoop and fenced it in for a chicken-run.

Sunday 31st January
Poured all day. Baby took up most of the time. She's found her toes now, and catches them one in each hand. Sara's to be vaccinated tomorrow. Listened to the

wireless. At last the Germans have surrendered at Stalingrad; their army is in full retreat, after eighteen months of bitter conflict. Fighting is still going on, many hundreds of thousands of German prisoners have been taken.

Thursday 4th February
Letter from Alex this morning. TWELVE PAGES!! Full of good news. He is working hard for his exams; has decided his career will be in journalism; is learning Spanish and Italian. He has a free day on 21st February and will try to visit Aberdare either by bike or bus. Wrote quotation from Shakespeare: "In delay there lies no plenty" (how true!) and songs: 'My Devotion'; 'Every Night About This Time'; 'Miss You' – so I've been singing all day. Worked out a complete food chart for Sara up to 1 year, with different meals every day. Sara isn't a bit affected by her vaccination and is lovely.

Sunday 7th February
Mum and Uncle went to Pen' this evening. I stayed in and listened to the last two parts of *War and Peace* – was a really wonderful production – one of the best I've ever listened to. Went to bed gone 12 and to sleep, of course, much later.

Tuesday 9th February
Took baby out in the afternoon, and went with Uncle and Mum to pics. at 7 p.m. Saw *Desperate Journey* with Errol Flynn and Ronald Reagan. Film about a "downed bomber crew" trying to get back to England from occupied France – more like the Marx Bros. acting Dumas's *Four Musketeers*. Awful dialogue – e.g. Errol Flynn, handsome as ever, to Ronald Reagan: "Let's blow up this German factory and then off we go to Australia to take a crack at those Japs." I really didn't enjoy it – I seemed to be much too aware that I was in a cinema just watching a film, and not lost in it at all. Felt very tired afterwards – and rather unstuck emotionally – I've managed not too badly over the last five weeks, keeping my mind off the track it's in the habit of following till I'm in bed – and then I let it run along for a couple of hours. (I suppose four or five hours' sleep a night is not enough.) I really don't feel like going to pics. for quite a while if I can't enjoy them more than I did this. The second feature *was* very good – but still something (or someone) was missing. Did plan to see *Wake Island* this week, but don't know if I will. Went to bed 11.45 still in the same mood.

Wednesday 10th February
Joyce had her call-up paper this morning to say she's to go to a training school in Newport on Monday. Sara was very fretful, cried when bathing, and then had most of her feed back up. Took her to Doc's about her septic thumb – he said it was the vaccination making her fretful. Joyce went to Kahns' to discuss with Bernard how to arrange to eat Kosher food and keep Shabbos in Newport. He suggested she stay in Cardiff, which is only a 20-minute train ride away.

Thursday 11th February

Baby off feeds again today, and left at least an ounce from each, but as the milk is stronger it doesn't matter much. Little spots have broken out on her legs and they itch – she keeps on rubbing her legs together (put on zinc and starch powder to cool them). Grandma came up and, of course, started grumbling about this and that – but I suppose it's to be expected. Strange how older people ridicule the new methods of feeding babies – "We grew up all right without all this potch!" they say – but not *all* of them grew up, and the death rate was definitely higher twenty years ago than it is now. *And* people would be healthier on the whole if their parents had been particular about food years ago. One woman I know gave her baby chocolate from three months of age; Mrs. Rees gives Robert (eight months) *chips* and another gave her baby bread and jam at *three weeks*! Mary continually gives her evacuee, Ruth, sweets and lemonade all day, and is very proud of the big plate of chips she eats. All these children *will* grow up but will they be *just* the same? Baby woke at 2 a.m. and at 5.20 – fed her at 5.50.

Friday 12th February

Raining. Doc came to see Sara. Said the vaccination had taken and gave me calamine lotion to put on the rash to stop the spots itching and methylated spirit on the one that was septic. Sara cried a lot. Mum went to Cardiff. Listened to the news. The U.S. forces have finally defeated the Japs at Guadalcanal and, after months of desperate fighting, the German 6th Army has surrendered to the Russians at Stalingrad.

Saturday 13th February

Joyce had an airgraph from India, from Leslie Munitz this morning!!! Leslie is *very* fond of Joyce – but Joyce is *not* interested! Told her to reply at least, as Leslie is so far from home with the troops fighting the Japs on the Burma–Indian border. Sara much better – 12th day of vaccination today, so it should be better now. No letter from Alex yet – I do so want to hear from him – and yet I'm glad he hasn't written. When I do get a letter I shall have to reply. Seven weeks gone! Went up to Bernard's at 8. Bernard translated a wonderful chapter from a German book – wish I could read it again. Couple of good bits:

> "Jews have always died martyred deaths and gone through terrible persecution for thousands of years and still kept faith in G-d."
>
> "Although Jews have been tried so many times over the last 2000 years they have still clung to their original belief, which is unaltered to this day."
>
> "One must accept the Laws of Israel whether one has a different opinion of G-d or not; as with the laws of one's country, one must obey, whether one agrees or not. The Torah *is* our country, and therefore its laws must be kept, whatever we think of G-d."

> "Look in the Torah [Bible] for G-d and one will surely find Him – look to criticise, and one will never come across Him."

> "The land [Palestine] was given for the Torah, not the Torah for the land ..."

I am amazed at Bernard's strength of conviction after all he's been through, but Bernard says that if he would give up his religion, then Hitler would have won! In fact, everything he has experienced has made his commitment stronger.

Monday 15th February

Joyce went to Newport today. Mum and Uncle went to Cardiff in the afternoon. They saw Joyce. Said she has to get up at 5.30 a.m. Work starts at 7. Her job is drawing blueprints.

Tuesday 16th February

Took baby to the clinic. She is now 17lb 10oz having gained 23oz in three weeks *with* being off feeds and vaccination. Stayed in on my own in the evening; listened to the radio. Had an air-raid from 10 p.m. till 11.

Thursday 18th February

Heard there was an air-raid in Swansea – 14 killed and many injured. Mum rang the farm. They said the raid had been pretty bad, but everyone's O.K. So glad Alex and family have moved away from the centre. Went to Cardiff in the afternoon. Talked to a woman on the bus – she said *Sketty*, just outside Swansea, had the raid badly! Glad Mum rang up – I suppose they wouldn't say everything was O.K. if it wasn't. Went to Uncle Harris's in Crewys Road. Met Joyce there. She says she quite enjoys working. Bought material for blouses – got home very tired. Raid on now. Stayed in the cellar until 1 a.m.

Friday 19th February

Had letter from Alex this morning! Says he may come over Monday! Whoopee! Went about the rest of the day in a haze of happiness. Alex wrote about South Wales Coast Town which was attacked Tuesday:

> "I would like to say a lot about this attack because it seemed of great importance (to me); but I'll reserve my impressions until I see you. But one thing I will say; two impressions have been left in me which I shan't forget soon. Firstly, I remember waiting impotently while about eight very bright flares hung insolently above my head before drifting slowly away, re-lighting as they went. And secondly, how really scared I felt to see a Junker 88 (I suppose) beetling off across my line of sight. I watched this Hun dart from North to South at high speed, before being hit by Ack-Ack and later crashing with tremendous noise. Anyway, it was the first time I really was frightened; teeth chattering, knees knocking, eyes popping – and that Jerry was probably feeling the same as me. Cynth! Was I scared! Went over to Rifka's. She was in a bit of a fix – alone with baby Malcolm – quite some

damage, and no windows left. Ivor came at 4 a.m. to take them to the farm. I got to bed at 6 and had 2½ hours' sleep …"

Sunday 21st February
Joyce came; said she *had* to work yesterday. She wants to keep Shabbos from now on. Will be very hard for her to get exemption. Felt rather upset about it. Gran and Berta came up. Made trifles and did chalk drawings in the evening. Took long time to sleep, thinking of tomorrow.

Monday 22nd February
Got up at 8 a.m. Joyce left. Did kitchen and bedrooms – washed woodwork. Gwyn asked what had happened to the place – it looked so tidy. Decided that, if Alex didn't come by 1 o'clock, he wouldn't come at all – changed to 2, and 2 to 3, but then gave up. Felt very funny – decided to have photo taken and send it to Alex. If he couldn't see me, at least he shall have a photo of me – I hope it turns out O.K. Felt all wobbly kneed going to have it. Met Moya and arranged to go to pics. with her. Saw *The Forest Rangers* with Paulette Goddard, Fred McMurray and Susan Hayward. Ever so good – laughed till I nearly rolled off my seat. Just what I needed.

Wednesday 24th February
Went down to Pen. this morning, and brought back my lead animals, and sculpted models. Took baby to clinic. She really looked, to me, the nicest one there. Had photos today – not struck – but definitely *me*. Went up to Kahns'. Talked about careers. Bernard said he'd got Shabbos off for Joyce. So glad!

Friday 26th February
Uncle went to London. Tried to finish letter to Alex, but didn't succeed. Mr. Mealing [the accountant] came to check the books (Jane Cooper's) and started grumbling about them. Anyway, I soon put him to right, and that was that! Joyce came in about 2 p.m. and told me that she gave her Certificate of Orthodoxy to the under-manager to give to the manager, but she's sure he didn't. Anyway, she's not going to work tomorrow.

Saturday 27th February
Went to Kahns' in the evening. Talked about G-d's knowledge of things to come versus man's free will, and also about the first plague in Egypt – when all the water had been turned to blood – where did Pharaoh's magicians get the water from to try out their experiments? Answer: from the land of Goshen [where the Israelites lived], which was unaffected by the plague. Joyce told Bernard that Chief Rabbi Hertz had made a ruling that Jews could disregard religious laws entirely if they interfered with the war effort. Bernard said that *that* probably

applied to people on active service but not to those in factories who could do the same work on another day. Joyce is worried what will happen when she returns to Newport. Got home at 10 p.m. Fed baby. Got up with her at 5.30 a.m., fed her, but didn't sleep again afterwards.

Monday 1st March
Too tired to write tonight.

Tuesday 2nd March
Reason so tired last night – baby has a cold and woke up four times on Sunday night. Uncle Charlie, Mr Curitz and boys called in. Men talked about Mr. Kahn – all against. They said he's a religious fanatic with old-fashioned ideas. Went to see Greer Garson and Walter Pigeon in *Mrs. Miniver* – was as good as all the publicity made out – thoroughly enjoyed it – felt Alex's absence, very badly, occasionally. Fed baby, went to bed 11.20 p.m., very tired.

Wednesday 3rd March
Dressed the shop windows today. Bought present for Mum. Went to Kahns' and read first three chapters of the Bible. Bernard was very upset, as a fox had got into his chicken shed on the Craig and killed *every* chicken (those lovely chicks he had incubated under his bed).

Thursday 4th March
Mum's birthday. She was delighted with her present, as she had forgotten it was her birthday. Uncle came back from London, for once quite shattered. He usually ignores the bombing, as he says: "You only cop it if it's got your name on it!" His sisters spend every night in the Underground. Yesterday a terrible tragedy happened in Bethnal Green Underground. As people were descending to be safe from the bombing a woman and baby tripped going down the stairs and *over* 170 people fell on top of her and suffocated or were crushed to death! The Golding family used to live three minutes from that station; they only moved to Cazenove Road N.16 two years ago; still, it could have happened anywhere! Mum has suggested that his five sisters should come here, however, I can't see them agreeing. Uncle didn't dare tell them he had *married* Mum until two years after their wedding – a woman with *two* children and he fifty years old! Spent some time drawing. Doreen called and we went to pics. Saw *My Sister Eileen* with Rosalind Russell – funniest film I've seen for ages.

Friday 5th March
Sorted out papers and entered them this morning. At 1.40 p.m. – knock at the door. Mum went and took person upstairs. Mrs. Prosser told me it was Alex – I wouldn't believe her until Doreen came down and confirmed it. It was Alex!!

My feelings were so mixed I could never define them. After feeding Sara we went around town looking for a book for Eva. Alex bought himself a cycle-bag in the Co-op, then we walked to Aberaman where Alex got some razor blades from Uncle Charlie (they're practically unobtainable). Gloriously warm day. Had tea and went upstairs to talk. Before I really realised that Alex had come, he had gone – he caught the 6.25 p.m. bus to Swansea. Went home from the bus station feeling very funny. Not disappointed, not happy, but more or less very puzzled over my own feelings – and feeling like kicking myself for not telling Alex what I wanted to and being so weak as to actually act against those feelings. Went to bed *very* tired, been awake since 6.10 a.m.

Saturday 6th March

Lovely day. Went up to Bernard's at 8 p.m. Went over Chapters 4 and 5 of the Bible. Didn't do much Hebrew, as Kahns have a young woman staying with them. She's from London and has come for a few weeks' rest. The recent heavy raids have shattered her nerves – especially after she was dug out from her home. She seems very sweet, and is about Joyce's age. Started *The Pastures of Heaven* by John Steinbeck (recommended by Alex).

Sunday 7th March

Went out with Gwyneth and baby this morning and to Schwartz's at 3 p.m. to see Mrs. Schwartz and new baby Saul. Sara looked lovely, and *so big* compared to Saul. Dashed home, bathed baby and rushed to Liberal Club at 6.30. The lecturer, Chaim Pearl from Cefn Coed Hostel, didn't turn up, so Mr. Bedash spoke about his visit to George Hall M.P. Began at last to realise that Alex actually did come Friday, and to miss him more than ever. It seems whenever I begin to settle down to being without him – we meet for a second – and then I start off again, missing his presence and wanting his company. Am rather worried about two things which I must resolve to tell him next time – I should have this time, but couldn't bring myself to, although I feel quite annoyed with myself on that account. 1) The Jewish Question (e.g. would he be prepared to stop smoking and travelling by bus on Shabbos?) and 2) The film influence in the drama. (How much are we affected by the romantic films we see?) Do hope I'll see him soon if only for this reason.

Monday 8th March

Joyce came home for an hour or two and brought me a play to type six copies of. Thirty-six pages! Began straight away and would have finished by 10.30 tonight (excluding Sara's interruptions) but for one page which came out back to front – carbon in the wrong way! Fingers awfully stiff. Baby had teaspoon of egg this morning.

Wednesday 10th March
Went to Cardiff to look for shoes – couldn't get any. Saw Aunty Millie and Bernard (Schwartz). Bernard hopes to join the forces. Aunty Millie rather concerned, but Bernard very keen. Went to Kahns' at 8 p.m. Talked about Purim and did some Hebrew writing. Bernard [Kahn] showed me a letter from Newport saying that Joyce's application was receiving attention. Joyce told me the answer was definitely NO, and therefore she had to work last Saturday. Bernard thinks there's been a mistake.

Thursday 11th March
Sara had all her breakfast with a cup and spoon. Mum and Uncle went to Cardiff. Doctor called, said we could bath baby. At last! Pulled off her plaster. Darned and washed stockings – need new ones, but they are almost impossible to get. Finished *The Pastures of Heaven*. Did some drawing.

Tuesday 16th March
Saw baby's first tooth coming through! Mrs. Schwartz came in and told Mum baby should be starting regular meals by now. Mum's comment: "Doesn't she *get* regular meals?" Will start tomorrow. Did some Hebrew in the evening. Beginning to read quite well. Find the spelling impossible!

Wednesday 17th March
Awful gas smell in the scullery – has been since Monday – like a real gas chamber – and it can't be seen to till *Thursday*! Got up 6.30 a.m., gave baby orange juice and rusk. Went back to bed and read. Woke Sara at 8.30 and gave her breakfast. Went to clinic (19½ lbs), then gave her lunch. Gave her tea at 4. Baby very happy all day – sat up in the pram. Went to Kahns' at 8. Went over the Purim story and Megillat Esther [Book of Esther]. Fed baby at 10.30, went to bed. Took up breakfast ready for tomorrow.

Thursday 18th March
Ta'anis Esther [Fast of Esther]. Had breakfast *early,* before daybreak! Mum and Uncle went to Cardiff, so didn't notice I was fasting. Felt O.K. Baby had Benjer's food pudding, and enjoyed it. Read Barrie's plays in the evening.

Saturday 20th March
Went to shul at 7.30 p.m. Ellen Kahn – er – Bodenheimer rather, showed me the place, and I found I could follow fairly well and even understand what was happening as it was being read. Came home at 9, fed baby at 10.30.

Sunday 21st March
Took Sara to Aberdare Park this morning. Fed, dressed her etc. Doreen came in to see how I put Sara to bed. Got to Windsor Place, Cardiff by 7.30 p.m., where

they had a Purim Dance. Of course they played quite a few of "our" tunes – so I didn't dance, but spoke to a lot of people. The play went off well. Caught 9.30 bus home. Met Ken and Idris from "train gang". Had an interesting talk with them. Very pleased to find I *could* talk without shyness and awkward pauses. Must be growing up!

Thursday 25th March
Mum and Uncle went to London for the day. Baby cried all morning, has nasty pimple behind her ear from vaccination; spots haven't gone yet and we have to bath her with sulphur soap and bicarbonate in the water. Doreen stayed with me. I hope Sara will get used to her by Sunday. (My cousin Leah's wedding in Merthyr.) Made some cakes in the evening with (almost) real chocolate covering made of custard powder, cocoa and syrup. Fed Sara and went to bed just gone 1 a.m.

Wednesday 31st March
Went to Cardiff and met Joyce at 3 p.m. She has *not* got permission to take Saturdays off, even though one of her friends is prepared to change days with her. She is being sent to a factory in Bristol next month. Went to pics. and saw *Man and His Mate* with Victor Mature. Quite enjoyable. Got home at 7 p.m. Baby O.K. so went to Kahns' as usual at 8. Started reading Exodus [second of the Five Books of Moses].

Sunday 4th April – Leah's Wedding
Went to catch 11.20 a.m. train to Merthyr. Had to wait one hour at Abercynon for connection! Met Joyce and rest of family on the train. Also Harold Cohen whom I haven't met before. All went up to Aunty Rosie's. Everyone there, i.e. *all* (or most) of the family – 25 first cousins, and 18 uncles and aunts – and what a crowd. Sadie looked really stunning, and Leah looked nice too. Her husband – a Czech, Mr. Weisl – gave a wonderful speech. He's in the Czech Air Force. Uncle Solly was also there with Aunty Phoebe and their baby son Lawrence. Came home at 9 with Joyce. Doreen had put Sara to bed, so I only had to give her the 10 o'clock feed. Talked about the wedding with Joyce until 12 – mainly about how nice *our* family is and how maddening it is that Uncle won't let us have anything to do with them. He doesn't know about today – and Mum, who of course knows, doesn't want Uncle to be told, to avoid a row.

Wednesday 7th April
Terribly windy today. Took baby to clinic; pram almost overturned with the wind. No letter from Alex yet. I *would* like to write – but – NO! Continued reading Exodus with Bernard. Moses was brought up in Pharaoh's palace as a prince. Very interesting chapter.

Guests at the wedding of Leah Shipman to Otto Weisl in Merthyr on Sunday 4th April 1943 (Author circled)

Thursday 8th April
No letter *today* – still! Thought of our walk to the Cwm (8th April 1941). Mum went to London. Made a pair of slippers. Uncle gave me a shirt; altered it into a blouse for myself. Baby cried all night, so no sleep for me. Definitely get the Doctor tomorrow.

Friday 9th April
Doctor came. Sara has a septic foot and has to be bathed in salt water and then bread poulticed. I really felt like crying when Uncle did it for her, she was in so much pain. Rifka came in the afternoon to buy some dresses. Wrote to Alex and gave it to Rifka to give to him. She made some jokes about Alex but I don't mind when she does. Read in the evening.

Thursday 15th April
Very hot day today. Went to park with Sara – roasted in my coat. Went to pics. and saw *The Major and the Minor* with Ginger Rogers and Ray Milland. Enjoyed it very much. Thought a lot about Alex today. The three inseparables: Alex, myself and the sun, separated as usual. Baby very naughty, won't go to sleep anymore without me nursing her or singing to her.

Friday 16th April
Ben and Rae came to visit Gran. They came to us this afternoon. Uncle Ben picks up all the gossip; told us about his friend Ivor Pritchard the Pub. A year after his first wife died – he'd been married for 20 with no children – he married Edna from Cardiff, his new barmaid. She was only 18, so there were quite a few jokes in the pub – but none so proud as Pritchard, when it became obvious she was having his baby.

After the birth, Doctor Hall came downstairs to give him the good news. "It's a boy," he said. "Hold on a minute …" Doctor held Ivor's arm. "There's nothing wrong, mother and baby are fine – but I think you're in for a surprise."

"Well!" said Ben, "he certainly was – the baby was *black*!"

"It's all those Yanks in Cardiff," said the men, "or that black beer you've been drinking. He'll be fine down the pit!"

To everyone's surprise, Ivor said, "A baby's a baby! Drinks all round!"

Uncle's face when I said: "I've always wanted a black baby!" was quite a sight.

Mum laughed; she knows as a child I only wanted black dolls since Joyce sat on my black celluloid doll and squashed it.

Ben and Rae stayed the night (in my bed). I slept in the spare room. Bed awful! Hard as iron and it creaks like matchboard!

Saturday 17th April
Went to Kahns' at 8 p.m. Did more about Pesach, and was invited up there for Seder. Accepted. Mum said she'd ask Uncle if he'd do a Seder here, but he refused

of course. Strange to realise Uncle knows so much – he was brought up Orthodox – but when his parents died young, leaving him the oldest of nine, he became an atheist. Question: How can he blame G-d for the death of his parents *and* be an atheist?

Monday 19th, Tuesday 20th, Wednesday 21st April
Went up to Bernard's Monday and Tuesday evening – enjoyed myself. Arrived home 12.25 a.m. and 12.45 respectively. Uncle in a furious temper. For once Mum stuck up for me. Result: Uncle cross all day! Miriam and Phoebe [Mum's cousins] came and picked dresses. Thought Sara was gorgeous – she is! Had a letter from Alex, Wednesday. Started writing an answer – gave it to Phoebe who was going to Swansea to see Aunty Ray. Went to bed at 12, very tired.

Thursday 22nd April
Mum and Uncle made it up and went to Cardiff. I went to see *Pride of the Yankees* with Gary Cooper. Enjoyed it a lot. Uncle still annoyed because I went up to Bernard's for *both* Seder nights.

Saturday 24th April
Stayed in shop in the afternoon. Joyce came; we went to Bernard's at 8 p.m. Talked all evening. I am surprised how determined Joyce is to keep Shabbos and the other dinim [laws] – she was always so happy-go-lucky and the first to give in on anything. Mum is still thinking about my suggestion of *not* waiting till the war is over before I start learning dress design in London – a sure way to stop the arguments here.

Tuesday 27th April – Yom Tov
Went to shul this morning. Had to go through the shop. Dark looks from Mum, Uncle, and shop girls, all busy with customers, expecting me to help – wish we had another exit so I could go out without everyone noticing. Lunch-time had a row with Mum over milk/meat and meshuggeners [madmen], Mum's name for religious fanatics (like the Kahns).

Bernard showed us a book by Rabbi S. R. Hirsch, a 19th century Rabbi, in which it said: "I have learned from experience that there can be no compromise between observant and non-observant Jews in religious matters. Any compromise only brings renewed trouble all over again." – What about us caught in the middle? He also said: "In every action the Jew must bear the stamp of the Torah he received at Sinai and reflect the refining power of the Torah – amidst all the developments of changing times."

Wednesday 28th April
Pesach over! And am I glad! – This year anyway. Baby had first taste of bread and butter today and liked it. Changed my hairstyle to a crop curl and it makes me feel very naughty. I like it very much.

Saturday 1st May
May!! I'm glad! Although it rained part of today. Went up to Bernard's at 8 p.m. and to my surprise he said he'd been thinking of writing to Alex to invite him down. Told him I didn't mind, but it would seem odd for a stranger to invite someone down for a weekend. Decided to ask Alex down for a day and then introduce him to Bernard first. Shall have to think it over a bit. Bernard stated, as his reasons, that it seemed that Alex and I had a firm friendship with no moorings, which is quite true. We are both changing every day and have never really had time to exchange our ideas and, in that sense, we do not even know each other. At least I'm sure Alex doesn't really know me, which is mainly my fault for not explaining to him what goes on in my mind. I must rectify that in the near future, and *no* evading it like last time.

Monday 3rd May
Miriam [Mum's cousin] and her son Carl came from Cardiff. Stayed till 5 p.m. Carl is the smallest eater I've ever seen. His ribs are sticking out – he's four and Sara eats more than he does. Miriam doesn't seem to worry as long as he doesn't dirty anything. Kept washing him all day. Baby woke twice – cutting second tooth. Jerry plane just passing overhead. We are doing very well in Tunisia. General Montgomery has won us all of Egypt up to Mersa Matruh so far. The Russians are quiet lately, holding their front.

Wednesday 5th May
Weather not bad. Went to see *Bambi*. Enjoyed it thoroughly. Tonight Mum told me a ridiculously funny thing. Uncle thinks that it's a tie between Joyce and me as to who likes Bernard the most. What a thought!!!

Friday 7th May
Allies captured Tunis and Bizerta!!! At 4 p.m. today. Wonderful news! General Alexander praised to the skies, and he deserves it. Germans have no hope now in North Africa; only remaining troops in Cape Bon Peninsula and we'll soon get them out of there.

Monday 10th May
Uncle went to London. Baby good. Knows where "flowers" are – "pussy", Mama, Dada, Baba, although she can't say anything but "Ga-Ga" yet. Can stand holding on to something. Taken ever so many prisoners in North Africa (about 150,000), many are surrendering. Got accounts book up to date.

Wednesday 12th May

Had busier day today. Mrs. Prosser whitewashed the back an awful yellow colour. She's in an odd sort of mood. A friend of her son wrote to say he'd definitely seen Alan picked up from the water by one of the lifeboats near Singapore. This may mean that he's a prisoner of the Japanese, which is of small comfort to Mrs. Prosser. Rained a bit. Thought of Alex of course, constantly, as I always do. Wish he'd write. Mrs. Gardiner (Meg) called in. She looks marvellous. Her baby is due on 12th November, so she says. I stayed in to listen to Tchaikovsky's Opera *Eugene Onegin*. Enjoyed it too. Baby Sara slept last night from 6.30 p.m. to 7 a.m., for the first time all through. Hope she does it tonight too.

Thursday 13th May

Went to Cardiff at 1 p.m., met Joyce. Bought two sailor hats. Seem to suit me. Read *Messiah of Ismir* by Josef Kastein in the train. Very good book. Everyone happy that the fighting in North Africa is over – many generals captured, including General von Arnim. Hope Myer will now get leave and be sent home.

Saturday 15th May

Went up to Bernard's as usual. Stayed part of the time in the garden. Talked all the time about free will. I am still finding this a problem – regarding:

1: My career – I am now a nurse-maid, cook, book-keeper, sales-girl, alteration hand – none of which I had planned to do.

2: Living my life according to Torah precepts. This is almost impossible to keep 100% and causes such trouble. Mum and Uncle say the Kahns are intolerant, but Mum and Uncle are quite intolerant to my wishes.

3: Alex and me: unexpected opposition from Mrs. Winter has made so many difficulties – all of which I could resolve except for my biggest enemy – my own conscience!

Bernard also read from the Book of Job – a parable (?) possibly written by Moses. It deals with the problem of suffering. Job, a happy wealthy man, loses everything, home, family, wealth, health, but never blames G-d, and never loses faith. The book is quite long, and beautifully written ("For wrath killeth the foolish man, and envy slayeth the silly one … When I lie down, I say, 'When shall I arise, and the night be gone?' And I am full of tossings to and fro unto the dawning of the day.") Eventually his wealth, family, herds etc. are restored to him, which makes a happy-ever-after ending. To me, this is not like real life. Talked so much; Bernard walked me home. Got in at 10.30.

Sunday 16th May

Baked a flan this morning for a change. Gwyn came in to say she may be called up, so she's trying for a job on the "Western Welsh" buses. I shall miss her. We took baby to the park this afternoon. She's got a little cold and was very cross – her top teeth are coming through. Wonder why we can't be *born* with teeth (like we have nails) and keep them for life! I've had ten years of toothache – six front teeth out (damaged in an accident on a ride on the dodgems in Barry Island) and quite a few pulled out by the school "dentist". Also seen scores of teeth pulled out by Uncle Ben in Gran's kitchen before taking impressions. It is most unfair that Joyce, the biggest chocolate eater I know, has marvellous *strong* teeth! Finished *Messiah of Ismir* and started *Going Home* by Ernst Hathern. Not bad so far.

Tuesday 18th May
Lovely day today. Walked with Sara to Cwmbach, Aberaman etc. to call on Jewish children to invite them to join a Youth Club Bernard is starting. Hope at least nine will come. Went to Penrhiwceiber to speak to Mr. Fine to let his son come. Listened to a well-acted play, *The Wild Duck* by Ibsen, in the evening.

Saturday 22nd May
Rained today. Read a little of *Going Home* – thought with amazement that a year or so back, I didn't even know or care what a Zionist was! I was quite content, like most Anglo-Jews, with my home here, my only home. And now I find myself actually reading books on Palestine, with an appetite for learning what the home of my forebears is like today – and also with a longing – homesick longing, for it, too. Went to Bernard's. Talked about Palestine and the possibility of reclaiming the desert for food production. Bernard intends to go there as soon as the war is over. His experience with farming will be very useful.

Sunday 23rd May
Lovely day. Wings for the Victory Parade. WAAFs, Home Guard, R.A.F., A.T.C., O.T.C., G.T.C., Wardens, First Aid etc. WAAFs' band very smart, also A.T.C.'s. Took Sara up to the park to watch. She didn't take her eyes off the parade except to occasionally smile at me, as if I was the cause of it. Three "tough" nine-year-old boys stood behind the pram – of course not deigning to look at a baby – Sara started playing with their fingers, while they unwillingly smirked at her.

Monday 31st May
Doreen got the sack for "borrowing" Mum's shoes without permission. I wanted her to stay as she's so good with Sara and helps with the housework. Mum said we'll advertise for someone else. Joyce came and dressed the corner windows, and they look great. Read in the evening, and did some Hebrew with Berta. (What a job!)

Tuesday 1st June
Hooray!! June! Then July! Alex's exams in a month! New woman came to replace Doreen. Marvellous worker, but Sara won't have anything to do with her. Sara's so sweet, but is she wicked! All the shop girls spoil her. Our bombers have

dropped bombs on the dams and area around Dortmund where a large number of munition factories are sited. Large area of the Ruhr valley flooded. Mum went to London. Mrs. Prosser distempered the scullery. We worked like navvies all day. Now the scullery looks nicer than the kitchen.

Friday 4th June

LETTER this morning!! Result: feeling wonderful! Started reply. Woman can't come because of her children – they can't manage without her. Pity. She was very good with the housework.

Saturday 5th June

Went to shul in the morning; then to Bernard's at 8 p.m. Did more about Shavuoth. Asked him at last *the* question! How do religious couples show their affection for each other before marriage? Very surprised at answer. Certain acts are permitted – or at least not punishable. Even living together as man and wife without a chuppah [religious marriage] in olden days was considered a marriage and needed a "Get" [divorce] if they parted. This seems a very proper idea – their children would not be stigmatised, and have full rights. Many more aspects discussed – in general of course.

Thursday 10th June

Uncle cross again. Went up Clifton Street to a Youth Meeting. Nine children came and I think they thoroughly enjoyed it. Bernard is marvellous with young people and very stimulating. Berta told me afterwards that she was bored! I was amazed, and told her that it was because she didn't take enough interest in what was being said. Came home at 10 p.m., Mrs. Chinn here [Gran's sister-in-law]. Aunty Chinn has the most marvellous smile, it lights up the room – she has such a wonderful nature.

Friday 11th June

Joyce came from Bristol and brought *strawberries* and chocolate *Halva* – haven't seen strawberries in three years. The Halva was not as nice as the ordinary vanilla – but still nice. Tried on a new frock at 10 p.m. – Sara has ruined my two dresses. It fits – so I'm having it!

Sunday 13th June

Only five children came to the Youth Club owing to the parents of the other four visiting them from London. Enjoyed myself. Joyce came and also enjoyed it, but Berta was bored again.

Monday 14th June

Becky [Mum's cousin] and Eli's wedding today. Got up at 7, caught the 1 o'clock train. Sara looks marvellous. She has enough hair to comb into small curls – she behaved very well the whole day. Bride wore blue. Didn't have a very good time, as no one there my age. Went to pics. in the evening. Saw Deanna Durbin in *The Amazing Mrs. Holliday*. Quite good. Heard that Miriam from Cardiff was ill today – lost her baby – a boy – but says she'll try again!

Thursday 17th June

Went to Penrhiwceiber this morning. Had a *bath*. Forgot to bring soap, so Gran gave me a huge hard block of scrubbing soap. Went to see Mr. Fine about Jacky coming to Youth Meeting. He was ever so nice about it – Mr. Fine has a furniture shop in Penrhiwceiber. We all went to Cardiff in the afternoon to see Miriam. Everyone in the train looked at Sara, she's so lovely. Slept in my arms on the way home. Bernard called at 10.30 p.m. to ask if I could go to see Fines – of course told him I had. We talked in the shop doorway. Bernard suddenly leaned forward and for a moment I thought he was going to kiss me – but he didn't – he was just lighting his pipe.

Sunday 20th June

Vera, Dita, the Shane girls and most of the evacuees came to Youth Club at 5 p.m. Spoke about 'What is a Jew?' (strange to think it's taken a war to make me realise I *am* one) – also what should be the aims and ideals of the Club – both drew a blank! Had a Brains Trust, but not many questions. Most enjoyed it. Bernard asked me if I would teach one of the boys Hebrew. I'm rather looking forward to it. It will at least be something interesting to do.

Saturday 26th June

Went to Bernard's at 8 p.m. Talked about Moses. Next week we're going to do Trumpeldor. Joyce was here. She's having a lot of problems in Bristol. They may "court martial" her, or the civilian equivalent, for not working on Shabbos.

Monday 28th June

Joyce went back this morning. Had a new girl today – Betty. She's terribly rough and coarse compared to all the other girls we've had. Went for a ride on the bike with Violet and Gwyneth. Went down Cwmbach Road and wanted to return on it, but Violet and Gwyneth said we'd go the main roadway. Got as far as Aberaman Bridge O.K. Coming down the steep hill the other side, the front wheel suddenly (swerved) and in a second I was spread out on the road with one knee jammed between the lower bars of the bike, and the rest of me on top of it. The road had just been tarred! The girls and a man helped me to his house – I felt awful. Wife bathed my knees and arms with TCP and tried to get tar off my hands with butter. Covered with tar. Right leg feels awful. Sent Violet to tell Mum to go to Pen. as she was waiting for us to return before going to Gran's. Violet told her we'd be following. Couldn't bear to think of her seeing me in this state. Caught Council bus outside house. Felt sick and dizzy for a moment. Got off outside our house – job to walk. Believe I've *sprained* my right knee – swelling terribly. Sent up for doctor – *out*. Came at last at 10 p.m. – and then – Gestapo! Cleaned wounds, gashes rather, with Liquid Paraffin – then sent Violet downstairs for nailbrush to scrub them – she brought back a *scrubbing brush*! Had to laugh – although very nervously. After the first torture he decided to probe out the tar with a sort of outsize needle. Lips very sore from biting them, then Doc said if he left the tar in I'd have awful blue scars left on my legs, arms etc., but I didn't care two hoots as long as he stopped quickly, I couldn't have held out much longer. Mum and Uncle came back – very annoyed at my sending them away – but I'm very glad I did. Doc finished at last at 12. I'm nearly finished too – so after it was all over I had to break down and cry like a baby – not because of the wounds, but the cross way Mum and Uncle spoke to me. (I knew I couldn't have held out if they had been there.) Doc was furious with them! Said: "She's been so brave until you came in and upset her!" Doc admitted afterwards that he should have taken me to hospital and given me chloroform, but I'm not really sorry he didn't, I'd rather be home. Didn't sleep all night. Listened to the clock chiming out the hours. At last the sky began to go from purple to blue and it was tomorrow.

Tuesday 29th June
Feel pretty dead today, and I'm sure I look much worse. Effects of last night working out today and I feel very sensitive. Sara came in and crawled to my bed – I could hardly move, except my right arm. She reached up and stroked my cheek – and the tears nearly came. New girl very kind to Sara. Told her what to make for her lunch. Thought a lot about Alex, and missed him more than usual – which is a lot. Read a little, can't remember what. Feel dreadfully tired, but unable to go to sleep. Must have dozed for about 3 hours, till 5 a.m.

Wednesday 30th June
Very slightly better. Feel awfully sore from keeping still, and in pain from wounds. Read *Palestine Stories* today. Doctor came and – what a relief from my imaginings – put healing ointment on. Exact details are – gashes to knees and left elbow and a grazed wrist – also fluid on right knee, and of course numerous bruises all over. New girl ever so comical. Tells me all about people who have died from infections; gone mad, and ill, and also about all the boys that are mad about her – and does she look a mess! Privately she thinks she's glamorous. Read *Hitler Through the Ages*. Ever so good. Mum still cross that I fell off a *bike*! Gran and Mrs. Chinn came to visit me.

Thursday 1st July
Hurray once again! Another month gone – another month nearer to what I'm waiting for – whom rather! Finished book and read some of Barrie's plays. Cuts hurting, but not too much now. Fluid on knee hurting most. Have had so far: *peaches*, *nectarines*, *grapes* and loads of cherries! Doing quite nicely!

Saturday 3rd July
Read a little from book called *Roots*, but only my eyes read it. Weather is glorious of course. Tough luck! Feel, as our new girl would put it, very lovesick today. Thought continuously of Alex and missed him so – wish more than ever that I could see him, if only for an hour. 'I've Got You Under My Skin' – and you're making me ache there too, for you. 'The Day Is Long and You're So Far Away' – but 'Wishing Won't Make You Here!' Oh blow!

Sunday 4th July
Quite a few visitors: Mrs. Brodie and Stella; Grandma; Mrs. Chinn; Berta. Mr. and Mrs. Kahn came in to see me and brought the loveliest roses I've ever seen. Gold colour – my favourite. They brought a few books from Bernard – he's working late on the farm. How I wish Alex was one of the visitors!

Tuesday 6th July
Started reading *Ye Are My Witnesses* by students of Rabbi Daiches – but didn't get very far. Rained a bit today – secretly rather glad – feeling a bit jealous of the nice weather. Did some drawings. Doc came and said I can try to get up! Tried, but couldn't balance at all. Got as far as the tallboy and went flying back, to fall, luckily, onto the bed. Can't bend my knee at all, or my left arm. Anyway, persevered and went as far as Mum's bedroom – Uncle ill with lumbago. Miss the wireless [only wireless was downstairs in the cellar]. Newspapers write about destruction of Cologne Cathedral (Germany). Tried to go to sleep at 8.30 p.m., but didn't sleep till 1 a.m. Alex, you're ruining my beauty sleep.

Friday 9th July
Knee dreadful. The Doctor came and dressed wounds. Sat up for two hours reading. Feel miserable! Can't think what's the matter with me. How I wish it was August. It's hard having to wait so long.

Sunday 11th July
Finished reading *Roots* by Naomi Jacobs this morning. Did some drawing in the afternoon. Friend of Bernard, Miriam from London called, together with Bernard, to see me. Miriam went to the Paris Academy of Dress Design in Bond Street. It's supposed to be very expensive. Showed her my drawings – she said I had quite good "expression" – whatever that meant! Wrote letter to *Drapers' Record* requesting address of Dress Design Colleges in London. Went downstairs (one step at a time) to hear the news. Our troops (Brits, American and Canadian) have invaded Sicily! General Eisenhower is in command. If they succeed it'll be Italy next!

Monday 12th July
Read *The Jewish Problem* by Louis Golding. Quite good. Got up from 3 p.m. to 5. Doc took the bandage off my wrist and right leg. Tut-tutted when he saw deep tar scars on knees. Left leg still hurts a lot. Had *raspberries* and *cream* (off the milk) after supper. They were delicious. Oh, well – another day gone!

Wednesday 14th July
Read *Iphigenia* by Euripides. Bernard came at 8 p.m. We did an essay by Wasserman on Genesis Chaps. 32 and 35. (Jacob's fight with the man/angel – who said to him: "Thy name shall be called no more Jacob, but Israel." – "And G-d said the land which I gave Abraham and Isaac, to thee I will give it, and to thy seed after thee.") Had an argument afterwards about Joshua's conquest of Canaan. If the land of Canaan had been promised to Abraham by G-d to be an eternal homeland for his people, why then did Joshua have to fight for it? Answer – the people who lived in the land at that time were fierce, a race of giants (anakim) who lived in fortified cities. They never would have allowed the Israelites to settle peaceably amongst them. Without G-d's help, Joshua's army, very untrained, would never have succeeded in conquering the land. Deut. XI is particularly impressive, and Joshua VI (12–20) describes the destruction of the walls of Jericho. Jericho, the oldest city in the world, was the first city to suffer from *blast*! "So the people shouted when the priests blew with the trumpets: and it came to pass, when the people heard the sound of the trumpet, the people shouted with a great shout, that the wall fell down flat – and they took the city." We also talked of the one sure way to break the Jewish people's faith – as Balaam advised: "Send down the girls to the camp!" Bernard went at 10 p.m. Awfully tired. Got a nasty boil coming. Lip swollen.

Thursday 15th July
Lip like a barrage balloon today. Bathed it, but didn't do much good. Read *Eyeless in Gaza* by Aldous Huxley. Got up and washed blouses and hair. Tried to wash tar out of white shorts – impossible! I was so proud of the way they had turned out – should have known better – *pride* goes before a *fall*!!! Went to bed at 6 p.m. … Oh Alex! Wish I could write, but don't dare until his Higher is over – oh, I wish, and wish, and wish, and wish – well – what? – You know – well!

Saturday 17th July
Was up a lot, but legs aching. The doctor came. Took off all my bandages – Hurray!! Lovely day. Read *Keys of the Kingdom* by A. J. Cronin. Awfully good. Bernard came in. Talked about 17th of Tammuz and Tisha B'Av – the two fasts commemorating the destruction of the Temple in Jerusalem. He didn't notice my still swollen face – at least he seemed not to.

Monday 19th July
Betty in as usual, with her "You been in the wars, bach?" … and "Two customers downstairs *buying black*! 'Ope you don't get blood poisoning." Shortly after, "knock, knock." Wonder of wonders! Violet with a letter! *His* letter. Oh Joy! I was delighted, naturally, and replied instantly, asking Alex to come as soon as his Higher is over (Wednesday). Went to pics. with Sheila in the afternoon. Saw *Virginia* – l.o.u.s.y. Still, first time out, and glad to be, but – *must* exercise more.

Tuesday 20th July
Mum told me to get up quickly as Bernard was here. Puzzled! Got up. It was Bernard Schwartz from Cardiff. He was surprised to see me so changed. I can't see it – he only saw me about three months ago. He's 6ft 1in and very good looking – naturally – as he's *my* cousin! He's travelling with some lighter fuel and hoped to sell some in Aberdare. Talked with him for a long time – and, surprisingly, found it quite easy – no awkward pauses. Cynthia, you must be growing up! Conceited me thinks he was a tiny bit impressed – he's going to the Army next month and said if he had leave he'd most certainly call in to Aberdare – to see the baby! Anyway, I hope he doesn't come, as nothing could come of it. Went up Cwmbach Road to see the "house with a garden", as Mrs. Smith heard it was being sold. (It would be perfect for Sara.) It *wasn't* for sale. I thought it was too good to be true! It's like a real fairyland. Legs very tired on the way home – just about made it!

Wednesday 21st July
Well, by English law I'm 17 today. Seems so silly – I've been 17 for years! Had a few cards, but Alex's was the only one that made me really happy that it was my birthday, and I do hope he'll come this week. Mum gave me a blouse, but it was awful – more for her age than mine – so she had it. I'm awful for anyone to buy presents for. I don't wear much jewellery and I've the most finicky taste in clothes. No one can ever tell if I'll like a dress or not. Most of all I need a summer frock or skirt. Similar to Joyce's birthday, Uncle cross over the silliest thing. Very glad that he may go (for good?), but didn't today at any rate. Baby woke at 7.30 a.m. and it was a job to put her back to sleep. Had a headache and felt rather sick. (Doc says I'm run down – war-time rations, sleepless nights etc.) Then Mrs. Prosser came in and cheered me up – made me roar with laughter. She had met Bernard Schwartz who told her that he'd had a shock to see how much I've changed – that I was most fascinating (?!!?) and that he just couldn't leave me, and couldn't do any business after he had! Mrs. Prosser was tickled – but I didn't know whether to believe her.

Thursday 22nd July
Woke up before 7 a.m. Fed Sara, don't feel too grand, left leg still hurting – but at least the boil has disappeared! At last Higher is over! I wonder …? More X (Uncle in bad mood) all day. Went to Lily Pond in afternoon, but didn't stay. The

place looked so *dead* and deserted, a sort of eerie atmosphere hung about it in the heat. Alex didn't come. I rang up and spoke to Mrs. Winter – she said he'd gone out for the day. Didn't quite believe her. Wish I could get out of it all. I've waited so long – more delay is quite unbearable.

Friday 23rd July

Went for a walk with Sara – wished Alex would come – but was in a hopefully – disappointed mood, in case he came, or did not – and then he *did*, at 1.30 p.m. After we had had lunch we went for a walk up the park. Told me he was too tired yesterday to go anywhere (!) and we must decide how we can spend some time together. Said he'd try to come to Aberdare Sunday if he could and I will go there Monday. Got home 6.30 p.m., Uncle bathed my leg, which he thinks is going septic. Felt like crying that my leg had to be bandaged up again. Couldn't eat much supper – I don't know why. Still feel out of contact with Alex somehow. I feel so unlike me – I don't say the things I want to say and can't help feeling Alex doesn't know the real me – and yet I adore him.

Oh! D—! If only – a lot of things! Hang it all – I'm not happy! What am I doing? Just wasting my youth in Aberdare! Rotting! Getting out of contact with Youth, Modern Thoughts, and above all Alex! What can I look forward to in life? Plain *Nothing*! It's h— here with Uncle shouting and continually making rows and upsetting Mum. Joyce is d— lucky! And Alex telling me of all the fun he has with his friends. Hmm. What fun do I get? Dear, Dear – ain't life awful! And don't you sympathise with yourself! Not 'arf you don't! You little twerp! Stoppit! Oh h—!!!

Saturday 24th July

Hopeless day – seemed endless, the time just wouldn't go. Can't understand why Alex's arrival, at the first possible moment, didn't have me walking on air the rest of the day, spreading joy all around me, instead of feeling so unhappy. Went up to Bernard's at 8 p.m. Talked about Shabbos prayers in shul, about orthodoxy and my going to college etc. Can realise why I was so pessimistic about "life" yesterday. There is no sense to life without Torah, and, as I haven't got much of that, I naturally feel fed up with life. If I had none of it at all I wouldn't wonder why life is, but just take it as it comes. As it is I can neither do that, nor live my reason for being, i.e. live Torah as I would love to live it. Until I do that, I cannot live, I can only exist, and perhaps live just enough of it to long to live it entirely and feel exasperated that I can't. One thing is certain, if I sojourn here much longer, I shall go nuts, barmy, or loopy, as the above denotes! I *must* get away. I really do feel I can't stand it much longer, "it" being Uncle and my own nagging accusations against the way I'm living. Pardon – did I say living? Well then – the way I'm partly living. Why is life so hard?

Sunday 25th July

No, Alex didn't come. Tidied around in the morning – just in case. Gave up hope at 4 p.m. Limping badly; the Doctor came and said my leg has to be bathed etc. again. Dita called in. Said she was going to the Aguda Harvest Camp for a fortnight. Asked me if I would go too. Would like to go, but will see when we get particulars. Rang Alex at 8 – going there tomorrow. Will have to come home tomorrow night because of my leg. Bathed it and went to bed. A few good things have come from my accident. First, and most important, Sara has accepted that someone other than me (Betty or Violet) can be trusted to look after her (I really think she *understands*). Secondly, in spite of the pain, my body feels rested – not so totally exhausted as I was. I've had a few good nights' sleep, except for one air-raid when I felt a bit vulnerable stuck up here on the second floor listening to the sound of German planes overhead; however by 12 we heard the all-clear. Lastly, I feel *taller* (5ft 5½ ins).

Monday 26th July

Got up at 7.30 and got ready to go. Went to the square, but the bus was too full. Went home, then round to the allotments to get some vegetables from Uncle Solly. Passed station and enquired about trains to Swansea. Caught 12.15 p.m. and got in at 1.50. Went to Alex's house, met him just going to meet me. Went to Rifka's – she asked me to stay a few days. Wired Mum. Went to Winters' and had tea there, also supper. Listened to J. B. Priestley on the wireless – was very good and then!!! – *the news*! Mussolini has been *sacked* (honourably abdicated) and King Victor Emanuel and Bagdolio have taken over in Italy. By the way, Bagdolio, a member of the Axis, is supposed to be anti-fascist!!!? Talked with Rifka till 11.30 p.m. She's a wow – and what a tease! Wonder how soon it'll be until Italy surrenders?

Tuesday 27th July

Alex came at 11 a.m. and we went to town (what was left of it), then to lunch at Rifka's, then went to the farm together. Wandered over our favourite haunts – past the white heather bank – down to the stream. Had tea at farm and got back to Rifka's at 7 p.m. Had a snack and went down to the sands for a walk. Very nice too! Alex left at 10. Had my clothes from Mum this morning. Plan to go to Langland Bay tomorrow if it's fine.

Wednesday 28th July

Alex came for a little while this morning. Very dull weather. Came again at 2 p.m. Went to catch bus for Sketty, but decided to walk through Singleton Park instead. Talked till 6.30 about Religion; Palestine (I'm glad he feels the same way about it as I do) and Careers. Arrived at Winters' still talking about careers – when his mother came in, she disagreed with Alex's ideas, at which Alex got quite annoyed. Left at 9 and walked down to Swansea beach, stayed there till gone 10. The last hour I was amazingly, completely happy, for which I have to thank Alex. For over an hour I was completely unaware of all problems and people except us two – and a superb realisation that I was *with* Alex at last. He said I was drunk. No doubt I was, and he was the alcohol. Alex, thanks for that hour. It must be at least two or more years since I was so completely happy. Got in feeling tired (knee throbbing – but determined not to let it spoil anything). Wandered about the room for a bit and just thought of my recent mood. When I was small, I had these moods at very short intervals – but the older I got, the more difficult and less frequent they became. To have complete happiness one's mind must go a complete blank. It's a mood that can't be willed – it just happens. I think this time it came more or less from a feeling of relief – after having poured out most of my thoughts to Alex – a willing receiver, and I was really superbly happy. I could have walked on like that, not saying a thing for hours, but Alex just wouldn't let me – my mood just vanished when he spoke about his, not impossible, embarkation to a fighter or bomber squadron. He said I'd kill him if he came back dead, but although I laughed, it was a meaningless one. I've known so many who will never come back – and so I was my usual self again. Alex said I was very unnatural all evening, but then I've never been in that mood in his presence before, so I can understand his feeling.

Thursday 29th July

Wonderful day today. Alex had to go to school in the morning for a farewell assembly. Had tea together at 4.30, then caught train (electric) to Mumbles. Lovely! Walked from there to top of a high cliff, stayed there for an hour. Took two snaps, but don't think they'll come out. Feel lovely in the wind and sun. Walked down to Langland, passed Cyril Wyman (in Air Force uniform) on the sands. Caught 9.25 train back. Came in about 10, had supper, bathed leg and finally went to bed.

Friday 30th July

Decided to go to Pobbles Bay this afternoon. Made sandwiches, wrote to Mum, put on my shorts – Alex had his "tropical kit" on too. Caught 3.30 p.m. bus to Pobbles. Most lovely bay I've seen. Stayed on sands for about half an hour – Alex went in the sea for a bathe. Didn't join him, as I don't have a swimsuit and the last time I swam I was ten. (Told Alex about the "wonderful swimsuit of many colours" that I knitted myself. Proudly entering Mountain Ash swimming pool, the cold water caused the wool to stretch until the swimsuit reached my knees! Embarrassed, I ran out clutching the wet folds around me! Everyone there collapsed with laughter.) About 5.15 the tide was coming in, so we went up on top of the cliffs to have tea. Tea made in flask tasted awful! Went further over the cliff where we could look down on another bay. Simply lovely. Sky: blue, flecked with the most tempting clouds, the sand, beautifully warm and golden. Sunbathed till about 8.30, but didn't get at all brown. Talked most of the time about

Photo of me at the Mumbles taken by Alex

careers and a lot about our future (?) and the disadvantages of the Army … "How can one keep a wife decently on Army pay?" I assured him I shall soon get a job and will "keep" myself. Walked over to Park Hill, passed an old castle; took one snap; waited for a bus. Got one at 9 and was in Uplands by 9.15. Felt very tired. Alex took me to Rifka's and then went home. We tried to put the blackout up, but couldn't, so went to bed in the dark. Took a long time to go to sleep.

Saturday 31st July

Air-raid warning last night, but I didn't hear it – however it must have awakened me, as I was awake for hours thinking of one thing in general, and one in particular. Had a letter from Mum. Went to Winters' for lunch. They had all been to shul. Their shop is shut on Shabbos. Went out for a walk and got caught in the rain. Got in very wet. My frock dried without leaving a sign of anything. Mr. and Mrs. Winter went out about 8 p.m. We talked *etc. etc.* until 9.30. Walked to Rifka's and got in at 10. Alex put up the blackout in a second. He had a grey suit on today and it did look nice on him. Yetta slept with me, but I was still able to hold "private thoughts corner" and "unforgettable memories".

Sunday 1st August
Got up at 9 a.m. Did some washing. Alex came to say he'd take Yetta and me to the farm at 2 p.m. Had tea in Rochale's. She had a visitor, a Lt. Fink. He stayed for dinner; we all had an enjoyable time. Joyce rang up to ask if I was coming home and what to do about the Aguda Camp? Said I'd like to stay, and she should ask Mum about the Aguda Camp. Answer was "Yes" to first and "No" to second.

Monday 2nd August
Alex called early – we talked about Italy – the Fascist Party there has been abolished! After he left, Rifka told me something that Mrs. Winter had said, which quite unsettled me. It seems she will never get used to my "friendship" with HER son! Alex came, but I hardly said a word to him the whole afternoon. Went to Winters', but just couldn't have tea. Came home 7.30 feeling awful. Went up to bedroom and had an old fashioned weep. Alex came up and caught me at it. Made me say what was wrong. Now that his exams are over he'll probably leave home soon anyway. I felt much better after I had told him what the problem had been over the past year. Came down and sat in the lounge discussing it. Alex said his mother could never influence the way he felt about me and that I should stop worrying about it. Went to Alex's home. Talked about marriage etc. Went to bed rather relieved – and with a few good memories to end a troubled day.

Tuesday 3rd August
Went to town with Alex this morning to send Berta a birthday telegram. Arranged to go to Pwll Du this afternoon. Made sandwiches and waited. Mrs. Winter rang to say Alex couldn't come, as he had to take Eva somewhere. Had very little time to feel disappointed, for Alex *did* come, with a big grin, and soon we were on our way to Langland. Walked from there ever such a long way along the cliffs to Pwll Du. Alex went for a bathe. Some Polish airmen were having some fun with a couple of girls. It was quite a pantomime! Got to Brandy Cove at 8 p.m. and climbed up a really steep mountain. Amazed that I had done so when we got to the top. It felt like only the two of us, on top of the world – but – couldn't find a way back. Began to feel a little downhearted. Walked to the edge of the cliff, and there, to our surprise, saw a path (if it could be called that) going down. Relieved and a bit scared at the prospect of climbing down it, but we did so. Began to walk from Caswell to Langland, where we waited until 10.30 p.m. for a train. Got into Rochale's after 11 p.m. Said she'd just rung up Winters'. (Hope they thought we'd eloped!) Very tired. Feet *very* sore. Didn't sleep for hours.

Wednesday 4th August

Poured all day. Stayed in and read *You Never Can Tell* by G. B. Shaw. What a good title! Alex came, but left early as he had to fire-watch in town. Rifka played the piano for a long time, then we talked till 1.30 a.m.!!! About all sorts of things. Glad too, as it stopped me thinking painfully of Alex. Rather tired, but as usual found tiredness no barrier to my thoughts.

Friday 6th August

Got up at 9.30 a.m., had breakfast and then a bath. Alex came at 12, and again at 2 and then at 3. Stayed in the lounge talking until it was time for me to leave. Went at 5. I caught bus; Alex took my parcel down on his bike. Met at the station. Felt peculiarly "unfeeling". Train went out at 5.45 p.m. Had to stand. Spent first part of the journey already composing a letter to Alex in my mind and the rest of the time read *Too Much Money* by Israel Zangwill. Got to Aberdare at 7.50 feeling awful, not wanting to go home. Tired from standing all the way, I arrived at Jane Cooper's. Felt very surprised at being a lot happier at being home than I had imagined. Sara grown tremendously. For tonight I have only pleasant memories of Alex. I hope he's feeling the same about me. Very pleased to greet my old room again. Amazed still at my happiness at being home. Oozing with affection for everyone. I'm sure it's because of Alex that I'm in my "happy mood" – still feel the effect of being with him.

Saturday 7th August

Stayed in today. Nasty weather. Thought of Swansea, Mumbles, etc. Happy mood vanished to a more morose one. Shabbos! Home! How much those words mean, how much they should mean, and how much *do* they mean – here? It makes me feel like crying to see the Shabbos candles lit in front of the day's takings, to hear the wireless pealing forth "swing" on the Shabbos before Tisha B'Av. And Uncle! How much he helps to make this house "home"! Went to bed early.

Sunday 8th August

Made a cake this morning. Was really delicious. Went up to Youth Club at 5 p.m. Raining. Very few came. Bernard said he wanted to speak to me after 9. Meanwhile I'm in an awful mood. No, Alex, not even the thought of you helps me to be happy. Bernard said he doesn't think Mum will let me go to London, but she *must*. Why should I *have* to live with the man she married? She had a choice, but I seem to have none! And I doubt if I could spend many more Shabboses here. My whole being revolts against the things that are done and the things that I do myself. Mum I love, with all the love a daughter can give – but I just cannot stay here. I'm quite ruining myself – if I don't go I shall end up hating myself and very soon that leads to hating everyone else. Mum – "Let your daughter go!" I cannot, must not, dare not, stay here much longer.

Bernard called at 9 and we talked for about an hour. I wish Bernard would meet Alex. He could explain to him much better than I can the need to keep the laws of the Torah.

Monday 9th August

Mum came in with Joyce's letter saying she'd given up her job because they would not allow her to have Shabbos free. Good for her! Factories are working a seven-day week – Joyce offered to work every Sunday – but her offer was refused. She's going to try and get transferred to a Hachsharah. Mum was very upset. She resented Bernard's interference more than Joyce's actions. ("He's made the two of you into fanatics!" etc. etc.) When she simmered down we took Sara with us and went to Bridgend where I bought a pair of navy shoes. One can't realise how mountainous Wales is until one has travelled from Aberdare to Bridgend. Sara was wonderful all day. Came home, Joyce came at 7 p.m. Found Alex's letter waiting for me. Mum and Joyce had a good laugh over my face after I had read it – I know it was glowing. Went to shul 9.30 to 11. Read Lamentations in Hebrew/English. Very moving. Written by Jeremiah. Also very apt description of the suffering of Jews in our own times – from news coming from the occupied countries. Chapter 5 verse 7: "Our fathers have sinned, and are not; and we have borne their iniquities." Definitely!

Tuesday 10th August

Tisha B'Av. Went to shul in the morning. Uncle in London – so no problem with fasting. Broke fast at 10 p.m. and started to write to Alex before I went to bed. Re-read Alex's letter written from Harvest Camp. He's feeling very lonely and wrote:

> "Let's hope things become a little better, because otherwise I shall be leaving this camp in order to come to Aberdare to elope with you on my ten shillings per week – and we could live happily on that, and love. Perhaps … So, thanks for being in Swansea those two weeks. I shall be able to talk about, and remember them, for longer than I will any other event in my youth. May we live those days again soon. P.S. For my views on *vous*, see Shakespeare's Sonnets No. CIV beginning "To me, fair friend, you never can be old," and read it *carefully* …

Apt Quotation by Drayton:

> Dear, why should you command me to my rest
> When now the night doth summon all to sleep?
> Methinks this time becometh lovers best,
> Night was ordained together friends to keep.

Wednesday 11th August

Entered in two months' accumulation of papers this morning. Went with Joyce to see *Random Harvest* with Ronald Colman and Greer Garson. Excellent. Came home and finished letter to Alex. Felt in a real "A1" mood; really, wonderfully, gloriously, happy. Beautiful moon out tonight. Gazed at it for about half an hour humming a couple of our tunes. Baby went to clinic today – weighs 24lb. She's one today! Yes, and I'm seventeen (Jewish date) today too. Sara had 15 birthday cards, 5 telegrams and one registered letter! We stuck them on the mantelpiece and Sara kept pointing to them all day. She splashed all the water out of her bath this evening and roared with delight. She walked right across the shop on her own! She's lovely, but I'm afraid she'll be spoilt when I leave.

Friday 13th August

This morning Dita brought a small parcel for me from Bernard for my birthday (Wednesday). Inside was a Singer's Prayer Book in Hebrew with English translation. I was thrilled, especially as his grandfather had written the following in Hebrew in the flyleaf: "Present to my friend Sheina Breiyna Cohen on her 17th birthday, 10th Av in the year 5703."

> The L--d is nigh unto all them that call upon Him,
> to all that call upon Him in truth.
>
> Psalm 145
> Dov Kahn

Hope I shall keep it *always*! [I have – as you can see from the copy below!]

THE AUTHORISED

DAILY PRAYER BOOK

OF THE

UNITED HEBREW CONGREGATIONS

OF THE BRITISH EMPIRE.

PRINTED IN ENGLAND BY
EYRE AND SPOTTISWOODE LIMITED, HIS MAJESTY'S PRINTERS, LONDON

מתנה לחברתי שיינא ברײנא
קאהען
ביום מלאתה שבע עשרה שנה
י' מנחם אב תש"ג לפ"ק
קרוב ה' לכל קראיו
לכל אשר יקראהו באמת

The Lord is nigh unto all them
that call upon him,
to all that call upon him
in truth. Psalm 145

דב בן שמואל הכהן

Brought coupon book up to date. Read *School for Scandal*. Listened to play on wireless; *1066 and All That!* Very good. Today I ate the sweetest plums I have ever tasted. I must have eaten *pounds* of them – and I don't feel full!

Monday 16th August

Went to office for ration book. Sara almost walking on her own now. Bernard called in to say I shall have to take over the meeting on Sunday, as he'll be working all day. Talked a lot about what I'm going to do. (Mum and Uncle went to pics.) He left at 9 p.m. Felt dreadfully unhappy. After struggling with myself for half an hour not to give in to tears, as Alex asked me not to, I just couldn't help it. He's never experienced anything like the state I'm in now, so he didn't know he was really asking too much. Although it wasn't over *him* that I cried – I thought of him, but the three reasons that caused it were:

(1) How am I going to go away and keep the Torah, as my whole being yearns to?
(2) How can I keep still my hands that long to do dress-designing, especially on Shabbos – when one isn't allowed to draw or write?
(3) How can I marry the one – who is my all – who does not at the moment correspond with the way I want to live – can I be sure that one day, P.G. he might?

Re (1) I could go without Mum's permission – but that I wouldn't do. Not because I wouldn't like to, although it would be unpleasant enough, but because Mum has suffered so many losses (her father, who died when she was three-and-a-half, her favourite brother when he was 23, and, when I was two – my father. How strange it is to write that word! I know that in some ways I am like him – although I've no recollection of what he was like). What would Alex think of me if I did? What would his mother think? I know only too well! Again, if I don't, how can I get Mum to allow me to go? It seems well nigh impossible – but for how long can I stand it here, breaking Shabbos and having to bear Uncle, both of which I loathe doing. And then: this house. It's not a home – I am in truth a typical, wandering, homeless Jew. Mum will always retain my love, whatever happens – but these rooms – I know them – but they are strange and unwelcoming, and Mum's love doesn't alleviate the sadness I feel. Once I did know and love a house – I did feel at home in my home – but that was so very long ago – if only I could recapture "that first, fine, careless rapture". Will I ever? Or will I never feel settled? Will life continue to be a depressing puzzle for me, with just a glimpse of sunlight, that, while I'm with Alex, dances through me – or will I soon be denied that too? How dreadful it is to be a prisoner to one's own thoughts. How fervently I hope that one day I'll read this again and be unable to understand my feelings – only wondering how I was unable to see how simply I could (and did) make everything come out right and with the glad thought that my happiness is as complete as it can be and will continue to be. How I long for that day! And Alex how I need you!

Tuesday 17th August
Uncle went to London this morning. Mum, Sara and I went to Cardiff. Managed to buy a pair of shoes. Delighted, as there are none to be bought in Aberdare. Put Sara to bed, and then went to pics. to see Leslie Howard (who was killed recently in a plane coming back from Spain) in *The First of the Few*. Was I thrilled with it! Only now can I understand Alex's enthusiasm on seeing aeroplanes – and feel it myself. Am in a different frame of mind tonight. Would rather be young with an uncertain future ahead of me, than very old, with hardly any future to be uncertain about!

Friday 20th August
Sweep came this morning and sooted us out. Spent most of the day cleaning and washing woodwork. Looks nice now – till tomorrow! Spent about an hour toying with a piece of wonderful silk I found in the sewing room. Plan to make a skirt out of it. Joyce came home. She has had a temporary release and acceptance at a Hachsharah. Bernard went to Oxford.

Monday 23rd August
Felt awfully sick and head-achy lunch-time. Didn't eat much. Went upstairs and actually fell asleep for an hour in a chair. Felt like a horse afterwards. Had a letter from Alex! High Spirits, Glowing Cheeks, Shining Eyes and an abundance of energy followed as a result. Thoroughly cleaned scullery out. Coal delivery came this morning. First the grating in the pavement was removed and bags of coal were opened and poured down the chute into the back cellar causing clouds of coal dust to settle everywhere. This cellar is our scullery where the cooker, dresser and fridge stand – it's also our "bathroom" where we have a "bath" in a basin of water à la Degas (we have a "Keep Out" notice handy to put on the kitchen door). Wrote reply to Alex in the evening. Also wrote to Slade School of Art for Admission Form.

Tuesday 24th August
Joyce and I went to Cardiff to see Anglo-Polish Ballet. Terrific!! I especially liked the Polish *Faust*, which was breathtaking. Also *The Cow that Spoke*. Came home 10.30 p.m.

Wednesday 25th August
Decided at 11 a.m. to go to Tredegar to Sylvia's wedding. Joyce and I caught the 1.30 p.m. bus and got to the house just in time. Sylvia looked lovely. All her family were there and a few more of Joyce's friends. At dinner I sat next to Marcus who is *not* a good conversationalist. After the speeches the rooms were cleared and records put on for dancing. Everyone danced, except for myself and one Czech boy eighteen-and-a-half years old called Harry – so of course we were introduced and spent the rest of the evening talking together. We had a very

interesting conversation, which, I think, we both enjoyed. Sylvia danced every dance, bouncing around the floor; no one seemed to mind that she was at least 5 or 6 months pregnant. She and her handsome husband are so obviously deeply in love. Later on I talked to a girl about my age who also keeps Shabbos – she was surprised to meet someone else who did. I don't wonder!

Thursday 26th August

Went, at 5 p.m., to see *Journey for Margaret* with Robert Young, Laraine Day and Margaret O'Brien. It was excellent! I then wrote to Alex to confirm Sunday's arrangements. Re-read parts of his letter:

> "You talk about the loveliness of the moon. Well, sleeping outdoors as I do, it can hardly be missed. And, last Sunday night there was an eclipse, which kept me occupied for quite a while – especially as I know what Cynthia (lovely name!) means – Goddess of the Moon! I too keep thinking it's about time we viewed it together, and I *would* like to sing 'Moonlight Becomes You' (as I've no doubt it does) to you. *Please* meet the Chepstow bus. Let's hope we can find a café open in Cardiff on Sunday, by which time the fateful results will have been published."

Sunday 29th August

Got ready to catch 11.20 a.m. train to Cardiff. Got into Cardiff 12.30. Raining!!! Went as far as the Club. Saw Aunty Millie, then went to meet Chepstow bus at the beginning of Newport Road. Came in at 1.15 and Alex was there!! Hurried to the Club and had quite a nice lunch. Alex showed me a newspaper. I didn't want to look at it, but did so – to find in the Higher Results: Alexander Winter: English; Physics and Mathematics. Felt inexpressibly happy, relieved and proud. Alex's moustache looks really grand and suits him wonderfully well. His new glasses are nice too. He's been promoted to Corporal in the A.T.C.. Talked about what he'll do for the few months before H.M. the King needs him at the beginning of January 1944. Went to Park Hall and heard Liverpool Philharmonic Orchestra conducted by Malcolm Sargent. Solo pianist: Noël Newton-Wood. They played the *Overture* and *Venusberg Music* by Wagner; *Shepherd Fennel's Dance*; Tchaikovsky's *Concerto No I* in B Flat Minor – was terrific, and Rimsky Korsakov's *Scheherazade*, which, I think, I liked best of all. Stupendous two hours! Went for a walk – still raining. Went back to Club, had supper, then hurried for Alex's bus which went out 7.35 p.m. Dashed back to Queen Street. Stopped by Harold Shipman and two other chaps. Finally got away, hurried to bus stop. Bus had gone – waited half-an-hour for the next one – wrote to Alex during the time. Got home 9.15 and finished letter.

Tuesday 31st August

Went with Mum to Bridgend (bus to Cardiff, then train from General Station). Train packed, so we went into dining car and had very comfortable seats. Ordered tea. Waiter came along and put on our plates ½ inch × ½ inch square of butter; another came with a teaspoonful of jam. After a few minutes the first waiter brought a jug of milk. This continued with tea, water, toast and cake. Ever so amused – most comical tea I've ever had. Met Aunty Annie with Shirley. Noticed that Shirley had a small forehead like me – feel more reconciled to it. Got a nice pair of brown shoes – really grown up pair, do hope my feet have finally stopped growing. Got a train, which went straight to Ponty. Changed trains, talked with a chap until we got to Aberdare. Joyce and I went to see *White Cargo* with Clark Gable and Hedy Lamarr. Quite enjoyable. Heard Churchill's speech, nothing new – Russians are in Kharkov; American and British forces have taken Sicily. Talked continually to Mum about London. Finally said I shall go after the winter. Think I'll be satisfied, if everything is arranged *now*, to wait till then. Joyce and I, like fools, stayed up till 12.30 a.m., reading alternately our respective diaries. Very amusing, but still, I'm hellish tired.

Wednesday 1st September

New clothing coupons out today. Sorted papers and did books solidly all afternoon until 7 p.m. Finished them. Went up to Bernard's with Joyce. We did some Bible reading and Hebrew. Talked about the meaning of a blessing. A blessing is like saying to someone: "May your wishes and aims come true." It is said in gratitude for receipt of food, or other good occurrences, e.g. on seeing a rainbow; eating a fruit for the first time (in a year); smelling something wonderful; seeing a fruit tree in blossom; escape from a dangerous accident or illness etc. Also talked a lot, of course. Came home at 10, wrote to Alex. Went to bed at 12.

Thursday 2nd September

Got up at 6.30 and gave Sara her orange juice. Mum went to London. Went to the chemist's and the snaps had come. One of Alex and one of me came out and they're both really good. Spent a long time looking at them. Alex looks so great on his – it's the best one of him I've ever seen. Mine is the best snap I've had taken too. I think the secret was pure happiness – and don't we look it. Finished sorting papers, then went with Joyce and Sara up to Frank Vining's den to see his paintings. Were awfully good. He's very surrealist minded. One abstract he did was really good – he'll go very far before he's finished. Gwyneth called in for tea; Grandma, Berta and Aunty Gwen also here. Taught Berta from 6 to 8, did quite a lot too. This week seems to be an extremely lucky week for me. First, I saw Alex, then heard he'd passed Higher; went to see the Philharmonic Orchestra; met quite a few of my cousins during the week; Mum agreed to me going to London – and the snaps were good! I hope the luck holds out and I see Alex again. Our Allied forces have done well in Sicily and the Pacific Islands – though not without cost. Waited up until Mum and Uncle returned from London.

Friday 3rd September
Four years of war today! 8th Army has invaded Italy! Russians are doing well too. Four long years ago – what a *child* I was, just thirteen, and shocked because we were actually at war – and almost as much because Olive and Megan had told me how babies were made – and even more incredible, where they grew before they were born! All that week every woman I saw seemed to be having a baby! Three days before the war started twelve-year-old Berta came to us from Germany looking so lost and fragile – I was glad then that I had taken German instead of Art, as I was the only one able to speak to her. Berta's arrival made the war, and the German's insane anti-Semitism – even against children, seem real to me! No one thought then that it would last so long or engulf so many countries – or bring bombs to our quiet valley … Had a letter from Alex today! Gosh, he does put me into happy moods. Met Dita – very brown – back from Harvest Camp. Finished Zangwill's book.

Monday 6th September
Letter from Alex this morning (second this week, and the last from Harvest Camp). Had to laugh at his feelings towards my cousins, Bernard Schwartz, Harold Cohen and Harold Shipman. He wrote:

> "Got into a frightful sweat because of your cousins. Hell! Was I jealous! How dare anyone say 'Hello *Cynth*' to you! What impudence! My gosh, was I jealous of those three dashing cavaliers – all of whom I imagined to be tall, dark, handsome young stalwarts, impeccably dressed and with their eyes and tongues hanging out at the sight of such a fine young lady. I bet their scheming minds were busy. Anyway, I was so jealous that I gnashed my teeth, and pitched up sheaves all in the wrong place, much too fast. So you see, I knew for certain then, just what my real feelings were, and are …"

Alex is right about Bernard, Harold C. and Harold S. They *are* handsome, but only Bernard S. has taken any interest in me – delighted that anyone could feel jealous over me. Danced around doing my favourite tango, 'Jealousy'. Saw *Star Spangled Rhythm* – film made for the Navy – huge cast of stars – Dick Powell, Franchot Tone, Alan Ladd, Dorothy Lamour, Bob Hope, Bing Crosby etc. Liked the song 'That Old Black Magic' the best. Very good, but expected much more.

Wednesday 8th September
Almost finished sewing dress I cut out on Sunday. Letter from Alex, and, of course, I replied. Did papers for most of the day. Mum is going to pay me £4 a week for doing (more than) a full time job, probably as an incentive for me to stay in Aberdare. She's pleased the books are all up to date. I intend to save most of what I get to pay for food and rent when I go to London. Forces' wives get only 25/- [25 shillings –£1.25] a week to live on! Mum pays most of the girls £2.

On 6 o'clock news heard – ITALY HAS GIVEN IN!!! Wonderful news! I do hope the war will be over soon so that both Alex and I may carry on with our plans uninterruptedly. Heard Laurence Rosenbaum won a State Scholarship! Listened to news again at 9. Unknown to us, General Eisenhower had already signed an Armistice treaty 3rd September with Italy.

Thursday 9th September

Gave Sara lunch – then, at 12.30, Alex came in! Very surprised – thought he was coming tomorrow. After lunch we talked upstairs until teatime. Went to catch bus at 6.25. Too full – wouldn't pick up anyone. Went to phone box; Alex phoned his parents. After supper took Alex to meet Bernard. Dita was there; we talked about Youth Group till 10.30. Talked on the way home about religion. Alex interested in, and surprised at, Aberdare community. He said there's more going on here for the youth than there is in Swansea, which has a much larger community. Told him it was entirely due to Bernard's enthusiasm and work. Alex was also pleased with my religious efforts – as long as I didn't become a fanatic and start to look down on those who kept little, but were kind, generous and community spirited. Promised I'd try not to – although I must admit I *have* been patronising! We talked while Alex had a fume (on his new pipe). He slept (!) on camp bed. Don't think I slept all night. Dozed from about 4 to 6.

Friday 10th September

Called Alex at 7 a.m. He was reading from the Talmud. Had breakfast and went to Fire Station bus stop at 8.10. Bus came at 8.25 and off Alex went. Feel awfully tired in a heavy–hot sort of way. Saw to usual things. Joyce went to Bristol at 2. Listened to *The Bartered Bride* on wireless. Can *not* realise that I saw Alex this morning – that he stayed the night. News from Italy! The Germans are now fighting the ITALIANS! More of our troops are landing in Italy, but the situation is very odd.

Saturday 11th September

Went to Kahns' at 5 p.m., home at 8. Finished sewing my dress, then phoned Alex in Whitchurch at 10. Three minutes of heaven – but, oh, so short they were! Told him I would see him in Cardiff at 11 a.m., Monday. Can still hear his voice! Three minutes is just *too* little. Never mind! Sunday will go – and worse luck, so will Monday! On the whole was quite a nice weekend except for one row with Mum over my thoughtlessness for not helping her this evening – I'm so preoccupied with other thoughts – still, I'm sorry it happened.

Sunday 12th September

Helped Mum this morning bottling fruit. Went to Youth Club at 5 p.m. Dita and I gave a talk on King David – worse than even *I* thought it would be! Sang and played games with the children. A storm started at 5.30. Terrific lightning and thunder. As always, I loved it, but some of the children were very scared and I didn't go home until 8. Bernard called in at 9 and we talked till 11. I suggested asking the two Friedman boys to come to the Youth Club. To my surprise, he said: "No! Definitely not! There's a problem –" I said they were very nice boys aged 12½ and 10. Mr. and Mrs. Friedman are Mum's friends; they had all been born in Penrhiwceiber and grown up together. I didn't continue the subject as it was so late. Bernard is going to Bangor this week to represent the Farmers' Union at their conference.

Monday 13th September

Got up at 7 a.m. Uncle went to London. I went to catch 10 a.m. bus. Full up. Rang Alex to tell him to meet the 10.25 train arriving in Cardiff at 11.40. Waited outside Cardiff station till 12.10. No sign of Alex. Rushed to Kingsway, met Whitchurch bus – empty! Went back to station – still no Alex. Caught tram to the Club. Alex was outside. Said he'd waited at the station for over half an hour. Then he went to the Club – then Kingsway – then back to the Club again. He was just about to go back home. We had lunch and then went to Roath Park. Sun came out! Went rowing on the lake; had tea in Kardomah, then went to see *Forever and a Day*. Wasn't very good! Much too Americanised Englishisms. Went for a stroll for half an hour. On the way to the station Alex turned down towards the General Station instead of the G.W.R. [Great Western Railway] Valley Branch off Queens Street. Both understood this morning's mistake, and both feel equally mad about it! My train was in and went out at 9 p.m. Got home 10.30. Joyce back from Bristol.

Wednesday 15th September

Did papers today. Board of Trade man here asking for invoices for cosmetics. In a stew, as we cannot find any for the exact date required. Drew in the evening till 11.30 and did two really fine drawings. The best I've done so far. Got typewriter out again today. Not too bad either, considering. (Left elbow almost better, except for a bump and some tar scars.)

Friday 17th September

Letter this morning! Pure happiness!! Carried me through the day. Really nice letter replying to all my concerns:

> "You say that since our meeting in April 1941, we have been pleased to find ourselves thinking and reasoning in the same way. But now, you suggest, we are beginning to diverge philosophically. Are our ideas and ideals still alike? My answer is, that if we really were alike in April 1941, and were the same until recently, then our changes are not important. You see, if we are alike in temperament and character, then these changes (hereinafter called developments) will cause no trouble. We two are developing along converging lines. We *have* formed new ideas, values, views; but

we don't change – we *do* develop. The 'basic elements' are still there, and it is these, you will agree, that really matter. You have said much of importance, but I'd like to modify your statements. *I* think it would be better to say that we are bound together by *corresponding* ideas rather than the *same* ideas. There'd be no fun in sharing one's life with a person having the *same* ideas as oneself – it would be the same as living on one's own …"

Wednesday 22nd September
Worked hard this morning. I had a bust-up with Mum this afternoon, as a culmination of all the previous small ones. Went to Kahns' at 8. Talked about the Yomim Noraim [10 Days of Awe from New Year to Fast of Yom Kippur] and finished Chapter 22 of the Bible. On the way home I was struck by the ironic beauty of six or more searchlights lighting up an enemy aeroplane. Looked like a silver moth caught in a shining web. Really remarkable. No siren. Heard the ack-ack – so hurried home. Wrote to Alex.

Thursday 23rd September
Mussolini has been rescued from prison by the Germans. Well! They're welcome to him. Joyce said: "One look at him, and you can believe in Darwin's Theory!" Joyce is going to spend the weekend at Kinnersley Hachsharah. Alex phoned to say he would come tomorrow. Spoke to Bernard at 9 p.m. and told him so.

Friday 24th September
Tidied around this morning. Alex did not come! Saw Bernard at 6 p.m. – as surprised as I was – although hardly as disappointed. He couldn't understand how Alex could change his mind at the last moment – didn't make me feel too good. Bernard said if *he'd* promised to meet someone he was fond of, *nothing* would get in his way – but then he doesn't have Mrs. Winter for a mother – and he's financially independent and always does exactly what he wants. Started reading *The Master* by Zangwill.

Monday 27th September
Letter this morning explaining why Alex had not come on Friday. Really feel quite different after reading it. Went to see *Casablanca* with Humphrey Bogart, Ingrid Bergman and Paul Heinreid. Liked it very, very much. Felt in a very sentimental mood afterwards – especially hearing Alex's "What watch? Ten watch. Such Much!" – didn't laugh at it, just felt funny. [In the film an elderly German Jewish couple are sitting in Rick Blaine's gin joint celebrating obtaining their visas for America. Determined to speak to each other in English in preparation for life in the U.S.A., the man turns to his wife and asks: "Vot Votch?" (Wie viel Uhr – What's the time?) She replies, "Ten Votch," (Zehn Uhr – 10 o'clock) to which he

exclaims: "*Such* much!" (So viel – *so* late!)] Alex does a hilarious impersonation of this "Vot Votch?" whenever he asks me the time.

Thursday 30th September – Jewish New Year
Went to shul at 9.30 a.m. and stayed till 1.30 p.m. Uncle Solly in charge of the service together with Mr. Bodenheimer. Had lunch – very nice too. Went up to Youth Meeting at 4.30. We talked about Rosh Hashanah and about the play. I am to be the father! Dita – the mother, Freda – Rachel, and Bernard will be David. Went for a ramble up the Craig. Quite nice time. Spoke to Bernard again about the Friedman boys, Steven and Keith. Bernard explained that, in Jewish law, a child is Jewish if he has a Jewish mother. One can't be half this or half that. If the child has a non-Jewish mother, as in this case, the child isn't Jewish and therefore is not obliged to keep the laws of the Torah. To make him do so puts unnecessary demands on him and takes away his free will at a young age. When he grows up, he can decide for himself to become Jewish or not. To be Jewish (particularly in our time) is hard enough without imposing the distinction on those who are not. Bernard said I should read the Book of Ruth.

Friday 1st October – second day of Jewish New Year
Shul this morning – Mr. Ginsberger taken ill during the service. Finished reading *The Master* and the Book of Ruth. Very moving story, especially where Ruth tells her mother-in-law, Naomi, "Entreat me not to leave thee, for whither thou goest, I will go; and whither thou lodgest, I will lodge; thy people shall be my people, and thy G-d my G-d …" Ruth, a Moabite woman became the great-grandmother of King David! So it's possible for anyone to convert, if they really want to. (The Vogel family have converted to Christianity and take their two boys to Church!) Went to Bernard's at 4 p.m. His grandfather is a little better, he has a heart problem. Dr. Jacobs from Merthyr there to see him. I left quite soon. Sky beautiful. No painter could possibly have done it justice.

Friday 8th – Saturday 9th October
Had delicious supper Friday, felt very festive. Fasted on Yom Kippur. Didn't feel a bit hungry the whole day. Had a headache though, from continuous reading. Followed the service well. Home at 7.30 p.m. Read Alex's letter – wrote reply till 2 a.m.!

Wednesday 13th October
Mum went to London. Uncle also there. Read *Ur of the Chaldees*. Succot [Festival of Tabernacles] tomorrow. Took Sara to Kahns' to see their Succah. First time for both of us! We had tea there. Told Bernard there's going to be trouble – the Coren family are determined to bring the Friedman boys to shul on Simchat Torah. They are going to insist on the boys taking part in the service.

Friday 15th October
Mrs. Friedman was here and told Mum about the fuss over Steven and Keith. Mum terribly angry with the Kahns. Just couldn't say anything to her, the mood she's in. Didn't go to Bernard's as arranged. Went to bed early to avoid the arguments.

Saturday 16th October
Italy has now officially declared war on Germany! The Germans are fighting for every town – it's no walkover. Mum still awfully cross. Went to Bernard's at 4 p.m. and talked about the whole affair, also the group and Succot. Mum told Uncle about the matter. Not as mad as expected. Being an atheist I suppose it's hard for him to say much!

Sunday 17th October
Went to Youth Club at 5 p.m. Two visitors there, a girl from Merthyr – Hilda (a refugee girl from Germany who lives with the Sherman family – Bernard has been teaching her Jewish studies), and a boy from Gateshead Yeshiva, Herman Stern. Practised play – everyone did quite well. The play is about a young man who wants to go to Palestine to be a chalutz [pioneer] and help re-build the land as a homeland for the Jewish people. His family object and friends try to argue against his idea. At the end Bernard sings:

> Hoi Ad Matai, Hoi Ad Matai? [(Trans.) Oh, how long (shall it be?)]
> Oh, how long (must we wait?)
> Until our people join together to become one nation.
> Until they all keep their Law (the Torah).
> Then will they return to their land.

Bernard in best mood. Realised, although I did not speak to Herman, how very similarly we must think about Judaism etc. Also realised that Alex has never really had any opposition as far as I'm concerned. He's the only "sensible" Jewish boy I've known. Are our ties too strong to weaken when I get acquainted with other youth who have the same love of Torah as I have, which Alex hasn't got yet? I also realised how very much Judaism means to me – it isn't the unimportant sideline I've tried to kid myself it is, and that I've told Alex it is. It is an all-important deciding factor, and it is going to be the thing that will decide whether Alex and I are to remain as we are now. Would he stand the test amongst other more committed orthodox young men? I must find out. Alternatively, the other way around. But at the moment, I can't see how this can be managed. When I go to London I shall meet plenty of people, but that won't be a fair test, as Alex will not be there to stick up for himself. So what's to be done? I'm in an awfully doubting mood tonight. If only I could see Alex, I would be clear about it.

Monday 18th October
Had a letter this morning, but I'm afraid it did not help to clear up my doubts. Wrote him a short note to say I couldn't possibly go to Swansea tomorrow. Busy

day – books – shop – Sara. Went to meet Dita and Bernard to discuss "dress" of characters in the play. Joyce came – filled her in on all the news till gone 1 a.m.

Tuesday 19th October

Wrote to Alex today. Worked in Barbara Gold's. Gwyneth there – not too happy. She has to start work in a factory in Treforest in a fortnight. Uncle in London. To my surprise, when I got home, Mum had lit Yom Tov candles for Succot.

Wednesday 20th October

Went to shul in the morning with Joyce – but too late – the doors were closed. Had lovely row from Mum for keeping various Yom Tov observances, and was disgusted when returning to shul this evening that it wasn't Yom Tov until tonight! We'd kept the wrong day! Still, Joyce and I had a good laugh over the whole affair – although we were a bit mad that we had had so much trouble for nothing. Didn't tell Mum that she'd lit candles a day early.

Thursday 21st October

Shul this morning. Mum very cross about "Friedman" affair. I feel very mixed about it. My reason says Kahns are right – it's a matter of principle – however I *like* the Friedman family and don't wish them any harm. It's odd that I am Jewish because I have a Jewish mother who keeps almost no Judaism and has taught me very little – and Keith and Steven are not, although their mother buys Kosher meat and always lights candles Friday night. (She also keeps Xmas!) The Corens are stirring up a real hornet's nest! Went to shul. Keith and Steven there. Kahns all went home! The first thing that met our eyes was the curtain between the men's and women's department had been thrown over the rail – everyone talking Loshen-Hora [evil gossip]. It seemed as if the whole spirit of holiness and sincerity had departed from the shul. On this night, "The Rejoicing of the Law" – Simchat Torah night – people who openly despise the laws of Judaism and the Torah – carried round the Sefarim [Scrolls]. Freda Rish was disgusted, and asked me what I thought about it. I agreed. Mrs. Coren heard, and jumped up from her seat and screamed at me, "Who do you think you are?" After calling me this and that, and saying that as a Non-Member (I am only a member's "child" remember!) I should keep my mouth shut, etc. etc. I did! Joyce, Dita and I left before the end, so disgusted were we, the way the women gossiped all through the service and not one of them with a prayer book in their hands. Outside the synagogue (how fresh, and cool, and clean the air was), Mrs. Coren carried on, arm in arm with Mrs. Friedman. They all came to our house. Mr. Coren made Kiddush [prayer said over wine on holy days]. Mrs. Coren spoke about the interference of the Kahns – and said they had no right to "persecute" innocent children (as if to keep children *from* Judaism was persecuting them). Mr. Coren said he was disgusted that we continued to go up to the Kahns and said that if we had any respect or duty to our family and friends, we wouldn't.

It was useless to mention that *they* had started the whole "affair". When they went, Joyce and I went to bed absolutely in hatred of this small clique – their low ideals – crazed minds – gossipy tongues, and pleasure in besmirching things that are clean, pure and divine. These people are supposed to show an example to the world of G-d's way of life! Then let us open the gaols and asylums and rather take an example from them! Thank G-d there are some people in the world who *do* show that G-d's law is worth following – who don't rush from shul on Shabbos to catch the bus home to their businesses, and who don't talk about one another whenever the opportunity arises. I am *sick of Aberdare*! SICK OF IT!

Friday 22nd October

Shul in the morning. Dita didn't come. Bernard and Adolf Bodenheimer there. All the children. Some fuss about calling them up for the blessing over the Sefer Torah [Scroll of the Law]. Uncle Solly in a predicament (as Minister). In the end, no child was. Mr. Goldsmith started shouting, but was shouted down. Mr. Coren gave out sweets to the kids – asked me to take a bag – I told him to give mine to the children. He threw them at me! They scattered on the floor – where they remained. After the service (!) Bernard and Adolf started to go out, to avoid rows in shul. Mr. Stein barred the way, and went to strike Adolf – Bernard just picked up Mr. Stein and put him aside – on the floor – and walked out! Mr. Stein grabbed the partition wall of the Ladies' shul to pull himself up – the whole partition fell down on him! I thought, what a lovely impression the children will have of Judaism this morning?! But they were delighted with the "action" – instead of being bored – and happy with the sweets and threepence they were given. Dorothy (Mrs. Friedman) came to us in the afternoon, very hot and bothered – told Mum she was going to make a case against Mr. Kahn. I asked her to come with me to Kahns' to sort it all out, but she wouldn't. Went up ourselves at 4.30, Mr. Kahn said not to worry – the congregation are just making up the whole affair to ease their animosity. Before Kahns came the shul was only open for three days a year and now there are services every week, so there's a feeling of guilt and resentment towards a "modern orthodox" family, in a valley community who thought religion "old-fashioned" and not relevant to the 20th century. Went home to find Uncle back from London. Doesn't say a lot, but is sufficiently annoyed about the whole affair.

Saturday 23rd October

Shul this morning. Mum just glared at me as I went through the shop. Came home to find Dorothy Friedman there. Spoke with her until lunch. Tried to appease her – told her she could go to the Rabbi in Cardiff and straighten out the whole matter if she really wanted to. She said she didn't have the time, as she had to return to her business in Wolverhampton. She won't be back till Xmas. She usually spends ten months of the year there. Then Mrs. Schwartz called in with Saul just as we were leaving to go to Kahns'. She said she was surprised, as she didn't think we'd bother with them again. Mum and Uncle went to pics. Bernard called in to talk about the Youth Meeting tomorrow. When Mum and Uncle came in, they started! Why did he come? Why must we go there? We're disgusting because we shun the shop on Shabbos. We've no right to. Bernard is *not* to come here, and we're not to go there. We are *not* allowed to keep Shabbos as we want to here, because it's not fair to show up those who don't believe in keeping Shabbos! Why should we be able to keep Shabbos when others couldn't? If the shop is good enough for a living on other days, why don't we work there on Saturday? etc. etc. I told Mum, if she thought I didn't deserve her keeping me because I didn't work one day, then I'd better get off her hands as soon as possible and keep myself. And I could too. Went to bed at 1 a.m. Felt determined to leave as soon as possible, but after some thought I decided that perhaps it's better to wait for a few weeks until Mum agrees to send me to London. One change of plan. I shall not send the Slade Form back or apply for the London School of Fashion. I shall find a job so that I can be financially independent.

Sunday 24th October
Helped in the house this morning. Didn't go to Youth Meeting, as Mum objected. Told her: "You'd think Bernard has led me into a life of crime, instead of just teaching me my own religion!" Bernard called to see if I was all right, but didn't come in.

Tuesday 26th October
Went to catch 9.45 a.m. train to Swansea. Went first to Alex's home. Very shaky. Saw Mrs. Winter. Alex came in at 12. Surprised to see me. Has clipped his moustache. I like it. Stayed for lunch, then both went to farm and stayed there. Talked about our plans – both very vague, except our resolve to see as much as possible of each other while we can. Caught 8.05 bus home. Songs: 'In The Blue of the Evening'; 'Deep Purple'; 'As Time Goes By'. Subjects: College – University, Jobs: Judaism – not much, unfortunately, and the future. Went to bed at 12. Alex lent me a book – *Noah Pandre* by Zalman Shneour.

Wednesday 27th October
Coffee fell on baby's face, lunch-time. Put Burn-oil on immediately. She was O.K. in an hour. I had a terrific scare! Went to pics. and saw *Five Graves to Cairo* with Franchot Tone. Very good.

Saturday 30th October
Stayed in bed. Cold bad. Read *Noah Pandre* and finished it. Beautifully written book. Started Shakespeare's *Love's Labour's Lost*. All went to pics. except me. Joyce is going to LONDON to work in the Bachad Office. If Joyce is in London

– well – then *I* too can go. She's going Thursday to see about it. So very happy. Perhaps I'll be there too in a month.

Thursday 4th November

Joyce, Mum and Uncle went to London today. I phoned Alex. Lovely to hear his voice. Told me he couldn't get tickets for Opera (*Faust*) but he'll still try. Saw picture *The Black Swan* – wasn't very good. Mum came home at 12.10 a.m., said Joyce is staying in Polly's.

Friday 5th November

Raids in London last night. Mum worried. Not very anxious for me to go. Thousands of *our* planes went to Germany and dropped tons of bombs on Dusseldorf. Hope I can do something really useful myself when I get to London. Can understand now why people volunteer.

Sunday 7th November

Was going to Youth Meeting today, but Trudy Stein came up, and anger waxed hotly once more against Kahns. Thought it better not to go. Trudy said they've *ruined* us! The cheeky so and so. Phoned Alex, spoke for quite a while. Weather getting very cold. Put an electric bar on in Sara's room. When she woke up this morning her hands were blue with cold. My bedroom is like an icebox.

Tuesday 9th November

Saw *Hitler's Children* this afternoon. Stunning, Stirring, and Stupendous. Made me feel awful! Things like that are happening at this very moment – and worse! Only now can I realise that fact. T.G. the Russians are doing so well – they have taken Kiev – the sooner we win, the sooner the enslaved people will be freed from their beastly torturers.

Thursday 11th November

Aunty Ray here. Gran came up to see her sister. Talked about the Friedman affair. To my amazement, Aunty Ray said – "Kahns are perfectly right. Steven and Keith are Gentiles and there's nothing wrong with that. What is wrong is for Mr. Coren, however well-meaning, to stir up trouble – he's an ignorant busy-body!" Well! Mum's *face*! Aunty Ray is her *favourite* aunt – mine too! It was like hearing words from an oracle! Aunty Ray is very lady-like and the most learned of Gran's sisters. Spoke to her about religion. Told her that my husband would have to keep Shabbos too. Felt sick when I thought it over. Will it mean giving up Alex? … I *couldn't*! We all went to Cardiff to see Aunty Fanny. Sara wonderful all day, laughing and smiling. Slept in my arms on the way back. Lovely feeling. Phoned Alex when we got back.

Friday 12th November
Saw to papers. Joyce and Uncle came home. Joyce not very thrilled with London. Is trying to persuade me to stay here for a few months – but I'm afraid she won't succeed. Brought me a newspaper with Ads for jobs – skilled personnel. Looked for something where my Shorthand, Typing, Bookkeeping, Drawing and German (a little French) and of course, Maths, would be needed. Wrote to a few.

Sunday 14th November
Went for a walk with Sara in the morning, then with Berta to Youth Meeting. Dita and Bernard talked about the German Pogrom of 1938. Felt awful, remembering *Hitler's Children* and how much more terrible the reality had been. Feel hopeless about Berta's family – pleased, for once, that she wasn't really listening. Asked Mr. Kahn if he knew of digs for me, outside London. Said he'd try. Read *Pygmalion* by G. B. Shaw in the evening. Very, very good!

Tuesday 16th November
Weather extremely cold. Wonderfully starry night. Re-read Alex's last ten letters (October–November). 1st October he wrote:

> "Before I went to bed I assembled all of your letters (all 46 of them). I started by reading your letter of the 11th inst. and ended by reading one dated January *1940* and a few dated August *1938*. I recall quite well my elegant pre-war writing paper with a silver 'A' on it. My, how you've changed! No longer only fifteen, you write (with vastly improved spelling – please note) almost as you did in 1941. At least with the same sentiments. D'you know, I think it would be fun to read each other's own letters again some day. Well, here's to the next few years, and may our friendship last and increase till such a time when we have to, unwillingly I suppose, part for the last time on this earth."

Alex's reaction to my discussion about the keeping of the Torah's laws was, unfortunately, predictable. Alex comments:

> "While I admire your pluck and tenacity in keeping the laws at all, especially amidst so much hard feeling, I beg you to retain a *little* of your old self, and to reserve a modicum of common sense. Regarding the changes Bernard has made in you and Joyce, there is a great deal of danger that you step over the line between reason and eccentricity. You see, you have undergone a reaction: you were formerly irreligious and disinterested; now you have gone quite the other way and become totally religious and pious. I have always tended to be fairly frum, and, although I do not follow *blindly* every letter of the law, I think my way of life, prayers etc. is every bit as acceptable to the Al-mighty as is Bernard's …"

Friday 19th November
Checked up on year's takings today. After lunch, helped Joyce paint kitchen and living room. Joyce had a letter to say she's to go to Hachsharah in *Bromsgrove*

December 1st. What luck! Took Sara for a walk. Very cold, but we both enjoyed it. Sara calls Uncle (her father) – "Harry" now – the little monkey! She's full of fun. Taught Berta in the evening. The Government has asked everyone to cut down on electricity – I'm writing this with gloves on, but I'm too cold to continue.

Sunday 21st November

Finished distempering scullery on my own. Went up to Youth Meeting at 5 p.m. with Berta. Had a very interesting discussion about History. What it is? – Who makes it? – What good is it? – What does it teach us, etc.? Of course, we finally concluded that only by having a Torah-true nation can we achieve peace for future generations – all other remedies will fail. Was very good.

Wednesday 24th November

Went to Penrhiwceiber in morning. Gran in bed with a cold. Served in shop. Bitterly cold with the large double door opening onto the street. Went to Kahns' at 8 p.m. Met Mr. Lichtig there. He was a former MP in Czechoslovakia and is now in the Czech Government [in exile] in this country. Had a nice conversation. Continued translating the Siddur [Prayer book]. Discussed various points from Alex's recent letters, e.g. "the keeping of outdated rituals". Bernard said there are two kinds of laws in the Torah; ones you can understand and find reasons for – not stealing – not killing – not bearing false witness etc. and Chukim [Statutes] which are beyond man's understanding, e.g. eating of Kosher food; not wearing garments woven together from linen and wool. One can sometimes suggest a reason – Kosher food for health and cleanliness – but food that is not Kosher can be clean, healthy – and also taste nice! (Don't I know! – How I *loved* the bacon I had in Gwen's home in Llangenech when I was four!) So one has to keep *all* the laws because they have been given to us by a superior, godly intelligence. One can't just pick out the laws that are "convenient" or "attractive" and not bother with any that may interfere with one's daily life. I know that Alex doesn't put on Tefillin – rides a bus and smokes on Shabbos, yet considers himself fairly frum. My arguments don't seem to convince him. It's like seeing a beautiful painting, with half the paint fallen off – one can't appreciate the beauty of the whole work.

Thursday 25th November

Went to pics. and saw *The Life and Death of Colonel Blimp* with Deborah Kerr, Roger Livesey and Anton Walbrook. Was really exceptional.

Sunday 28th November

Got ready to go to Agudas Yisrael Meeting in Porth. Caught bus at 2.40 p.m. with Mr. Bodenheimer, Mr. & Mrs. Kahn, Bernard, Dita and Joyce. Mountainous journey thrilled me as before. Got to Porth at 4. Had tea, then meeting began. Those present were: Dr. & Mrs. S. Katz, Mr. & Mrs. M. Katz (brothers), Mr. and

Mrs. Stern and their son Max, another boy – Benny Eschwege. Speaker was Rev. Morris from Ponty. Spoke about Torah, and gave quite a good speech. I was surprised though, to find that everyone there had accepted, and tried to keep, a Torah-true life, *young* people included! Joyce, Bernard and I were invited to Dr. Katz for supper. Walked home with Mrs. M. Katz and had a very interesting conversation with her. She was a Beth Jacob teacher – learned in Vienna – taught in Hungary and Bavaria. Very nice person. Mrs. S. Katz showed me her baby Yitzchak (Isaac) – born last Rosh Hashanah. Lovely atmosphere of absolute brotherhood and comradeship, both at the meeting, and in the house. Enjoyed the day very much.

Tuesday 30th November

Worked in Barbara Gold's today, as Mrs. Prosser has 'flu. Still no letter from Alex. Joyce had a letter today to say she would have to wait another fortnight before going to Kinnersley. She's so disappointed. Saw *So Proudly We Hail* with Veronica Lake, Paulette Goddard, Claudette Colbert. Terrific!

Thursday 2nd December

Letter came for Joyce from the Appointments Office in Cardiff to say she had to report there *today*! Decided to catch 12.55 p.m. bus. Dashed upstairs, changed, dashed down – washed etc. and dashed out to queue for ten minutes before the bus came in. Everyone got on except us and two or three others. Went home – Mum had a brain wave and suggested we went to Cross Inn and catch the bus from Swansea to be sure of a seat. Caught 1.30 bus to Cross Inn to be told that the Cardiff bus had passed ten minutes before. Waited till 1.50 for bus back to Aberdare. Bus stopped every hundred feet for the driver to go out and post a letter, chat with friends – stopping at the Square. Got there at 2 and ran towards bus stop. Bus there! – But it went out full before our turn came. Joyce said: "All right, let's hitch." "O.K." says I and off we go to New Road and stop a car. "Only going to Aberaman 1 mile away." Told us we wouldn't get to Cardiff on that road. Missed three cars most certainly going to Cardiff as we walked back. Started to rain. Caught the train and had to change twice. Walked to the Parade, to Appointments Office, only the chickens didn't live there anymore, it seems the birds had flown. Joyce thought very hard until she had the bright idea of looking for the address on her letter. We walked wet and wearily to High Street. Meanwhile Joyce's sole came off the heel! Joyce was told by the Appointment Officer that she could have a job as a jig-borer – drilling holes in jigs – with Saturday free – of course she refused it. (Anyway, she's used to boring people – and holes in me!) (Space for comment by Joyce … * ! * ! * ! …) – Oh quite! Went to Prince of Wales Theatre but couldn't get in. Booked two tickets for next Thursday – *La Bohème*. Went to Palladium and saw *We Dive At Dawn* with Eric Portman. Very good – only we saw the end first and didn't see the middle at all.

On the way to the station two Yanks tried to "get off" with us, but we weren't having any of it. Joyce said emphatically: "That's all I needed to finish a lovely day!" But it was not all. We had to change twice again on the way home, at Pontypridd and Abercwmboi! On the station wall our torch lit up the familiar poster – IS YOUR JOURNEY REALLY NECESSARY? "Grr! * ! * ! * !" said Joyce. Glad to get home (for a change).

Reproduced courtesy of the Imperial War Museum, London

Thursday 9th December

Joyce went to Bristol today. She thinks she may be able to get a drawing office job. I went to Cardiff to see *La Bohème* (on my own) and enjoyed it fairly well. Came home on 6 p.m. train. Awful journey. Train almost dark – only girl in a full carriage of men. One boy kept a torch shining on me nearly all the way up – moving it around my body. No one spoke and I felt d— uncomfortable. Ran all the way home – nearly flattened my nose on a lamppost – but saw it just in time. Spent some time drawing. Joyce came home late, she had fallen downstairs while in Bristol; has a swollen knee.

Saturday 11th December
Went to Bernard's at 8 p.m. Told me about his trip to London. Had letter from Alex to say he'll be here Monday. Very upset thinking about his visit and what I'm going to say to him about my more active participation in Judaism and my plans to leave home. Had nasty argument with Uncle and Mum; not worth recording. Uncle thinks because he knows a lot, he knows everything. No one is allowed any opinion except his.

Monday 13th December
Tidied around. Went to meet the 12.15 train. Waited and Alex and "tasche" [moustache] came off it. Felt very strange with Alex for quite a long time. Went out for a walk after lunch. Alex talked about the Varsity revue. Very amusing. Alex said it's funny how on day visits we can never talk anything but small talk. He's right too – I just couldn't say what I'd decided to say last night. Alex caught the 7.30 train home.

Wednesday 15th December
Everyone has 'flu, so worked hard in both Jane Cooper's and Barbara Gold's. Heard Mrs. Jenkins in 'Ceiber has died (from the 'flu). Glad Gran is better – over 700 people in Britain have died of it in *one week*!

Thursday 16th December
Mum went to London to buy Xmas stock, so I was up early. Dylis has left the shop and gone to work at a factory in Treforest. Brian (her boyfriend) has gone to the Navy. Dylis was very cut up about it – "But he's *a musician*, what can he do in the Navy?" "Maybe," I said, "he can go into ENSA" [Entertainment National Service Association], but with so many ships being sunk by mines, subs. and bombings, I can understand her fears. I made her laugh, reminding her of the time she explained to me the difference between a "polite" kiss and a "passionate" kiss! Arranged to go to pics. to see *The Gentle Sex*. Waited up for Mum, but *she didn't* come. Very worried. Finally Mum came in at 1 a.m! She had missed the Ponty station, and gone all the way up the Rhondda. She managed to get a car from Tonypandy. Went to bed at 1.30, deadbeat.

Monday 20th – Friday 24th December
Worked in Barbara Gold's all week. Very busy with Xmas shoppers. Went to Kahns' Wednesday. Was told a place had been found for me to stay; a Mr. Katz living in Berkhamsted just outside London. Hope I can go soon. Miriam and Carl came for the weekend.

Saturday 25th December
Went for a walk with Miriam (Fred's abroad in the Army), Carl, Sara and Gwyneth. Wonderful "quiet" Xmas atmosphere everywhere. Weather cold and

clear – my head filled with familiar hymns. Sara looked like a doll. Went up to Bernard's at 4 p.m. Talked about Chanukah [Festival of Lights]. Bernard surprised I have only once seen Chanukah candles lit – in Alex's parents' house when I was six. Wished Bernard "Happy Birthday!" Talked in bed with Miriam till 2 a.m.

Monday 27th December
Dena, Aunty Fanny, Gran here for the day, also Becky and Eli. Uncle let off steam about a small thing, and although he was right he did make us awfully embarrassed behaving so badly in company. Dena and Berta came with me to Youth Meeting. Hymina Nevies from Pontypridd also came. Had quite a good discussion on 'The Place of Women in Jewish Life'. Bernard said the woman is the pivot of a home and very respected. Also talked of famous biblical women: Deborah, Hannah, Judith, Miriam (Moses' sister). Started letter to Alex.

Tuesday 28th December
Finished letter. Explained to Alex that my decision to become more orthodox is *not* a phase of piety, or a reaction to my former ignorance or difficult home situation. I have *argued*, *resisted*, and *accepted nothing* unless I was 100% convinced of its relevance to my life. I'm inclined to be an "all or nothing" person and feel fortunate that, in this crumbling world, I have found a way of life that is spiritually rewarding and makes a lot of sense.

Wednesday 29th December
Went up to Bernard's at 8 p.m. Did some of Isaac Breuer's book; good too. Had two replies to my job applications. One refusal, and one acceptance – in an Architect's Office – but the vacancy is for June 1944; secretarial and drawing office position – hopeful!?

Thursday 30th December
Went to pics. with Gwen Walters; saw *Action in the North Atlantic* with Raymond Massey and Humphrey Bogart. Very good! Great acting!

Friday 31st December
Worked fairly hard all day. A lot of customers; quite a few staff still away with 'flu. Started reading *The Seven Pillars of Wisdom* by T. E. Lawrence. 1944 tomorrow! What will the New Year bring?

1944

Saturday 1st January
1944! What a nice number. Added together it comes to "18". Mentioned this to Bernard when I went there at *4 p.m.* (another 4). He said: "18 is a special number in Hebrew, meaning 'Life'." Hope this is a good sign for this year. Started well, with the Germans retreating from hundreds of small towns in Russia; Russians moving towards Leningrad.

Sunday 2nd January
Very busy this morning. Went over to Liberal Club to help with the party preparations. Sara wore the suit I made her and everyone remarked how sweet she looked. Affair, which was a mild tea party, finished at 7.30 p.m. Not very interesting. Wrote to Alex.

Monday 3rd January
Sent Alex's letter to London where he's seeing off a cousin "to foreign lands", and probably spending the £6.0.05 he earned at the Post Office (over Xmas). Uncle went to London. I worked all day in Barbara Gold's.

Tuesday 4th January
Barbara Gold's all day. Went with Berta to Ezra meeting at 7 p.m. Bernard spoke about 10th of Teves – Fast in memory of the breaching of the walls of Jerusalem – death of Ezra the Scribe – and the translation of the Torah into Greek by 70 translators on the command of Ptolemy – in Alexandria. This translation is called *The Septuagint*. Asked Mum about London tonight. More or less agreed to let me go.

Wednesday 5th January
Mum changed her mind about London. Joyce stuck up for her, so I had little chance of success.

Saturday 8th January
Had letter from Alex this morning. Wrote about London trip. Also he's received date for his medical for the Air Force. Bound to pass A1 – all that stooking and cycling! – He wants me to go to Swansea for "… at least three days – instead of

moping or rushing about like mad in Aberdare, you can rest and be happy here". Went to Bernard's in the afternoon. Phoned Alex. Whoopee!

Wednesday 12th January
Felt cold coming on, so went to bed early.

Thursday 13th January
Cold much worse. Mum went to London. Read part of *The Seven Pillars of Wisdom*.

Saturday 15th January
Cold bit better. Sara also has a cold now. Cancelled Swansea trip – shall do my moping in Aberdare!

Thursday 20th January
Mum in London again today. Busy with Sara all day – her cough's really bad. Read more of *The Seven Pillars of Wisdom*. Listened to the news. *At last* the long siege of Leningrad (sixteen months of German blockade) has been ended by a final bombardment from Russian troops – imagine how joyful the people left alive must be – starving but full of courage and now at last victorious! Mum home "early" – 11.20 p.m. Her last two visits she came home at 1 a.m. and 2.

Saturday (Shabbos) 22nd January
Raining. Went up to Bernard's at 4 p.m. Did part of the Mincha [afternoon] Service. Very stormy. Bernard took me home – we discussed London, or other places where I might find work.

Sunday 23rd January
Joyce's 21st birthday. Made trifle. Went to Ponty with Bernard and Esther at 5 p.m. Listened to Youth Group there. Rather bored. Rev. Harris hopeless, even as a spiritual leader. He skirts around questions too much for my liking. Yesterday our troops landed at Anzio, which is just below Rome. They used "ducks" [amphibious troop carriers] to get ashore.

Monday 24th January
Went to meet the London train to take Bernard's friend Nathan up to Clifton Street. He's been directed to go down the mines – our Ernest Bevin's idea! Bernard, who knows the pit manager, is trying to get him an exemption or at least a deferment until he has finished his studies. Nathan is learning to become an optician; like Berta, he has also not heard from his parents since before the war. We got on well; he's quite good looking and has a great sense of humour. Can't imagine him digging coal! Found out he's related to Mum's friend Jack Davies.

Told me Danko (who started the Ezra Youth Group in England) is already working down the pits in Durham. Listened to news of beachhead landing at Anzio. Here we've had a few air-raids, but the bombers have mainly targeted Cardiff.

Saturday 29th January
Very heavy raid on Cardiff last night. Many casualties, fires and damage – more to the town than the docks. Aunty Fanny has sent Dena, Miriam and Carl to stay with us for a few days. I'm sleeping in Sara's room on the folding camp bed. Didn't sleep much because of Sara's cough and … de-luxe model bed! Who designed this!!? Dena feels safer sleeping in the cellar.

Tuesday 1st February
Coupons released today at last! Weren't very busy though. Did books etc. Saw *Victory Through Air Power*. Not bad. Finished skirt for Judy Schwartz. Looks quite nice too. Same as Sara's – except I embroidered "Judy" on it.

Sunday 6th February
Had meeting at 5 p.m. Leslie Nevies came (from Ponty). Interesting discussion on what to take literally in the Torah, and what not to. What is a miracle? When did they stop? Could one occur now, etc.? Finished at 8. Half of one of my teeth broke off. Had toothache.

Monday 7th February
Persuaded myself all morning to go to dentist. Had tooth out in the afternoon. Woke up "laughing". Don't think I'll be scared again to have tooth out under gas. It's O.K. Stayed in of course.

Tuesday 8th February … **day of a real MIRACLE!**
Went to pics. this afternoon. Saw *Mission to Moscow* with Walter Hudson and Ann Harding. Quite good. On the way home stopped in at Barbara Gold's to be told that **Berta's brother MANFRED was here**!!! He's here with the American forces. Arrived this week, and came straight down to see her. When Berta came to us from Germany, on the last ship before the war started, she was just twelve – she'd left her parents and four brothers and gone alone by train, ship, and train again, to arrive at last, in our tiny village of Penrhiwceiber. She knew not one word of English. Although we all loved her, especially Gran, she's never made much attempt to take part in anything – always bored or disinterested, and sometimes seemed "not quite with it". We knew she'd never see her family again – they had never written to her, so we never mentioned them in order not to upset her. I'd been the only Jewish girl in my school, but Berta is the only *German* Jewish girl in hers. After she'd heard that two of her brothers had made it to America she was thrilled, but now, *today,* that news is *real*! Manfred is actually *here*. Met them going for a

walk as I went home. Berta proud as anything – and she has something to be proud of too! He's very good looking, and smart, in his forces uniform. Mum couldn't get over the quality of the material. Berta is really glowing. I made supper for them, Berta talking *non-stop*! Manfred is a really nice person. They caught the 9.40 p.m. train to 'Ceiber.

Wednesday 9th February

Went down to Pen. to ask Berta and Manfred to come for dinner. Had dinner, then we all went to Watsons' to have photos taken.

Took bus to Aberaman to see Uncle Charlie. Uncle Charlie was also born in America but left there for Wales when he was only two. Berta seems to have grown inches overnight. All went to see *Heaven Can Wait* with Don Ameche. Not bad. Very good second picture – Laurel and Hardy. After supper we went to see Mr. and Mrs. Kahn. Manfred is a Corporal in the American Air Force, Ground Staff. He's twenty-three and looks a lot like Berta. His motto word is "*Swell*". Everything's "Swell" – and today it certainly was.

Thursday 10th February

Went to Cardiff at 12.45 p.m. Wandered round Civic Centre, then to General Station. Manfred's train left at 4.20. As a parting gift Manfred gave Berta £10 to spend on all of us! We three went to pics. *again* and saw *And the Angels Sing*

Joyce and I with Berta and Manfred

with Dorothy Lamour and Betty Hutton. Came home 10.20. Now we need another miracle, to keep Manfred safe. It would be too cruel if anything happened to him now. Glad he's Ground Staff.

Monday 14th February
Sara has been coughing badly all week. Had doctor in today to see her. She has *whooping cough*!! Went in afternoon to see *Bataan* with Robert Taylor and Lloyd Nolan. Excellent film about the war in the Pacific. Had letter from Manfred today, Joyce replied. Did some Hebrew *writing* in the evening. Got on much better with it than I thought.

Tuesday 15th February
Stayed with Sara most of today and slept with her in the front room in the night. She's really quite ill – I think I'm getting whooping cough too, on the quiet.

Wednesday 16th February
Doc gave Sara injection today. I didn't go to Bernard's, so listened to wireless. Very big raid on Germany – over 1,000 planes bombed Berlin. Most of them American bombers. In Italy, the Germans are fighting hard to stop our troops getting to Rome. Slept with Sara again.

Saturday 19th February
Stayed in with Sara. Although her cough's bad, she's quite cheerful. Says most things now – "Shut-the-door"; "Howareyou"; "Window"; "Fire"; "Shoos"; "Sara Beca Doughbing" (Sara Rebecca Golding); "Aunty Dowa"; "Aunty Dosie". [Dora and Rosie, two of Uncle Harry's sisters.] Made her a pinny this evening. Quite pretty too. Sara looks like a real doll. Mischievous as a monkey! ("Mon-tey"!)

Sunday 20th February
Had a bumper meeting today. Benny and Sophie came from Porth, plus Hilda, Freda and "We Three". Dr. Katz gave a discussion starting off with "Why do we think?" Answer – to find the "Truth". There is only one truth. "Can we find it by reason?" Answer – "No, for reality cannot be proven." How do we know that *our* reality is right? Everyone's reality is different. It is impossible to prove to bees (who have no colour sight) that something is blue and not black. Reality is only conceived by our own reasoning, and therefore it can be doubted. Revelation is something beyond our faculties and reason, it is something independent of ourselves – beyond our reason – therefore it must be true. Conclusion: Revelation is the only means by which we can get at the truth.

Friday 25th February
Not feeling so good today after "trying" to sleep with Sara. At 12 Joyce told me, to my incredulous surprise, that Alex was here! Little wonder I was shocked. Yes,

there he was, large as life, with moustache perhaps a little larger, and the same old lovable smile. After lunch we went for a long walk, but didn't talk about anything serious. I thought he would stay the weekend, but he wouldn't, because he would have to stay with Bernard (who might have started a religious discussion with him). He went back at 7.30 – I felt awful and didn't sleep much, despite Sara's lapses of quietness. He said today: "Religion is a private affair." Well I hope he considers an intended partner as having some little right to interfere. Feel awfully miserable.

Sunday 27th February
Meeting as usual. Leslie Nevies was there. We discussed Isaac Breuer's ideas. Am Yisrael – Am Torah [Nation of Israel – Nation of Torah]. People of Israel kept together as a people by the will of G-d for the sake of bringing His Law to the world. Those who do not bother to do so gradually fall away from the Jewish People with time, and get lost to our nation.

Tuesday 29th February – **Leap Year!**
Went to see Roddy McDowall in *My Friend Flicka* today. Very good too. Sara much better. She can say almost everything now, and knows lots of Nursery Rhymes. She seems to have a wonderful memory – or have all babies?

Wednesday 1st March
Had a letter from Alex today. Reference to: "… the ghastly details of my visit last Friday (the busiest day of your week), the subsequent childish acting which I performed with such skill and ease, and my seemingly hurried retreat from your desirable company. I feel terrible about it all, so much so that I rose with the intention of riding back to the scene of my folly, only to find the first snow of winter barring the way to Aberdare … Today I met your cousin Shirley Collins – she is attending that Paragon of Art Schools, that Peak of Perfect Artistic Instruction, that Acme of Arteducation – the Art School of Swansea – I'll say no more."

Went up to Bernard's for Shiur [lesson]. Mr. Rosenblum from a London Yeshivah there. He wants to go to Swansea tomorrow collecting for charity. Joyce volunteered to show him round. Mum said it would be better if *I* went – so I spent a restless night in anticipation.

Thursday 2nd March
Got up at 7 and got ready to go. Snowing!! Caught 8.05 bus with Mr. Rosenblum. Read on the way down. I admired the lovely snow-covered scenery. Went first to Mr. Winters'. He gave us names and addresses etc., also 3 guineas [1 guinea = £1.05]. Went to see Mr. Palto, who was out, therefore went up to the farm in the meantime. Uncle Harris gave us 1gn and suggested we asked Palto if he can give

some of the money collected for United Appeal to the Mifal [Charity for Torah Education]. Had lunch in Rochale's. Went back to Palto. Had a long talk with him: he said he would put the idea before the Committee. Took Mr. Rosenblum back to bus depot. Had long talk with him about Mizrachi and Aguda. [Mizrachi – Religious Zionist Pioneer. Aguda – Orthodox movement involved with establishing religious educational establishments.] He said he would rather me be an Agudist, for then he would be sure I was Orthodox, and that was the main thing. I was a bit confused, as he himself is Mizrachi. His bus went at 4.25 and I hurried back to Alex's. Had long talk with Mrs. Winter about my plans to find work in Leeds/London; she, very enthusiastic as long as it would take me as far away from Swansea as possible! Alex came in at 6 with Cyril, and whew – what a comedian Cyril is – every second word he said made me laugh. Everyone left at 7.30. Alex rang up to find out time of bus. It went out at 8.05. Got there at 8 p.m. and talked for ten minutes 'In the Blue of Evening' before the bus moved off. I jumped on at the very last second and spent the journey in a pleasant frame of mind – lovely memories – nice day altogether.

Saturday 4th March

Mum's birthday. Yes, I forgot again. Cricked my neck badly this morning, so stayed in all day. Hurting too. Drew in the evening and read Alex's letter: ("You make me completely happy or completely miserable; you complete all I am and do; and for that I do so much want you to be with me as long as I am in this world. Maybe these words are the idiosyncrasies of a lovelorn, short-sighted eighteen-year-old, but right now I mean what I say.")

Tuesday 7th March

Went to pics. Saw *Mr. Lucky* with Cary Grant and Laraine Day. Very good too. Sara still not completely better. Joyce went to Swansea this morning to ask if Aunty Mary has room for her (on the farm), if the Appeal Board lets her go there. Appeal is tomorrow, as Joyce refused to go to the factory at Stonehouse because of Shabbos! Stayed in with Sara and finished her dress.

Wednesday 8th March

Couldn't resist trying blue chiffon dress on Sara, even tho' it's for summer. The piqué edging that had been done professionally made all the difference. Sara looked adorable; wonderful colour with her dark brown curls. Sara immediately rushed into the shop, pirouetting between the counters, being admired by all the shop-girls. Suddenly she overbalanced, knocked into the desk, a whole inkpot full of dark blue ink spilt all over the front of the dress! Iris screamed: "Duw! Oh! Duw!" Sara, seeing her face and the large navy spots growing larger on her dress, burst into a fit of giggles. I soaked the dress in cold water, but only after about six washes it's come clean. Sadly, all the frilling looks floppy, and the whole dress

Mum with Sara wearing new dress

looks worn out. I should have known better – it was Ta'anis Esther. Fasted O.K. Went to shul at 7.35 p.m. just in time to hear the Megillah [Scroll]. Came home and packed into supper. Read *Seven Pillars of Wisdom* – and *finished* it! It's really a work of genius!

Saturday 11th March
Stayed in until 8 p.m. Went up to Bernard's and did Parah Adumah [Biblical laws of the red heifer]. Talked about Laws of Purification (in Biblical Times). Mrs. Andrew's "Pontypool" grandson came in this afternoon. He's been fighting in Africa for three years; typical cockney soldier. Couldn't sleep much during the night. Alex on my mind. Don't know what I'll do about it all.

Monday 13th March
Did books today at last, and feel pleased that I've got them up to date. Saw *Adventures of Tartu* in evening. Enjoyed it very much; awfully thrilling.

Wednesday 19th April
The happenings of the last five weeks have been so many and so varied that I've sadly neglected to recall each day's happenings as I have done heretofore. However, I must try to do my best to record, as faithfully as memory permits, my thoughts and occupations that have crowded each day. Though it would seem

considerably easier to start with today and work backwards, which I would really prefer to do, I think it would really serve me better to start where my memory is somewhat clouded, and keep this week's happenings which are still quite clear in my mind – and will therefore last long enough (if not longer) to allow me to record those dim memories that will fade 'ere the fresher ones are written. (It will be needless to note that the book I'm in the middle of is *Lorna Doone*!)

Saturday 1st April

Iris came in to say there were ORANGES in the shops. Of course we all thought it was an April Fool's joke – but no, Megan came in with THREE! Sara's face, when she saw them being peeled, was full of amazement. She kept one "whole" – "not spoilt", all day. I went to shul in the morning and to Bernard's in the afternoon. Talked about Pesach and what Joyce and I could do for the Sedorim [Passover night services].

Sunday 2nd – Monday 3rd April

Worked jolly hard doing my bedroom etc. Cleaned kitchen cupboards and put fresh paper in them ready for Pesach.

4th April '44!!!

Wrote to Alex. Received letter from him (on the 6th) dated 4/4/44. He wrote:

> "I simply must write today because one can only write the same *four* figures in the date once in eleven years – what a thrill, eh? Have arranged to be in Aberdare on the 10th – just find a nice secluded sunny spot where we can sit down and talk, and talk. We can discuss wider issues, birth, the world, life, death, religion, cult, pictures and Eira's 'last boy-friend' … And at night I can take you out under the moon and sing all the love songs I know to you. (Remember me on the '8th' – our special anniversary.) I think it is a sign of the failure of education, when we have to get professional composers – or shall we call them 'jongleurs' – to make love for us – still, I'm certain I couldn't unblushingly make up some of the things which come into such songs as 'Besame Mucho'; 'You'll Never Know'; 'Intermezzo' etc."

Thursday 6th April

Work, work, work.

Friday 7th April

More work. Got everything beautiful by 5.30 p.m. Really pleased with myself. Joyce and I caught 6.05 bus to Cardiff and went to Rosens'. Had Seder there. They had two American soldiers besides the family, Miriam and Hetty [their daughters], Jack and baby etc. Baby rather underweight. Quite enjoyed Seder. Followed very well. Went to bed at 12.

Saturday 8th April
Three years today! [Since Alex and I walked to the Cwm]. Went to shul in the morning. Dena brought a soldier home to lunch. Went back to town – town bursting with American soldiers, jeeps, lorries etc. Returned to Rosens' Seder: had a dashing American sailor, Bob, for company together with a soldier who was quite the opposite. Bob stayed till 3 a.m!!

Sunday 9th April
Went to shul with Jack this morning. Followed everything. Unterman gave a good sermon, and Zucker sang wonderfully. Met David Steiner (Alex's friend) and was invited to a Neshef [party] at 6 p.m. at Habonim. Accepted. Went to bed and dozed till 5.30. Went to Windsor Place, Joyce and Dena came too but left straight away – too childish for them no doubt. Enjoyed it very much.

Monday 10th April
Took 11 a.m. bus to Aberdare. Alex came at 5. Really wonderful to see him. Went to meeting at 6. Subject: Isaiah X:32–XII:6. Was not a good meeting. I was sorry for Alex's sake. Talked till 11 with Bernard (Alex did, I listened).

Tuesday 11th April
Alex and I walked around town in the morning, and went to Gran's in the afternoon. Came back – were going to go to Bernard's. Mum was annoyed and stopped us. She told Alex about the "Friedman Affair"! I felt awfully upset. Had to make use of Alex's shoulder. He told me I should go away – at last he realises that. Went to bed at 11 p.m. – OR SO.

Wednesday 12th April
Went to Cardiff by 10.25 a.m. train. Shopped for shoes for Alex, but couldn't find any. Went to Rosens'; Hetty and Jack had a Pidyon Haben [special ceremony for the arrival of a first-born son]. Mum etc. there, Aunty Mary, Yetta – and Arnold Shepherd from the Cardiff Habonim – who was there, so Dena told me, because he'd been "struck" by me, Sunday. He must have been disappointed when Alex came in. Went to Roath Park. Watched three wonderful planes in the sky making "clouds". Thrilled. Alex amused me all the way home by telling me funny stories.

Went to bed at 11 or so … (* * * !) – Happy memories!

Thursday 13th April
We went as far as the Lily Pond in the morning. Didn't talk much, too full of feelings. We watched the broken shafts of sunlight move over the dark green leaves and delicate wax-like petals of the water lilies; there must be hundreds of them, crammed together in the old rusty tank. We sat, mesmerised by the humming of dragon-flies darting about, until we heard a different droning, a

plane passing overhead. The mood broken, we returned to the present. In the time left before Alex caught the 12.30 bus to Swansea we managed to have quite a good discussion. In the afternoon I took Sara to the park. She was still grumpy after this morning's tantrums when I had left her with Mum. I think she felt jealous of Alex when she saw us together. A few rides on the swings soon had her chuckling and beaming as usual.

Friday 14th April
Yom Tov today – didn't do much accordingly. Went to Bernard's at 4 p.m. as usual.

Sunday 16th April
Had meeting today on "Ich-heit", or Ego. Very good. Ego is made up of:

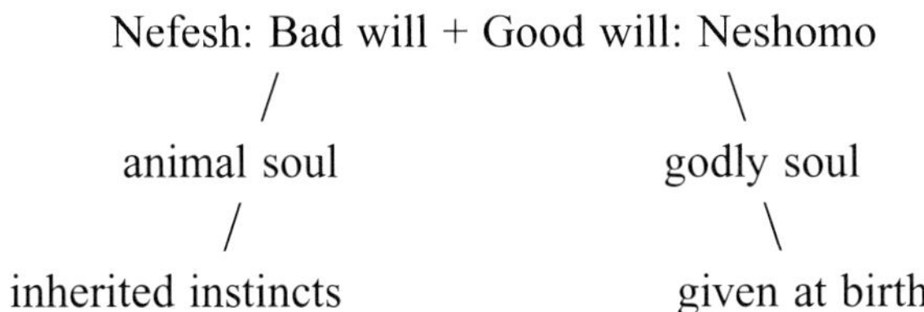

We humans are all descended from the first breath of G-d – or of oxygen, and derive from the same origin. Only G-d is independent of a prescribed existence in time. Contrasted our own ego with sentence in Exodus III:14, when Moses asks G-d his name. G-d replied: I AM THAT I AM or more correctly: I SHALL BE THAT WHICH I WILL BE. G-d is both past, present and future – i.e. eternal. What man sometimes imagines to be his own free decisions are but the product of unconscious influences arising out of his past. However, we have the power to choose "Good Will" to carve our immediate future in G-d's service, in this way the Good Will will triumph over the Bad Will. (Ideas mostly from Rabbi S. R. Hirsch.) Also talked about Descartes, "I think, therefore I am". He also believed in the innate idea of a G-dly being. Also about Kant – (Das ding an sich) [The thing in itself] – everything perceived has first its own identity – but we only know how something appears to us, and that differs according to time, place and person; e.g. does a tree appear the same to an artist as it does to a woodcutter – in different centuries? And so on … Enjoyed it very much.

Tuesday 18th April
Long letter from Alex – very pleased. In it he wrote:

> "As for my visit to Aberdare last Thursday, I really have a good deal to be thankful for. At least we got down to some of the basic facts, and I hope we get on from there to some kind of understanding. Though in my present state of mind I don't see that an understanding is going to go a long way to finding happiness, permanent and

imperturbable for us two. And after these last few years of deep feeling between us, I'm afraid I cannot imagine happiness with anyone but you amie très chère."

Monday 24th April
Joyce went to Cardiff. Aunty Millie called in. Talked about her son Bernard [Schwartz] and the army. Went to pics. and saw *Flesh and Fantasy* with Edward G. Robinson and Barbara Stanwyck. Strange picture. Quite good.

Wednesday 26th April
Went up to Bernard's at 8 p.m. Talked about Moshiach Zeiten [the coming of the Messiah] – resurrection and the future Eden. Don't understand it of course – does anyone? Had to read Hebrew without vowel signs! Very difficult. Went to bed at 11. Dreamt all night I was missing bus to Swansea – went to Palestine instead! Didn't miss 10 a.m. bus to Swansea. Went to Beck's [Mum's cousin] and was invited to sleep there. Went to Winters' at 3. Alex took me to University at 6. Saw George Bernard Shaw's *Pygmalion* – and never enjoyed a play so much in all my life. Quite superb acting from all – it was really terrific! Met Alex outside and went to Sketty for supper. Went out for a walk – and walked, and walked. Got home at 11.30.

Friday 28th April
Got up 8.30 a.m. (Had sleepless night – three hours at the most.) Listened to the birds from 5. Had breakfast. Alex came; took me to Cocket bus stop – he went on to college. I saw Aunty Mary on the farm and gave her Joyce's letter. Caught 2.30 bus from Cross to Llanelly. Loved Llanelly as always. Saw all the family there. Had tea with Aunty Sarah. Caught 7 p.m. bus back. Alex came after supper and we went for a walk down Mumbles Road. Walked in a small park. Told Alex what Torah meant to me and how I couldn't live my life all Nefesh (body) and no Neshomoh (soul). He understood. Wished I could have talked more, but had to go in.

Saturday 29th, Sunday 30th April
Two wonderful days. Walked a lot – to Caswell Bay, Langland and Mumbles.

Monday 1st May
Went up to farm this morning to say G'bye to everyone. Alex came at 4 p.m. with a squashed gardenia in his pocket. He'd picked it for me in the college grounds. We went to the Empire and saw the International Ballet, which included *Carnival*, *Swan Lake* and *Everyman*, the last of which I really enjoyed. Got to Beck's at 11. She had bad news for me; Joyce was going away (or had gone), and I was to catch the first possible bus or train in the morning. Awfully upset about it, as I haven't said G'bye to Alex: I was to meet him at 12 tomorrow. Worst of all, we had planned to *talk* tomorrow, and I had hoped to achieve something positive. Wrote him a note; didn't sleep for a long time.

Tuesday 2nd May
Got up at 7 a.m. Phoned farm and Alex. Caught 10 a.m. bus and was home at 12. Mum in Cardiff. Phoned Alex to give my belated farewells – so near and clear and yet so far and distant! Sara also said "Aw-wow" to him. Mum came home at 2.30, and, to my grief, said there had been no *urgent* need for me to leave Swansea and that her message had been misunderstood. Still home I am and that's all there is to it.

Wednesday 3rd May
Joyce went to Cheltenham yesterday – she has a job near there, in Stroud. Her appeal was not granted, but she's going to take Shabbos off in any case. Hope she doesn't get into trouble or get sent to prison over it.

Sunday 7th May
Dr. S. Katz gave a talk on Revelation. Rather hard to understand. Ellen had a baby boy today! My cousin Sadie Shipman [Barton] also had a baby. Mazeltov!

Mr and Mrs Ginsberger with Ellen and baby Simon

Thursday 11th May
Went to pics. this evening. Saw *Dear Octopus* with Margaret Lockwood. I could understand why Alex wanted me to see it, and why he liked it. Also the great similarity between it and our affair.

Sunday 14th May
Went to the Brit Milah [Circumcision Ceremony] of Ellen's baby. They have called him Simon. Afterwards ten of us went down to Cardiff in one carriage. Bernard and I went to a lecture in the Civic Centre, on 'The British Colonies and the Negro Question'. Cardiff is simply packed with Americans and many of them are coloured. They are all here to help *us* win the war!

Monday 15th May
Papers, papers. Did a lot of washing this morning. All my underwear of last month. *Clean* too mind you!

Tuesday 16th May
Had a letter from Joyce, also a parcel from Manfred – chocolates and NYLON STOCKINGS! Went up to Bernard's to discuss plans for me leaving Aberdare. Tonight, after writing out pros and cons of Swansea, Cheltenham or Leeds – Leeds won. Worked out a plan of campaign. Feel upset at having to relinquish Swansea. Nefesh cried, but Neshomo had peace.

Wednesday 17th May
Went up to Bernard's at 8 p.m. Told him my decision. He gave me some help. I feel pleased about it now and *very determined* to carry it through.

Thursday 18th May
Did papers in the morning – handed them over to Mrs. Prosser who will be doing them when I leave. Went to M.A.C.S. in afternoon to get my Matric Certificate. Very strange going to the school after three years. So pleased that the Headmaster still had my certificate in his desk. Dashed back. All rush today! Got ready to go to Cheltenham. Listened to news. Monte Cassino has been taken by the Allies after months of heavy fighting. Rome next!?

Friday 19th May
Caught 2.30 p.m. train to Cheltenham. Had nice company down. R.A.F. chap helped me with my parcels. Got to Cheltenham 7.15. Joyce met me, and we went to Mrs. Rose's. Had supper, then went across to Rev. Ferber's. Told Joyce that Alex had had a directive to go DOWN THE MINES! However, as his medical for the R.A.F. has been arranged, he probably won't have to go.

Saturday 20th May
Went to shul in the morning – nice building. Met Jack Davies and his sister Cynthia (whose real name is Cecilia). Both very nice people. Jack suggested I could find work in a drawing office in London. He said he'd find out for me. Cold terrible; stayed in bed the rest of the day.

Monday 22nd May
Caught 9 a.m. train to Leeds. No change, got there at 3 p.m. Miriam seemed glad to see me. Went to see Mr. Spiro, the employment officer. He seemed to think he could get me a job in Burton's [Gents' Tailors]. Wrote to Mum.

Thursday 25th May
Phoned Mr. Spiro, but he didn't have anything definite to tell me. Went to town and did a lot of shopping. Found I'd run out of money, and was quite embarrassed. Gave back everything except the elephant I had bought for Sara, and the halo hat. Kept 8d [eight pence] – went at 12.30 p.m., cost 2d in tram. Had to change at Derby. Had quite enjoyable ride, except one hour over-due [to Cheltenham]. Got bus to town – cost 2d – so 4d left. [Approximately £1.50 in today's money.] Relieved to get back to Mrs. Rose's. Resolved never to go away again without *more* than sufficient money. Joyce fancied my "Mrs. Miniver" hat [as worn by Greer Garson in the film], so I gave it to her.

Friday 26th May
Met Joyce in Gloucester. Arrived home at 8.30 p.m. after travelling since 3. Mum home, Uncle away. Bit of a rubdown for going to Leeds without asking. Letter from Alex waiting for me, a week old. He's coming here to put on *Pygmalion*, the play for the Red Cross Appeal, in a few weeks' time. Will I be here to see it? Alex has *failed* his medical for the R.A.F. After two years in the Air Cadets: he's bitterly disappointed. They have put him down as "Category 3" *because of his specs*! His eyesight is too poor to enable him to join an aircrew. Of course, I'm a little relieved. But what now? Army, Navy or – maybe he can carry on with his studies? He wrote: "I have no money, and too much pride to ask for any. The R.A.F. has slammed the door in my face – and I don't have to tell you how that is smarting. Now I'm hanging around hoping that something will turn up, and I do hate being a Mr. Micawber."

Sunday 28th May – Shavuoth
Went for a ramble to Hirwaun with usual gang. Very hot. Wore my new yellow dress. Joyce told me that she thinks Bernard has a crush on me – but it's a ridiculous thing for her to imagine. I have no doubt at all that she's wrong.

Tuesday 30th May
Joyce went back to Cheltenham this morning. Dita and I wrote out forms for Harvest Camp. I also wrote to London, re. jobs. Bernard is going to Hachsharah

next Tuesday. I have to give a speech on 'Duty of Jewish Youth Today', so spent half the night writing.

Sunday 4th June
Big meeting today. Bernard Rose was there and all the others. Gave my speech. Spoke for one-and-a-half hours!! – and wasn't bad. Bernard [Kahn] spoke about the ideals of chalutziut [pioneering], and on the whole we had a very enjoyable meeting, the best I ever remember. Bernard also spoke to me afterwards and congratulated me on my speech, which he said was very good. I was so pleased.

Monday 5th June
Yesterday, after four months of heavy fighting, our troops, together with the Americans, have entered *Rome*!!! Did books etc. Went with Dita to Bernard's in the evening to finish everything to do with the Youth Group. Said "Good-bye" to Bernard – don't feel somehow as if he's really going for good. I should be upset, but I'm not!

Tuesday 6th June – INVASION DAY
Had to go to Mr. Staines in Port Talbot today for clothing coupons owing to us. Had a good journey there and back. Came home in time to hear 1 o'clock news. D-DAY! At last! Monty and Eisenhower in charge of the landings. Thousands of ships, aircraft, tanks and lorries are crossing the Channel into France. Shop empty of customers – everyone glued to the wireless listening to the frequent reports. Went up to Bernard's for two seconds to give him the advert to place in the *Jewish Chronicle* for the Ezra Holiday Camp. Got back in time to hear King's Speech.

[D-Day was the first day of Operation Overlord, the greatest air and sea invasion in history. On its success depended the liberation of all of Nazi-occupied Western Europe. More than 200,000 men were involved on that first day in 6,000 ships and landing craft and 10,000 aircraft. In all over two million personnel from the Allied forces took part in the operation.]

Wednesday 7th June
Usual day. "Nutin' speshal."

Thursday 8th June
Unusual day. *Very* "speshul" – Alex came. He had to go to see Mrs. Jones and Ivor Davies, 2 Gladwyn Gardens, about the sale of tickets for *Pygmalion*. Walked back through the Park. Sara kept awake *all* evening, so Alex spent it alone, while I spent it with Sara. Mum came home from London normal time. Went to bed very late.

Friday 9th June
Walked up the Craig this afternoon. Raining slightly. Talked about Alex's future, and mine too. Alex went at 6.25 p.m., but I'll see him again at the end of the month. He left me feeling slightly disturbed.

Saturday 10th June
Had a letter from Jack Davies asking me to go to London on Tuesday to meet him. Thrilled about the drawing office job. Mum suddenly most agreeable to the idea. By amazing coincidence it was Jack Davies who had introduced Mum to Uncle Harry, so, obviously, anything Jack suggests *must* be O.K. Mum and Uncle think that London will now be much safer, as the Germans have enough to do fighting our advancing troops in Normandy. Went to Kahns' where Mr. Bodenheimer taught me. We translated part of the Sidra [weekly portion of the Torah]. Did some Hebrew verb conjugations too.

Monday 12th June
Wrote to Alex today in answer to his letter, which both disturbed and surprised me. He had written:

> "I'm sorry to say that for the first time I left you feeling very small instead of the opposite. Though I feel years older than I felt recently, I still feel very humble and childish before you. Which idea reinforces the dread thought expressed in the old song which Ben and Myer liked so much – 'Darling, Here Lies Love.' The first words of this song are:
>
> The end has come,
> My heart is numb,
> There's only one thing I'm conscious of –
>
> "No, I'm sorry but I cannot rid myself of the feeling that I cannot hold you anymore. You've outgrown me by far, and I can no longer hope to compete with you and for you. Your every action points out to me, that what you do, you do well. How proud I felt when I watched you dealing with Sara after your mother had failed to manage her. And how very small I felt when I realised that you use the same method, with similar effectiveness, on me, to act like a child yourself – to make me happy when I need patting, or to make me happy by establishing a sham superiority over you. I feel it more than ever impossible to rise to the very high standard you demand. It seems we will have to spend many, many, many hours yet, arguing over all that has gone before, sparing no thought, however personal, following every trail however remote. The only medium I can see is far too sweeping for us, and will inevitably cause sorrow and heartbreak. I little realised what our elders had meant by all their warnings and head shakings. When I see you acting and living above the minds and bodies of everyone with whom I have seen you in contact with, then I know that I could never attend the same camp as you. Again your clear-sighted common sense would appear superior to my intellectual myopia, and this fear can overcome the love I bear you – united of course with my childish jealousy."

Hope my "clear-sighted common sense" arguments will persuade him to come!(?) Told him that I shall be in London tomorrow – wired Jack also. Got together my certificates, drawings, and exam results.

Tuesday 13th June

Up at 6 a.m. Caught 6.50 train with Mum. (At last moment had to hunt for Jack's card – so relieved to find it.) Had rather embarrassing journey up with Mum. ("Your make-up isn't on quite right! See that you don't crease your skirt when you sit down! Are you *sure* you're sitting on it properly?" etc. etc. etc.) I felt about two years old by the time we got to London. Last time I was there I was eleven. Took taxi to restaurant and phoned the Welbeck number. Had to phone again at 4 p.m. Meanwhile, looked around the shops. Saw smashing nightdress and costume that I liked but didn't get. Went to Bickenhall Mansions at 4 and met Jack. Mr. Haut, the director of the firm, wasn't there so I have to see him tomorrow morning. Mum went home on 5.55 train. Went back to Jack's for tea and had a good chat with him. Later, went to Louis Chinn's furniture shop, talked about Rosser, his brother, who was born opposite Gran's in Penrhiwceiber. Even though Gran and their mother are sisters-in-law, they always call each other *MRS.* Britz and *MRS.* Chinn. Mrs. Chinn's other sister is called *MRS.* Levinson. Louis took me to his home in Wembley. He has three children, boy seventeen-and-a-half, girls fourteen and eleven. Stayed the night.

Wednesday 14th June

Got up at 9 a.m. and, after breakfast and G'bye's, went to Underground and caught a train to Baker Street. Tried to phone Paddington to find out times of trains, but couldn't get through. Went to see Mr. Haut and had a long chat with him. He

Left to right: Gran's sister (Aunty Ray), Mrs Chinn and Gran

thought I should go to the Barnet Office as a Secretary with the opportunity of going into the drawing office at any time, if I preferred it. He would confirm all the details tomorrow – when I should start, salary etc. Met Jack for lunch, and thanked him for his help. Decided to go to E.N.A. [Ezra Noar Agudati]. Caught bus, changed once for Stamford Hill. Took taxi to 83, Lordship Park and met Jenny Wechsler. Got on very well with Jenny and had a meal there. Surprised and relieved to find "83" is a boarding house and a sort of restaurant, and E.N.A. is really at 85. So I struck lucky! Decided to stay there the first week I'll be in London while I find something better, as I'd prefer to live with a family. (I don't think I shall want to travel every night to Berkhamsted.) Talked together all evening about Aberdare Groups and London activities.

Thursday 15th June

Saw Mr. Haut this morning. He said I could start *next Monday*. Thrilled, I skipped down the outside stairs, walking on air. "I've got the job!" The thought filled my mind – but a few yards further on I really *was* flying through the air! I landed heavily on the pavement, my right arm twisted beneath me. I lay there stunned, ears ringing, and with a mouth full of dust. A postman helped me to my feet and sat me on a low wall. "You all right?" he asked. "Of course," I said – "I just fell." "Your arm – are you sure?" he persisted. "You should go to the hospital." Just then we heard ambulances and fire engines chasing down the road. I looked back

Photograph courtesy of the Imperial War Museum, London

– wordlessly I noticed the destroyed buildings – the clouds of dust – and that staircase I had just come down, now like a jutting monument, reaching skywards, leading to nowhere. "What was it?" I asked.

There had been no air-raid siren or sound of bombers flying over us. A taxi stopped, unable to pass the débris that had fallen onto the road. I ran over to it. "Can you take me to Paddington?" I asked the driver. He nodded, and half an hour later I stood in the Ladies' Waiting Room at Paddington. I looked a mess; covered with dust; my right arm throbbed badly and both knees smarting. With my left arm I felt beneath my torn skirt. There were two gaping holes in my new non-run nylons … On the way to the train I bought *Druid's Rest*. Tried to read it most of the way home. Train left at 4 p.m. and I arrived in Aberdare at 11.15. Hand feels terrible. Mum of course shocked at my hand. Me too, as my wrist seems three times as big as usual. Bathed it. Went to bed, but did I sleep? Heard Alex was here Tuesday. Left a letter – the darling.

Friday 16th June

Went up to the doctor's. He thinks I've broken something. Hope, and hope, and hope not! Went to the library and picked *Brain and Ten Fingers* – though I've only five at present! Went up to the hospital and had wrist X-rayed. Have it in a sling! – and a splint! Felt like sobbing on way there and back, to think of my job in London that I wanted to go to next week. Mum rang Jack to tell him I was O.K. (!) and to find out what had happened. Jack said he'd heard the Germans were sending over a new pilot-less bomb. Some more came over today. Took my misery to pics. in afternoon and saw *Appointment in Berlin*. I was interested for the short time that I was able to forget the pain in my arm. Phoned Alex at 5.30. Felt terribly shaken and nervy before I rang up, but when I heard his voice and told him the black news, I felt so much better. He said he *knew* and *felt* that something had happened!

Saturday 17th June

Had result of X-ray today. Yes it *is* broken! This evening typed one-finger letter to Alex. Took hours. Wrote also with left hand. (Even tried writing with the toes on my right foot – not bad either!) Read *Escape from Berlin* by Catharine Klein and a 'William' book.

Sunday 18th June

Went up doc's and had plaster put on arm. Feels one hundred times better with it, although a bit strange and rather heavy. Mum's eyes lit up when she saw the plaster: "How long?" she asked.

"Six weeks!" I groaned.

"FATE!" Mum said. "You weren't MEANT to go and get yourself killed in London!"

What can I say? Uncle and Mum have been to London hundreds of times since the beginning of the war, without a scratch. I go *once* and …

Monday 19th June

Read Noël Coward's plays most of the day. Wrote to Bernard to tell him the news. In the Kibbutz he is known by his Hebrew name "Dov". (My Hebrew name is Shaina, but it doesn't feel like me.) Dressing, undressing, combing hair, call for acrobatics!

Wednesday 21st June

Can use hand a little. Letter from Bernard. He wrote from the Kibbutz in Basildon: "The raids in London are getting worse every day. Today, it was supposed to have been terrible. All day long. Hundreds killed."

Listened to news – the pilot-less bombs are reaching London day and night. Started selling tickets for *Pygmalion*. Sold 25! (Out of 300!!!)

Friday 23rd June

Letter from Mr. Haut: they have found new premises: everyone O.K. except for minor injuries. Do I still want the job? Sold almost 50 tickets. Saw Ivor Williams – Treasurer for the Red Cross, and told him the bad news [re: the poor ticket sales], but he'd expected as much.

Saturday 24th June

Dov (Bernard) was home today. Talked all afternoon, about wrist, job, and London. He advised me not to go till the raids stopped. I *would* be mad! Told me all about Kibbutz. The owners of the farmhouse are moving there from London, so the members will have to sleep on the top floor.

Sunday 25th June

Youth Meeting. Went for a ramble up the Craig. Lottie Lehman from London was there. Told us all about London Ezra. Had an argument with Leslie Nevies about instituting Torah in Palestine. He thinks it'll be easy! Ha! Ha! – still, it isn't really very funny.

Monday 26th June

Tickets, Tickets, Tickets!!! No thanks! Can't go! Too dear! Blast! I'm fed up!

Tuesday 27th June

More tickets; more blast! New furniture came today. L.O.U.S.Y. Uncle impossible! Is doing everything over twice – because he won't listen to us the first time. Correction – the furniture is not new but Edwardian. Uncle has bought a complete house-full of second-hand furniture.

Wednesday 28th June
Furniture half in. WHAT AY MESS THEE PLACE HIS HIN! It's unbelievable! In my bedroom X marks the spot.

Thursday 29th June
This is wonderful. Mess. Mess. Mess – and Alex walks in! – and I walk out (but with him). Went to see Mrs. Davies about the tickets. Had a not-so-nice chat. She doesn't seem to care if the play is a flop. Pouring! Got soaked, but didn't care – "What do I care whenever rain falls – I've got my lurve to …" Alex told me about last week's performance in Ystradgynlais – small audience, but well received. He was concerned about my wrist – also Sara's constant requests for me to do everything for her. Uncle went to London this morning – as Alex remarked – to personally control the new counter-measures that are being used against the "glider" or "robot" bombs. Unfortunately there is no way to stop them. Alex went back on the 6.25 bus. Worked solidly till 12 to get straight.

A.R.P—Patrons will be notified from the stage if an air raid warning has been sounded during the performance. If you wish to leave for home or official Air Raid Shelter, you are at liberty to do so. All we ask is that you will depart quietly and without excitement.

There will be a five minute interval between Acts

PROCEEDS TO THE RED CROSS
PENNY-A-WEEK FUND.

Will YOU Give an EXTRA PENNY Each Week ?

Programme note to wartime theatre audience

Friday 30th June
Went to Pen'ceiber for a bath. Met Alex at 1 p.m.; hurried to Coliseum and met others in the cast; went hunting for speaker; came back with John and a few others, gave them tea – then took them to the bus stop. Came home to find Alex (who'd gone to Cwmdare for a pick-up truck) placidly eating tea at 6 p.m!! Show goes on at 6.30!! He caught 6.10 bus, Berta and I walked. Poor audience, but the play was tops! Showed the boys where I'd arranged digs for them. Alex had supper with us and about 11 we went to bed.

Saturday 1st July – Shabbos
Got up about 9.45. Went to shul with Alex 10.30. I was the only girl there. Rained all day. Stayed upstairs and read *Quiet Wedding* by Esther McCracken with Alex. Awfully good. Went with Alex to Coliseum at 6. I came back to put Sara to bed. She kept on talking. I lay in spare bedroom and dozed for half an hour. Just got downstairs at 9, when Alex came. Gave him and myself supper. Mum and Uncle came in later at 10.30. They had gone to pics. after the play. We went to bed about 11 p.m!

Sunday 2nd July
Got up at 10 a.m. and cleaned out scullery. It needed it too. Alex went to Coliseum at 11 to clear up props; came back 1.30 p.m. We had lunch, then stayed upstairs reading. I did a drawing of Alex, which seemed quite like him. Like him? – Yes, I like him immensely. Family came to visit, but we didn't go down until supper. (Fooled around with our hair in the evening and had fun.) Went to bed 10.30; awfully sleepy.

Monday 3rd July
Got up at 9 a.m. Alex cleaned his suit and packed. Walked around town until lunch, then went to Park. Chased by summer flies. Talked about Summer Harvest Camp. Alex not sure his parents will agree to his going there – with me! Took Alex to catch 6.25 p.m. bus. Full. Awfully glad. Went as far as the Lily Pond. It was wonderfully peaceful and lovely. The sun came out. Walked back feeling tremendously happy. Took Alex to station where he presented me with his own pocket Siddur. Pleased as a Cheshire cat. Train went at 7.25, but Alex stayed with me for hours afterwards – in my heart. Went home and began letter to him. Went to bed at 10 p.m.

Tuesday 4th July
Had a good rest last night. Took Sara out all afternoon in the sun. Had an itch under my plaster; the swelling has gone down, so the plaster moves and can be quite uncomfortable; can type well and do most things normally. Finished letter.

Thursday 6th July

Had a letter from Alex today!!! Wrote a letter in reply. All on *Pygmalion* tickets as I felt so happy I *had* to do something crazy; used up thirty of them. Sent them together with his watch, now in working order. Joyce came home; she's now working in Stonehouse, near Stroud, in a factory making gyroscopes for planes. In this factory the workers have every other Saturday free. Joyce explained her objections to working Saturday to the Manager – she offered to work late, lunch-time or any other time except Saturday. He told her he understood and would see what could be done. So far she's had no trouble – so after so many months of struggle it seems she's found the right place. She's staying in digs in Cheltenham.

Saturday 8th July

Had a letter from Bernard asking if I could find homes for some London evacuees. He wrote: "London is dead. Mass evacuation is taking place. Wolf and Anny have gone to Manchester. There is hardly a Minyan [Congregation] left in the Adass. All activities have stopped. Last Sunday it seems to have been terrible; it sent a new wave of evacuees into the country. There seems to be no defence, as one after another of these flying-bombs come through to London."

Heard on the news that all those who have no work in London should leave. Meaningful looks from Mum – she's convinced that G-d (the unacknowledged One) arranged my accident on the first day of this terrible new attack on the capital so that *I* wouldn't be one of the people working in London.

Saturday 15th July

Went to shul. Two of the new evacuees there. We all went to Kahns' for tea. Yesterday Vilna was recaptured by the Russians! It seems that the whole large community of Jews in Vilna has been wiped out! Odd to think that had Grandparents Cohen not fled from there in the 1880s after a pogrom [anti-Jewish riots – in which their parents were killed] and come to live in Wales, I would not be here now.

Sunday 16th July

Youth meeting today. Dr. Katz gave a Sicha [lecture] and I enjoyed it. Hannah, one of the evacuees, was there. She came with me for a walk up the Craig. We went to the *top*. She was thrilled! She'd never seen a sheep so close, or the town looking so small before. She's cockney, which amuses me very much. Came home at 10.30 p.m., and boy – was I hungry!

Wednesday 19th July

Had letter from Alex and *he's going to camp*! Am in 7th Heaven. Will see him tomorrow maybe. Had another letter by 11 a.m. parcel post together with a book of J. B. Priestley's plays. Delighted with both. Rang him at 8 p.m. – excited at seeing him tomorrow.

Thursday 20th July

Went to Cardiff with Mum and Sara. Waited quite some time for Alex at the station. He came at 2.15 p.m. Wandered around town, and finally landed up in Roath Park as always; but it was nice there. Talked about Camp etc. Alex took the tram to Steiners' and I caught the train home. It was packed. Met Dora Schwartz – stood and chatted as far as Abercynon where I changed trains.

Friday 21st July

Went to Cardiff at 11 a.m. Met Alex and went to Rosens' for lunch. Cyril Wyman walked in, which caused Alex much surprise; Cyril too. Went to Roath – stayed until my bus came at 7 p.m. On the way home watched the most wonderful red-gold glory of the sun, setting behind the blue-grey clouds – and thought – how wonderful the splendour of G-d's creation – how much more splendid must He be! And also, how great the gift G-d has given us of imitating His beauties, though our imitations fall to a far lower standard. But what pleasure we get from those imitations if they are really good! It is because we strive to attain that attribute of G-d's, of creating beauty, and are pleased when we almost do so. Should we not then also strive to attain those other attributes of G-d – those of creating peace, love and kindness? G-d has given us the ability of creating beauty – He has shown us the way to Art. He has also shown us how to live, to create life, and to make life worth living; should we not then accept this gift too – for surely, is not the art of living the greatest Art of all? Almost forgot it was *my birthday* today. It's silly but I am supposed to be eighteen – 18, no I don't like the figure at all. Now seventeen was just right. But – horror – think how awful nineteen is going to be – but why worry? I've another year yet till then. At home a beautiful spread of fruit was laid out for me, but I didn't pitch in with enjoyment. During our walk in Roath Park, Alex had told me that he'd kept Shabbos twice doing everything *I* think is important – not smoking; not riding a bus to shul; not cycling, etc. – but those two days he'd been miserable, all the joy had gone out of Shabbos; he'd been irritable and certainly did *not* feel a better person for it. He had tried it out for *me* – he would do anything to make me happy. I told him one can only keep religious observances one believes in oneself, otherwise it's not sincere and I wouldn't want him to make changes in his life just for me. I hope I didn't sound too "preaching". Very concerned about Alex's last remark, "It'll be all right when we're married," – but will it? Went to bed at 11.30 and spent a conscience-stricken night. Finally satisfied myself re. my future, and went to sleep. Must write this on the 21st! An attack on Hitler's *life* was reported today. Unfortunately not a successful one – still it does show some disarray – is the Third Reich starting to crumble?

Monday 24th July
Had *plaster off* today. Hand feels terrible and looks a horrid shape. Tried to write to Alex this evening, but quite unable to.

Tuesday 25th July
Had awful dream just before I woke up. Felt I'd been tossed in the air and was lying on the ground. Couldn't move my legs or *both* my arms. Worse still I couldn't SEE! Awoke very relieved to *see*, and only a slight pain in my disfigured right hand. (Exactly a year ago – last June – I injured my legs and left arm, when my bike skidded into fresh tar.) Mrs. Prosser in to take over the books. She said I should grip and press a rubber ball to get the movement back. Gran said I should wrap the arm and hand in hot wax, which I can buy in the Chemist's. Had a bit of an argument with Mum over Camp: doesn't seem as if I can go August 1st as the new clothing coupons come out then. Had barely washed (fortunately *not* "bare"ly) when Alex walked down to the cellar/kitchen. Stayed upstairs till lunch, then went to Food Office to report lost food points. We've looked everywhere for them and are in urgent need of food tins, dried eggs, pilchards etc. Alex told us our phone number is to be ABERDARE 285 – but we haven't even got it yet! He just knows everything! Even told me where my lost points were! Enjoyed today; he went at 7.30 p.m., but I'm to ring him tomorrow at 6.30 p.m. May go to Porthcawl with him Thursday.

Wednesday 26th July
Can go to Porthcawl tomorrow, so phoned Alex and enjoyed speaking to him as I always do. Queued outside the telephone box in the pouring rain. Poured all day. Grandma not very well, so don't think Berta can go to camp either on 1st August. Spent most of today changing price tickets on the clothes, as Mum intends to have a SALE to coincide with the new coupons. Sent adverts to *Rhondda Leader* and *Aberdare Leader*. Made skirt from striped silk remnant.

Thursday 27th July
Rushed to catch 9.40 a.m. bus to Neath. Waited there for half an hour before Alex came. Rained all morning, but not where we were! Caught bus to Port Talbot, then bus to Porthcawl. Got there at 2.25 and walked to Rest Bay. Found ourselves a nice seat in the rocks, and had lunch/tea there. And was I hungry! Both of us have colds, but the fresh sea air blew mine away. Had quite an unpleasant incident – for me anyway – as I was most embarrassed. [Alex had looked at me and smiled, and for no reason I felt a blush creep over my face for the first time in my life.] Caught 6.25 p.m. back to Neath. (Had a lift from Rest Bay to Porthcawl with two of the "Bohemians" we had seen on the beach – we were quite surprised how different they were from our first impressions, and also with the lift.) At 8 the bus left – and at 9 I was home. Wrote to Alex afterwards.

Friday 28th July
Had phone in today! It stands on a shelf half way up the stairs. Rang up Jenny in London and found out that the Camp doesn't start till 6th August. Not disappointed, as I couldn't go anyway.

Sunday 30th July – Tisha B'Av [Fast of Av]
Fasted very well. Shul until 11 a.m. and then park with Hannah, Dita and Pippa, Dita's little cousin, also new evacuee, Marcus, fifteen-and-a-half – staying in Kahns'. Doesn't talk much – and when he does I can't understand him. Hurt my hand (pushing Sara in the pram), and it feels bad again. Got home at 6 p.m. to find a bike lying on the floor, and the most wonderful person sitting beside it, grinning up at me. I couldn't get in quickly enough, and when I did, it was so wonderful being with Alex – my Alex, once again. Somehow, mainly through Tisha B'Av I expect, we didn't hit it off today – I was fasting, and he, of course, wasn't. I took him as far as Trecynon and hoped he'd get home O.K. (26 miles!) with his two bandaged punctures. Tonight, 10th Av according to the Jewish calendar, is my birthday. After everyone was in bed, and Alex had rung up to say he'd arrived safely, Mum and I had a blow-out over the fast and many other things. Small X. Wrote to Alex to console myself, and got to sleep about 2.

Tuesday 1st August
Coupons came out today, but we weren't so extra busy. It seems everyone has got used to not buying clothes. (Make Do and Mend!) Anyway most of the men are away – the women in uniforms or boiler suits. An old black coat will do for funerals – there are few weddings, though plenty of romances, mostly with the Yanks. Dressed the windows and enjoyed doing them. Went to Pen. in the afternoon and enjoyed my bath. Berta showed me a letter from Manfred.

Wednesday 2nd August
Arranged about Camp. Going there on Sunday. Leslie rang up about the railway transfers [Government-paid tickets]. Jenny had sent them to Porth by mistake. Letter from Alex left me in a troubled mood. He wrote:

> "My picture of an ideal Jew is of a very ordinary man who leads a very normal life and who is quite at peace with the world and with himself. He has a religion quite like that of his fellow men and so is never in trouble with them. Your picture is of a member of a sect; a man with a one-sided education; with an ethereal ideal and with the ability to transport himself out of the toil and troubles of this world, where he finds himself hemmed in and tortured, threatened and imprisoned. A man in fact, who, in order to prepare himself for another world lives the otherworldly life here, and whose cult of self-denial becomes an indulgence. One man practises self-denial in little matters as I do, the other practises self-denial above all else – as I'm afraid you might want to do. And Cynthia, it isn't *you* who *should* do it. I know that you

are going to be upset, perplexed, annoyed and surprised at what I've said, and I may have revealed too much ..."

No, I am not surprised, but hope and pray that when Alex meets a large group of committed young people in Chieveley he will be impressed and that this matter which has divided us will be resolved – in fact I'm *sure* it will be.

Thursday 3rd August
Mrs. Davies and Sheila came from London to stay with us. Mrs. Davies said that more than 6,000 people have been killed or injured by the flying bombs and thousands of homes have been damaged or destroyed! Gran said they can stay with her as long as the raids continue. Told Mrs. Davies about my job with the R. G. Engineering Co. – she said I was lucky to have only a broken wrist. Good news tonight – our troops are moving forward in France; the Americans are slowly recapturing many Pacific Islands and the Japs are retreating in Burma.

Friday 4th August
Had busy day. Did a little packing. At 7.30 p.m. who walks in – Alex. I knew he might come, but wasn't certain. Very pleased. Joyce also back for the weekend.

Saturday (Shabbos) 5th August
Alex wouldn't come to shul today for some obscure reason. Stayed home most of the day. Joyce and I went up to Kahns', just to say "G'bye". Packed after Shabbos.

Sunday 6th August
Caught train at 9.05 a.m. for Reading. Terribly tired. Missed Leslie at Ponty and Cardiff. Got to Reading at 3 p.m. Had to wait four hours (till 7.10) for train to Newbury. Alex and I walked around Reading and ate sandwiches in the Park. Lovely there. Feel wonderfully happy! Last few moments together before being "on best behaviour" in camp (no one there knows we're practically engaged). Discovered Leslie waiting on platform and travelled with him to Newbury. At the station I noticed a very foreign, rather Spanish looking person, and discovered he belonged to the Camp; in fact, he had a lorry there, and the three of us and Rachel and Hannah Pels – twins – got on. We travelled 5 or 6 miles through lovely countryside to Chieveley and got to the Camp just as they were having supper. Introduced to some of the others; met Jenny [Secretary of the London Ezra], then we were allocated our tents. Alex and Leslie were sent to a far field where the boys had their tents. I was allotted Tent No. 1 with Minna Igelfeld and her Ma. First time I've ever slept on the floor in a tent. I don't know anyone here besides Jenny – Alex seems so far away ... Feel very, very, strange.

Monday 7th August
Bank Holiday and therefore no work. Got up early – tidied bed (!) – straw palliasses on the floor. Alex biked to Oxford. I helped peel spuds in the morning and enjoyed it. Most of the people here are refugees from Germany – and speak German nearly all the time. Listened to a talk given by Rabbi Jakobovits. Palled up with Edith Meyer. At 1 p.m. went to try to hitch to Newbury. No luck, but eventually a bus came and I managed to catch a train to Oxford. Met Alex and his friend Gary there. Liked Gary, as I knew I would. Gary took us to his University and Christ Church College. Wonderful buildings. Just plain thrilled. Caught 6 p.m. train back on my own. Felt very tired. Got back to camp at 8. Had supper; Alex came about 10.

Tuesday 8th August
Alex went to work. I didn't, as nothing had been arranged for us. Went to Newbury with Hymina Woolf and Miriam Eisemann. Walked into a hotel there and asked if we could pay to have a bath. Answer: yes, but only one, and of course only the regulation 5 inches of water. We took turns – but had no soap. Went to Post Office and sent telegram to Mum: "Please send soap. Love Cynthia." Did some shopping. Got back for lunch. Food isn't very good, especially the sandwiches – all the boys returned them uneaten in the evening. Alex very, very critical. Conditions here are: one cold tap attached to a hosepipe for over sixty people. Lavatories! – situated in the Chieveley Junior School consist of small buckets (for 5 to 6 year olds) underneath low-lying wooden planks with a hole cut in the middle. Ugh! There is a rota for the boys to empty the buckets every night – no volunteers, obviously.

Alex said: "You should see how the Scouts run their camps – they're fantastic – so well organised. Nothing could be worse than this place!"

I spoke to quite a few people today. They don't seem to be a bit enthusiastic about Ezra – or work. Terribly disappointed. Feel like giving the whole thing up. What an Ezra! The girls are not so bad, but the boys are impossible: they made a dreadful fuss this morning when Alex took out his razor and started shaving – a single KNIFE is not allowed! Even the girls don't seem to want to do anything. There's no feeling of Chaverut [friendship] here at all. Started for bed feeling fed up, after a social given when everyone was dead beat; they sang a few Hebrew songs which would have been nice if there'd been a bit of enthusiasm with them. Alex disagreed with everything today, and I don't feel too happy at all. Talked with one girl, Miriam, who even asked me what the Ezra ideals were! But at least she was genuinely anxious to know more. Suddenly, like a clean breath of air in a hot house, I saw Bernard standing in the field; I left Miriam and went over to him quickly. Told him – poured out to him – all I thought about the people here. Worked myself up and let out all that had stirred inside me since I came. Bernard spoke to Felix, one of the leaders, and I let Felix know how I felt – quite disgusted with everything. Bernard said that I should not give up an ideal because the

Reproduced courtesy of the Imperial War Museum, London

War-time Government poster calling for volunteers

society does not live up to it. He pointed out that most of the people here are refugees from Nazi Germany who have lost their homes, possessions, schooling and many of them also parents or close relatives. They, like Berta, have not much to be enthusiastic about – even keeping the traditions and rituals of orthodoxy is a great achievement, coming from such a background. Many people would have completely lost their faith under similar circumstances. I agreed. At least *he* stood for what I call Ezra and real faith, though he seemed to stand out too much, compared to the others.

Bernard told me he had worked for a week to set up the tents together with his *Italian* prisoners of war. The Spanish-looking person who had driven the lorry was Italian. "Imagine me, a so-called enemy alien being put in charge of war prisoners! They helped me to erect the whole camp," Bernard said with some amazement. "Of course, knowing what it's like to be locked up myself, I give them a lot of freedom, only locking them up at night."

After he left I mentioned him to some of the others. Most did not know him – after all he's done! I described him in glowing colours, and told them about the Kibbutz he had set up, and all the groups in Wales. Felt very upset at supper – feeling so very alone. Miriam asked if Bernard was my boyfriend. I told her he's been a friend for some years, but platonic only. Went out on a bike ride with Alex. First time since my accident last year. Felt awfully shaky. Rode as far as the phone box and a bit further.

Wednesday 9th August

Got up early. Lorry called for us at 9.30 a.m. Alex went to a farm on his own. Fifteen to twenty of us went out singing enthusiastically. Grand feeling – though a wee bit scared after hearing about the "terrible" work. *Very* hot day. Had to do weeding – awful for hands, but enjoyable in company. Spoke to a lot of people. Finished all our work by 12.45 p.m.; washed hands in stream. Had lunch, then lay in the sun by canal bridge. Lovely. Spoke to Edith about Judaism, then started arguing with Moshe, to which everyone joined in; got quite heated and was enjoyed by all. At least they spoke their views and thoughts. Only wish that the proper person had been there to lead them to the right conclusion. Dov (Bernard), for instance, could have made something out of it. Spoke to Hymina about Socialism. Lorry came at 6, and we went home singing and feeling very tired, but happy. Evening Shiur [lecture] by Immanuel Jakobovits on 'Reward and Punishment'. Spoke to Alex in the evening and disagreed – or rather agreed to disagree. He was horrid to me and more or less left me in the cold! Because of his Liberal attitude he has been cold-shouldered by the others, and no one has bothered to try to influence him, as I had hoped they would. Saw Bernard on the way back and once more poured out my troubles to him. Now I have the chance, shall I make the final break or not? He told me to decide myself, and I suppose there's only one answer, "Yes, it must finish." Feel terrible. Went to bed in pieces and didn't sleep.

Thursday 10th August

Hardly looked at Alex this morning. Didn't dare. Went to the farm with eight others stooking (we were taught how to hold the sheaves, one under each arm, and push them together with force against our partner's sheaves so that they stood upright in the field to dry – hard and thirsty work). Didn't like it in the morning – had terrible headache. Enjoyed the afternoon as the sun came out and we did oats. Worked together with Betty Emanuel; argued with Moshe because he wouldn't work; he just lay down and went to sleep! Enjoyed the work. Finished at 5 p.m. Suddenly feel terrible. Temperature and what a headache! Went to bed at 9, but got up at 10 to see Alex so he wouldn't think I was ignoring him. Made me go for a walk, but felt I could drop at any moment. Wasn't any use talking as my mind is made up. How I got to bed I don't know. Head terrible. Met Toni in my tent.

Friday 11th August
Got up late. Feel a bit better. Helped in kitchen, then went with Toni to Newbury. Bought sunglasses. SARA'S BIRTHDAY. Sent a wire. Had bath in hotel. Feel grand after wash and change to Shabbos clothes. Hitched back to camp. People from the Kibbutz here too, also many other new people. Service, then supper. In between courses we sang Zemirot [Sabbath songs] which, although I didn't know many, I really enjoyed. Then followed a long talk by Rabbi Jakobovits. We were all so tired that most people fell asleep. I almost did. After that a few songs were sung and we went to bed.

Shabbos 12th August
Spent a really enjoyable Shabbos! Got up late and heard end of service. Had lunch, then sat for a time in the sun with Malka Igelfeld. I've made quite a few friends, contrary to Alex's experience this week. Went for a walk with Alex, but conversation very flat. Went to Sam Brazil's Shiur on week's Sidra – also to Jack Katz's. They were very different, but both interesting. Talked to Bernard the rest of the afternoon about Aberdare activities. Alex and Leslie joined us, also a boy from the Kibbutz. Had a nice "tea" on our own. Had supper and then a Shiur by Rabbi Jakobovits on 'Position of Women in Jewish Life'. At question time people's views astonished me! As always I had a few questions to put to Rabbi Jakobovits. Service and Havdallah [lighting of candle at the end of the Sabbath]. Then we sang and poems were read out about the camp. Some quite good. Gaby "gabbled" away as usual. Was quite enjoyable. Heard lots of mysterious comments about the Kibbutz, and remembered Bernard's statement that "Things are even worse there!" Except for Bernard no one knows anything about agriculture. Feel rather miserable about it. Boys made fools of themselves in the night by pouring water into our tents – but mine, like the Land of Goshen – was saved. Either because of Mrs. Igelfeld, our cook – or luck!

Sunday 13th August
Got up late. More than half the camp is ill with stomach upsets – either from the food, water or "toilet" facilities. After lunch went for a ride with Edith and Alex to Boxford four miles away. Prettiest village I've ever seen. All thatched cottages – lovely! Wished Joyce could have seen it. Enjoyed the *ride* too and felt quite at home on the bike after one great scare at the first hill I went down. Got back late and had some sandwiches. Went for a walk with Alex. He said he also has stomach cramps and is going home tomorrow. Our conversation was very restrained. For a while we could hear the sound of singing coming from the camp and then only the sound of our footsteps on the country lane. Alex suggested he would leave college

and find a job. Then in a few months we could be married. Within marriage I would "get over" this religious phase, and be content to live and love in "this world". I told him that my decision to part was irrevocable. I *did* want to live an Orthodox life and my husband would have to have a similar aim. He had tried to change for my sake, but his heart wasn't in it and he was happy the way he was. I didn't want to bring up children in a home of conflicting ideas. When I marry I want "both horses to pull the cart in the same direction" so my children would have a life of love and security, all the things I never had.

I said, "This really is Goodbye!" And as I said it all life seemed to drain out of me – I had no idea I would feel like this! I ceased to feel, and even the noise of a large lorry rumbling along the narrow road at some speed didn't penetrate my head. I just walked on in the middle of the dark road.

Suddenly I felt Alex pull me sharply into the hedge – the edge of the lorry glanced against my skirt. "A fine way to start your new life," Alex said shakily, "by getting yourself killed!" We walked silently back, returning to our respective tents. I never thought the price of principles would be so high! Will I ever lose the habit of thinking of Alex every minute of the day? Will the closeness of the last few months fade in my memory? I think not. I didn't sleep – only the sound of an owl hooting, and the sarcastic crowing of an early morning cock, mocked me. I should feel happy – was it only ONE WEEK since we walked with such joy in Reading Park? What I *do* feel is a large hollow inside me. I look the same, I got up, dressed, but it's just a shell.

Monday 14th August

Went to work at 9.30 a.m. after saying goodbye to Alex. Many of last week's campers have gone and new ones have come in their place. We did weeding all day, Clara Jeidel, Edith, Judith and Moshe. Of course Moshe didn't work! Work very tiring, but enjoyed it nevertheless as it dulled my thoughts. Got back, feeling rather strange to find Alex gone. Slightly relieved, no 10 p.m. walk and discussions. Washed – and did I need it. Mum's parcel arrived this morning with soap and biscuits. Biscuits tasted of soap but ate them gratefully.

Tuesday 15th – Friday 18th August

Unable to write much; days pass in a blur. Worked hard stooking.

Saturday 19th August

Rabbi Dr. Munk came for the weekend. Heard a very good Shiur from him on '6 Days of Creation or Maybe 100 Million?' He explained that during the first days of the Creation of the World, as described in the Bible, when there was no sun or moon, a day cannot be considered like a "day" in "our time" – as we count a day by the rising and setting of the sun and moon. When the earth brought forth animals etc. they could have evolved as science describes – there is no

Rabbi Dr. E. Munk surrounded by members of the Ezra Harvest Camp

contradiction – because G-d said: “Let the earth bring forth”, and it did. Even the dating of the earth from the time of creation must take into account the Flood. The weight of water, its heat and cooling, could have seemingly “aged” the earth, making the scientific process of dating incorrect. Of course he developed the theme more than the above, quoting sources. A lively debate followed. In the afternoon I went to him to ask a few She’eillahs [questions] on various points of ritual observance which I was unsure of. To my amazement he said he’d prefer not to give me any answers. “Why not?” I asked, puzzled. He replied: “If you do something wrong now, it’s due to ignorance, but if I tell you something you do is wrong – and you continue to do it – then you’ll have laws you choose to keep and those you choose not to, which is not a good way of life.” “What if I tell you I shall keep the dinim?” I assured him. “Well, what do you want to know?” he asked, smiling. We talked, and a lot of small points were cleared up.

Sunday 20th August

This morning a photographer came to take a group picture of everyone. Very sunny day. Met Judith Fisch carrying a large bowl of ripe plums. I asked her if she’d like to have cream with them. “Cream!” she cried, “I haven’t tasted cream since before the war. Where will you get it from?” I walked over to the milk churn and scooped out a few spoons of cream from the top. It was the most delicious “meal” we’d had in camp. At 4 p.m. Shifra, Gerdi and Miriam asked if they could hitch to the Kibbutz in Pangbourne. They were told they had to go two together [for safety], so they asked me to make up a second pair. I didn't want to go, as I wasn't anxious to see Bernard there. Last night he'd popped in to the camp and I had a feeling that his interest in me was a little more than usual. I didn't want to get my fingers burned (playing with fire). At last I gave in, and we hitched the eleven miles to Nachlat Zvi. There were two girls both named Ruth there. Bernard said: "All good things are three," and named the cow Ruth as well! Bernard was quite surprised to see me there. I showed Ruth Wolf how to make toast from the stale bread by holding it in front of the fire on a wire prong. After supper Bernard spread some hay on the floor of one of the rooms – and with a blanket on the top, that was our bed.

Monday 21st August

We all woke early (doubt if we slept much), and got up in time to see Bernard taking a huge Shire horse out of its stable. The nearby fields were still misty with early morning dew – it seemed almost foggy. Gerdi and Shifra asked for a ride, and Bernard easily lifted them onto the horse and took each one slowly around the field. Then Miriam had a turn. Bernard turned to me and said, "You next." I refused – but he just smiled and lifted me onto the horse. It seemed very high, but luckily I'm not scared of heights. Bernard walked the horse sedately to the far side of the field. Just when I was feeling relaxed he suddenly pulled the horse's reins and started to run; the horse cantered faster – and faster. "Stop!" I cried; he went faster still. "Say you'll marry me," he called out, "then I'll slow down." Swaying from side to side, grasping the horse's mane tightly, "You're killing me!" I shouted. "Well! Say yes!" Bernard called up to me. "I'll think about it," I gasped, "that's a promise!" Bernard nodded and brought the horse to a trot, and then slowly we returned to where my friends were waiting. No one had seen anything untoward, and we all went in to breakfast. I felt furious, partly with myself for coming – but at least I *felt* something for the first time since Alex left. We managed to stay together for the journey back, as an army lorry stopped for us, and we all got into the back. I was quiet, thinking about the last time Bernard asked me to marry him, I was fifteen-and-a-half! I thought he had forgotten all about it, but it seems he was just waiting – anyway, he'll get the same answer.

Sunday 27th August

Returned to Aberdare, travelled as far as Ponty with Leslie. Sara awfully strange at first, hid behind a chair, but afterwards wouldn't leave my side all day. How she's grown!

Friday 1st September

Radio bulletins all day reporting our great advance through France towards Germany! Paris was liberated last week and General de Gaulle has already been there amidst wild rejoicing.

Sunday 3rd September – **Five years since the beginning of the war!** National Day of Prayer. Service in shul at 11 a.m. Very moving. After lunch, Mum, Uncle and Sara went to see Gran. I'm alone above the shop – everything dead quiet – no cinema noise or dance hall or radio blaring. Time to catch up – and think. The last two weeks of camp I made many good friends: Judith Fisch, Annette Broza, Clara Jeidel and her sister, Rachel Pels, Celia and Miriam – of the boys, Nathan Vogel, Nathan M., Avrom Yankel Katz, Felix Wolkenfeld, Manno Feldman – all extremely nice people and very knowledgeable. I enjoyed meeting Rabbi Dr. Munk, who, besides being a Rabbi, has a Doctorate in English Poetry. Two couples who seem to be heading for romance – Celia and Danko, Judith and Felix. Still think my decision to break with Alex is the right one. Last Thursday, a very hot day, worked digging out potatoes all day. Backbreaking work. Bernard called in after supper, I deliberately stayed with Annette, so all he could say was: "Don't forget your promise!" Well, it's bad timing for him, as I can't turn love OFF–ON like a switch – at the moment I've got a major fuse! The habit of "Alex thinking" still continues, and I feel quite drained. I wonder if he's told his parents? At least his mother will be overjoyed at the news.

Tuesday 5th September
Letter came today from the Ministry of National Service with a form to fill in so that an interview can be arranged for me, as I'm now eligible for war work. I have a choice of factory, forces or farm. To go to a war factory or the forces would put me in the same difficult position (with Shabbos, etc.) as Joyce, so I have two possibilities. Work on Aunty Mary's farm in Swansea – this is now not an option with Alex only half an hour away. Go to the Kibbutz in Basildon. This would solve all religious difficulties – but Bernard would also be there – and Mum would have a fit, besides being awkward for me. Joyce thinks that I would be exempt if I took a teacher's course; she's finding out more from Cheltenham College of Art. Don't know if they'll accept me, as I've never had any Art lessons. Imagine, Joyce and I could rent a small place together! Spoke to Mum – she said she'd give £2 a week to help with our rent! No reply yet from Alex to my letter of 29th August. Dita called in this evening. She has agreed to take over my position as Secretary of the South Wales Branch of Ezra Noar Agudati. Typed and sent out invitation to Sunday's meeting – Leslie will give a talk on the Yomim Noraim.

Wednesday 13th September
Letter came from Alex with instructions: "For Heaven's Sake preserve this letter. I may want to refer to it one day."

Took the letter to the Lily Pond where I could re-read the nine pages quietly without interruptions. Alex wrote:

"Since arriving home I have been utterly miserable. The first ten days I was ill with colic. From various obvious signs the doctor was able to deduce that my illness was due to irregular and unusual meals, so I put it down to the wurst and sardines – I'm thinking of suing the E.N.A. for ptomaine poisoning. However during that painful period I was able to settle my mind on quite a few matters and decided that I was very glad to have escaped being seduced and misled by a gang of rampant fanatics. That was followed by sympathy for you, that the girl I (had) loved so much and esteemed so greatly should have wandered so pitifully from her proper path. This mood was followed by a wave of agnosticism – and at present I feel entirely antagonistic to all religious feeling. You, poor errant, say in your letter 'I have found something to live for', in fact you believe in living for death; how utterly hopeless is your desire for a husband who would 'help you live your ideal' (unnamed and untranslatable into terms of this life). This hardly helped to smother the ghastly flame of jealousy burning in me. I am on and of this earth, whereas you are becoming too otherworldly for me to handle. My life is carried on in terms of Austin Sevens and good food; your life *should* be carried on in terms of your latest design and whether you'll be able to pop over to Paris for the weekend. I never thought when I promised I'd go through fire and water for you that that would mean passing you in Heaven on *my* way to Hell. You see, I can live a reasonably *good* life; but what I mean by a *good* life does not coincide with a life of Torah. I have tried to argue you out of your 'madness' but that only tends to make you magnanimous – like your friend Bernard, you think to yourself 'Poor fellow! His ignorance needs to be rectified.' Fanaticism is a horrible thing; in a woman it's terrible; in a girl it's unforgivable. Where has all your clear-sighted common sense gone? So you see, Cynthia, my illusions are gone; I have only one thing left, a hope that one day I will find you again, and that you too will find yourself. That small glimpse I had of one life for two has left a very deep impression on me and I still want to give all I have for you. If only I had held the reins when you started charging along the path of religion and crashed off into the broad high road of adolescent fanatical idealism. I shall try and come to Aberdare the day after Yom Kippur, when you can refute my arguments face to face. Meanwhile – there's no love like an old love ... I have seen *This Happy Breed*. You are in this story of ordinary life – twice. And I'm in there once. I win you in the end, so you see I still have hope."

I sat for a while in "my" secluded "Lily Pond" and thought of Dr. Katz's ideas on the different perceptions of reality. I could see the rusty, weed clogged, abandoned factory(?), now open to the skies and filled with rusting pieces of machinery, or I could focus on the water-filled rectangular iron tank, crammed full with glorious water lilies, yellow and pinky-white, and watch the dragonflies drinking from their nectar – it's all a question of what one focuses on. Alex and I had both gone to the same camp, but where he saw "fanatics" I saw ordinary people convinced that Torah was the basis of their life; people who encouraged questions, as long as they were genuine and a real search for truth. In fact, I had expected *more* idealism, but had found a balanced normality; certainly not a religion based on preparation for Death – but one that enriched *this* Life. Bernard once compared life to a shaky wooden bridge over a ravine that has strong handrails either side. The handrails represent Torah, which is always there to cling to when difficulties arise and to guide us on our way. Alex's religion is one of convenience – if it suits him, he keeps it – if not, it's not relevant to his way of life. This last year our love has become deeper and more passionate, but we have taken different paths, and I *need* the handrail of Torah. I realise that pure love has its pitfalls – I can't afford to make the same mistakes that have occurred in my family – a past that has affected both Joyce and myself. A cool autumn breeze lifted the golden and brown leaves. I walked away sadly, with a feeling that I would never go there again.

Friday 15th September
Very busy today. Peggy came in – and *was* I glad to see her. Went back with her to 'Ceiber. We talked non-stop. She's enjoying studying at Aberystwyth University; I told her about Summer Camp and the outcome. I knew she'd understand, as her family are very devout Christians – they go to chapel three times on Sunday – and no one considers them "fanatics"! Called in at Gran's for a bath, but the coal had run out and the water was cold. Gran wasn't bothered, as she prefers to wash in cold water. She said I looked washed-out and gave me cabbage water to drink. She also gave me a piece of fresh yeast to eat, but I couldn't. Gave me a lovely Challah [plaited bread] and some eggs to take home for Mum. Bernard phoned to say he's home for Yom Tov (New Year). Joyce also came – she invited Mrs. Rose, her landlady, who is coming on Sunday. Bernard said the Germans are dropping a new type of rocket-bomb on London, worse than the doodlebugs, silent and capable of much more destruction. Uncle is very concerned, as his sisters refuse to leave.

Shabbos 16th September
Shul, then went to tea at Kahns'. Talked with Bernard about the Kibbutz. Quite a few members (doodlebug refugees), have joined. Went home for supper, then walked up to Adolf and Ellen's for Havdallah. Walked down from Llwydcoed with Bernard. He dropped many gentle hints regarding "our" future. Remembered last time we walked down. That was three years ago when I was only fifteen-and-a-half and he had so rudely walked off – annoyed that he'd fallen in love with me! Met Joyce in Kahns' and got home at almost 11.15 p.m.

Sunday 17th September
Extremely busy. Two evacuees came, Marie and Helena. Had quite a job fixing them up with homes. Bernard rang up and offered to give me some help. He went to see Cohen's "Aberaman". As he entered their shop he was quite shocked to be greeted by a very loud voice shouting at him: "Bl—dy Fu—er, Bl—dy Fu—er!" Seeing no one there, he was astonished to find the voice coming from a large

parrot. "That's nothing!" I laughed, "that parrot has a most colourful vocabulary." Took the two girls to Schwartz's and Curitz's. Grandma, Berta, Jean and Maurice came up. Slept in one bed with Joyce and Jean. Did I say sleep? Jean's a handful, and then some!

Monday 18th September
Rosh Hashanah. Feel pretty rotten today, went to shul in the morning. Meeting of children's group at 4 p.m. – had a good gathering. Met Bernard at 9.30 with Joyce and Berta; walked up the Craig. LIGHTS were put on. BLACKOUT GONE! We looked down at the sparkling town in amazement and wonder. My mood lifted – though I had too much to think about to feel happy. All the way home lights were streaming out of open doorways; people busy chatting and pulling down blackout curtains. A strong smell of dust filled the air – and the slap, slap of death to spiders as they emerged from their five years' hideout. Moira's parents had opened their fish and chip shop and were giving out free chips to a queue of pyjama-clad children. It was strange to *see* the pavement without the help of the moon. At home neat piles of blackout material covered the counter – Uncle, with his capable upholsterer's hands had stripped every window in the shop and was almost finished upstairs. Went to bed feeling sick, can't think why.

Tuesday 19th September – second day of Jewish New Year
Shul in morning. Went to Kahns' for tea. Hannah there. After she'd gone Bernard became very blunt – and there's no mistaking what he wants (an answer to his proposal of August), but I don't feel like giving it to him for many reasons. He's been offered a job as Madrich [leader] of a children's transport going from Portugal to Eretz Yisrael [the Land of Israel]. Said the decision rests on me whether he takes up the offer. Went as far as shul with him and said G'bye. Alex rang up in the evening to say he wants to come to see me tomorrow. Took Joyce to station. Met Jean Lodwick there. She's M.A.C.S. secretary!! Jean of all people! And going out with the headmaster's son! Didn't sleep much and feel awful. Too much to think about. I have to block out "romantic love" and come to grips with what really happened in camp in Chieveley. (Both Alex and Bernard):

Justification No 1 – **Alex**
He was hateful to Minna.
He was hateful to Felix.
He was hateful to everyone.
He was *hateful* to me.
He was hateful to *me*!
He complained about the food – which *was* bad.
He complained about the spirit, which was also bad.
He complained about the organisation, which was also bad.

He complained about the tents, which were O.K.
He complained about the lavatories, which were terrible.
He complained about me.
He spoke civilly only to people outside the camp (Gary etc.) with the exception of Monty because Monty is English-born.
He rejected all the ritual of Yiddishkeit in spirit, if not in action.
He tried to make everyone feel uncomfortable, and he made me feel I didn't care what he felt like or what he did.
He made me feel ashamed of him.
He made me feel uncomfortable with the others in the camp, as they were unaware of our relationship.
He made it difficult for me to speak to him, and when I did, he didn't seem to understand – or want to.
His face was in a perpetual frown as he let drop the mask of love that had once transformed it.
He made me go out when I felt I could faint with headache and sickness, just to satisfy his peace of mind. He seemed so enormously selfish. All this proved to me that ours was an adolescent (?) and physical love; even now this powerful force within me wants to blind me to the true picture that I had of him in Camp. I must not gloss over these facts, for they were honestly true. It remains that I like him because – he can satisfy my romantic needs; I like his voice; I like his versatility; because he loved me but NOT because he is who he really is. Q.E.D. – I hope desperately! It's written in Exodus that "G-d hardened Pharaoh's heart" not to let the Hebrew slaves depart – now, *I* need help to harden *my* heart when I see Alex tomorrow – I mean today, or else the memory of all the wonderful moments we spent together will soften my resolve. Now it seems only fair to assess my true feelings towards Bernard, as he will not let the matter rest:

Justification No 2 – **Bernard**
He has no sense of humour.
He has a volatile temper.
He dislikes, and is disliked by people who don't live up to his standards.
He is extremely tactless.
I *admire* his capability.
I admire his foresight; his willingness to work unceasingly; his ability to speak well in public, and to influence the youth towards Yiddishkeit.
I admire his self-sacrifice in his efforts to do as much as possible for Judaism and in his service to G-d.
I admire his sincerity; his frequent acts of unusual kindness.
I like him for his ideals, because I like *them*.
I like him for his rare and unexpected tenderness.
I like him for his ability to do what he wants.

I like him because he has done so much for me, taught me so much, and I am grateful to him.

<u>BUT</u>:
I did not mind him going away.
I did not mind his absence.
I did not feel any attraction towards him, or any need for him. But now that he does, if I do, it will be only because I miss the satisfactions of No 1 physically; or feel lonely mentally, or am talked into it by him.

To sum it up: Love is made up of two things – (1) Sexual attraction (2) Respect. (1) is impossible because of faults; (2) doubtful – same reason. He brings out the serious me – the sarcastic me – the servant of G-d me, but *not* the happy silly me whom I like. If I knew it to be G-d's will to marry Bernard then I would say "Yes" and make a success of it, knowing that I could absolutely rely on his constancy as a husband, and his role as a father, and a pivot of Jewish family life. I shall show Bernard this, so that he knows where he stands.

Wednesday 20th September

Slept late; can't imagine why I feel so ill; head terrible – chilly etc. Rang Alex not to come, but he arrived at 11.30 a.m. We stayed upstairs until lunch. Alex looked pale and upset – and I suppose I did too. I told him that ours was an *all* or *nothing* situation, – "all" meaning two partners joined in marriage soon – for how long could we hold out? Alex had always said we fell in love too young, and, at not quite 19, he wasn't ready for marriage – therefore it has to be "nothing" – however much that hurts. Didn't eat lunch as it was a fast (Fast of Gedaliah), and anyway we both had no appetite. Took Alex to the station at 2 p.m., and waited until the train had left. A strong feeling hit me that I would never see Alex again – and I admit my eyes were wet – a typical "train station G'bye" only no music to accompany "Le Dénouement". After dinner Mum and Uncle had a terrible row. It seemed like a film – I just watched calmly, as it didn't seem real. Never ever seen a temper to equal Uncle's. Went to bed and stayed there. Got a temperature.

Thursday 21st September

Got up about 11 a.m., but couldn't do a thing. Wanted to go back to bed, but Mum wouldn't let me, as Uncle was packing his trunk in my bedroom, and she wanted him to go away first. Doc came and ordered me straight to bed. Shocked that I was up. Uncle picked up his heavy case and almost threw it into the back stock room. Perspired all night and didn't sleep. It's years since I've felt so ill. It's influenza and fever. Phew! The things I've had this year. It's really too bad!

Friday 22nd September
Nothing to eat since Tuesday. Feel unreal – horrible. Nearly fainted in the evening and Mum had to call the doctor at 12.

Shabbos (Saturday) 23rd September
Not much better. If only I could eat! Feel too weak to move a finger, and feel sick when I do. Doc called in this evening and said I could *eat!* Had some soup with breadcrumbs in it, but could hardly chew. Feel like a baby learning to eat! Felt worse after eating and didn't sleep much.

Sunday 24th September
Want to eat, but can't, everything makes me feel sick. Temperature down a little. Was able to read a little Chumash [Bible], but soon got too tired.

Monday 25th September
Read a little from *So Little Time* by John P. Marquand. Uncle *still* here, in spite of everything. Ten-page letter from Alex. Page 8:

> "Cynthia, darling, it's become clear to me these last few days that there is, after all, no hope for me where you are concerned. I simply cannot make myself worthy of you. My love for you is still a consuming flame, and the memories I have of you will always feed that fire. But I'll never be able to share the warmth of this fire with you, having lived in an impossible situation for so many months, there remains for me only the course of refusing to stand in your way, to stand aside and let someone else, someone more deserving than me, enjoy the pleasure of your company, the beauty of your person, and the warmth of your feelings. I want *so* much of you *so* much, I can't hope to pay for my desires."

How can I face the letter-less days ahead? Dozed quite a lot – old memories drifting through my dreams (Alex and I, about twelve, lying on top of the hay in the barn, reading his comics; running down together to the lower pastures, looking for lucky white heather). I awoke to the "unreality" of two wars still in progress; the world war, and our own private war. I could hear the frequent explosions of anger, and the meaningful silences … "Why d'you put up with it?" I asked Mum.

"You wait till *you're* married, then you'll see!" she answered – which leaves me with two ambitions – (1) to get better and (2) to stay SINGLE!

Tuesday 26th September
Gone all yellow! Rather scared it's jaundice. Couldn't eat much. Looked in the mirror – my face, eyes, *all* of me more yellow than a buttercup.

Wednesday 27th September
Yom Kippur. Davened [prayed] most of the day until I was too weak. Dita came in the afternoon, and I made an effort to speak to her – she said Mr. Ginsberger

had been ill – but was better. I was so relieved, as I felt concerned about him. Knowing his weakness (he's 82) and yet his strong emunah [faith] helped me in my resolve to last out. Mum wasn't pleased, of course, about me fasting. Doc came and said I had jaundice (probably caught it in camp) – I mustn't eat any fat at all. Broke fast at 8 p.m., but once again felt ill after eating. Poor tummy, I've treated you badly this week!

Letter from Bernard: "Please answer me, yes or no. If no, it will be no shock to me, otherwise I shall get enthusiastic about it – has Alex been to see you again? Fast well, look after yourself."

Slept very little.

Thursday 28th September

Heard this evening that Bernard's grandfather, Mr. Ginsberger, died last night! Feel really upset – more than over any of my own relatives – for he was my ideal of Judaism characterised – personified. Feel too upset to write more.

Friday 29th September

Wired Dov [Bernard] – couldn't go to the Kibbutz for Succot. Doc came, said I can get up tomorrow.

Shabbos 30th September

Got up for lunch, stayed up about three hours; sat in a chair all the time. Went to bed "wore out". Dita called, said Bernard was home.

Sunday 1st October

Got up today for longer. Bernard rang up and spoke for one hour. Dead beat afterwards, though pleased he rang. Rifka came from Swansea as a messenger from *Mrs.* Winter. She *begs* me to continue my "friendship" with her son. *Now*, after three years of doing everything possible to stop us being together! Rifka says Alex is *very* upset, quite sick in fact. I told Rifka the only good thing about my decision is that I won't have *Mrs.* Winter for a mother-in-law. Really upset about Alex, but I'm pretty sick too! Rifka told Mum why she had come – Mum very shocked that I hadn't said a word to her. Went to bed early.

Tuesday 3rd October – second day of Succot

Would have liked to have gone to shul, but Mum said it was too soon. Bernard called in to see me. Tried to persuade me again, but didn't get very far – or I think he didn't. Not quite sure. Went up to Kahns' at 3 p.m. Dita, Vera and Maurice there. Bernard gave a Shiur on Succot. Was quite good, "because I was there" – Bernard said! Went at 7, the others went to shul, but I was much too tired to go.

Had supper and went to bed. Wrote to Bernard, mostly the ideas from my list of pros and cons. Wonder what he'll make of it?

Thursday 5th October

Letter from Joyce. Great news! The Cheltenham School of Art has accepted me! She showed them my recent drawings – they say I can start immediately. Joyce has already started to look for a flat for us. Got up full of energy, but didn't stay up long.

Shabbos 7th October

The colour of my skin is almost back to its normal "sallow". Mrs. Prosser said she couldn't bear to look at me when I was yellow, as it reminded her of the Japs – and Alan. Poor Mrs. Prosser – the chance of Alan being alive after all this time is very slim. My "diet" is keeping *me* slim, my fat ration is used by Mum and Uncle. Went to Kahns' at 4 p.m. Mr. Bodenheimer gave a Shiur to Maurice and me. Maurice is going to help me edit *Koleinu* [South Wales' *Ezra* monthly magazine]. Hope he takes over when I go to Cheltenham.

Monday 9th October

Letter from Alex written on the 5th:

> "First I will report a recent conversation I had. I was gloomily staring into the fire last week, when my Mother said 'Something's wrong between Cynthia and you, isn't there? – I, of course answered 'No-o-o', and Mum said 'I think you must have treated her very badly in camp, and she, having seen just what your temper is like has decided to have nothing to do with you! – and I'm not surprised either!' This was repeated almost word for word in your letter of the 28th, following our tête-à-tête. I can see the situation is beyond redemption, and believe me, I *am* sorry.
>
> "So, after all, our idyllic love was as normal and usual as the growth of any flower. The bud of love reached the stage when it was due to blossom, but then, when the moment of supreme beauty should have been attained the canker got into it. And the death (the one-sided, death so far) that followed was painful but natural too. Obviously then, artificial respiration will not be enough. We must both await the arrival of a new seed and hope that the new flower will be almost as beauteous as the first – only this time different combinations will have to be tried.
>
> "And so, at last, we come to the final and formal farewell. Please take care of yourself; treasure as something you will never have again the memory of your first devoted admirer; think of me sometimes, and remember the many wonderful years we have had together …"

I could hear Vera Lynn on the radio singing one of "our" songs downstairs: 'Yours': "I'll never love anyone the way I love you …" How can I ever forget? The memories will be with me always and will stay fresh and not dim with time … Sat in the dark next to Sara sleeping peacefully and worried about the effect my leaving will have on her. At least with Sara it won't be a final farewell.

Wednesday 11th October

Amazing letter from Bernard. Long; typed; and *pleased* with my criticisms! He said the remarks I'd made about his faults were correct – he wrote:

> "As far as I can see only one thing can change me and that is You. It is gone 1 a.m., but I have to write to you, as then I might be able to sleep for a change. I have to tell you I was proud of your letter as it showed me that you reason every step of your life and that you look at it in the right way. Still, I hope that in the meantime you have reasoned out to the wretched word YES, but still your letter was a masterpiece. I am glad you know my faults as then you won't be disappointed; I enjoy your frankness, as only that way can we live together. These last few nights one great light burns in me – to have you entirely as my own, and then together we will work for the good of our people. About my language in general – since I was imprisoned in Germany, I had strange ideas and came to dislike humanity as a whole, but with time I noticed that there was one thing in this world which is worth working for – living and teaching Torah, but one thing remained inside me – the dislike for all people that don't know what they live for. Besides, being a workman and a farmer, my language may be rather blunt. After all that I have seen in my childhood – murder, pogrom, Sifrei Torah burnt in public, shul's burning etc. – I have become different from other boys of my age. I can't for instance waste my time playing football, listening to the radio, etc., for I consider it wasted for the cause for which I am living. How, Cynthia, I would like you to make me young again, as, especially lately, I have noticed that I have aged. You could be just plain silly, and I would fall in with you in plain silliness. How I would love to see you laugh. Since I left you last week I was nervous and happy all day knowing that you are after all considering it. How we would be united in the education of our children, how I would look after you and try my best to be a father in the real sense …"

After four more pages written until 6 a.m. and the horse "Cynthia" waiting to be fed, Bernard wished me: "All the best for your future life which is at a decisive point at this moment."

Re-read the letter tonight, but *cannot* come to any decision.

Thursday 12th October

Quiet day. Mum and Uncle went to Cardiff (he's *still* here – because of the flying bombs in London, a truce has been declared at No 11, Cardiff Street). Read all last week's *Echo*. British Commandos have liberated an island called CYTHERA. It's the first of the Greek Islands to be re-captured. Renewed assault on the last German troops in Aachen. The Canadians are clearing Antwerp. A Ponty boy, missing since the fall of Singapore in '42, has sent a message home to say he is alive! On the personal front – re-read Bernard's letter again – no comment except a grin – and a worried frown. Danko is engaged to Celia! Just as I thought!

Shabbos 14th October
Went to shul with Maurice, then to Kahns'. Mrs. Ginsberger was up and seemed better. Rochale had a baby girl today – just heard, and was very pleased about it – though my chances of going to Swansea to see her are rather slim.

Wednesday 18th October
Busy day. Typed *Koleinu* and took it to the printers. Joyce rang up. Told her I was coming to Cheltenham for the weekend to look over the flat she'd found. She said Bernard would be there – but I already "almost" knew. A bit excited. He's to give a talk to the Cheltenham Youth Group.

Thursday 19th October
Did correspondence; got things ready. Collected *Koleinu* from printers in Treforest. Twisted ankle – but I'm *still* going tomorrow. Saw *100 Men and a Girl* with Deanna Durbin. Very enjoyable.

Friday 20th October
Got up to catch the 8.25 a.m. train, but caught the 7.50 instead and arrived in Cheltenham at 12. Quick … I'll say! Went to Mrs. Rose's. Letter from Joyce waiting for me; asked me to meet the train Bernard would be on. Surprised and glad that he's coming today; thought he would come Sunday. Met 2.15 train – but – no Bernard. Wandered around town. Raining. Went to station at 4 to be told there was no train at 4.25 as I'd been informed. Next train 6 o'clock. Very disillusioned; went home saying, "Curse love! It's a disease! Damn it! It isn't worth the worry!" – and so on. Went to shul 5.30 – just in case Bernard would be there, but the shul was closed. Returned to station to meet Joyce on the 6.15. Train came in late at 6.30 *and* Joyce came with BERNARD!! Surprised and excited. Rushed home to Mrs. Rose; had supper then went to Mrs. Galinski's. Pouring!! Left Bernard there. On the way back told Joyce about it all (Bernard's proposal) and she's horrified at the idea! What a day!

Shabbos – sorry – Shabbat 21st October [Modern Hebrew]
Couldn't go to shul this morning, as my shoes were wet (from last night's soaking). Bernard and Joyce came in at 1 a.m. and we had lunch; then to Galinski's at 3 for the meeting; seven people there besides us. Bernard spoke very well, and I felt quite pleased. In the evening, went to station with him to find out times of return trains. Had supper, went with Bernard to phone the Kibbutz to tell them he was catching the midnight train back. Joyce came with us to see him off.

Went to bed gone 2 a.m. – after a long discussion about Bernard. Joyce says Mum would NEVER give permission for me to marry him so I would have to wait 2½ years! Well, I'm not "*in love*" – but in principle I don't see why I have to have Mum's approval.

Sunday 22nd October

Picked up the key to the flat from Mr. Galinski. We shall pay him £2 a week – lucky to get one. It's a ground floor flat with one large bedroom, large living room and a tiny L-shaped kitchen with a bathroom (bath and hot water geyser), partitioned off it. The kitchen has a cooker, small sink, 2ft-square table, two chairs and no space. One can fill the kettle, put it on the gas, make a cup of tea – all without moving from the chair. Some shelving and drawers cover part of the long wall. It is absolutely filthy, and all kinds of crawly insects have made their home in it. Erwin, from the flat upstairs has promised to fumigate it for us.

Monday 23rd October

Caught 10 a.m. train home. No seats, so stood until Cardiff. Feel like I've left America and come back to Wales! There are ten American servicemen to every eight civilians in Cheltenham. Sorted out a few things to send to Cheltenham. Found my only souvenir of Llanelly amongst them, *The Snow Queen* by Hans Christian Andersen, beautifully illustrated by Honor Appleton – my consolation prize for having had my perfectly healthy tonsils removed (Mum was always fashionable!) when I was six. Sara had scrawled all over the illustrations with blue and red crayons. On the back page Linda, who's been looking after her, had written: "When Kay and Gerda grew up they had a baby girl which they called Sara. And Linda loved Sara very much." This makes me feel better about leaving Sara. I hope when *I'm* married Sara can come and live with me. Decided to pack *all* my books to keep them in good condition.

Tuesday 24th – Sunday 29th October

Very busy week; I'm leaving on Sunday. Saw Mostyn on Tuesday. He's been invalided out of the Air Force. His plane was shot up over Germany; he managed to coax it back, but he's got a lot of shrapnel wounds. Seemed a bit withdrawn – hope Ben will come down to cheer him up. Phoned Ben, who said he'd try and get leave. Bernard phoned Wednesday, but I was in 'Ceiber to say G'bye to Gran and Berta. Mum wanted to know why Bernard had phoned. Told her it's probably to do with me becoming a land-girl – which is partly true, as Bernard would like me to join the Kibbutz. Tonight I'm in a strange, sad mood: sad about Mostyn; about leaving Sara; about packing away Alex's three hundred or more letters; about leaving my beloved Welsh hills. I know I'll be back for visits, but I also know I'll never live here again. Goodbye my Wild Lily Pond.

Monday 30th October

CHELTENHAM

My own flat. It's in a filthy condition, but cleaned some of the bedroom. Slept in Mrs. Rose's. College! – Loved it! Did Life Drawing in the morning, drawing from the Antique in the afternoon; drew 'The Discus Thrower'. Made friends with others – young men and women about my age. Tutors absolutely great. The course also consists of Anatomy; Costume Drawing; Oil and Watercolour lessons; Outdoor sketching and Architecture. Stone Carving in the evening is optional.

Tuesday 31st October
Went to buy rations in lunch break. Continued cleaning in evening. Still some itchy creatures (lice?) in the kitchen. Erwin came down and opened the bottom drawers of the kitchen cabinet. They were filled to the top with filthy, blood-stained chicken feathers! The last tenant, a shochet [slaughterer], had stuffed all the feathers into the drawers and left them there. They were crawling! What a job! Burned the lot – disgusting smell – Erwin said he'd fumigate the kitchen again.

Wednesday 1st November
Letter from Bernard. Full of conviction that I am in love with him; but like Kay in the *Snow Queen* I am left with no more feeling than a lump of ice; still and cold as the ice walls. Our flat really is *cold*, as we've got no coal. Bernard wrote he had phoned Aberdare to speak to me, but I was already in Cheltenham. He spoke to Mum – surprised to get his call. Read his four-pages long, interesting letter, full of his plans and hopes.

Thursday 2nd November
Finished bedroom and it looks quite clean at last! Joyce stayed home and cleaned out the bathroom. Max, our American friend, called in to say G'bye. He'll be away with his unit for a few weeks. Made some coffee (his) with tinned milk (also his) – the Americans are not allowed to drink our milk for fear of catching T.B. Offered him some of Gran's biscuits; first visitor in our new flat. Front room looks really nice. Two window seats, an antique desk, antique chaise longue, table and chairs. But COLD, we've still got no coal. Went to Mrs. Rose's to hear the news. She loaned us a small electric fire.

Friday 3rd November
Cleaned and scrubbed and disinfected etc. etc. etc. the kitchen. Started cooking at 2.30 p.m. and got everything done. Had supper (quite nice, but room wasn't very warm), felt quite ill from laughing so much at our discomfort. Went to bed at 9. Strange to light my own Shabbos candles without a husband – but I've nursed a baby without being a mother – so what!

Shabbos 4th November
Got up at 10 a.m. and went to shul. No Chumash there, so had to go without. Very few women: prefer Aberdare. Came home to find electric fire in front room gone out. Still, had dinner, and then, from lack of fuel more than anything else, went to bed for an hour. Wore our coats and gloves; talked, and sang and laughed! Shabbos, Shabbos, Menucha! Went to Cynthia Davies, but she was out. Came home to find parcels arrived. So relieved. Had "bean-feast" on the contents. Said Mincha [afternoon service] and made Havdallah, then made supper for Mrs. Rose, Mrs. Feld and her daughter. They stayed until 10.20 p.m. and then I washed up *all* the dishes; *everything* was dirty. Joyce started distempering the kitchen. Went to bed at 2.

Sunday 5th November
Went out this morning to sketch. Drew a cart-horse – and also drew a crowd of Yanks – "Hi-ya babe? C'm for a cawfee? How about a ride?" Put on a serious, concentrated look – and then a hurried, purposeful stride, back to Evesham Road. I have to learn not to smile and say "G'morning" to everyone as I do in Wales – it's asking for trouble, even of a good-natured kind.

Helped Joyce distemper the kitchen. Did I say "helped"? "Look Joyce, a WALL!" We had a great time drawing on it à la Rubens, Cézanne, Goya. Terrific Mural! After supper we started covering our masterpiece with cream distemper. At 10 p.m. it had dried – and our drawing emerged *through the paint*! We redid it. Again, and again! At 4 a.m. we decided the figures were too faint to be noticed, and finally got to bed.

Monday 6th November

Letter from Bernard asking me: "Cynth, be frank, tell me outright – do you still not feel anything for me? I must have an answer soon, so as to satisfy the restlessness of my mind. I stand before you, asking something of you of which you yourself know that it will be so, earlier or later – so why not let me have the assurance now?"

Five long pages and a lot to think about. Question? Am I just too choosy? First I say no to Alex, and now I'm keeping Bernard on tenterhooks – when I *know* he would make a good husband. I've studied with him every week for 4–5 hours for the last two years. He's taught me that I can choose, not only what I want to do (which is not always possible) but what I want *to be*, changing direction away from the influences of the past and be "my own person". I like the fact that even though he knows my family background and problems, he still wants me, having, as he wrote, worked on myself to attain a higher Madrega [spiritual level]. He said that he, himself, is on a lower step of Kedusha [holiness] than me, having lived a Torah-life since childhood (and not having to fight for it).

Finally wrote to Bernard "Yes", but he should understand that I don't feel "love" at this point – but do hope that this will come later. Went straight out and posted the letter. Told Joyce about it. She said Mum would never agree to it – so I expect I'll have trouble with Uncle and Mum. For once Uncle Harry has been proved right when he said: "There is *no* such thing as a platonic friendship between a young man and woman!"

Wednesday 8th November

Went with Joyce to see *Phantom of the Opera* with Claude Rains. Great film. Wonder if Bernard will accompany me to films, operas, concerts? The newsreel showed MacArthur's advance on the Philippines; the bombing of Tokyo by the Americans – the slow advance of our forces in Italy and Belgium. Besides fighting, there are many mines to defuse everywhere, hidden by the retreating Germans. Our troops (British, Polish and Canadian) have begun to liberate the south of Holland – they have got as far as Breda.

Thursday 9th November

Found Max fast asleep on our couch when I got in from college. Invited him for supper Friday night. He asked if he could bring a friend. He left some food tins, so we should have enough for four. Did some cooking in the evening. Meanwhile read from *The Nineteen Letters of Ben Uziel* by Rabbi S. R. Hirsch. Quote: "We must also read the Torah in Hebrew – that is to say, in accordance with the spirit of that language. It describes but little, but through the rich significance of its verbal roots, it paints in the word a picture of the thing – it presupposes the listening soul, so watchful and attentive, that the deeper sense and profounder meaning, which lie not upon, but below the surface, may be supplied by the independent action of the mind itself."

Typical *long* German sentence – but I like the idea.

Friday 10th November

Came home to find a letter from Bernard. Max came with his friend Arthur, so I hardly had time to read it. Arthur looks about seventeen, much too young to be a soldier, and very sweet. We had a lovely evening. Max made Kiddush for us, then we ate and sang until quite late. Went to bed about 12.

Saturday 11th November

Went to shul in the morning. Spoke to Danny Friedland, an American who's from an Orthodox family. Invited him for next Friday night. Max is going back to his unit tomorrow, so it'll be company for Arthur. Spent some time studying Hebrew verbs – my weakest point – and some vocabulary. Had time to re-read Bernard's letter. Quite amazed! I've known Bernard since I was fifteen, but I don't *know* the loving, happy person who wrote this letter. Bernard wrote:

> "Well, whoever thought when I started teaching you – a hearty Mazel Tov! I hardly trusted my eyes when I received your letter lunch-time today. So I rang up just to make sure whether it was not just a mood, and indeed it was not. Cynthia is mine and I am Cynthia's and together we will struggle in this world. Believe me, nothing shall be too hard for me if I know you feel better with my accomplishment. Cynth, I still can't get it, 'Bernard engaged to Cynthia'. You sure you did not make a mistake? When shall we make it official, and when do we get married? … Thank you ever so much for the lovely picture. I never thought that one needs a picture to keep someone that one loves in mind, but now, since I have it, I can hardly go six hours without looking at it. By a strange coincidence, today a letter came from the Home Office granting me an exit permit – my ship is going on the 29th – so it will go to Eretz without me. The *Koleinu* is a great success of yours, indeed the entire movement can be proud of the South Wales group, as it's the best group in the country … Do be happy that you have said "Yes", and don't be afraid of your mother and all the rest. I shall write again tomorrow."

Thursday 16th November

Cold, damp day – but – our COAL arrived this morning! Made a roaring fire tonight and did *nothing* except sit in front of it – thinking about, and reading, Bernard's letter. Lots of questions in it. When do we tell his parents? Mum and Uncle? His boss has refused permission for him to have time off to come and see me. Asks me to phone Saturday night.

Friday 17th November

Hurried home from college to prepare supper. Joyce had baked a cake. Arthur and

Danny enjoyed being away from the camp and eating with Shabbos candles on the table. Danny taught us some new Shabbos songs. Lovely atmosphere sitting around the warm glowing fire. Phoned Bernard after Shabbos – he was *waiting* by the phone!

Monday 20th November
Stayed on for evening class in stone carving. Wonderful experience, using hammer, chisel and stone. Got covered with white dust – hair, face, clothes – should have brought an overall and headscarf.

Tuesday 21st November
Went to pics. with Joyce. Saw *Now Voyager* with Bette Davis and Paul Henried. Not so good. Talked with Joyce about her friend Paul.

Wednesday 22nd November
Days fly by; the artwork in college needs complete concentration and seems to blot out the whole world; I enjoy everything I do. Joyce and I are getting on better than we ever have – actually beginning to like each other. Miss the news on the radio "becos" we have no radio – however no love songs to remind me of Alex. Shoals (!) of happy smiling GI's remind one there's a war on – but in an unreal way. Letter from Bernard this morning to: "My very own (?) unquestionably dear Cynthia" – three full, typed pages, setting out his views on politics, religion and Zionism. He believes girls should only do certain jobs that remind them of motherhood – (I don't agree!). Asks "Do I want children?" Well, I've no illusions about babies – the "little darlings" mean hard work; broken nights; constant worries and I don't want the responsibility soon – but yes, I would eventually like children of my own. (Seems as if I may have to wait two-and-a-half years, as I doubt Mum will give me permission to marry Bernard.) Bernard wants to announce our official engagement when he's 21 – that is on 25th December! Just four weeks away! Couldn't get to sleep. Too many doubts – also one very private fear: was Mrs. Winter right about my nature? Deep down I *know* that I am a faithful person. From my father I have inherited a passionate spirit and an independent mind – a love of music, writing poetry, my artistic ability – and from Mum a strong romantic love which enables her, now that she has Uncle Harry in her life, to continue to love my father, as I do Alex, even though I have someone new in *my* life – hardly new! Got up at 2 a.m. and wrote to Bernard all my fears and doubts.

Thursday 23rd November
Joyce went home as she had a free day – she'll be back tomorrow. I went to Mrs. Rose to listen to the news. We heard Frank Gillard's war report direct from the front – the awful weather conditions there are holding up our advance – the tanks and jeeps stuck deep in mud. The Russians are almost at the Danube. Churchill

now fears victory may not come before the spring. On a brighter note – the lights in London (Piccadilly etc.) have been put back on. Started cooking for Shabbos; boiled three carrots, two potatoes, to make a pie – kept the carrot/potato water for soup. Dropped in a mixture of dried egg, flour and salt. It looked interesting, but hope it doesn't taste like rubber bands!

Friday 24th November

Really cold day. Joyce came back in the afternoon with a note from Mum to phone her IMMEDIATELY! Asked Joyce if she knew what was wrong? – Is Sara O.K? She said it's about Bernard and me – she had told Mum all about us!!! Well, it had to come out sooner or later – but I *was* cross. Phoned Mum – the wires went hot and crackled, she was so mad. How could I *do* this to her? What would her friends think? It's a slap in the face for the whole family – marrying someone frum [orthodox]. What about Alex? What will we live on, Bernard's only a farm manager – suddenly my doubts of this week disappeared – I told her I'd made up my mind – to which amazingly she replied: "Oh, well – if that's what you want I won't stand in your way." And the phone went dead. Came in to find Max fast asleep on the couch. He looked exhausted and only woke up for Kiddush and supper. He's got two days' leave and came straight here from the fighting in France/Germany. Phoned Bernard after Shabbos.

Wednesday 29th November

Four-page letter from Bernard in answer to my letters and phone call:

> "Your phone call was like a light in the darkness. A small dim hope that came indeed at the last moment. If there had been a possibility for me to go with the ship that sails next week I would have done so. So please write whether you still love me and want to finish our days together for the aims which I have so clearly stated during the last three years. It must be YES as otherwise I am ruined. If you had never said 'Yes' I never would have been happy for the last fortnight. I would not know what I have lost, but every minute I am not clear about us and our future, is a misery. You said you are looking forward to seeing me, and how sure are you, dear, that your mother will let you go. Yes Cynth, your mother has victored once again, for did she not keep you in Aberdare for the last two years against your will? In this way your mother is clever and gets you to agree with her … To carry on with your letter; yes, Yitzchok loved Rebecca, but as soon as he saw her, he took her for a wife. No time lost whatever for quarrels before marriage. I always believed in early marriage, as it is ten times healthier, morally, physically and spiritually. You tell me that your love for me would have to be encouraged, but how can I do so when you are so far away? Yes, I would try to be a good father to my children, especially when I know that you have given birth to them. Hopefully they may be born and reared in the air of Eretz Hakodesh [the Holy Land]. Not only shall they learn of this land and its laws, but experience the peace for which we had to fight so bitterly. I know that you like children, and your love for them will be far greater than the love you will ever be able to show me – so when do we meet and where?"

Thursday 7th December

So cold all the water pipes have frozen, even the geyser in the bathroom. Went to Youth Meeting in the evening to arrange Sunday's Chanucah Party. Joyce decided to leave the oven on, as it backs onto the bathroom partition – hopefully we can have a bath when we return – well, not exactly – Erwin dashed into the meeting to tell us to come home immediately, as the water pipes had burst and flooded the downstairs flat. We rushed back, put off the mains and went downstairs to help clear up the mess. The water had brought the ceiling down. Didn't get to bed until 3 a.m.

Sunday 10th December

Got up at 10 a.m! Cut up meat and made lunch. Joyce helped washing up. Erwin and Jeffrey came, to go with us to the Chanucah Party. Went and enjoyed it; play went off really well. Came home, lit Chanucah lights. Had to wait up for meat to cook, so answered Bernard's letters. He wrote:

> "Funny your mother changed round so quickly that she now gives permission for you to marry me straight away. Yes, even easier than to get your permission. It is hard to accept that she thinks I am the worst person on earth to marry her daughter. I am sure my parents will be overjoyed with you as a daughter. You write about my strong ideals, my seriousness. Have you ever been imprisoned or seen a pogrom? Has your heart ever bled in pain for the suffering of your people? Did you ever for a second realise the terrible disaster in which we and all Jewry are in? Then how can I look on? How can I have pleasure or be materialistic? I told you from the beginning that you would have to give me back my youth, which I have lost these last years. We must meet soon. Yours in eternal love, yet to be saved for the future and our common good."

Letter No 2:

> "There is no need to tell me that the old Cynthia is dead, how else would I have approached you? They are two entirely different persons. Two different worlds which will never go together. A contrast which can best be seen when one compares you with others of your age. Don't imagine that my will power is so very strong, you seem to have much too good an opinion of me. How can one have a strong will power when one sees your two dark eyes shining in happiness?"

Am amazed that "distant", "serious", "idealistic", "controlled" Bernard could have written the rest of this letter!

Thursday 14th December

Went to pics. to see *This Is The Army*, music by Irving Berlin, with Ronald Reagan and Joe Louis. Quite good. Newsreel showed tremendous battle between the American and Japanese fleets. The U.S. used subs. and aircraft carriers – the Japs used suicide bombers to which, like the V-2s, there is no defence. Many ships sunk on both sides. The shocking news of the unbelievable mass slaughter of Jews by the Germans in their concentration camps – possibly millions, has now been confirmed. Bernard has been saying this for years – mostly to deaf ears!

Sunday 17th December
Went out early to do some sketching; drew a farm scene; lovely old cart, thatch roofed barn etc. [See copy of original, overleaf.] It was cold but sunny. Came back to find *Bernard* in our flat! He'd cycled the 63 miles from Pangbourne to come and see me. (Flattered? I'll say – and pleased.) We had lunch, then he slept like a log for a few hours. Talked about the holidays. Decided that I should go home for Xmas, and then go on to the Kibbutz for a few days. At 5 p.m. he left to cycle back in the dark. I walked the first mile with him. Didn't have much time together for all that effort (126 miles!) but Bernard said it was worth it.

Wednesday 20th December
Got to Aberdare at 2.30 p.m. Stood ALL the way! Trains packed! Glad to see Sara – Linda has been looking after her very well. Took Sara with me to Kahns' to say "Hello". They seemed pleased to see me, especially Mrs. Ginsberger. Thought of Bernard's letter: "Why should not the world take part in the happiness of two people – I should shout it out, tell everybody how I feel," but so far Bernard has not told his parents. Mum is behaving quite ostrich-like – quite "MUM" on the subject – she thinks it's just a passing phase and will go away if she doesn't acknowledge it. Uncle, however, is *very* sarcastic at every possible opportunity.

Thursday 21st December
Spent the whole day getting the books up to date, writing to firms, sending out cheques. Shop stayed open all day and was very hectic.

Friday 22nd December
Helped serve in the shop, did quite a few hurried dress alterations – Uncle pinned the hems. I asked Mum if I could light candles for Shabbos – she said *she* would.

Saturday 23rd December
Did not help in the shop! Very difficult situation as it's the busiest day of the year. Went to visit Adolf and Ellen in the afternoon. Black looks greeted my return as I walked through the packed shop and up to my room. This is definitely my *last* Xmas at home.

Sunday 24th – Monday 25th December
Gran and Berta came. Listened to the King's Speech at 3 p.m. Gran of the same opinion as Mum, but said, "at least he's a *worker*", meaning Bernard. Persuaded Joyce to come to Basildon with me tomorrow. She agreed. Told Mum we were going back tomorrow – she thinks to our flat in Cheltenham. Mum gave me a thick tweed coat, double-breasted and rust coloured. I had my eye on a dark-red swagger, but the rust one is more practical and warm.

Tuesday 26th December
Took train to Reading, and then hitched to the Kibbutz. Great fun, nice welcome, and best of all – a roaring fire. After supper Joyce and I went upstairs to bed. So cold we both slept in all our clothes – coats, gloves – but at least we had beds! (Last time we slept on straw on the floor.) Joyce has at last come to the conclusion that Bernard and I do seem right for each other. We talked until 3 a.m. – mostly about my ability to "change" Bernard. Can one ever really change another person's personality? Maybe just pure happiness and love will give him back his youth; and, of course, children (ours – but *not yet*). One thing I like is his generosity – I could *never* marry a mean man.

Wednesday 27th, Thursday 28th, Friday 29th December
Snow, snow, blizzard, snow. Took Joyce to the station at Pangbourne and waited almost an hour for the train. She went back to Cheltenham, but I'm staying on here until Monday. Met the Kriegers (the owners of the farm). Had tea there; lovely people. They seem to think the world of Bernard. I'm beginning to agree with them. The last few days have been pure enchantment: the scenery – snow covered fields, stark black skeletons of trees pasted onto a grey-white sky. The warmth of the cowshed – me, watching Bernard milking seventy-two cows! He's so loving and gentle with them. Everyone here says they knew last August that we would get engaged – that is everyone except ME!

Sunday 31st December
Took three snaps of Bernard, two on the horse – "Cynthia", and one in front of the cart. Quite misty. Talked about our future. It's likely that the Kibbutz will soon close for lack of members, so Bernard will have to find another job. This evening we finally finished our letters to Aberdare – to Kahns and Mum, telling them of our marriage plans. It was quite late when we left the warmth of the farmhouse, in a buoyant, happy mood. The branches of the trees hung heavy with snow. Suddenly, the moonlight burst onto the ice particles coating the leaves, making the whole place look magical. We walked "crunch, crunch" towards the postbox at the end of the lane. I snuggled into Bernard's short, warm jacket – his large capable hands are amazingly warm – together we placed our letters in the box –

it seemed to seal our decision. We walked on as far as the riverbank – the water black and silver, flowing quietly on its way. Our feet made deep marks in the thick snow. Through the muffled silence we heard the sound of the Italians singing. When we arrived back, it was 1945!

Bernard on Shire-horse in the mist

1945

Monday 1st January

This morning I faced the first day of the New Year with one of the hardest tasks I've ever attempted – to write to Alex telling him that I'm engaged – in such a short space of time – and to Bernard Kahn, who is *not* his most favourite person. After a few attempts I managed a reasonable, unemotional letter, hiding my true feelings which, from now on, will have to remain locked deep inside me. Retraced my footsteps of last night to the post-box, the path now a slushy track between the unspoilt white banks of the lane. Relieved when I heard the letter drop into the post-box – I should hate Alex to hear about my plans through a chance phone call from Mum to the family in Swansea. Bernard came in lunch-time – he'd managed to get the afternoon off. On the way to the station I was in my "happy non-thinking" mood. As we passed the Italian P.O.W.'s caravan, Bernard knocked on their door, took a key out of his pocket and unlocked it. "Meet my fiancée!" he announced. The four men jumped up beaming, put their arms around him, then courteously bowed to me, "To you and to the New Year," they said smiling. An hour later I was alone in the train on my way back to Cheltenham. Arrived at Cheltenham at 9 p.m. Met Rev. Braier; he walked me home; told me that one of "our" GI's, George Nagel, had been killed in the fighting – not a regular visitor to our flat – still, my "up in the air" mood vanished. These last few days in Basildon – the isolation – the snow-covered scenery – made it seem as if the whole world had retreated, the war as unreal as the land-scape. Now I'm again "normal", worrying about Arthur and Max, and all the other young men who make up the headlines: Our troops are pushing back the Germans, overcoming fierce resistance – but at what cost!

Wednesday 3rd January

Talked with Joyce about Cynthia–Bernard – she is now quite convinced that we *do* look a couple. Very pleased, as it would be difficult if she resented our engagement, especially if Bernard doesn't find work in London and, as I hope, looks for work here. Leaving tomorrow for Aberdare to meet Bernard there – and face our families!!

Thursday 4th January

Got to Aberdare at 8 p.m. Mum and Uncle were in 'Ceiber visiting Gran. Sara sleeping; Linda baby-sitting. To avoid arguments I was in bed by 10. Read *Design for Living* by Noël Coward.

Friday 5th January
Very large X! Uncle exploded and said if Bernard *dared* come here, he'd throw him out! Mum said, glaring at me, "You know he really *will*!" And yes, Uncle's quite capable of doing so. (It would have been rather funny, if this was a Victorian melodrama and didn't concern *me*!) Walked to Clifton Street to prevent Bernard coming to the shop. We met at the Clock Tower, and, before I could say anything, Bernard said – "My parents don't want you to visit them anymore – they are completely against me marrying you." Then he announced, in typical Bernard style, "Don't worry, they'll just have to get used to it, come on, let's walk up the Craig." So we spent some wonderful hours walking on the high ridge of the mountain. The sky was grey, but not menacing. In a great mood we ran down the mountain paths and arrived breathless at the top of Clifton Street. We arranged to do the same tomorrow.

Sunday 7th January
Got the train to Cardiff with Bernard, then changed platforms – he to catch the train for Pangbourne – I to catch the Cheltenham train, which came in almost an hour late – and full – had to stand all the way. Felt very cold. Used two eggs, that Gran had given us, for supper. Told Joyce about my reception in Aberdare. Joyce speechless. I feel very upset at Kahns' attitude towards me – never expected them to react like Alex's parents. *My mistake* is in thinking people who know me, KNOW ME! – In fact I'm either seen as Joyce's younger sister, "Jane Cooper's daughter", Ruth's girl, Alex's or Bernard's future wife – Sara thinks I'm her *mother*! Poor Juliet! She never stood a chance with those Montagues – she was *just* a *Capulet*. "What's in a name? That which we call a rose by any other name would smell so sweet." Actually *my* surname is the same as Bernard's – Kahn – Cohen [Priest].

Monday 8th – Thursday 11th January
College every day. Good to be back. Joyce in a great mood as she had a letter from Paul. I had a letter from Alex thanking me for my birthday wishes. Since September he's been ill, and only now beginning to eat food again. He says I'm mistaken in hoping he will find someone else soon, for, he writes:

> "I'm a fool, I know, but unfortunately, I am a faithful fool with a constant heart. As for your announcement, week by week I have sought (with fearful heart and trembling hand) for just such an announcement in the pages of the *Jewish Chronicle*. Now, I suppose I must do the honours in the timeworn traditional way, the only way left to the conquered. May I offer you heartiest congratulations, and may you both know constant happiness such as I have never known. I know

> Cynthia, that your decision is no rash one, and that you have come to it only after much careful consideration, wise deliberation, and examination of all your feelings, memories and experiences. I know too that it is no idle decision, but one you wish to stick to and make worthy, one to cherish all your life and never regret. I must say that even I can see the prospects are indeed bright. Lastly, since you are now attending an art school, I wish you much success in your long desired career. Once more, goodbye, my Scheherezade, goodbye, ma jeune dame aux longues cheveux – if I am denied the happiness I so much strove for, at least may you find what I lost. I shall finish conventionally and formally; it is certainly better that you never know how *I* feel.
>
> P.S. I have asked that all my shirts be changed to have button cuffs. I have no use for links at all anymore. Alex Winter."

Went to bed early, wondering how I could cause someone I've cherished so much pain. Alex's P.S. was like a wound in my heart. There can be no "au revoir" or "aufweidersehen" – just – "goodbye ..."

Friday 12th January

Came home from college to find letter from Bernard. Had no time to read it, as so much to prepare for Shabbos. Will read it tonight. Arthur and Jack are coming for supper. News from the Ardennes so-so, the weather not helping either side. Better news from the Americans in the Philippines – Luzon has been captured! Read Bernard's letter – three long closely typed pages, which began:

> "I still can't believe that we are not together anymore, and that I can't come to you for advice. Those miles that are between us seem like thousands, and as if we had not spoken to one another for over a month, so much do I long to be with you and to be able to look after you. The weekend seems to me as if it had been a dream, even though not everything went the way we wanted, nevertheless we were still able to be together. Yes, together with you all my life, that in itself is an ideal which is worth working for, and for which I am going to concentrate all my time. How did you get back to Cheltenham? You know, at the moment when I had a last glimpse of you, a tear came out of my eyes – I felt like jumping out of the train to run back to you. I stood at the window looking back at you, and even when I could not see you anymore, I still looked back as if I knew you were still looking at me from the other side. And indeed I dreamt I could still see you, and only woke up when the train stopped at the next station, then I realised I was *in* the train and took my seat. At Pangbourne I went to see if there was a bus, but there wasn't one, so I walked the five miles home. It was pitch dark and one could hardly see a thing. I arrived to find Felix had been on the same train, also Mr. Rauchman – we had all walked the same way, one behind the other without knowing of each other! Mr. Rauchman had come to sort out Segal/Kreiger's light fittings which are stored in the barn to be safe from the London bombings. The Kibbutz is definitely closing down, so I shall try to find work in London – failing that, perhaps on a small-holding in Cheltenham."

I'm amazed at the confidence Bernard has in planning his life – if things don't work out one way, he's already thought out another. I'm surprised too, that *I'm* part of them; at times, in college I have to remind myself – I'M ENGAGED!

Wednesday 17th January

Bought Joyce's birthday present from an antique shop. It's a glass bowl on top of a silver tree with a deer standing beside it. Didn't have enough money, but seeing my disappointment the shopkeeper let me have it for less. Letter from Bernard waiting for me when I got back from college. I had thought love would grow slowly between us, but I was wrong! My "controlled, sensible, idealistic" fiancé is head over heels in love and doesn't need poets or jongleurs to describe his feelings. Bernard wrote:

> "In my dreams I think of you, when I speak I talk of you, while I eat I think of you, when I work I imagine I work together with you, you, you – You. Yes, indeed, I can't get my thoughts away from you and wish we were together – forever. When I think of the few days we had together, it seems as if it was only yesterday; when I think – when shall I see you again, then it seems like years since I saw you last."

Thursday 18th January

Went to Mrs. Rose's to hear 9 o'clock news. The Russians have taken WARSAW and are advancing towards Lodz in Poland. Rang Bernard from phone box – freezing! Told him about the Hatchery (a partnership) advertised in the Gloucester paper – gave him the Box Number. Bernard told me he had spoken to his father about us. Mr. Kahn said he knew no one suitable to marry Bernard in Aberdare, Cardiff or even London – so if Bernard has found an orthodox girl for himself they are happy about it – in any case he has always liked me! Well!! I walked home with a big smile on my face.

Friday 19th – Monday 22nd January

Letters every day from Bernard. On the 18th he went to London to look for a job. One offered £3 a week, another as cutter and bookkeeper in a gown factory – well he's certainly *not* "cut out" for that. He's not sure he would get released from farm work. One letter described his London visit:

> "When I got there it was dark; when I came to Manor House I could not walk the usual way to Lordship Park as a V-2 had come down there and had hit a block of flats. The building fell right onto the main road – all the windows, doors and very many roofs are down. Lordship Park looks terrible as another V-2 came down nearby. The last fortnight was one of the worst of the last three months; while I was there it was quite noisy! Berthold Strauss leaves London every night for Berkhamsted as do many other people although most of the bombs come by day. In fact most of the V-2s come by day but everyone is still in fear of night-time bombing."

Tuesday 23rd January
Joyce's birthday – she was thrilled with my present. Finished my stone sculpture last night. It is a semi-abstract idea of "the beginning of life". The forms suggest living creatures not quite formed, evolving from the stone. It feels good to touch and I'm very pleased with it. Too heavy to bring home.

Wednesday 24th January
So cold in college today, the life class was cancelled – shivering model only has one bar electric fire – we wore our coats. Did Anatomy instead, muscles of shoulders and arms; drew muscles and tendons in different positions; found it fascinating. Teacher demonstrated the way muscles change shape (under the skin) as they contract or lengthen. (Remember to look for convex, concave and straight lines of the body.)

Thursday 25th January
Used the last of our coal tonight. Mrs. Rose offered us a bed in her kitchen, but we decided to stay here. Instead we put the oven on, placed *all* our baking tins in it – pillows on top. When they were really hot we placed them in our beds, and after half an hour took them out. Then we jumped quickly into bed, both of us decked out with scarves and gloves. Had to put the oven off in case the pipes freeze, defrost too quickly and burst, causing a flood like we had before. This is the most severe cold spell since January 1940.

Friday 26th January
Newspapers say we are held "in an Arctic Grip". Yesterday was the coldest day for *fifty years*! In the Channel ports the *sea froze*! I stayed in all day. Wrote to Bernard. Dentons gave us some coal for tonight – two Yanks coming for supper, Arthur and a friend. Letter from Berta. She's very excited, as Manfred wrote to her that he will take her back to America with him "after the war". What a magical three words! The GI's are always so optimistic. I'm thrilled for Berta, as Penrhiwceiber has little to offer her – Gran, of course, will miss her.

Wrote to Mr. and Mrs. Kahn. Imagine I might be calling them Father and Mother one day soon!!! I've never called ANYONE Father! I feel a lot of affection and respect for Mr. Kahn, so it'll be strange, but nice.

Sunday 28th January
Bernard came for a few hours. He gave a talk in the Allies Club: 'Torah in the Twentieth Century'. It was well attended with many Yanks from the Camp. Quite a few questions were asked. Went with Bernard to the station; he caught the night train to Pangbourne. Had only a few minutes to discuss the adverts before the train left. I'm really *fed* up saying "G'bye" at stations – walking back alone – feeling like Ingrid Bergman leaving Humphrey Bogart in *Casablanca*.

Monday 29th January

Telegram from Mum this morning to say that Sara is very ill, and that one of us must go home immediately to look after her. I wanted to go, but doubt if I could stand the atmosphere under present circumstances. To my surprise, Joyce said she'd go, she'll take a week off work. Costume drawing in college. Freezing. Mr. Willoughby said we should remember Michelangelo lying on his back for four years painting the ceiling of the Sistine Chapel. If *we're* cold and hungry then maybe *we'll* be geniuses!! I never notice that I'm cold or hungry while I'm drawing or painting – so maybe there's hope for me yet!

Wednesday 31st January

Joyce left this morning for Aberdare. Letter from Bernard. He's going to Brighton tomorrow to see a farm (bailiff's job). If nothing comes of it then he'll come to Cheltenham next Wednesday to see Lewis in Gloucester about the chicken farm. He wrote:

> "I don't think there is any need for you to look for a bed for me, as we would be talking all through the night to make the most of it. Please go to bed a bit earlier this week so that you won't be too tired when I get there. And not a word to me about the shoulders dear, you hear, or I shall go back the same night!"

I *do* nag him about his posture – he has what I call "ploughman's shoulders" – while I used to walk to school with a book on my head! Dita is coming here for Shabbos so I shall have company. She's been fond of Bernard for years.

Friday 2nd February

Met Dita at the station. She brought me a letter from Joyce. It seems Sara had a bad asthma attack – Mum is convinced it came from a *rat's bite* (a rat from the tobacconist/confectioners next door). *I* think it's from all the fluff from the dress alterations – there are three sewing machines in Sara's "bedroom". Joyce thinks it's because Sara is missing me, which is very likely (I wish Sara could stay with me when I'm married). Joyce is coming back Tuesday.

Saturday 3rd February

Danny Friedland came for lunch, Erwin joined us. We took turns reading from *The Book of Jewish Thoughts* – an anthology originally produced for servicemen in the First World War and recently reprinted. This small slim book – more than 300 pages, contains writings from the Talmud, Churchill, Einstein, General Smuts, G. B. Shaw, William Blake – even Olive Schreiner (*African Farm*) and many others. We came across an English translation of the well-known Sabbath Table song, 'Shabbos Menuchoh' [Sabbath of Rest], composed by Isaac Luria (1534–1572). Danny showed us how, in the Hebrew song, Yitzchak (Isaac) had used an acrostic – the first letter of his name to start each line. He was surprised when I said that Luria (according to Aunty Sarah) was my great-great-gr-gr-gr-etc grandfather, for my grandmother had been a Lurie/a, a direct descendant of the famous mystic. It was almost dark when we stopped reading, then sang until Danny had to leave to return to camp. Dita and I went to Mrs. Rose's to hear the news and to GET WARM!

Wednesday 7th February
Bernard came lunch-time – great to see him, then he went on to Gloucester to meet Mr. Lewis. Lewis owns an orchard outside Cheltenham – about six acres of land with three hundred fruit trees where Bernard could keep chickens and sell the eggs, splitting the profit between them. There's also a small stable on the land where Bernard says he would sleep to save renting a room. Arthur also came at 5 p.m. and arranged to come for a long weekend leave. He told us Manila has been captured. We talked about the film *Bataan* which we had both seen. Great film. We looked up Bataan on the map. It's a tiny island at the top of the Philippines. There was an enormous bombing raid on Berlin this week. Arthur is actually worried that the war in Europe will soon be over and he'll be sent to fight the Japs. The Japanese are the most vicious and deadly fighters. After supper Bernard went to see Mr. Russell. He is about seventy-eight years old and needs help looking after his half an acre of garden. He grows vegetables and fruit to exhibit at the Royal Show in Windsor and has won a lot of cups and medals. He also has a printing firm, one of the biggest in the country, printing bank notes etc. for the government, and books and pamphlets for Germany and Europe. Bernard liked him; thinks he can learn a lot from him. He was offered the job at 2/- [two shillings – 10p] an hour for as many hours as he wants to work. Bernard accepted it as a part-time job. As promised, we talked all night. At 8.30 a.m. I left for college and Bernard went to catch the train for Aberdare. I told him to try and see Mum while he's there.

Thursday 8th February
Went to a Dress Designing course after college. Enjoyed it and did some good drawings. Read Giorgio Vasari's *Lives of the Painters, Sculptors and Architects* written about 1550. Fascinating. Very cold night. *Hope* our pipes don't freeze again. Last week we were a whole week without any water! (We *mashed* snow!)

Friday 9th – Saturday 10th February
Arthur came early; brought some welcome food tins and three bars of chocolate, which made Joyce's eyes sparkle. He helped us get ready for Shabbos, even helping with the cooking! We lit the fire in the kitchen; it was much more comfortable and cosy. Erwin came down Friday evening and we did some Hebrew together; later I did some Chumosh [Bible] with Joyce and Arthur. Went to shul in the morning – didn't enjoy the service very much. Spoke to Rev. Braier.

He's very much looking forward to Bernard coming to stay in Cheltenham. He's been married three months, has few friends; he studied in Gateshead Yeshiva. Suggested Bernard would read the weekly Sidra. Imagine REV. Bernard Kahn! Mrs. Rose came for tea. After she had gone we studied part of the Bensching [Grace after Meals], then sat around the fire and sang all the songs we remembered, while the dusk gradually fell and night softly made its appearance. Joyce made Havdallah [Ceremony with wine, candle and spices marking Sabbath's end] for a change, and did it quite well. I tried to imagine Bernard was here – and wrote him a long letter. Since our recent adventures, I feel so serious, and yet it is a "serious happiness", for, just to think I have brought Bernard happiness gives me immense pleasure. I want to spend my life smoothing away his worries and helping him to solve them. Finishing the letter, I experienced that strangely wonderful feeling that love brings, and the desire to let the whole world know how we feel about each other.

Sunday 11th February

Managed to do a lot of Architecture this morning – Joyce in work. I went out to post Bernard's letter. The sun shone as if to tell us Spring is on its way; met Cynthia Davies and her brother Jack and talked – or rather Jack talked and we listened. Jack talks faster than any man I know, as if his thoughts are on a speed track and pour out like an avalanche. At least he talks a lot of sense. He is a fervent Zionist – a great admirer of the Revisionist leader Vladimir Jabotinsky and believes that settling in Palestine (with our OWN government and our own defence forces) is the only way ahead for the Jewish people. I told him a little of Bernard's and my plans, and Mum and Uncle Harry's objections – Jack spluttered x*x*x*x*! For he had been the one to introduce Mum to Uncle Harry! Cynthia is very attractive and much in demand in the social life of forces-choked Cheltenham. Ran home to make lunch for Arthur – to find a letter from him on the table apologising for his abrupt departure and not taking proper leave of us before returning to his battalion. On reporting to base his unit was called back earlier than expected. He just had time to return Joyce's bicycle and write:

> "Indubitably it is unnecessary to say that, as usual, I enjoyed every minute of my stay with you people. Indeed, I find it difficult to express my genuine appreciation for such a pleasant 'Shabbos'. It is inspiring to witness how you two girls follow the beautiful traditions of our people even while away from home and family."

I thought how right Bernard is when he says one influences or impresses someone more by *example* than by brainwashing. Had lunch alone, and mused about my situation:

(1) *Being away from home*, Joyce and I for the first time are able to keep our religion as we have wanted to for so long. It was far easier to get away than I had expected. The war – Joyce's war work – my imminent call-up unless I was at a

teacher's college – made this flat in Cheltenham an ideal solution and best of all, obtained Mum's consent – especially as it would take me away from Bernard's influence – or so she thought!

(2) At last I am studying Art – doing something I love – and, unlike school, which I hated, I enjoy every day. How '3' will affect this is yet to be seen.

(3) My marriage plans. Bernard is impatient to marry soon, and, in a way, I am too. Bernard is very mature, and being twenty-one has no problems; I, on the other hand, am old enough to be called up for army service but not old enough to marry without Mum's written consent! When she hears Bernard is *living* in Cheltenham she might be persuaded to agree.

Tuesday 13th February

Went to the pictures for the first time in three months. Saw *Dangerous Moonlight*. Very good, especially the music – Addinsell's *Warsaw Concerto* was superb; put me in a sad, romantic mood. The moon has always had a strong effect on me – especially when it's full – after all, my name in Greek means Moon Goddess. Felt safer walking home alone now that the streets are filled with the headlights of the American jeeps tearing around – we don't have to rely on the moon to see by any more. "Thank you, Moon, you've been a good friend these last five years." Wrote letter to Bernard telling him how unreal my life here seems; only the ten days I spent with him in Basildon seem real – and very wonderful. I can't forget Bernard, in his short jacket and tyrolean hat, taking me to the Park Farm across those frost covered meadows, singing and laughing; Ruth, the cow, so placid and contented, and "Cynthia" (the horse) whom I didn't have a ride on after all; the countryside so new and clean with its brilliant white coat on and the new splendour it attained at the setting of the sun. I'll never forget how Bernard looked in the moonlight when we sat at the window with our tea and cake. (*Dangerous Moonlight*!) I wonder how I shall feel when he comes here for good. Asked him a few dinim – whether plastic or bakelite dishes can be used for meat and milk, like glass – are they porous like china or not? Lighting the Shabbos candles – so far I have only lit them twice in succession. Will lighting them next week mean that I shall *have* to every week from then on – (three times in a row makes it compulsory) – not that it matters, I shall have to in any case, very soon, when I am married i.e. in a year or two!

Wednesday 14th February

Found a temporary room for Bernard at 22, Albert Close. Joyce said that I needn't have bothered, as Bernard is the only boy she'd trust to sleep *here*, as he is so naive. What an honour! Little Bernard with such a sweet innocent face and with such little knowledge of girls, etc. Don't know how I kept a straight face! Told her not to worry as he intends to sleep at The Orchard in the stable. Joyce's comment – "The two of you are quite mad!" Since Sunday the pipes have been frozen once again, so no water. Wrote to Mum saying I was fatter, but not from noshing [over-eating] (hope this worries her!) but from dirt – but not ORDINARY dirt, as I've drawn patterns all over myself with the two drops of water that were left in the tap! Thanked her for the parcel, although it's a pity we can't make use of the towels as we can't wash anyway – if we get too bad we'll use 'Modene', our sink cleaner, instead.

Thursday 15th February

Spent lunch-time looking for a paraffin stove for The Orchard – no luck. Wrote to Bernard – missing him. How I wish we knew when we can be married. Asked Bernard if he intends to wear a top hat – or an open-necked shirt? It appears that our plans to live in Eretz Yisrael are receding into the distant future. It's strange how much I long to go there; if we could go this week, I would, and yet I realise it's not all going to be fun – at least it'll be warm! I can't believe Mum would really make us wait two years! Joyce met a really frum Yank at the Allies Club last week. He's been to Yeshivah in America: he's bringing a friend with him to supper tomorrow night. Joyce and I stayed up late cooking – that is, I cooked, she baked, and we sang all our favourite arias, somewhat theatrically, finally falling onto our beds in "The Ice Room", dying, dying … "My tiny hand is frozen, no one to warm it into life."

Saturday 17th February

Really enjoyed last night. Our GI's came with some welcome tins (pineapple!!) and even more welcome news – the old city of Dresden has been bombed to pieces, also the Americans have carried out a huge attack on Tokyo. We all felt elated – no one has any pre-war "normal" emotions left – no turning the other cheek. The V-2s are still falling on London, and at last the Germans and Japs are getting back some of their own medicine. Tomorrow there'll be a debate in the Allies Club: 'Has Science improved Mankind?' I have to speak against it – i.e. that it hasn't. Have to think up some ideas about it – actually I believe Science *has* improved mankind, both materially and physically (what about the war!!! – the Germans have used Science for barbaric purposes). Dictionary Definitions: *Science* – Knowledge … (Like the Tree of Knowledge of Good and Evil, Science can be used for both good and bad ends.) *Scientific*: Knowledge depending on deductions from self-evident truths (as in maths) or based on observation or experiment of material phenomena.

The search for scientific knowledge was started by the ancient Greeks; one of the earliest scientists – Arestarchus, suggested that the earth revolves around the sun – more than eight hundred years before Copernicus came to the same conclusion. To us, nowadays, "Science" has a different meaning, almost as if it's the opposite of religious belief. Man can either use or abuse a moral code, but Science has no morality – no feelings. "Scientists" have come to consider themselves superior to other more modest professions, their ideas and conclusions inviolate. But have they brought us benefits?

Example 1. For defence or attack, early man used bows and arrows. Today we have the rockets (V-1s and V-2s) and aerial bombers. Early man used catapults and swords, while we have machine-guns and heavy artillery. Early man used horses and boats – we have tanks, ducks, subs. and destroyers – so has science improved mankind?

Example 2. Two men start out to cross a desert, one on a camel, one in a jeep; they both take the same amount of food and water. Two days after they leave, the man in the jeep is far ahead. Suddenly there is a terrific sandstorm. The man and the camel cover up and wait until the storm has passed and then carry on with their journey. The jeep is clogged with sand and cannot start – the man has to decide whether to wait for help (which may never come) or walk, carrying his food and water. With luck he may survive and reach his destination – but has modern scientific advancement proved to be better than the ancient well-tried ways?

I *do* think that science has greatly benefited the world of medicine/surgery for, in olden days, Mum could never have survived a Caesarean together with a hysterectomy – and a new baby – and be fit and glamorous too.

Last thought: I *hope* I'm the second speaker tomorrow!

Monday 19th February

Very good debate yesterday. Jeffrey Galinski spoke *for* the motion – he's so brainy – his arguments were very persuasive. It was fun picking holes in his ideas and, to my surprise, I put mine over with confidence. There was a good turnout, many new faces, mainly GI's. Wrote Bernard a long letter. He's coming here Monday on his way to Gloucester (to see Mr. Lewis and finalise arrangements for The Orchard). Then it'll be "Good-bye" again as he intends to spend Purim in Aberdare.

Sunday 25th February

Bright sunny day, so I got to the orchard at 10 a.m. to distemper the inside stable. Ugh! Took me almost two hours just to clean out the cobwebs, dust, straw and old horse manure. Finished painting one wall when Erwin turned up with sandwiches and a hot flask of tea. What a friend! We took it in turns to paint the rest – (only one brush). When we'd finished it was almost dark. I sang 'Away in a manger' … Erwin asked, "Is Bernard really going to live here?" I said: "It'll suit him – he was born on 25th December!" Of course Erwin thought I was joking. Got back to Evesham Road by 5 p.m., covered with dirt and distemper. Put on the geyser for a bath. No luck! Geyser on strike – used kettle of hot water and a bowl, à la Aberdare. Spots of white on my hair make me look quite bohemian – so they can stay there, as I'm too whacked to wash them out. Hope Bernard brings a few planks of wood from Basildon, so we can put up shelves. Bought two kitchen chairs last week (5 sh. each), also a small table. Bernard is sending his bed. Acc. [Accomodation] will look like this:

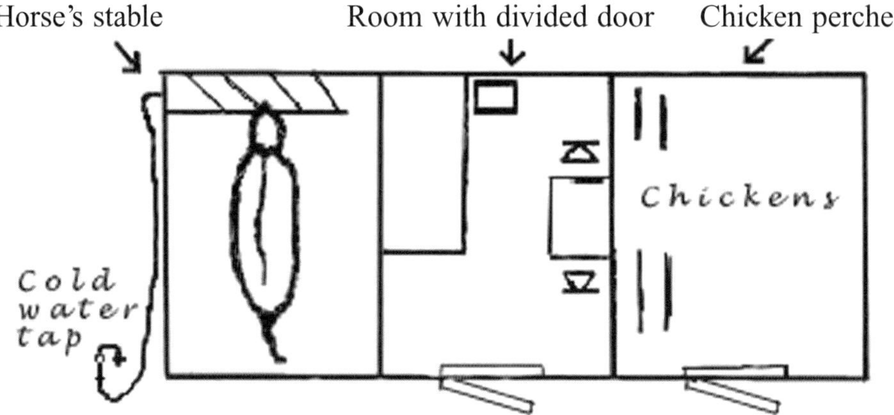

"Luxury Room with a View". From his bed (with top part of door open) he'll be able to see the sky at night – the fruit trees at dawn. When they're in flower, it'll be a fantastic sight.

Monday 26th February

Went straight from college to meet Bernard's train. He took his bike from the Goods' Van, and another ladies' bike – *for me*! "Sorry it's second-hand," he said, "it only cost £5, but I know you've never had one of your own." I was thrilled! What freedom! No more slinking along the crammed Yank-filled streets alone – I shall sail by their octopus arms on my chariot! Bernard left almost immediately for Gloucester. Tonight I've looked at my bike a dozen times – remembering how sweetly Bernard gave it to me, apologising for its few rust marks. Erwin said he'd see to the brakes. Wrote Bernard a painted letter, every word a different colour with many illustrations – something special for Purim.

Thursday 1st March

On Tuesday I went to shul to hear the Megillah. Atmosphere a bit muted, as it's difficult to rejoice about Esther's triumph over Haman, and the deliverance of the Jewish People in the Persian Empire more than two thousand years ago, when our present day Haman – Hitler – is still alive and even more bestial. The Russians who liberated the "death camp" of Auschwitz a few weeks ago, described it as "the worst 'Death Camp' captured". Many people in shul have family members on the Continent and still live in hope of seeing them once victory has been achieved. The presence of the Yanks brightened everyone, especially as they doled out pocketsful of sweets and chocolates to the children. They are putting up a plaque in the Synagogue to commemorate their time here and the hospitality they have received. The wooden plaque will be unveiled by Captain A. P. Schwartz, American Army Chaplain. Chaplain Shoemaker, Captain M. Routtenberg and Corporal Landau will be present. Rev. Braier is leaving Cheltenham – and so far no one has applied for the job. Sent a telegram to Bernard on Purim morning to phone me at the phone box (539771) at 4.30 p.m. I got there five minutes early and only waited a few more minutes before the phone rang. Bernard said he'd not met Mr. Lewis in Gloucester, as Lewis did not arrive. Bernard got a very cold reception from Mum and Uncle. Mum said, "What d'you think you're going to live on when you're married – peanuts?" Bernard was very hurt – told her he's always kept himself (farm worker, shepherd's pay 29/- a week!!) and we would not expect any financial help from her. I told him I had some savings from my work in Aberdare – it would be enough to start the partnership with Lewis: I could be a "sleeping partner". Bernard was quite shocked until I explained what that meant. We often have misunderstandings over English expressions. Sent a birthday card to Mum for the 4th of March. Went to see Mr. Galinski (our landlord) to pay him for March. Showed him the report in the *Cheltenham Gazette* – a local marine, John Connolly, home on leave, who had survived years of active service, died from gas poisoning while having a bath. The bath was heated by a geyser installed more than thirty years ago and had no flue pipe to convey the fumes outside. Told Mr. Galinski our geyser looks *ancient*; we can't see any flue and it doesn't work – so *please* send someone round so we can have a *hot* bath! Joyce went to the Regal with Max to see *Dragon Seed* with Katharine Hepburn. I stayed home as Bernard is coming here tomorrow. Cooked until 12.

Friday 2nd March

Went to Lloyds' Bank with Bernard to open an account. Saw the manager – who I'm sure thought we had a large sum to deposit – Bernard told him a bit about his background, so he was very pleasant; I put in the £300 that I'd saved from my earnings in Aberdare. Bernard didn't really want me to, but was pleased when we came out with our first chequebook. Told Bernard not to worry, as with his business mind it will come out all right. I *do* trust Bernard but certainly *not* Lewis! (I don't have a good feeling about him.) Arthur, Max and Joe are coming for supper. Bernard is staying at Albert Close (12/6 a week) until the weather gets warmer. Our first *real* Shabbos!

Sunday 4th March

Really enjoyed Shabbos! What a difference it makes having Bernard here to make Kiddush, lead the Zemirot and join in the conversation, answering our guests' many questions. Joe was thrilled with the shul (Shabbos morning) as it's over one hundred years old – and that to the Americans is *OLD*! [It was opened in 1839. The Ark, Bimah, benches and reading desk, originally made for the New Synagogue, Leadenhall Street, London in 1761, were donated to Cheltenham when the New Synagogue moved to Bishopsgate. The plaque showing the prayer for the Royal Family is even older, having originally been made for the Great Synagogue, Dukes Place in the late 1720s during the reign of George I.]

We promised to take them to Tewkesbury; I expect they'll be in raptures as much as I was with the ancient timbered streets; the houses and shops leaning onto each other at odd angles; the gleaming old glass windows. Joyce had a letter from Paul inviting her to see a play at Stratford-on-Avon. Paul is an Intelligence Officer with our forces in Europe where his fluent German is much needed. After hard fighting, Cologne has been captured by General Patton's Third Army; in Burma, our forces have taken Mandalay and the Russians continue to advance; the whole of Russian Lithuania is now free. Good news, but nine months after D-Day, we are *still* waiting for the total defeat of Germany and Japan.

Sunday 11th March

Had evening classes all week – dress designing. Bernard met Mr. Lewis; they agreed to both put up £50 to start the poultry business. Bernard worked twenty-eight hours for Russell, so earned almost £3! He also bought a few live chickens and sold them to the shochet [butcher] who comes from Birmingham every week. Bernard brought us long white radishes – the orchard is full of them, (at least he *thinks* they're radishes) – sold some to the vegetable shop and got potatoes in return. He also brought some wild mushrooms, but when we had them tested by the chemist they were found to be poisonous … Tomorrow is half-term, so we are going to an auction in Droitwich. Bernard wants to buy a cow so that he can make and sell cream cheese. He was delighted with the painted stable – Jack Spelman came today with a *paraffin stove*!

Monday 12th March

To save the train fare we hitchhiked to Droitwich – but got to the Manor House too late to bid on any of the cattle. It was the first time I'd attended an auction, and watched fascinated as a lovely 15th century dresser went for £850! The other lots all sold quickly. Then to my amazement I saw Bernard bidding for the last lot, No.135 – *four* bee-hives together with inhabitants. No one wanted them, so he got them for £7.10/-. He said the bees would be good for the trees in the orchard, and he could sell the honey. One small problem – how do we transport them to Cheltenham??? We went to the Goods Yard at the station to enquire about transport – they had a good laugh, and said "Definitely NOT!" I said "Dov," (Bernard's Hebrew name, meaning Bear), – "you've got a bee in your bonnet!" Of course Bernard took this literally. We made our way back to the road, hoping

for a lift. It got very dark, and no cars or lorries came our way. After walking one-and-a-half hours an American lorry picked us up. He drove at seventy miles an hour or more, the fastest I've ever travelled. Our driver used the dark, winding roads like a speed track, but we were grateful, especially as he dropped us outside our door.

Tuesday 13th March

Cycled to The Orchard after College. Drew a sketch of some wind-blown trees, and of Bernard digging a trench, ready for planting beans. We discussed Pesach. Joyce is going to Bromsgrove Hachsharah [agricultural training centre for young Jewish youth who intend to go to Palestine]. Bernard is going home, and I shall write to the Sunderland Girls' Hostel, asking if they'll have me. Good job we didn't buy a cow until after Pesach.

Thursday 15th March

<u>MAN OF HARLECH!</u>

This week, eleven German prisoners of war escaped from the Bridgend P.O.W. camp. Some were caught immediately, but three got as far as the *Aberdare Valley* and were caught by Constable Ed Williams in Godreaman. Caught by *our own*

Mr. Williams; he must be thrilled to see his name in the *Echo*. The fruit trees in the orchard are completely covered with buds. Bernard says if we don't have frost it'll be a bumper crop. I'm looking forward to seeing it in blossom; it'll be a lovely sight. Tonight, two Yanks, who are going away, brought Bernard two *electric* shavers – one in excellent condition. He paid £3.10 and £3 for them. Tuesday, Joe brought him an almost new typewriter. A large number of GI's are leaving, needed to reinforce the Remagen bridgehead (Germany) etc. Joe is an expert in erecting Bailey bridges which will replace the damaged bridges across the Rhine. They can be erected in a night and are strong enough for tanks to cross.

Saturday 17th March

Bernard read the Sidra in shul this morning. He was very nervous, although he'd rehearsed it last night. Everyone thought he did it very well. One of the members spoke to him afterwards, asking him what he was doing in Cheltenham. He turned out to be Mr. Rakusen from the 'Matzo' Rakusens. He and his wife have a mansion in the Cotswold Hills, and keep a *chicken* farm! We have been invited to visit them tomorrow.

Sunday 18th March

Weather bright, so we left early to cycle to Rakusen's farm. The hills were as steep as in Wales – both of us too stubborn to get off our bikes until the last steep incline – when we were practically standing upright on the pedals and gasping for breath. Great view! Rakusen's house very beautiful – the chicken farm, enormous! At least two to three hundred chicken coops, all very neat. Had tea with Mr. and Mrs. Rakusen; we talked about farming; our future plans – and of course the war. Is this, as Mr. Churchill says: "The beginning of the end?" Bernard bought six chickens from them (12/- each). They were put into two boxes, which we tied onto the back of our bikes. The way down was a *dream*! Hair flying, wind tingling our cheeks, we arrived in Cheltenham without *once* using our pedals. The chickens tho' had *not* enjoyed the experience – two looked distinctly downcast – Bernard took them to the local hotel, and sold them for £1 each. [A good week's wage was about £4.00!]

Tuesday 27th March

Bernard left for Aberdare at 10 a.m., leaning out of the train until the last moment, as if we'd never see each other again. I caught the 10.30 train for Sunderland. Had very good connections arriving at 10.40 p.m. During the journey I wrote notes for a Sicha which I've been asked to give the girls – hope I won't be too shy! Betty Hamfling was waiting for me together with Hilda; they were both mystified why an "English" girl, with family here, should want to spend Pesach away from home. All the girls here are refugees from Germany and have no idea what has become of their families. Wrote to Bernard and got to bed at 1 a.m. P.G. next year, Bernard and I will be together.

Wednesday 28th March
Helped with the cleaning and cooking (for Pesach) – all the people here are very nice to me. (They say I don't seem ENGLISH; well I'm not – I'm Welsh.) Made friends with Helen, who, at twenty, is the oldest girl here. Some of the girls started a discussion about dreams and what Freud thought about it. Everything seems very empty without Bernard around – I miss him more than ever. I wonder what his parents had to say about us?

Tuesday 3rd April
Just received two letters and a telegram from Bernard. Poor thing, he's really in the thick of things. He wrote: "Darling, tonight is Pesach, the Time of Our Redemption. What a word, what for? What was the good of it?" The reason for his low mood – Mum and Uncle! They were invited to visit Kahns' the first day of Pesach, but never turned up. Mr. Kahn was furious, and questioned Bernard's intention to marry me. Oil and water are more likely to mix than the Kahns and my family. Bernard then went to see Mum, who told him, "Uncle doesn't know that Cynthia is in Sunderland as he would say it's Meshuggah [crazy]! What right do you have to stop the girls coming home for Pesach? I won't permit you to have anything more to do with any of my girls!" … and so on. Bernard felt so unwelcome, certainly not like a future son-in-law. I phoned Bernard and told him the day won't be long before we can be united together with a bond that cannot be broken by any human person – I am quite confident we can deal with whatever comes, however difficult life may be. I feel very responsible for Bernard's quarrel with his father and told him his people have had enough Tzorus [troubles] in the past – he should try to give them a little joy with his presence, especially as this is the first year without his grandfather there to give the Seder. Wrote to Kahns, and to his grandmother in GERMAN. I've decided to go straight to Aberdare rather than return to Cheltenham for I must see Mum to try to improve the situation.

Thursday 5th April
Gave a talk, which to my surprise went off very well; lively discussion afterwards … Notes … (written on train) … Title: 'Keeping Shabbos in this Modern Age: "Every age considers itself to be 'Modern', but we in our time have encountered an amazing number of new inventions – electric light; the telephone; the car; aeroplanes and cinema – how do the enduring laws of Shabbos 'fit in' with these advances? What does one say to someone who considers the switching on of a light on Shabbos not to be forbidden, as it can hardly be considered *WORK*. I would answer as follows: 'There are those who acknowledge G-d and His wisdom but who do not think that switching on a light on Shabbos makes that statement any the less sincere. But what is the idea behind the prohibition of light switching? I would interpret it this way. When Man was created, G-d gave him

the world to master. Man ruled the animals – he governed Nature and conquered the Elements. But of *man*, G-d was master. To ensure that Man did not forget this, G-d gave him the Shabbos. 'Six days of the week you are lord of all you survey – you will easily forget that I am the world's Maker, and it is by My hand and My doing that you are able to rule the earth. Therefore, on the seventh day, acknowledge that you are but My servants, and I, the true Ruler. Acknowledge Me by refraining from governing *anything* on that day. Hand over your crown and sceptre to Me, and do not assert your powers over My Works. By this I will see that you really do remember that I am the L--d your G-d.' Man accepted readily this demand (at Sinai) and has tried to keep the seventh day a day of rest. Rest from creating; rest from asserting his power; rest from dominating; a day of total servitude to G-d. Now do you see the reason for not switching on a light? It is your mastery of electricity and your denial that G-d rules the Elements that you show. Switching on the wireless shows the same superiority, also acquiring new things for yourself as you do when you buy or receive presents. When you leave here (the hostel) and go out into the wider world, you will be confronted by many arguments to sway you from a strictly religious life – you *must* be prepared for a challenge – and have suitable answers ready. It is not enough 'in these modern times' to say, 'I don't know why – that's how we've always done it'. Of course, we know that to some questions, such as the Chukim there is no simple answer, for they are beyond Man's understanding – but to all detractors one can reply with a positive recommendation – 'Go and Learn'."

Friday 6th April

These last ten days have gone so slowly – and another three days and four nights until I am with Bernard again. It will be almost two whole weeks since we were last together! Monday cannot come quickly enough. How I long to be with him again – to hear his voice – to see him; inside me is a vast yearning, eating me up! According to Professor Joad, "love" is just Nature's device to get Man to procreate – however, what I *feel* is much more complex than that. Wrote to Bernard yesterday telling him I would arrive in Aberdare late on Monday; that he should stop worrying about our financial situation, for even though our living standard may not be high, even the lowest can be spiritually heightened for me, working and living together would alone be sufficient, with an identical aim – that of having and bringing up children along the same path.

Now a chronicle of my time here. On Monday we went for a ramble – beautiful countryside. Must have walked twelve miles, and *was* I stiff afterwards! Tuesday we went to the sea-shore, quite unlike my beloved Llanelly, and one visit to Gateshead, which is even more dreary than Penrhiwceiber (also a coal-mining town, 'tho 'Ceiber is much smaller, just a few streets along a valley). Visited Celia and Danko – (Danko is one of Bevin's pit-boys). I've read only one book *The Laws of Jewish Marriage*, and as usual have plenty of questions, but think I understand most of it. It appears that the old adage "Absence makes the heart grow fonder" is a key factor in Jewish marriage – but in the form of abstention at certain times, bringing a more complete love into all aspects of daily life. It certainly is a different way of looking at marriage! Most nights we have talked until 2 a.m. – my troubles seem small compared to that of the girls here – we don't discuss the war, as it's too painful for them to be reminded of their families' situation, however we *do* listen to the news. According to reports there were "End of the World" scenes in Germany as the four cities of Hanover, Brunswick, Hamburg and Lubeck were set ablaze (Bernard's father was born in Lubeck). Our troops have crossed the Rhine (on some of Joe's bridges no doubt!) and are being supported by a large "Armada" of aeroplanes carrying supplies and men. In Tokyo, the whole centre has been devastated by firebombs dropped by the Yanks – they have also taken the island of Iwojima, an important position, but with the loss of many soldiers in the "to the death" fighting. Hope to get a little more sleep before I leave for Aberdare. I don't look blooming with life from my "holiday" and shall arrive home bleary-eyed to meet Mum's anger. (Is there no Prodigal *Daughter*???) Re: Uncle – If I have not been in Sunderland, where then am I supposed to have been?

Monday 9th April

Pesach is over for yet another year. I wonder where I shall be next year? Will there be Peace – and if so what kind of peace? During the long train journey, re-read Bernard's many letters that have been my daily support. Thought up endless arguments to have with Mum – I've always been contrary; therefore, if Mum disapproves of my marriage, I'm almost certain it's the right thing for me to do. I look at my reflection in the carriage window and say to myself – or rather to my old self, "Is this me? The me that was?" and the answer comes back quite definitely, "No it isn't." And I'm so glad it isn't, and feel so thankful to Bernard for giving me the opportunity of being different. He has given me not only knowledge, but a strong handrail that I can hold on to; a feeling of joy that by my own deeds I can affect my future and not be dragged down by the past and the deeds of others.

As the train moved into London there seemed to be a sudden lifting of spirit; we all smiled with relief – for the last two weeks no V-2s have brought havoc from the skies. I had a long wait in Paddington for a connection – but at least I got a seat.

At Newport, a smart, confident young man in uniform came in; I hardly recognised him – Cliff Pritchard – my childhood street-gang friend who had played Hiawatha to my Minni-ha-ha up and down the dark streets of 'Ceiber. "Duw!" he said, "Duw, there's bewtiful you are!"

"You too," I grinned. "How's the Tank Co.?"

He laughed, "Not *in* tanks, I'm serving in a submarine. Compared to lying in the dark wet pits hacking at coal, it's like living in luxury, I love it."

"But you can't swim!" I said, surprised.

"Well, I don't plan on getting *wet*! – Anyway, I've learned to swim – and many other things." He winked, "I got engaged last Xmas!"

"So did I!"

He gave me a look! "My Mam doesn't approve, my fiancée's ENGLISH! From Portsmouth, Da's taken it quite well." He left the train in Pontypridd, with a wave and, "If you can't be good, be careful!"

I watched him stride along the platform. Bernard was waiting when the train arrived at 9.10 p.m. After a wonderful reunion he walked with me as far as the shop and left. We are meeting tomorrow at 10 a.m. at the Clock Tower. Dead Tired! Looking forward to seeing Sara in the morning.

Tuesday 10th April

Sara woke me at 8 a.m.; "Ow Be?" she said. "Cynth?" She looked puzzled – was I really there? Would I disappear again? (Yes, I'm afraid so.) Sara is now a pretty brunette Shirley Temple straight out of *Curly Top* – with a very Welsh (Linda) accent. At breakfast Mum was very prickly: "You know, Bernard wouldn't even have a cup of tea and cake here," she said, miffed. "Not Kosher enough for him I expect!"

"Well – there are different standards of Kosher," I said.

"NO," Mum replied, "Kosher is Kosher!"

She's actually right about that! In this mood there was little point in discussion; decided to pack the last of my belongings to take with me to Cheltenham. Slid the large box from beneath the bed – and immediately felt something was wrong – the box was far too light! My books of essays, poems, drawings – boxes of complete sets of cigarette cards (hundreds of sets collected for me by the miners of Penrhiwceiber, and Uncle Ben's friends); the fifty or more plasticine models of children of different countries dressed in their national dress that I had made during my stay in Gran's; the hand-made trousseau I'd made for the Shirley Temple doll Uncle Harry bought me – all gone! Only the doll remained, dressed in her long pink dressing-gown and matching pyjamas. I tore downstairs …

"Oh," Mum said to my enquiry, "I didn't think you'd want those things anymore, now you're going away – I threw them out – anyway they were getting mouldy."

I felt bomb blasted! All my cherished souvenirs up in smoke! Ridiculous to care so much – but I do. Met Bernard as arranged. He told me his farming friend, Trevor Wigley had called on him last week to tell him Wag, the sheep-dog Bernard had trained, was pining for him, no one could do anything with him – perhaps Bernard would like to have him? Bernard was going to Cross Bychan to collect him. The walk up the mountain was just what I needed; we made plans to return to Cheltenham. When Wag saw Bernard he just went wild with delight, dancing around him on two legs, front paws around Bernard's neck, licking him, lying on the ground to be tickled. After this show of affection, Wag stayed glued to Bernard, but was reassured as we took him with us to Aberdare.

"He's not jealous of me," I remarked.

"Of course not – he's a male – he'll love you." Wag snorted happily, as if he understood.

Popped into the shop to tell Mum that I was leaving for Cheltenham immediately. *Great Scene*! "How could you? Linda has her holiday next week – WHO WILL LOOK AFTER SARA?"

I promised to return on Sunday, the last week of *my* holidays – and that I'd bring the books up to date. Had lunch in Kahns'. Mrs. Kahn gave me a jar of duck fat that remained from the four ducks Bernard had brought her – Bernard and Adolf had plucked them together – what a job! At 3 p.m. we caught a bus for Porth; Wag settled down happily between our feet. The Katzes, as usual made us very welcome. We told Dr. Katz our plans to stay in Cheltenham until we could be married.

"I don't like it," he said, "You two alone, without supervision."

"But we're engaged," I said.

"Just so," said Siegbert Katz.

"Well, Joyce will be with us – and Bernard will be sleeping at The Orchard."

Unconvinced, he said, "Get married soon! I'll speak to the Kahns and put a word in for you."

After an early meal we waited at the bus stop to get a bus for Cardiff … "No!" said the conductor, "we don't take dogs." Neither would the next bus. When the third bus came, we were ready: Wag – front legs around Bernard's shoulders, hidden by Bernard's tweed coat, his long black and white tail dangling below, me – close behind, hiding the tail, we ran quickly to the top deck and put Wag under the seat. Arrived at Cardiff to find the last train for Cheltenham had left. The stationmaster suggested we took the next train as far as Newport and caught a connection from there. *No* connection! *No* waiting room open, *no* lights. We sat on the cold bench all night waiting for the 6.30 a.m. train – how romantic! *Actually* we were both tired; Wag snored, and an aroma of farm manure and unwashed dog wafted upwards. By the time the train arrived the three of us were almost glued together looking like a marble Rodin sculpture. Arrived at Evesham Road to find Joyce frantic with worry, about to go to the police. Bernard went straight to Russell's to work. After a short rest I went with Joyce to buy bread (half-hour queue, and fish – one-hour queue). Told Joyce what had happened to my cherished mementoes of the last nine years. Sometimes Joyce surprises me! "Not Mum," she said, "Mum's a hoarder – only the doll Uncle Harry had given you was left – I think *he* did it in a rage and Mum was covering up for him." Glad now that I took my matric. certificate, diaries and *Children's Shakespeare* last time.

Caravans at The Orchard, April '45

Wednesday 11th April

Max called in today with a parcel for all of us: four packets of tobacco for Bernard, one pair of army gloves for me; one-and-a-half lbs of chocolate, sweets and gum for Joyce. He stayed for supper – told us that the Russians have taken Vienna. Bernard said, "My first girlfriend lived in Vienna, I wonder if she's still alive?"

Thursday 12th April

Hitch-hiked to Reading to buy some milk churns from a farmer – got there, but the farmer was out – I was pleased, remembering the bee-hives which are *still* in Droitwich; Bernard has received a *bill* for rent of the land they're standing on! Lewis came at 4 p.m., but not with the poultry as promised; he wants exclusive rights to sub-let the land to caravans – all the money to go to him! This is quite ridiculous. So far he has not put up one penny towards buying the laying hens.

Friday 13th April

Lovely sunny morning. Bernard went first to the Employment Exchange for permission to work at The Orchard, Warden Hill Road, then to the Police Station to have his Alien's book stamped. We worked in the orchard until 2 p.m. cutting off the dead branches from the fruit trees. Made a large pile of wood that we can use as firewood. Some of the pear trees are beginning to blossom. Spring has really come:

> In spring time, the only pretty ring time,
> When birds do sing, hey ding a ding, ding;
> Sweet lovers love the spring.

Sunday 15th April
Yesterday Arthur stayed with us most of the day. In shul the talk was of the death of President Roosevelt – what a great shame, now that his forces are doing so well. Bernard took me to the station at 12 – how many more times will we arrive together, only to say "G'bye"? Had to stand all the way from Gloucester. Wished I could have spent such a lovely day together with Bernard out in the country instead of being on my own in a terribly stuffy train. Mum looked really pleased to see me and is being very careful about food, she doesn't know what she can offer me and what not; it makes it a lot easier for me, as I don't have to make excuses. Although Mum buys Kosher meat, she never learnt the dietary laws – there was no one to teach us in Penrhiwceiber. I don't expect Mum to change because of me – just to be tolerant of my keeping the traditional customs. It's strange how these dietary laws alone can separate people, even within the same family.

Monday 16th April
Worked on the books for most of the day, apart from seeing to Sara. In the late afternoon took Sara to Clifton Street to visit Kahns'. I was very nervous, but they were very nice to me and I felt more at home there than I had ever done before. Sara was delighted to see Simon, who looks like a little doll, with long blond hair and big blue eyes. He smiled all the time; Bernard's mother said that Bernard was fair like that, but, different to her other children, his eyes were brown instead of blue, I wonder what ours will look like? Mrs. Kahn gave me her recipe for potato salad, and Zwetschkenkuchen [Damson tart] – exact to the one eighth of a gram. I have been invited to join them Friday night for supper.

Tuesday 17th April
Heard accounts on the radio of the monstrous crimes that have been committed by the Nazis in the concentration camps – Auschwitz and Buchenwald, which have been liberated. We are, like the American and Russian liberators, speechless with horror – the scenes are even worse than anyone could have imagined. That human beings could inflict such unspeakable persecution on such incredible numbers of men, women, children, even babies, makes us dumb with shock – we cannot even speak of it to each other. At moments we want not to believe it; army personnel who liberated the camps, and war correspondents that reported on it, are sickened by what they have found.

Wednesday 18th April
Went to Penrhiwceiber with Sara to see Gran and Berta. Emrys (the bus conductor) stopped the bus at Gran's door; Sara draws admiring glances from everyone we meet – some women remembered Mum at that age. Gran turned off the wireless when the news started; with a sigh she looked across at Berta, but Berta seems to have blocked out memories of parting with her family six years

ago; Gran's mother was killed in a pogrom by the Cossacks – maybe that's why she applied to take a refugee girl in 1939 when so few others did.

The smell of gefilte fish frying reminded me to ask Gran for some of her recipes. Gran is an instinctive cook (unlike Mrs. Kahn), e.g. Barley Soup:

"Soak some barley."

"How much?"

"As much as you want … Salt …"

"How much?"

"You'll know how much."

"How many onions and carrots?"

"As much as you need." Ditto for her bread and cinnamon cake. She is astonished that I don't know! Chopped herring? – Grated apples? Sugar! Eggs! – Gefilte fish? – "Don't forget to put some oil in to keep them moist."

At home a letter from Bernard was waiting, he will phone tomorrow night. So far Mum has avoided the subject – I know, from long experience, her "I'm busy, don't talk to me now" face.

Thursday 19th April

Went to Cardiff to buy a few things for Mum. In Gottleib's, I gave them Bernard's and my ration books for fats and sugar. Mrs. Gottlieb said she'd buy the cream cheese for 3/- a pound when we start making it. Such a lovely day, wished I could be in "The Orchard".

Returned to find two letters from Bernard – he wrote:

> "It was lovely to hear your voice, I could not get enough of it. I often feel as if we two have grown into one, and at the moment one part of me is missing. Oh, dearest, I will try to do my best for you forever, your wish shall be mine, and in what you find delight, I shall find delight. I shall try and ring you on Thursday night at 10.30 so please be near the phone. Last night I slept in "The Orchard" Warden Hill Road for the first time. I left Evesham Road gone 12 and when I got out there it was quite dark, all one could hear were the cows mooing in the neighbourhood. It was so peaceful. I imagined for a moment I was in Eretz [Israel]. How lovely it would be if we would just have a shed like that and a bit of land out there; I stopped and dreamt for a minute, but woke up to the fact that it was just wishful thinking. I opened the door, lit a candle, and here I was, I had a home of my own for the first time in my life. How lonely I felt without you. I thought of Bereshit [Genesis] and Odom VeChavah [Adam and Eve]."

Bernard phoned "on the dot" and I went to bed with the sound of his voice still in my head. What little time we've had together during my "holiday".

Saturday 21st April

Spent most of the day at the Kahns'. Tonight, *spoke* to Mum; told her that I'd be back at half-term when I'd be almost nineteen. I hoped she'd agree to sign the marriage permission then – as I don't want my mind to be influenced by a piece of paper – or have constant arguments over my future. I wouldn't want to hurt her in any way – 'She didn't say Yes – but she didn't say No!'

Sunday 22nd April

Got up early and decided to dress the windows (of Jane Cooper) – used lovely spring colours, blues, yellows, soft greens. Enjoyed myself; used some ideas picked up in Cheltenham; the clothes really looked stunning! Mum was delighted; she came with Sara to see me off and I left for Cardiff in a good mood. Waited a long time at Newport for a connection. Got a seat and passed the time drawing sleeping passengers opposite me until it got too dark.

The train stopped a few times and half an hour before we reached Cheltenham it stopped for good – everyone out! It could hardly be an air-raid or unexploded bomb, probably heavy troop movements. We were told no trains were allowed into the main station, so we'd have to make our own way home. Everyone departed except one man – a Chinaman. I saw a lone taxi moving along the dark road. It stopped and as I got in I asked the Chinaman if he'd like to join me for the ride to Cheltenham. We sat together in the back. "You are so kind," he said; my thoughts, as usual, were on seeing Bernard again.

Suddenly, the man took hold of my hand and said: "I want to marry you."

"Pardon?" I exclaimed. "I'm engaged to be married."

"No ploblem," he said. "You pletty, you kind, you be my wife – I take you back with me." With that, he gripped me tightly.

I felt pretty foolish – also a bit scared. He told me he was visiting relatives who had a laundry business in Cheltenham. In my wild imagination I had visions of me being drugged, put into a laundry basket and "shanghaied" out to China, never to be seen again.

My "suitor" was so serious and sure of himself, nothing I said made any impression on him. "Please," he said giving me a little bow, "give me your addless."

I wrote down a fictitious address in Lansdown Road and asked the driver to stop there. I paid and pretended to go into one of the houses – waited for the taxi to disappear, then ran like the wind to Evesham Road and straight into Bernard's arms. "You're shivering!" he said, "It's not cold."

"Hold me tight!" I gasped, then told him about my kind (?), foolish (!) gesture and its unexpected result. After a hot drink I calmed down – Bernard had been three times to the station to meet me – what a homecoming! He was very concerned and didn't want me to go to college tomorrow alone, but I assured him I'd be careful.

Monday 23rd April

Went to college this morning disguised with a headscarf, sunglasses and an old shawl; glad to arrive there safely. Bernard met me after college and we cycled to The Orchard. As he opened the gate for me, I stopped and drew breath in wonder – almost two hundred trees all in blossom! Delicate pink, cream and white petals covered the fresh green leaves – magical! I want to fix this sight in my mind forever. As I bumped over the grass towards the shed, another surprise awaited me. "Look," said Bernard, and there in the shed was a large soft-eyed brownish white cow. Bernard had bought her in Tewkesbury for £21.10/-. I watched him milk her, expertly directing the frothy creamy-white milk into a bucket. "What shall we call her?" I asked. Just as we watched the sun dropping, golden red behind the trees, Joyce came pedalling down the field; "Joycycle!" replied Bernard, giving the cow a loving pat. "This is Van Gogh's 'Orchard'," Joyce said. The three of us cycled back to the flat for supper, Wag trotting along beside us.

Wednesday 25th April

Bernard bought two poultry sheds for 7/6; also twelve hens – Plymouth Rock. Their feathers glisten in the sunlight, really beautiful birds. Joycycle (our Shorthorn × Ayreshire), is producing gallons of milk a day; He hopes to start making cheese in a day or two. Tonight Bernard brought four eggs, a bottle of fresh milk, and 15/-, which he insists on paying us for his food. Things are looking up – I shall save £1 this week from our housekeeping money. In Germany the Russians have surrounded Berlin; it's hoped that the Americans will meet up with them very soon. Bernard has written to Paul to see if he can find any trace of his brother and other members of his family – uncles, aunts and cousins. Paul is in Germany interrogating captured German soldiers – some even pretend to be Jewish and all of them claim to be innocent of any atrocity!

Friday 27th April

This morning Bernard received a letter from Rabbi Dr. Schonfeld of the C.R.R.E.C. [Chief Rabbi's Religious Emergency Council] asking him if he'd be willing to go on relief work in the camps on the Continent for *three months*. He says he cannot refuse, stating: "Do not the Jews on the Continent and the conditions in which they are in, make it our absolute duty to help them if one can?" I would not be able to join him – he would like us to be married before he goes. Worried about it all day. I have only seen happiness on his face these last few months, blotting out his terrible memories of the time he was imprisoned in Dachau before the war. If he goes, he will come back a completely changed person, yet I cannot be so selfish as to keep him here. What point would there be in marrying, only to say goodbye – Mum would never agree anyway. He has replied asking for more details, especially about re-entry into Britain. Having only an Enemy Alien's Passport he may not be allowed back. The weather is sunny, the news great – the Russians and the Americans have met near the Elbe. Arthur is coming tonight so I really must put on a cheerful face.

Sunday 29th April

"Don't cast a clout, till May is out …"

Yesterday was freezing, we were back in winter clothes. This morning Bernard arrived early, looking exhausted. "I've been up all night," he said, "trying to save the fruit." A bitter cold wind was blowing. All night Bernard had lit candles under the trees and made a few wood fires around them to try to keep the frost from damaging the fruit. We went back together with more candles – a hopeless job. We gave up when the weather got worse, a light snow covering everything. At the flat I heated up some soup, but it took some time until we thawed out. "That's the end of our fruit," Bernard sighed. "I feel like saying 'Eicho'." ['How doth the city sit solitary that was full of people …' from Book of Lamentations written by Jeremiah.] "Last week, everything looked lovely and I was hoping for a bumper crop, and now I have a lot of trees with no fruit on them."

Later, we went with Joyce to the Allies Club. The atmosphere there was electric, as a ripple of speculation and rumour intoxicated everyone – "Goering's dead", no – "Mussolini's been killed" – "Italy's surrendered" and so on – we all waited for the evening news. The Allies have asked the G.H.C. (German High Command) for an unconditional surrender and are waiting for a reply. Good news from Italy – the fighting is almost over and our forces have taken Milan. Two Yanks came back with us; we made a large fire and sat round it talking and singing. We persuaded Bernard to sleep on the couch as the orchard would be so cold – Wag was quite happy and curled up before the glowing coals. Went to bed very late.

Monday 30th April

No Life Class in college because of the cold – did drawing from the Antique instead. I love drawing the Discus Thrower. At 5 p.m. I cycled to the station with Bernard to send off our first box of cheese. It weighed 28lb and went to Margulies in London.

Tuesday 1st May
I went shopping lunch-time; food very scarce; heard we are dropping containers of food on Holland; there is great starvation there. Bernard came and brought eggs, milk and rhubarb. He told me he had bought more hens – sixty now, and found another market gardening job. Cooked the rhubarb – it was a lovely pink colour – tasted it – awful! No sugar or saccs. Made custard with the eggs, milk and corn flour, stirred in the rhubarb. Bernard then went to phone the C.R. Council to speak to Rabbi Schonfeld. They have decided to send someone else to the camps in Europe, as they cannot guarantee Bernard re-entry. I'm pleased, but not sure if Bernard is. Tonight he was very moody; we have all heard about the liberation of Dachau and the terrible scenes there – Bernard wouldn't stay for supper, just wanted to be alone. I hope Joycycle, Wag, and collecting the eggs will ease his gloom.

Wednesday 2nd May
Mrs. Rose came over after the 9 o'clock news, to tell us **Hitler is dead**! All fighting in Italy has stopped. The Russians are in Berlin. We can hardly believe that Hitler is no more. Mrs. Rose showed us pictures of her son who is in the Army. He was in Palestine on Pesach and wants to live there after the war.

Monday 7th May
College very disturbed today. Not much Architecture done. Everyone expecting the end of the war. At 3 p.m. two girls came in to say it was over, but we didn't believe them. We listened to the 4 p.m. news and heard that the German High Command has ordered all German troops to surrender unconditionally. Came home and told Bernard (who had just come back from Russell's) the news. Cycled out to the orchard to feed the chickens and Wag. Collected the eggs and brought some home. Heard that tomorrow is V. E. Day and therefore a holiday. Peace will be declared from one minute after midnight tomorrow, 8th May. Stayed up and read. Joyce had heard the news on her way home, but didn't believe it until Erwin came down to tell us he'd heard it confirmed again on the wireless. Bernard came back from The Orchard – he and Erwin had a celebration mock fight, slapping each other on the shoulders in fun. Suddenly Wag shot up at Erwin and attacked his throat; Bernard shouted "Down, Wag!" and Wag instantly obeyed. "Good dog," Bernard said, fondling his ears, adding, "he really thought I was in danger." At 8.30 Bernard and I went for a walk and stayed out until 1 a.m.

Tuesday 8th May – **V. E. Day**
As Joyce didn't have to go to work in Stroud, we both got up late. We went out into the crowded streets – most people queued for bread, while I queued for fish; I stood there for almost an hour. Everyone was in a good mood, although, this

being Cheltenham, quite reserved apart from a few smiles, everyone thinking their own thoughts; mostly, I expect, that we had lived through to see the defeat of Hitler and the destruction of his enormous war machine. I thought of the day in September 1939 when war was declared; I was barely thirteen …

By lunch-time the streets began to fill with Yanks from the Army base. When Joyce and I arrived back at the flat, our own GI's, Arthur, Max and Charlie, were already there. They had brought tins of butter, syrup, oil and peaches; Bernard arrived with some vegetables and a jar of fresh cream. We had a great celebration lunch! The other families in Evesham Road were making plans for a children's street party, which was to take place after Churchill's speech at 3 p.m. At 2.45 p.m. we went upstairs to the Denham's flat to listen to the radio. When Churchill started to speak we all gave each other the "V" sign. Afterwards we cycled out to the orchard, two balancing on each bike. Some of the plum trees were still in flower, Joycycle munching away at the fresh green grass. Our GI's are very concerned that they will now be sent to fight the Japs in the Pacific, instead of just "cleaning up" in Europe, as US losses there are high.

As we stood round watching Bernard milking the cow, he suddenly spurted a stream of milk all over Max's perfectly pressed uniform. Max took it in good part, and I wiped him down, making a big fuss over wiping his mouth, for the Yanks are not allowed to drink our milk because of T.B.! As it got dark, things began to liven up; everyone put all the lights on and Cheltenham became a fairyland. The main attraction was the beautiful façade of the Queen's Hotel, which, lit up, looked like a palace. All the main buildings had searchlights directed on them and looked wonderful; the Promenade was filled with people wandering up and down along the tree-lined streets, singing and dancing, many now quite tipsy. Our GI's and Bernard made a cordon around Joyce and me, so we wouldn't get too many unwanted hugs and kisses. At 9 p.m. we returned home to hear the King's Speech, which was even more moving because of his slight stutter. Bernard and I cycled to the hills to see the bonfires that were still burning. Indescribable feelings – it seemed as if the Milky Way had fallen into the valley.

So this great episode in history – and especially in Jewish History – is finished. There is a feeling of both joy and sadness, for as Bernard remarked: "How can we have the proper spirit to celebrate – as our losses have been so great." Still, without drinking one beer, we are too intoxicated with events to go to sleep. Lines from Baudelaire's 'Enivrez-Vous' run through my mind:

> You must always be drunk. It's everything – but on what? On wine, on poetry, or on virtue as you please. And if sometimes, on the steps of a palace, on the grass bank of a ditch, in the dismal loneliness of your room, you wake up – the intoxication already diminished – ask the wind, the wave, the star, the bird, the clock, all those things that groan, that sing, that speak, ask what time it is; they will reply to you: "It's time to get drunk! Intoxicate yourselves on wine, on poetry, or on virtue, as you please."

But *definitely*eeee!!! We are all quite drunk with happiness and relief!

Wednesday 9th to Tuesday 29th May

The last three weeks have passed quickly, like a dream – everything "normal" but no one knowing exactly what "normal" is, or what "peace" is. Although the killing and destruction in Europe have stopped, the upheaval is great; masses of people are moving about, trying to find their families or homes; many prisoners of war have returned home, after four or five years in captivity. Here, Joyce is not sure what to do when she is released from her job in Stroud. Charlie has been sent to the Pacific, Max has returned to America and Arthur is still with us. Mum has been ill with MUM-ps!!! The shop has been very busy, everyone wanting new clothes in which to meet returning husbands, lovers, sons. Food and many simple needs are scarcer than ever. Lucky we have the orchard – but we almost didn't. Last Thursday, Bernard had just finished the morning milking, four gallons a day now, when – what a shock! A policeman appeared with a summons for him and a notice for him to leave The Orchard immediately, as he had no right to be there! Bernard told the policeman about his agreement with the owner – Mr. Lewis – BUT – *Lewis* does not *own* The Orchard; it was all a *fraud*. (Am I surprised?) The real owners live in a village ten miles away in the Cotswold Hills. Bernard was upset and said he'd go to see them to try to make a new rent agreement and get their permission to stay on. I said I'd go with him. We arranged to go there Sunday afternoon. All Shabbos Bernard bit his nails to the quick – he said he always goes "derech ha-yoshor" [the straight path] and now it appears he has been cheating the real owners of their rent – I suggested paying them back from my savings. The episode of the policeman has brought back all Bernard's memories, of his imprisonment as a fifteen-year-old boy (because of his Enemy Alien's status); of the time he spent in a prisoner of war camp in England, and then being interned on the Isle of Man. Sunday we cycled to the Kingsleys' home. Just before the village we stopped for breath and to tidy ourselves; I found one boiled sweet in my pocket. We were both quite hungry, so I asked Bernard for his penknife to cut the sweet in two – suddenly I saw my hand covered in blood – I'd sliced through my middle two fingers (luckily it was my left hand). Bernard wrapped his hanky around the deep cuts and, holding my arm across my shoulder, we arrived at the Kingsleys' beautiful Georgian house. What they must have thought of us arriving like that – my clothes all spattered with blood. Mr. Kingsley expertly bandaged my two fingers, his wife gave me a hot sweet drink. They were surprised how young their trespassers were. Bernard showed them his agreement with Lewis (the rogue), and Lewis's advert in the *Cheltenham Gazette.* He told them about his refugee status, and a bit about his past, that now, when at last he felt free and happy, was making enough to keep himself, and saving up for us to get married – along came the summons. The Kingsleys took pity on Bernard and showered us with kindness. They gave permission for Bernard to stay at The Orchard for as long as he needed to, *rent free.* We cycled home in good spirits – except for my throbbing fingers. Phoned Mum Monday evening; she said she's not contagious anymore, so I shall go to Aberdare next Sunday to get her written permission for us to marry. As Siegbert Katz had forewarned, it really is quite hard being together with Bernard every day without being married.

Sunday 3rd, Monday 4th June

After a long tiring journey home, arrived to find Mum looking and feeling great – no more "Greer Garson", but "Marlene Dietrich" in a new red dress all ready to welcome home the troops. She had the same dress in blue, one size larger, in stock, and gave it to me. It has red and gold squares printed onto the material – a Hershell. I'm thrilled! Uncle has gone to London to see if he can re-start his upholstery factory. With only a warning to me not to do anything hasty, Mum *signed* the paper (the marriage consent form). She dropped a hint that Alex is doing well, studying for a degree in Cambridge. I said I was glad – I try so hard *not* to think of him. Visited Kahns', as usual very nice – only one *small* condition (?!!!), that I wouldn't marry Bernard until Mrs. Kahn had finished her one year's mourning for the death of her father (that's in October!) – that the Chaseneh [wedding] should take place in London where we would be able to hire a Kosher caterer. Mrs. Kahn would give me a list of her family and friends she wanted invited! Ellen said she's against an early marriage, as I need more time to learn how to keep a Kosher kitchen (I feel more than ready to be married). Ellen added that of course the wedding would take place outside, and not in a synagogue. (In October???) Began to wonder if Gretna Green is outside enough for her. Adolf said he'd lend Bernard his dinner jacket and top hat – which is very nice of him – except he's at least six inches shorter than Bernard. Mr. Kahn said he'd give me the silver Ziflounes belt [antique filigree wedding belt] to wear on my wedding dress – it's a heavy piece and really not my taste. Walked back to the shop, where, fortunately, Mum was too busy to ask questions – or to give me lists of *her* family and stipulations. I can't see Mum paying for a wedding she doesn't even want! Met Mrs. Prosser – who still hopes against all odds that her son may have survived in a camp in Japan. She said "not knowing" is the worst. I feel truly sorry for her. There's been no news of Bernard's brother Erich either – but Bernard has written to all the authorities to try and trace him. Slept (for the last time?) above the shop.

Tuesday 5th June

Took the bus to Cardiff, mentally saying good-bye to the green hills, the grey slag heaps and terraced houses, the Cynon Valley where every path is known to me. How I hated it all when at seven years of age I came from Llanelly – how dear it seems to me now that I'm leaving it, possibly forever.

Monday 25th June

Went to the doctor this morning. Shabbos I felt really ill, with an odd sort of feeling in my neck and throat. Told the doctor I've got mumps. He said, "How do you know?" So I told him about Mum and my visit to her three weeks ago. He examined me: "Yes, you do have mumps." I told him about Bernard – he said mumps is a nasty thing for a young man to catch – it can make them infertile. Bernard of course refuses to be careful – he rang his mother to ask if she remembers if he's had it – she didn't know. It's painful and I look a sight! Joyce definitely has not had it and has put me in purdah. She sits as far from me as possible, and uses her own plates, cups etc. Bernard has at last sold the bee-hives to the new owners of the Manor. I lie here thinking …

Where the bee sucks there suck I.
In a cowslip's bell I lie.
There I couch when owls do cry.
On the bat's back I do fly
After summer merrily.
Merrily, merrily shall I live now
Under the blossom that hangs on the bough.
Ariel in *The Tempest*

Invitation to our GI visitors for Friday night: "Only those who have had mumps need apply." Obviously, no college for me. My two fingers have healed nicely, only leaving a white scar across both of them. One of the GI's called in with some good news – Okinawa, an island only 350 miles from the coast of Japan, has been captured; the Americans are also fighting the Japs in Borneo. Arthur "sat" for me while I drew his portrait.

Left to right: Bernard, Arthur and A.Y. Katz, Summer '45

Friday 20th July [10th Av]
I'm nineteen today! [Hebrew date.] (Bernard said that every 19 years the Hebrew date and the English date fall on the same day – well not this year – the next time it may happen I'll be 38) Yesterday, that is until 3 hours ago, I fasted until 10.30 p.m. [Fast of 9th Av]. I couldn't eat much after, as my mumps gave me trouble. Yes, I've got mumps at nineteen years of age! I went to bed at 12 but couldn't sleep. Got up, came back to bed, tried to sleep, but too wide-awake! Decided to write something in you, my little neglected diary, just to let you know what's been happening to me lately.

One date, the 21st June, stands out in my memory. Bernard (the boy I'm still in love with, and always will be) went to London to try to get me a certificate (for entry to Palestine) – his was certain, but mine was unsure. At 10.30 p.m. he was supposed to return. I waited till 11 p.m. and went round to the station. Rang up London but couldn't get through. By now 11.30; no more trains, so sure he could not arrive. Rode up to The Orchard as quickly as I could – without lights, (the battery on my bicycle was kaput and the country lanes of course, are not lit) and got there at 11.45. Went straight to the next farm, woke the farmer and asked if he could milk the cow. He said his son might, when he came in. Went up to top gate and waited for the boy in the dark. Felt terribly tired. At last I saw a lantern light gleaming cheerfully through the grey-black darkness. Ran towards its moving beam and finally caught up with Ken, as I found it was. Explained about the problem of our unmilked cow getting mastitis [milk fever]. He was surprised that I was not frightened to come up alone with not a soul around except the wind rustling in the trees and the cows quietly chewing or lowing softly behind the tall hedges. The moon came up – white – picking out the silver dew hanging on the fruit-less trees and glistening in the tall grass. The sharp sound of milk dashing against the side of the bucket, in a perfect rhythm, soon joined with the regular chewing of our cow. Joycycle was glad we had come, but kicked occasionally at her strange master, for her bag was very full. We talked, and the lantern light hanging on the rafters picked out the dark shadows of the hens roosting in the shed. They slept on. Wag had not liked the dog that had followed Ken through the field and had barked, but now both dogs were silent and watched us from out of deep solemn eyes. The cow was milked and sent back to her field. Ken pushed my bike as far as the gate and wished me goodnight. I watched the lantern glow receding until eventually it was enveloped by the darkness. I waited a few minutes and then rode down once more to the shed. It was glorious riding down "'neath the pale moon" between the trees towards that grey ramshackle building. I locked the door after me and undressed by candlelight. I had luckily found one single match, and also a torch, but that didn't seem to work. I snuggled down into the soft feather bed, my skin thrilling to the touch of its smooth coolness. The flickering shadows melted into one as I snuffed out the orange flame. I lay there listening; the hens next door were snoring, occasionally moving their weight from one leg to the other. The moon found a crack between the door and roof to show herself. I watched her radiance, and the cool hay-scented air ran softly over my face. I thought of last year's camp, and snuggled deeper into the bed; I slept.

At 3 a.m., the sound of my name being called awoke me. I listened again and heard Bernard's voice calling softly "Cynthia, Cynthia." Covering myself, I walked across the stone floor, and after a few attempts opened the door. After Bernard's sharp words of enquiry, I explained how, when he had not come, I found someone to milk the cow, and then stayed at The Orchard, it being too late to cycle home alone. Pacified, he began to tell me his great news – *he had our certificates* – the boat sailed a week next Friday! It was already Thursday. Tomorrow we would go to London. We would have to be civilly married with a special licence, sell and pack all our things, say our goodbyes, and we had a week to do it in. Our excitement was indescribable! Suddenly Wag barked and we held our breath. He growled, grunted and then stopped. "There's someone here," said Bernard – but I put it down to the hens: "After all, who would come at 4 a.m. in the night, and what for?" The happenings of the day were unfolded to me; my head became weary with sleep, but worried with sleeplessness. My mind was busy; thinking, planning, dreaming, but no sleep came. The clear rousing cry of the cock rang out through the morning air – another joined in and soon the hens began to rouse themselves, one by one clumsily jumping from their perches to greet – for them – another monotonously senseless day. The morning brightened, and at 7 a.m. our day began.

Friday, (22nd June) we caught the first train to London and went immediately to the Jewish Agency. There our hopes were soon dashed, as the Secretary, Mr. Feuchtwanger, explained, it would be impossible to get my release through in time to catch the next boat. Bernard, being classed as an 'Enemy Alien' would have no problem. My age and British Nationality makes me liable for war work if I left the Art College. The only way would be for me to marry Bernard as quickly as possible then I too would be classed as an Enemy Alien (!!!) and could get an exit visa; getting all the relevant papers processed would take some time, therefore our certificates would go to two other people; we have been promised priority as soon as the Minister of Labour agrees to my release. We spent Shabbos with Family Bodenheimer, a cousin of Adolf's; Anny Bodenheimer said I could stay with her any time I needed to be in London. In a way it's quite a relief to have a few more weeks in which to:
Get married (Registry Office).
Sell the chickens – our beautiful Rhode Island Reds.
Sell the chicken hutches etc. Ugh! I'll have to clean them of all the droppings!
Sell Joycycle.
Send Wag back to Llwydcoed (regretfully).
Pack and be ready to leave Cheltenham as soon as we are allocated certificates.

Tuesday 24th July

Rather emotional parting with Wag, Bernard's most reliable guard and constant friend. Joyce is going to Aberdare, so she agreed (was persuaded) to take the dog back to his old home in Llwydcoed where he will be well looked after. Couldn't bear to look into his sad puzzled eyes as the train pulled out. We hired a horse and cart to take the chicken hutches to auction; hire of cart – £2, fee to auctioneer 10/- [ten shillings], grand sum received £3, which means I spent the whole of Sunday cleaning them for 10/- ! Mr. Barr has bought the chickens. Bernard had arranged to work on his land for 2/6 [two shillings and sixpence] an hour to supplement the money we get from the cheese. Every Tuesday and Thursday we cycle to the station with 28 or 29lbs of cheese, wrapped and packed in a cardboard box. We leave a three-mile trail of drops of whey along the road; the more moisture left in the cheese, the heavier it weighs on the scales. We send the weight receipts to Margulies, our London buyer, or Mrs. Gottlieb in Cardiff.

Sunday 29th July

At last I have been allowed back into the human race, after weeks of isolation; celebrated by going to the Allies Club today. The discussion was on: 'How soon Palestine might be a real Jewish Homeland?' How serious is the pledge by Hugh Dalton, Deputy Leader of our new Labour Government, for the creation of a free, happy and prosperous Jewish State of Palestine? How will it come about? With the certificate quota so restricted to Jews entering Palestine, one fears there will be no change in the situation until the British leave – and then what? Most of the Yanks here are obviously more interested in the ongoing war in the Pacific and their longing to return home to America. This week a huge attack was launched from Okinawa on mainland Japan. However no one expects the Japs to surrender – they think their Emperor Hirohito is divine and they are all prepared to fight to the last man. Arthur came back with us; he's certain he'll be sent out with the next posting.

Wednesday 1st August

Cycled to Gloucester, sat outside in the warm sunshine drawing the Cathedral. I marvelled at the work of the ancient sculptors, builders and craftsmen – so glad it hasn't been bombed to pieces like Coventry Cathedral. On my way out of Gloucester, riding down a steep hill, the brakes on my bike finally died on me. I charged down out of control – a tall Yank stepped into my path and I flew into his arms. "It's a pleasure, ma'am," he said when I thanked him. He then stopped a truck, put my bike in the back and escorted me back to Cheltenham. He and the driver came in for "cawfee".

Tuesday 7th August

Yesterday at 8.20 a.m. an atomic bomb was dropped on the Japanese town of Hiroshima. Reports said that smoke rose seven-and-a-half *miles* into the air! There was more power in that one bomb than twenty thousand tons of T.N.T; there is approximately four miles of destruction! It must have been like the biblical rain of brimstone on Sodom and Gomorrah: "When Abraham looked toward all the land of the Plain, he beheld the smoke of the land went up as the smoke of a furnace."

Tuesday 14th August

Another atom bomb has been dropped – this time on Nagasaki – with the same terrible effect as the first – but with a different result – THE JAPANESE HAVE SURRENDERED! Total Peace was announced at midnight. THE WAR IN THE PACIFIC HAS ENDED! Cheltenham erupted with sound, as all over we could hear railway engine whistles, foghorns, and cars beeping. We joined the thousands of people, many still in pyjamas or dressing gowns, dancing and cheering. Along the Promenade everyone danced the Hokey-Cokey and sang. Tomorrow will be a holiday – V. J. Day. The Denhams listened to the midnight broadcast given by Attlee, our new Prime Minister. Every light has been put on; the American troops here are crazy with relief and happiness. Even our old retired officers and generals "the Poona brigade", emblazoned with medals from their many years in India, are out on the streets waving their walking sticks and shouting "It's over, it's over!"

With all the excitement I almost forgot this morning's news – it seems like a week ago – Bernard and I went to see the Magistrate at the Registry Office to ask for a 3-day Special Marriage Licence. Our reasons were: (1) We had been engaged for seven months, (2) Bernard was a refugee now living in a stable, (3) We had my mother's written permission. The Magistrate granted us the licence and we made an appointment with the Registrar for 2 p.m. on Friday. So Friday we will be Civilly Married!

Wednesday 15th August – **V. J. Day**

Andy, one of the GI's, came at 10 a.m. – in tears of joy. We all went to hear the bands playing in Montpelier Gardens. We watched the dancing in the park, which went on all day and, in the afternoon, the church bells rang out. We went with Bernard to the orchard and waited for him to milk the cow. Dear Joycycle, she's to go to the auction in Tewkesbury next week. Bernard has got a temporary job at the Aguda Office in London. At the flat, Joyce and I used all our week's rations on a really grand supper. Sunday has been declared Victory Sunday. There'll be a special service in shul with the recitation of the Gomel Benediction [Blessing for being saved] and Hallel [Thanksgiving Psalms]: "I was brought low, and He saved me. For Thou hast delivered my soul from death, mine eyes from tears, my feet from falling. I shall walk before the L--d in the land of the living." The Kel Moleh Rachamim [Prayer said in memory of the dead] will also be recited.

I showed Andy and Bernard the poem I'd kept from the *Jewish Chronicle*, which was both apt and moving.

Poem: Thy Victory
by Gunner 1765994 R.A.

We turned to Thee, O G-d, in need.
Who knew not G-d in easy days,
Our little lives were marred by greed
And fickle, pleasure-loving ways;

We knew not G-d but prayed to Thee
When Mankind faced Calamity.
You heard our prayers O G-d of love
And spared once more thy frail Mankind.

Teach us, O G-d, Thy Law of Love
That we may see, who have been blind.
That we may make the peace to be
Worthy of this, Thy Victory.

Thursday 16th August

This morning a telegram came for Bernard; a letter from Paul for Joyce. The telegram was from the Administration of the Terezin Concentration Camp. It said: "erich kahn terezin is not your brother."

So Bernard's search for news of his brother goes on.

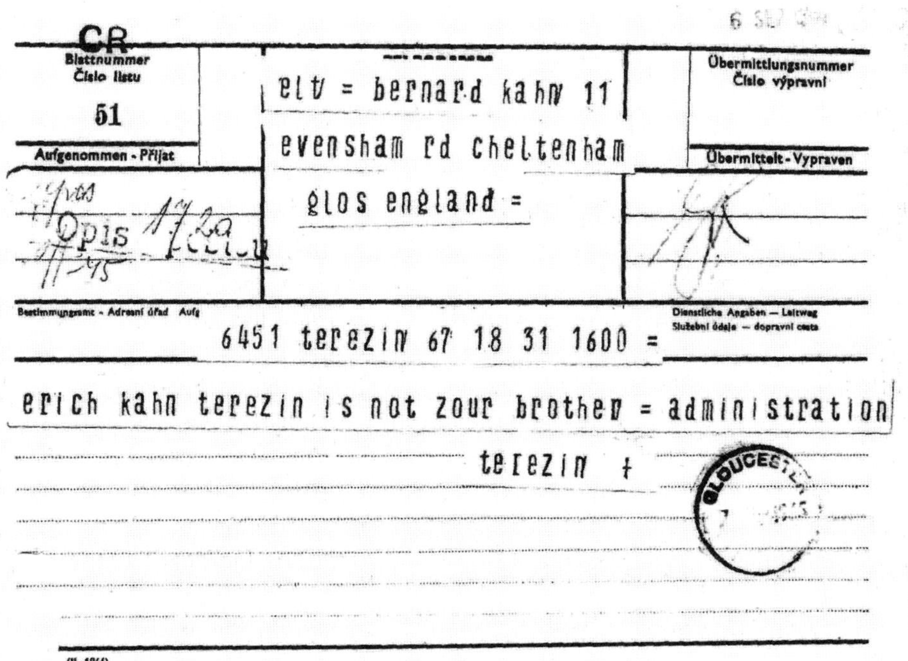

CR

Blattnummer
Číslo listu
51

Aufgenommen - Přijat

elt = bernard kahn 11
evensham rd cheltenham
glos england =

Übermittlungsnummer
Číslo výpravní

Übermittelt - Vypraven

Bestimmungsamt - Adresní úřad Aufg

Dienstliche Angaben — Leitweg
Služební údaje — dopravní cesta

6451 terezin 67 18 31 1600 =

erich kahn terezin is not zour brother = administration
terezin +

(II-1946)

Paul's letter said: "There are very few Jews left in Bohemia and Moravia – every one left alive is a Ness [miracle] and almost none in any of the former Nazi occupied countries. In Frankfurt about 250 people have returned." [Out of a Jewish Community of over 70,000.]

Paul is working with Intelligence collecting evidence for the trials.

For a while we were overwhelmed and subdued – but Charlie and Andy arrived with a jeep to take us out. We all went to Bromsgrove where there was much rejoicing and dancing – the streets and roads are awash with flags and jubilant with street parties. Bernard left at 10 p.m. saying, "See you tomorrow!" Joyce's comment: "You two are quite crazy!"

Friday 17th August

This morning I phoned Cynthia Davies to ask her if she would be a witness to our marriage, and could she bring a friend to be a second witness. Joyce persuaded me to wear my new blue dress and a hat; she made me a bouquet of wild flowers. We arrived at the Registry Office at 1.45 p.m. Bernard – in his Shabbos suit – Joyce, Andy, Cynthia, Jack and Doris, were the grand sum of our guests. The Registrar looked down his nose and asked: "Should we wait for the others?" Meaning our parents. It was quite obvious what he was thinking. At 2 p.m. the ceremony started – and well! …

"Repeat after me," the Registrar said to Bernard: "I, Bernard Kahn, take Cynthia Cohen to be my lawful wedded wife," etc.

"I, Bernard Kahn, take Sinsea Cohen to be my lorvul vedded wibe."

"No," said the Registrar and made him repeat it again. Yes, he did say, "Awful vedded vife"!

At the third try the Registrar, his face a picture of disgust, gave up – particularly as our guests were crying with laughter. Joyce, a hanky in her mouth, and Jack pretending to have a coughing fit.

"You may put the ring on now."

Bernard looked at me in alarm. "We're not using a ring." I said quickly.

"Oh, well," said the Registrar, now quite resigned, "you don't *have* to use a ring. Please sign this form."

Bernard read it. "She's not a spinster!" he said with disdain.

"What?" asked the Registrar. "Has she been married before?"

"I *am* a spinster," I whispered, "it's not what you think." [i.e. an old maid]. Then said the Registrar in one breath: "I now pronounce you man and wife and I hope you will be very happy in your future life together and that will cost you 7/6 [seven shillings and sixpence] and 5/- if you want a copy."

"That's cheap," replied Bernard, "my dog licence cost me 10/6."

Our wedding party stood outside on the steps. "Right, I'm off," said Bernard jumping on his bike, "I've got to milk the cow before Shabbos."

"That's the last straw," said Cynthia's friend Doris. "I've always wanted a Registry Office marriage, but after *this* I've decided to get married in church."

Joyce and I left; we still had to cook the food for Shabbos. Andy came with us. At 5 p.m., I phoned Mum to tell her the news. "What!!!" she exploded, "You *stupid* girl, now it'll take you three years before you can get a divorce!" What encouraging words! I told her I know life may be difficult with Bernard, but I also know he will always be constant, trustworthy and capable – and as far as being a good family man, he knew more about family life than I did. We were trying to arrange our Chuppah [religious wedding] in London for October; Dayan Posen, Bernard's teacher and friend from his Internment Camp days on the Isle of Man, has agreed to officiate. Sara can be my bridesmaid. "Well, it's done now …" Mum answered. We finished the phone call agreeably, Mum, I'm sure, already thinking about what special outfit she would wear and who she'd invite to a "London Wedding".

On the way back I felt free as a bird – no, more like a butterfly having crawled out of its chrysalis, spreading its wings and flying into an unknown world. So now I am a *Mrs.*! On Monday I shall have to register my new name on my ration book, identity card etc … Oh, yes, and now I am officially "*An Enemy Alien*" – *Stateless*. If I want to become British again I'll have to be *Naturalised,* having been born here and never having left the country in my life – *and* the war is over! The war that has lasted just three weeks less than *six years*! I was little more than a child when it started – now I'm a married woman – Cynthia Barbara Cohen is no more, I must try out my new signature: Cynthia B. Kahn.

What a momentous week this has been; when I think of the atomic bomb and its power of destruction, I'm filled with awe and amazement. What a finale to this frightful war that has taken so many lives – a war that forced Bernard to flee from his home in Frankfurt to find refuge in our remote Cynon valley, deep in the Welsh mountains – an event that has changed my life entirely. In a moment the steady lights of my Shabbos candles will glow in the twilight; I feel like saying the "Shehechionu" Blessing. ["Blessed are Thou O L--d our G-d, King of the universe, who has kept us in life, and hast preserved us, and has enabled us to reach this season."]

Sunday 19 August

VICTORY SUNDAY

This afternoon, Joyce, Bernard and I went to the service in shul; it was very moving – especially for us, as we said good-bye to our Cheltenham friends, some of whom we may meet again in London, and to the many GI's who we'll never see again. After the Kaddish was sung, the President gave an inspiring speech. He quoted from a report from Rev. I. Levy, Senior Jewish Chaplain to the Forces, who wrote:

> There are no words to convey the tragedy and misery of the gruesome camps and the condition of the pitiful remnants of our lost communities in Europe." He added,

> "Those of us who have remained alive and safe must surely ask themselves 'Why me?' and determine that the life we have been granted will be of some value in a future world, renewed and at peace.

After the reception we exchanged addresses – ours at Anny Bodenheimer's in London – as we have no idea where we will be living. Then we walked with Lenny, George and Elliot up Cleeve Hill from where we could see the racecourse almost completely covered with a sea of army tents and the whole town lit up below for the first time, after six years of blackout. Three or four bands were playing; the sound of celebration rose up around us. Our GI friends left, promising to keep in touch; Bernard and I stayed on in the warm dusk – the smell of wood smoke rising from the hundreds of bonfires that pierced the velvet darkness with their orange and yellow flames. For once, we were quiet, not wanting to break the magic, and for me, a rare moment of complete happiness; two lines of Baudelaire came to mind:

> With a contented heart, I climbed up the mountain,
> From where one can look at the city spread out below.

POSTSCRIPT

The benefits of peace did not come immediately. The first few years after the end of the war were a time for reconstruction and the rebuilding of people's lives. A short account follows of what became of some of the people mentioned in the *Diary*.

Bernard and Cynthia had their religious wedding in London in October 1945 and Bernard found temporary employment at the Aguda Office there, helping with the rehabilitation of refugees from the DP (Displaced Persons') Camps in Europe. They made two further attempts to emigrate to Palestine but were thwarted on both occasions.

Bernard's parents moved to Cardiff where his father restarted his chemical business, manufacturing supplies for the printing industry, and named it the South Wales Chemical Works. He had been forced to sell his pre-war business to the Germans. Two years after the war, Bernard's father suffered a heart attack, and Bernard returned to Wales to manage the factory. In 1953 the factory moved to Surrey, where the business flourished. As the years went by Bernard became a well-known figure in the printing world, where his expertise and experience later earned him the title "Father of the Printing Industry".

They had two sons and a daughter: David and Yaacov, who entered the family business; and Miriam now living in Israel. All three are long since married and have children and grandchildren of their own.

Bernard never forgot his love of agriculture and, when the opportunity arose, acquired the farm adjoining the factory, deriving years of pleasure from it. Not one to waste a moment, he spent his free time helping to establish schools and other educational institutions.

As soon as all her children were at school, Cynthia returned to studying sculpture and oil painting, this time at St Martin's School of Art. In 1971 she was delighted to be accepted with the first year's intake at the newly started Open University, later becoming one of the first students to obtain a BA degree there. Cynthia then continued studying English Art and Architecture in Richmond, and was much in demand for her lectures with slides on the history of art. She subsequently taught oil painting in an adult education college for thirteen years. In 1990 Cynthia joined a writing class in Hampstead, where she had a dynamic tutor, Sonia Ribeiro. After hearing Cynthia read out parts of the manuscript of her wartime diary, the class encouraged her bring it to publication.

Sam and Henny Kahn, Bernard's parents, became well known figures in the London community, with a warm and welcoming home. Shortly after the end of the war, they received news that their son Erich had perished doing slave labour in a salt mine in Austria. His name is recorded, amongst millions of others, at the Holocaust Memorial "Yad Vashem" in Jerusalem, and also on one of the walls of the Pinkas Synagogue in Prague where he had been studying when the Germans overran Czechoslovakia. (Luckily their eldest son, Walter, had escaped to Switzerland.) When the Germans offered Mr and Mrs Kahn restitution money for Erich's death, they initially refused to accept it, but when Mr Kahn found a plot of land suitable for building a new synagogue, it was decided to use the money to purchase it. In September 1958 he was proud to be given the honour of laying the foundation stone of this large new synagogue for the Golders Green Beth Hamedrash Congregation.

Joyce moved to London soon after the end of the war, and worked for a number of years managing the showrooms of various clothing manufacturers. She married Bernard's best friend, a widower with one daughter. They had a daughter and a son and later a number of grandchildren. In 1980 they moved to Israel, where she established a local lending library. Her interest in art continued and drawing remains one of her favourite activities.

Sara came to London at the age of eighteen to study Occupational Therapy, following which she went to Israel. Some years later, she obtained a degree in Biology at the Hebrew University. She married a Professor of Behavioural Psychology and lived for many years in America before returning to Jerusalem, where she currently works at the Hadassah Hospital. Sara has a large family with many grandchildren.

"**Gran**" continued working in her Hardware Store until she was eighty. She was well known for her generosity and warm hospitality to family and friends. After a bad fall, she went to live with her daughter in Aberdare, retaining her wonderful sense of humour and sound mind until the age of ninety. Her son Ben and his wife remained in Nottingham where he set up a Dental Laboratory which became renowned for its excellence.

Ruth and Harry eventually bought Ty-Clyd in Abernant Road, from Mrs Schwartz, the house where Sara spent so many of the first weeks of her life. They closed Jane Cooper, retired, and, for the first time in their lives, were able to take a holiday to visit Sara and her family in America.

"Uncle Harry" remained in good health until the age of ninety. He died sitting in his chair holding the birthday card Cynthia had sent him three months earlier. Ruth then moved to a small house close to her daughters in London and decided to lead a fully religious life. Bernard became the devoted son she had never had. She attended classes in millinery, piano and dressmaking and made many new friends. Ruth enjoyed a wonderful social life until the age of ninety-three, attending the weddings of a granddaughter and a great-grandson in Israel just two weeks before her death.

Berta Oppenheim left Penrhiwceiber after the war and went to live close to her brothers, Erich and Manfred, in Baltimore. She later married Jessie Sugarman and they had one son. By a strange coincidence, the best man at the wedding of one of Bernard and Cynthia's granddaughters in Israel turned out to be Erich Oppenheim's grandson! Berta still keeps in touch with Joyce and Cynthia.

Alex Winter fulfilled his wish to go to university and, some while after, met and married a lovely wife. They lived a happy life together and had children and grandchildren. When, many years later, Cynthia met Mrs Winter by chance at a reception, Mrs Winter gave her a warm embrace, which she reciprocated.

Mrs (Rachel) Chinn, née Britz (*First diary entry: 10th June 1943*), and her large family lived in a small house opposite "Gran" in Penrhiwceiber. Her husband died in an accident when their eldest son, Rosser, was only thirteen. "Gran" then gave Rosser goods from her shop to sell in the surrounding villages. Eventually the family moved to London and bought a furniture shop. In 1946, Rosser and his brother Norman, became partners in Lex Garages, which grew into a large, thriving business. Mrs Chinn achieved her wish of living to a hundred and died surrounded by all her family. Cynthia, who had always been close to her, was one of the last people to have a conversation with her.

Sarah Britz, 1906–1940. (*Last Diary entry: 25th September 1940.*)
After contacting the Commonwealth War Graves Commission, a letter was received containing the following information:

> Civilian SARAH BRITZ
> Died: 24th September 1940
> HACKNEY, METROPOLITAN BOROUGH
> London
> Age 34
> of 19 St Mark's Rise
> Died at Downs Park Road Shelter

During the Second World War, the Commission was given the task of compiling as complete a list as possible of Commonwealth civilians whose deaths were due to enemy action. The complete Roll of over 66,000 names is bound in seven volumes and kept in St. George's Chapel at Westminster Abbey. A different page is displayed each day. Her friend Mrs Robins is also listed.

Bernard Schwartz (*Diary entries between 11th June 1942 and 21st July 1943*), joined the Army at 18 and served in the Royal Armoured Corps. He trained at Sandhurst, where he became an officer before being posted overseas to Port Said on the Suez Canal. In 1944 he married Yolanda Shapirer in Cairo. By the time he was demobilised in 1948 and returned to Cardiff, Bernard had attained the rank of Major and was later awarded life membership of the British Legion, receiving a Gold Medal for Distinguished Service. His tall, imposing figure and humorous, outgoing and energetic personality were the reasons that, at the age of 32, he became the youngest ever President of the Cardiff United Synagogue. Bernard was immensely active in raising funds for various charities, particularly the Annual Poppy Day Appeal, and, with great pride, led the Remembrance Day Parade in Wales for over 50 years. The highlight of his long life was being invited to Buckingham Palace for his investiture as Deputy Lieutenant of Glamorgan.

Norma Glass MBE, née Corrick (*First diary entry: 2nd January 1942*), married an architect, Martin Glass, and still lives in Swansea. She runs workshops for schools on Judaism and interfaith dialogue, and is a member of The Board of Deputies of British Jews. Norma was awarded an MBE in the Queen's Birthday Honours for 2002 for Services to Racial Understanding in South Wales, and is often heard and seen on radio and television.

Lawrence Collins (*Diary entry for Sunday 4th April 1943*), became the Honourable Sir Lawrence Collins, LLD, FBA. He read for his Law degree at Downing College, Cambridge, continuing his studies in international law at Columbia University, New York, becoming a solicitor in 1968. Lawrence was a partner in the City firm, Herbert Smith, from 1971 to 2000. He specialised in international law, writing books and papers on European Community Law and private international law. In 1997, he became one of the first two solicitors to be appointed Queen's Counsel. In 2000, Lawrence became the first solicitor to be appointed directly to the High Court bench, and now sits in the Chancery Division. He married in 1982 and has a daughter, Hannah, and a son, Aaron.

Shirley Cohen (*Main entry on 1st March 1944*) met her first husband when he was serving in the American armed forces stationed in Wales and went to live with him in the United States after the war. They had two children, David and Judith. She married her second husband there and has become a renowned artist under the name Shirley Zena Brodoff. Her works have been exhibited at many venues world-wide.

Pamela Majaro, née Cohen (*Diary entry: 28th May 1942*), studied Law at University College, London, where she met her husband, Simon Majaro. They married in 1954 and had two daughters, Nadine and Nicola. She subsequently became a sculptor, then painter and photographer, but always had a deep-rooted love for classical music. In 1998, she and her husband set up the *Cavatina* Chamber Music Trust with the aim of increasing young audiences and helping young musicians.

Gerry Black (*Diary entries from 28th January to 3rd May 1942*), the 14-year-old evacuee boy whom Bernard taught for his Bar Mitzvah in 1942, moved back to Ilford the following year. During his exams for his School Certificate, a V1 flying bomb partially destroyed his mother's house, and Gerry received severe cuts. He joined the Army in 1946 and served in Germany from 1947 to 1948, spending much of his spare time helping Jewish children in the displaced persons' camp at Bergen-Belsen. On his return, he studied law at the London School of Economics, qualifying and practising, first as a barrister, and then as a solicitor. In 1987 he was awarded a PhD for his thesis on: Jewish Medical Care in the East End of London from 1880–1939; later becoming President of the Jewish Historical Society of England and a trustee of the Jewish Museum. He has written a number of books on the history of the Jews of London.

Through a chance meeting with his son, Rabbi P. Black, Bernard and Cynthia renewed their friendship with Gerry and came to know his wife, Anita.

Arthur S. Abramson (*Diary entries between 10th November 1944 and 29th July 1945*) had become a very close friend of Joyce, Cynthia and Bernard during his time as an American GI stationed near Cheltenham. In August 1945, he was transferred to France, but spent his month's leave with Bernard and Cynthia in their London home before returning to the USA. Once there, through Bernard's influence, he decided to study for his BA at Yeshiva University in New York City. In 1952, Bernard visited Arthur and his wife Ruby, at their home in New Jersey, after which they lost touch. However, at the beginning of January 2005, during the final edit of this Diary, it was decided to include a photo of Arthur standing outside a tent with Bernard (see p. 262). Bernard's son David decided to try his luck on the Internet to see if he could trace him. He sent an e-mail to two of the A. Abramsons that his search turned up: "Dear Dr Abramson, I am doing some research into my family's history. There was an Arthur Abramson stationed in Cheltenham during WW2 and I would like to know if this was you. If so I would appreciate it if you would get in touch. Regards. David Kahn."

To his surprise, the very next day, David received the following reply:

Dear Mr. Kahn,

I am very likely the person you are looking for; I was not stationed in Cheltenham as such but served as an x-ray technician at a U.S. Army hospital not far away in the countryside near Cirencester. During my time there, before being shipped to France, I used to visit Cheltenham whenever I could. Are you by any chance related to Bernard Kahn? He became a very good friend of mine in Cheltenham and later in London. His fiancée and later his wife, Cynthia, as well as her sister Joyce, were also my friends.

Arthur S. Abramson
Mansfield, Conn., U.S.A.

There ensued a flurry of e-mails flying back and forth across the Atlantic, culminating in two special phone calls from Joyce and Cynthia to Arthur on his birthday, the 26th January 2005.

Arthur had not been idle in the intervening years. Having obtained an MA from Columbia University, he spent two years in Thailand, teaching English, before returning there to finish his PhD in linguistics. He joined the research staff of Haskins Laboratories in 1959 and, later in life, became Professor of Linguistics at the University of Connecticut. During his long career, he often returned to carry out language research in Thailand, and has been awarded numerous honours and distinctions. On his retirement, he was granted the title of Emeritus Professor and is still active in his field.

Arthur has two married sons, Joseph Benjamin and David Nathan, and a grandson, Isaac Benjamin. The members of both families are delighted and intrigued by this renewal of old acquaintances. A most fitting ending to this postscript, which at times seems to have taken on a life of its own.

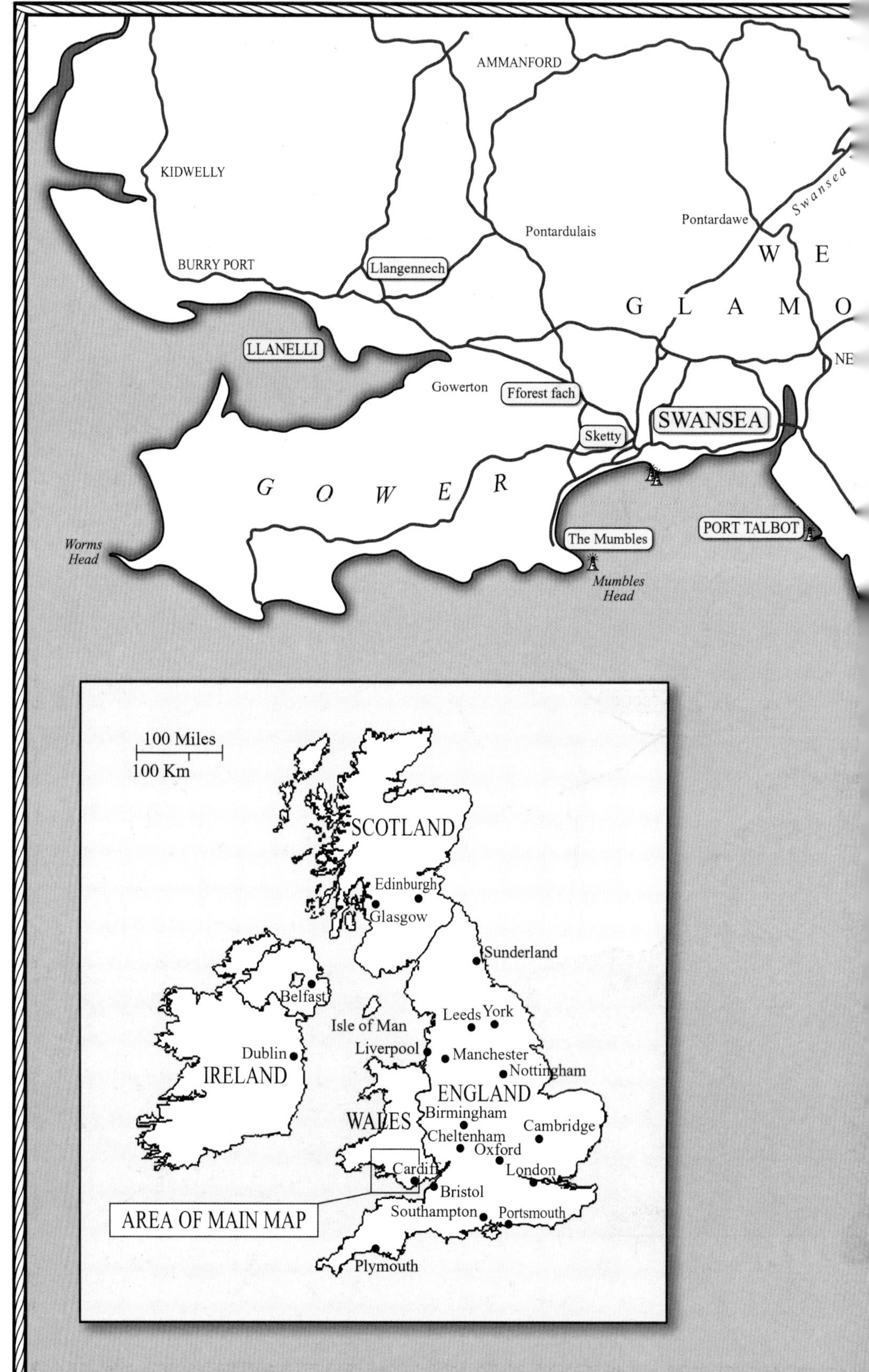
AMMANFORD
KIDWELLY
Swansea
Pontardawe
Pontardulais
BURRY PORT
Llangennech
W E
G L A M O
LLANELLI
NE
Gowerton
Fforest fach
SWANSEA
Sketty
G O W E R
PORT TALBOT
The Mumbles
Worms Head
Mumbles Head
100 Miles
100 Km
SCOTLAND
Edinburgh
Glasgow
Sunderland
Belfast
Leeds
York
Isle of Man
Liverpool
Manchester
Dublin
Nottingham
IRELAND
ENGLAND
Birmingham
WALES
Cambridge
Cheltenham
Oxford
Cardiff
London
Bristol
AREA OF MAIN MAP
Southampton
Portsmouth
Plymouth